OUT

IN THE FIELD

Reflections of Lesbian and Gay Anthropologists

Edited by Ellen Lewin and William L. Leap

University of Illinois Press   Urbana and Chicago

Manufactured in the United States of America
1 2 3 4 5 C P 5 4 3 2 1

This book is printed on acid-free paper.

Library of Congress Cataloging-in-Publication Data
Out in the field : reflections of lesbian and gay anthropologists
/ edited by Ellen Lewin and William L. Leap.
p.   cm.
Includes bibliographical references and index.
ISBN 0-252-02219-X — ISBN 0-252-06518-2 (pbk.)
1. Anthropology—Field work. 2. Gay anthropologists.
3. Lesbian anthropologists. I. Lewin, Ellen. II. Leap, William.
GN343.F53O87 1996 301—dc20 95-43456 CIP

Contents

3 REPRESENTATION

Preface
Ellen Lewin and William L. Leap

E very book and every new direction in scholarly writing are products of particular historical moments. *Out in the Field* draws its intellectual raison d'être, as our Introduction will detail, from the emphasis on reflexivity that has preoccupied anthropologists over the last decade and from the growing academic examination of sexuality, in particular homosexuality, that emerged in a variety of disciplines during this same period. In addition to the stimulus for such work provided by the burgeoning movement for lesbian and gay rights and the popular discussion fostered by public debates over such explosive issues as the AIDS epidemic and gays and lesbians in the military, the opportunity to produce this volume has emerged out of a series of specific developments in anthropology that took place over a period of more than twenty years.

In 1970 Clark Taylor introduced a resolution at the annual business meeting of the American Anthropological Association in San Diego. The resolution supported gay and lesbian rights and the study of gay and lesbian topics by anthropologists. He spoke eloquently in highly personal language of the discrimination faced by members of the profession who were known to be homosexual or whose scholarly interests focused on homosexuality. The resolution was passed by the liberal membership, but little attention was paid to its provisions for many years.

Although homosexuality did not become a key issue in anthropology in this period, over the next decade the status of women became a central topic in anthropology, giving rise to the elaboration of gender as an intellectual construct. Along with the growth of a feminist analytical perspective, feminists in the AAA began to exert pressure on the organization to recognize problems of sexism in the profession and to acknowledge the significant intellectual contributions coming from the new work on women. As a result, the AAA created the Commission on the Status of Women in Anthropology (COSWA), which undertook a number of studies of discrimination against women in the discipline. The AAA also sponsored a curriculum project called "Gender and Anthropology" that assembled materials on women for those teaching standard anthropological topics. Later, anthropologists who work on issues related to women and gender or who are concerned with using anthropological findings to promote policies beneficial to women formed the Association for Feminist Anthropology (AFA).

Although sexuality and sexual variation were presumably among the range of topics feminists might choose to examine, little work was done in feminist anthropology on homosexuality or lesbianism during the 1970s and 1980s. "Gender and Anthropology," for example, included little directly related to this topic, and many lesbian feminists active first in COSWA and later in AFA felt that their concerns were invisible despite the fact that they recognized sizable numbers of AFA members as lesbians. Some found that when they did suggest a focus on a lesbian or gay dimension of a particular issue there was polite agreement, but the discussion would rapidly shift away from homosexuality and the suggestion would be quickly forgotten. Others felt reluctant even to raise these issues, not wanting to call attention to themselves in this way.

In 1974 a small group of anthropologists, nearly all men, met to form the Anthropological Research Group on Homosexuality, whose members got together each year during the AAA's annual meeting. While the name of the group suggested that these were all scholars who studied homosexuality, many did not. The group became an unofficial gay support group, offering its members an opportunity to meet and socialize at the otherwise stressful convention. ARGOH published a newsletter and performed the vital function of informing its members about recent work related to the topic of homosexuality, but it was still generally understood that the name of the group concealed its actual function as an organization for gay anthropologists.

By 1986 a number of members of ARGOH had become frustrated with the group's secretive stance. By this time, some women, many of them also active in feminist activities, had joined the organization, and many more of the male members were open about their sexual orientation. At the next annual meeting (in Chicago in 1987), members voted to change the name to the Society of Lesbian and Gay Anthropologists (SOLGA) while intending to continue to serve as an interest group for anthropologists whose scholarly interests were in homosexuality, regardless of the sexual orientation of these individuals.

This name change invigorated the organization. Despite the objections of some members who feared that the new name would stigmatize the group, membership increased at a modest pace. More important, SOLGA became more active in sponsoring both scientific sessions and informal get-togethers at the annual meetings of the AAA and to some extent at meetings of the Society for Applied Anthropology and regional societies as well. The newsletter broadened its coverage of developments in the field and included a steady stream of book reviews and articles; its regular publication further facilitated the formation of informal networks and encouraged members to work together on a variety of projects.

By this time, the AIDS pandemic had become a prominent concern in the research agendas of many anthropologists, gay and straight, and the formation of the AIDS and Anthropology Research Group (AARG) and, simultaneously, the AAA Task Force on Anthropology and AIDS created networks of colleagues and friends that complemented and extended SOLGA's professional ties. AIDS research also brought SOLGA members out of the professional closet by creating forums where people could speak openly about sexuality and culture and find colleagues who shared these interests and by reinforcing SOLGA's commitments to public discussion of these themes within anthropology.

All of these trends came together at the AAA's annual meeting in New Orleans in 1990, when William Leap and Liz Goodman organized a symposium on "Lesbian/Gay Identity and Fieldwork." As far as we know, this was the first session at an AAA meeting to discuss lesbian and gay concerns regarding field research and data analysis or at which the lesbian or gay *identity* of the anthropologist was a primary focus. Despite its having been scheduled for eight o'clock on Sunday morning, the session was well attended and stimulated a great deal of intense discussion. A number of the chapters in this volume (Newton, Burkhart, Goodman, Wafer, and Walters) were originally prepared for this session.

The discussion that followed the papers was so heated, in fact, that during the year following the symposium we began to plan for this volume but decided to wait to complete the roster of contributors until after two other related symposia had been held. The first, organized by Ellen Lewin in early 1991, was "Writing Lesbian and Gay Ethnography" and took place not at the AAA meetings but at Out/Write, a national lesbian and gay writers' conference. Leap's and Weston's papers were originally prepared for that session. Later in 1991, at the AAA meetings in Chicago, Lewin organized a session called "Writing Lesbian and Gay Culture," which focused on issues of representation and followed from the Out/Write panel. The chapters by Kennedy and Roscoe that appear in this volume were first presented at that session. Additional contributions were drawn from other sources. Lewin's paper was originally presented at the Fourth Annual Lesbian, Bisexual, and Gay Studies Conference at Harvard University in 1990. Chapters by Murray, Bolton, Lang, and Williams were solicited during the preparation of the volume, as was the Afterword written by Sue-Ellen Jacobs.

The process that made possible the gathering of contributors that has resulted in this collection grows directly from the networks developed in SOLGA. SOLGA's existence allowed us to find each other, to know something of the experience each of us had had as lesbian or gay anthropologists, and, finally, made it possible for us to commit our diverse experiences to paper and begin to draw conclusions from them. At the same time that SOLGA has facilitated intellectual exchange and generated interpersonal support for its members, SOLGA members have continued efforts begun by Clark Taylor to combat discrimination against gays and lesbians. Most recently, a SOLGA report on the status of lesbian and gay anthropologists led to the formation of the AAA Commission on Lesbian and Gay Issues in Anthropology, a move that seems to demonstrate some level of official commitment to overcoming prejudice against lesbian and gay individuals in the profession and against the study of homosexuality in anthropology. Several of the authors in this volume— Bolton, Jacobs, Kennedy, Leap, Lewin, and Newton—are also members of that commission.

At this writing, we are still far from achieving equal opportunity in academic anthropology. Gay men and lesbians continue to find that they must keep a low profile if they are to avoid systematic, although sometimes subtle, discrimination in graduate school and in professional life. Those whose research focuses on lesbian and gay issues may experience obstacles to mobility, and most of those who have devoted their careers to these topics either lack regular employment or are unable to achieve positions commensurate with their accomplishments. With the partial exception of those who study or work at institutions that have adopted domestic partner policies with respect to benefits, most, regardless of their specialization, face serious hardships coordinating their family and professional lives. While hard economic times throughout the academy have meant that many heterosexual anthropologists are also blocked from realizing their full potential, lesbian and gay anthropologists continue to find their safest professional path in concealment and secrecy, even as the lesbian and gay civil rights movement begins to achieve some small victories.

It is our hope that this volume will help give a voice to those lesbian and gay anthropologists who have remained silent. Our process in producing this collection is like the continuing experience of coming out that lesbians and gay men have chronicled in recent literature: first, acknowledging one's identity to oneself; then, revealing that identity to selected and trusted others; and, finally, sharing that identity openly with everyone one encounters. These steps are not necessarily sequential, nor are they all necessary for individuals to reach a comfortable understanding of who they are. But the fear and self-consciousness that are recurring themes in these accounts have shaped and sometimes impeded our personal and professional development in many ways. Speaking openly is a step toward stripping homosexuality and lesbian and gay identity of their stigma. This volume is one effort among many to facilitate that process and disseminate our words.

The completion of this volume owed a tremendous debt to our editors at the University of Illinois Press: Carole Appel got the project off the ground, and then Karen Hewitt became our editor on Appel's retirement and saw the collection through to publication. We also want to thank Liz Goodman, who was actively involved in launching this project and who worked behind the scenes throughout the editorial process, and Angui Madera, who has supported our work in lesbian and gay anthropology in numerous ways. Finally, we would like to dedicate this book to the memory of Arnold Pilling.

Introduction
Ellen Lewin and William L. Leap

Current debates over the meaning of homosexuality, spurred on by growing demands by lesbians and gay men for the kinds of recognition and social entitlement afforded other minority groups, have inevitable consequences for the conduct of inquiry in all academic fields, but perhaps most insistently in cultural anthropology, in which the individual researcher, particularly as fieldworker, figures so prominently in the creation of the scholarly product—ethnography. From its earliest days, when the work of the founders of the field, E. B. Tylor, Adolf Bastian, Sir Henry Maine, and Louis Henry Morgan, had the effect of defending the superiority of their own cultures in comparison with the conditions that obtained in the non-Western world, anthropologists' comparative framework has always started implicitly from the self. Although notions that advanced societies (such as those that produce anthropologists) are more evolved, and hence superior, to the "primitive" societies long ago gave way to cultural relativism, comparison, often with the self as the implicit starting point, has remained a fundamental tool of both data-gathering and theory-building ventures in anthropology (Spiro 1992; Stocking 1987).

At the same time, however, efforts to qualify as a "science" sometimes have made anthropologists unwilling to reveal what they imagined was the unscientific, subjective process that occurred in the field. This reticence produced, as Myerhoff and Ruby (1992) have pointed out, a decidedly unscientific refusal to specify method. The tendency, anchored in a naive positivism, to assume uncritically that what was out there was simply there has begun to crumble, leaving the way open for a far more highly specified discussion of how the researcher and the research process interact to shape ethnographic writing.

The growing concern in anthropology with fieldwork as a situated and negotiated process and the associated understanding that ethnographic descriptions are the product of these shifting and sometimes poorly understood forces have led to calls for the opening of communications about every aspect of the researcher's being and have demanded that ethnography constitute itself in a more self-reflexive mode. Although discussion of these issues has hovered in the background of anthropology for some time, a number of works intensified scrutiny of both fieldwork and ethnographic writing and have had a profound impact on the degree of self-consciousness anthropologists now bring to both ventures. The chapters in Hymes's collection *Reinventing Anthropology* (1972) sketched the boundaries around many of these issues. Said's (1978) critiques of anthropology's tendency to "orientalize" its subjects and Clifford and Marcus's concerns with the problem of representation (1986) clarified this terrain, provoking debates that have continued unabated up to the present (see, for example, Harvey 1992).

The literature that has been spawned by this new consciousness is large and diverse, bearing on all areas of practice in social and cultural anthropology. With respect to fieldwork, Rabinow's *Reflections on Fieldwork in Morocco* (1977) is perhaps the most frequently cited contribution to the debate on reflexivity. Reacting against the contradictory assumptions promoted in anthropological training that "anthropology equals experience" but that the only valuable result of this experience is the "objective data" one brings back (1977:4), Rabinow's analysis of his experience in Morocco convinces him that fieldwork is a collaborative operation in which informants and anthropologist mutually construct explanations and interpretations (1977:164–65). This means that various aspects of one's identity, together with the specific events that unfold during the research, generate a particular and unreplicable field experience, which then becomes the stuff of ethnographic generalization. That such generalization must then be illusory at best is Rabinow's inescapable conclusion.

This shift to an increasingly reflexive stance also has particular relevance for the way in which gay and lesbian anthropologists constitute or understand their experiences as fieldworkers and as the producers of ethnographic writing. If reflexivity demands candor about the assumptions and desires one brings to the field, then one must be open about how one manages one's identity and how this contrasts with or resembles strategies one employs at home. To some extent it has been assumed that discussion of what it means to be gay or lesbian in the field must turn on a discussion of sexual desire and expression, and that any such discussion will begin to break down the longstanding reluctance of anthropologists to acknowledge sexuality wherever it be found in the field (cf. Vance 1991).[1]

That sexuality is virtually prohibited as an element of even the most candid fieldwork chronicles is demonstrated most clearly by reactions to those few sexual confessions as appear in the literature. Beyond the general alarm that greeted the revelations published in Malinowski's *Diary* (1967), those rare instances in which anthropologists have been willing (or some might say, eager) to reveal the sexual fantasies and experiences they had in the field only highlight the limited view of sexuality that the profession has been able to discuss. These few discussions have nearly always been heterosexual in nature (Rabinow 1977) and, with few exceptions (cf. Cesara 1982), the prerogative of men.[2] The notion that homosexuality might be an issue in the field, either between researchers and informants or between researchers and partners who might accompany them to the field, has until now rarely been discussed.[3]

For those of us who see ourselves as lesbian or gay, homosexuality is perhaps most influential in its implications for our social status. Although debates about the advisability of being open about homosexuality tend to focus on the sexual forces such revelations might unleash, the actual effect on lesbian and gay lives has to do most with questions of opportunity, personal emotional support, and the ability to undertake whatever activities—in this case professional ones—the individual wishes to pursue.[4] Like the recent debate over the presence of homosexuals in the U.S. military, the issue has not so much been whether lesbian and gay anthropologists exist, but whether and under what circumstances our existence ought to become manifest. While this issue has appropriately been approached mainly in terms of social equity, this volume will raise the question in terms of its significance for the anthropological enterprise, both as it is carried out in fieldwork and as it frames the creation of ethnographic writing.

Bringing the experience of gay and lesbian anthropologists into the open raises a number of significant questions for the discipline as a whole. First, it broadens the debate about reflexivity by making problematic aspects of the researcher's identity formerly assumed to be uniform. Second, by bringing additional dimensions of gender into the discussion of the conduct of research, it adds to the contributions already made by feminist anthropologists seeking to undermine masculine hegemony in the discipline. These issues are all relevant to discussions of fieldwork in traditional anthropological settings—locations far removed both physically and culturally from the researcher's home.

Fieldwork Dilemmas

Fieldwork has always been a subject of great fascination for social and cultural anthropologists. While some have rightly pointed out that the role of fieldwork in the socialization and professionalization of anthropologists has been romanticized and that its complexities have not always been adequately appreciated, anthropologists, particularly those working in specialties that demand extended contact with living informants, tend to have a lot to say about the experience and to continue to emphasize it as a critical dimension of professional practice. For many, the very decision to enter the profession was bound up with images of the field and of the experiences of particular anthropologists whose accounts we had read.[5]

This vision of anthropology suggested that it was fundamentally different from other academic fields in that one could not merely sit around and theorize: intrinsic to the discipline was the requirement of going out and living with those being studied; sharing the life circumstances of people in the less-developed world (where anthropologists traditionally worked) seemed to mean, in a more innocent age, that one could not use, debase, or otherwise objectify members of the cultures studied. For those who began their careers in anthropology before the onset of intense self-examination about the creation of the "other" and complicity in the West's orientalizing agenda, anthropology seemed to offer an authentic way to collapse the differences between themselves and other kinds of people, to eclipse separateness in the developed world, especially in academia.

The classic formulation of what anthropological fieldwork should be is by now well known. As Agar (1980) phrases it, the anthropologist is properly a "professional stranger," essentially justified to take up the enterprise by her or his differentness from the culture to be studied. "Participant observation" in a culturally alien community is the hallmark of the enterprise, with the researcher becoming "for a time and in a way part of its system of face-to-face relationships, so that the data collected in some sense reflect the native's own point of view" (Stocking 1983:7).

What is particularly significant about this method, in Stocking's formulation, is that it not only tells us what anthropological knowledge is but also offers the basis for constituting the identity of the anthropologist. Along with fieldwork, the emphasis on holism and relativism provides the "basis for anthropology's claim to special cognitive authority" (Stocking 1983:8).

A substantial literature on fieldwork methodology provides techniques and devices for bridging the distance assumed to be appropriate between the anthropologist's own culture and the field and for easing the pain of attempting to fit in where one is at best awkward and uncomfortable. Many fieldwork stories center on linguistic pitfalls attendant on trying to get started on one's research while still learning the local language (Conklin 1960; Samarin 1967). Others lead us through the difficulties that accompany properly situating oneself in the community: finding a place to live, engaging local people to help with the daily tasks of survival and act as research assistants, coping with illness and discomfort with the water, food, or level of hygiene, and, more significantly, figuring out who to believe, who to talk to, and how to behave in the research setting (Beals 1980; Chagnon 1983; Kimball and Partridge 1979). Still others, going back to the now rarely consulted *Notes and Queries* (Seligman, ed. 1951), offer specific recommendations on techniques and procedures for gathering data or taking notes (Sanjek 1990).

But despite these resources, fieldwork training has been largely absent, as generations of students have learned to proceed by trial and error, with success a marker of predestination for an anthropological career and missteps indicative of defective anthropological instincts. One learned to do anthropological fieldwork by doing it, and those who faltered had to confront their readiness for the task. Outside of the evangelical ministry, anthropology is perhaps the only discipline that operates with an implicit notion that professionals have a "call" or a "vocation" that they will uncover in the field if they are "meant" to continue.

No matter what the specific difficulties accounts of fieldwork focus on, they are virtually unanimous in emphasizing the importance of playing a suitable role in the setting one has chosen. Both the memoires of established anthropologists and various manuals that explain the mechanics of the fieldworker's craft place considerable emphasis on the ways in which one must self-consciously manage one's identity in order to complete the research successfully. Some recommend finding a way to fit into the local social structure, particularly if a kinlike role is appropriate (Briggs

1970). Others describe ways in which the specific expertise an anthropologist may bring to the field may legitimate his or her presence within the local community (Leap 1981; Wulf and Fiske, eds. 1986). Still other accounts focus on how an anthropologist can be part of a community for a sustained period of time, experience the way of life of the people in an authentic manner (yet one that does not interfere with collecting data), and not disrupt day-to-day existence (Foster et al., eds. 1979). We are counseled to locate a role we can play that fits into the structure of daily life and ongoing social organization and to take on activities that may allow us to reciprocate what we receive from the group with whom we are working.

The morals of most of these accounts are that fieldwork is uncomfortable and stressful, that the fact of difference is the most central demand of the work, and that difference must eventually be overcome through participant observation. One's success in learning a culture might, from this point of view, be measured by one's ability to begin to think and behave like a native, or at least to anticipate correctly how a native would behave in a particular situation (Frake 1962). But although finding a place, a role, in the field and eventually achieving closeness to the culture under study is essential to the success of one's enterprise, one still ought not study one's own culture.

Geographical distance is often assumed to assure the cultural distance required for an anthropologist to be a "professional stranger." This has meant traditionally that the location of the field site should be physically distant from the anthropologist's home (preferably in another country), that the field site should at least be culturally distinct from what the fieldworker is familiar with (an Indian tribe, for example), or that the economic level of the field community should be simpler and probably poorer than that the anthropologist is used to.[6]

Some scholars have vigorously criticized the limitations of this tradition. African American anthropologists spoke out some time ago (Gwaltney 1981; Jones 1970) about the often explicit expectations not only that they not work in their own communities in the United States but also that they forego research in Africa because they would lack objectivity about members of their own race. Other members of ethnic minorities have addressed the same issues in developing approaches to working in their own communities or in communities they identify as related to those in which they originated. As critiques of anthropology's tendency to operate in the shadow of colonialism in selecting for study people who seem sufficiently "other" have intensified, calls have increased for fieldwork to be shifted closer to home or for anthropologists to consider "studying up," that is, focus not on impoverished and relatively powerless people but on elites in their own societies and elsewhere (Nader 1972).

Recent work by "native anthropologists" has confronted the mystification of distance most directly. Limón, for example, evocatively describes his experiences working in a community in South Texas similar to his hometown. He self-consciously observes himself maneuvering between "participation" and "observation" while worrying about how to represent this world without feeding pejorative stereotypes (1991:129). In a somewhat different vein, Ohnuki-Tierney speaks of how the native anthropologist must struggle to distance herself while also taking advantage of her knowledge of ordinary life. "Native anthropologists," she suggests, "have easy access to not only the intellectual dimensions but also to the emotive and sensory dimensions of these behaviors" (1984:585). But Nayaran argues that the dichotomization of "native" and "outsider" is bound to be problematic insofar as the identities of all people—anthropologists included—are shifting, multiplex, and situated in specific historical and sociological contexts. She calls for "the *enactment of hybridity* . . . writing that depicts authors as minimally bicultural in terms of belonging simultaneously to the world of engaged scholarship and the world of everyday life" (1993:672, emphasis in original; see also Altorki and El-Solh, eds. 1988). Along the same lines, Tedlock has reminded us that the commitment to a specific field site required by long-term fieldwork may lead anthropologists to become bicultural and thus at least partial insiders (Tedlock 1991; see also Foster et al., eds. 1979).

In like fashion, anthropologists who have begun to work in locations neither remote nor exotic, their own Western cultures, have had to reconfigure the use of distance and objectivity in defining how they operate in the field. Aguilar (1981) enumerates some of the advantages to be realized by working in one's own culture—including the greater ease in fitting in without altering the setting and the economies that result from already possessing considerable amounts of background information—and contrasts these with the allegedly greater objectivity said to be possible when one comes into a community as an "outsider." He also points out that an insider's advantage may tend to be neutralized by conflicting professional demands, because even an insider may tend to organize observations in terms of ideas that prevail in the discipline.

Still other anthropologists may be frank in their desire to learn something about themselves in the process of studying populations they can regard as their "own people." Thus, doing ethnographic research among one's own may not only be beneficial because it frees the anthropologist from engaging in exploitation or offers the intellectual advantages of existing knowledge, but also because it enables the researcher to learn something about herself or himself. When Myerhoff, for example, decided to undertake research among elderly Eastern European Jewish immigrants, she asked herself whether she was doing anthropology or embarking on a personal quest. As Kirshenblatt-Gimblett reports (1992:x), Myerhoff wrote that her earlier work with the Huichol Indians would always be limited by the fact that she would never be a Huichol Indian. "But," she continued, "I would be a little old Jewish lady one day; thus it was essential for me to learn what the condition was like, in all its particulars . . . I consider myself very fortunate in having had, through this work, an opportunity to anticipate, rehearse, and contemplate my own future. This had given me a temporal integration to my life that seems to me an essential ingredient in the work of maturing."

The Feminist Critique of Fieldwork

Feminist anthropology has asked the most persistent questions about ethnographic distance and the struggle for objectivity, particularly by assailing the division between "scholarship" and "personal quest." During its early days in the 1970s, when the founders of the field sought to create a new "anthropology of women" in response to questions raised by the women's liberation movement, the emphasis was on women studying women as a way to know themselves. Feminist anthropologists, largely inspired by feminist politics, confronted an ethnographic record rarely informed by women's voices (Ardener 1975). The primary task was to restore women to active agency, to tell their stories in their own words, and to use these words to organize new, women-centered approaches to the study of traditional topics. Were women everywhere subordinated, or did specific cultural contexts accentuate gender inequality? Would the cross-cultural perspective that women anthropologists had been trained to apply to social issues tell them whether gender inequality could be changed?

Most salient in the 1970s was the view that some universal characteristics of women transcended other divisions; the task, then, was to identify and clarify the sources of women's status and generate broad cross-cultural generalizations about how gender operates. Taking dichotomous gender categories rather literally, it was often assumed that women's common experience would loom large in interactions among each other and that, for example, reproductive roles would transcend other sources of difference (DuBois 1983; Oakley 1981). Feminist anthropologists set themselves the task of ending the long silence of the ethnographic literature on women. This objective would require working with people like themselves—women.

Those skeptical about the new feminist scholarship claimed that these ideologically driven scholars could not be sufficiently disinterested and objective to do credible work; these objections were countered by a feminist epistemology that questioned the feasibility of any scholarship being entirely objective. This emphasis on positionality was grounded in the emerging understanding of male bias in the academy, as new work revealed the extent to which women's realities had rarely been considered sufficiently significant to fuel research agendas. Feminist researchers tried to erase the generations of female invisibility by allowing women to speak for themselves through various narrative strategies (Personal Narratives Group, ed. 1989) and by making clear, unapologetically, who they were and why they were undertaking research on women (see, for example, Fonow and Cook, eds. 1991; Harding, ed. 1987; Nielsen, ed. 1990; Roberts, ed. 1981). Mascia-Lees, Sharpe, and Cohen argue persuasively that the notion of the other that has recently come to preoccupy postmodernist anthropology was developed most fully by feminists who themselves "speak from the position of the 'other'" in regard to men (1989:11).

More even-handed treatment of women only began to be required when, inspired by the women's movement, (mainly) women anthropologists moved to challenge the assumptions that had long governed ethnographic research: that the "important" things to study were done by the men and that the prototypical ethnographer was a man. This new approach led to such provocative works as Golde's *Women in the Field* (1970), which confronted the image of the male anthropologist, and the numerous studies of women, including re-studies of classic ethnographies, that called for a reevaluation of much of the ethnographic corpus and demanded that women's stories be conveyed from women's point of view (see, for example, Goodale 1971; Reiter, ed. 1975; Rosaldo and Lamphere, eds. 1974; Weiner 1976).[7]

Abu-Lughod has brought these diverse perspectives together in calling for anthropologists to pay special attention to the perspectives of feminists and those she calls (borrowing a term from Narayan [1993]) "halfies"—"people whose national or cultural identity is mixed by virtue of migration, overseas eduation, or parentage" (1991:137). "What happens," she asks, "when the 'other' that the anthropologist is studying is simultaneously constructed as, at least partially, a self?" (1991:140). Her answer is that feminists and other halfies, by virtue of their "split selves," must mediate between speaking "for" and speaking "from" (1991:143). They can never fully remove themselves from the ambiguities of positionality and thus are pressured to deal with the incompleteness any representation of the culture must have. By drawing attention to the value of more particularistic representations, feminists and halfies can help disrupt the tendency toward seamless description of culture.

These are painful issues for all anthropologists, as demonstrated by the proliferating literature not only on fieldwork and ethnographic writing but also by the almost excruciating self-examination engaged in by many practitioners. In describing the loss of faith so many anthropologists have experienced in the nature of ethnographic representation, Geertz reminds us that our product is writing, or what he calls "ethnographic ventriloquism," and that "the un-get-roundable fact [is] that all ethnographical descriptions are homemade, that they are the describer's descriptions, not those of the described" (1988:145). Viewed as writing rather than "truth," ethnographies may be analyzed more productively, he would suggest, in terms of *how* they convince readers of their veracity rather than in terms of *whether* their accuracy can be proven.

These discussions have precipitated a moral crisis for many anthropologists and have spread beyond the profession to the extent that many nonanthropologists have taken up the critique of anthropology's colonialism and made it their mission (Trinh 1989). The popularity of Said's *Orientalism* (1978) among anthropologists and the broadening critique of the implicit colonialism of much of ethnographic writing (Clifford and Marcus, eds. 1986; Marcus and Fischer 1986) demonstrate the concern anthropologists have with this aspect of their work, whether they have done research with people they see as other or close to home. In the face of collapsing confidence in the solidity of ethnographic writing, some have shifted their careers to the dissection of anthropological epistemology, abandoning in the process the question of the use to which any of this work is to be put. Commitment and loyalty become reduced to questions of hermeneutics, and the ethical dilemmas that fueled the shift of the anthropological gaze closer to home in the 1960s float to the peripheries of the debate (Mascia-Lees, Sharpe, and Cohen 1989; Sanjek 1991).

Lesbians and Gay Men Join the Debate

The debates fostered by feminist anthropology, research "at home," and the emergence of "native anthropologists" all suggest a basis for considering the specific situation of gay and lesbian anthropologists both in terms of the redefinition of research topics and choice of field settings. Gay men and lesbians have been invisible as some of the professionals who create anthropological knowledge, and only a sparse body of research in the discipline has focused on homosexuality. As was the case with feminist research, it seems that most of the new anthropological work on homosexuality is being undertaken by lesbian and gay scholars. Whether the inspiration for this work stems from involvement in the gay rights movement, or whether gay researchers undertake such studies because they feel more able to address the subtleties of the topic, they must confront the issue of being "insiders" and how this will affect their professional status. While other insiders are unlikely to have concealed their gender, ethnicity, or national origin, lesbians and gay men have a long and necessary tradition of secrecy about their identity. Choosing to study a topic defined as "homosexual" almost means that others will suspect one of being gay and very likely regard one's work as tainted by personal concerns.[8]

As we noted earlier, the instructional manuals on fieldwork tend to be preoccupied with the mechanics of establishing oneself in the field and going about the business of collecting data. Because the central medium of data collection is, in fact, the anthropologist, getting settled satisfactorily in the field tends to be all about identity management, requiring a highly attuned awareness of how one is being perceived in a community and how this perception will further or impede the research venture. Besides the various accounts of how to undertake this correctly, the literature is full of humorous anecdotes about blunders and misunderstandings anthropologists have made that have had awkward, if not disastrous, implications for the progress of their work.

Fieldwork is seen as different from daily life at home, precisely because this sort of identity management is required; it is assumed that people don't have to do this in their own communities, at least not with the same urgency. But the ordinary life course of lesbians and gay men depends precisely on this sort of management on a regular basis, and this raises particular problems for fieldwork and ethnographic interpretation.

As Goffman explained in his important work on stigma (1963), persons who have a "spoiled identity" must manage information about themselves to create the impression they feel would be more favorable. Gay people in particular find both in their families and in work settings that they must create the impression of heterosexuality in order to avoid feared consequences of ostracism and isolation. Ordinary interactions may be scrutinized for evidence of exposure; hypervigilance is historically the interpersonal stance taken by gay men or lesbians, particularly when operating in contexts where exposure might have serious negative consequences. Most gay people, particularly those who came of age before the gay liberation movement of the 1970s, can testify to some period of secrecy about their sexuality, with passing as straight having been a valued strategy at some point in their lives. Accomplishing this involves careful use of language—no tell-tale, same-sex pronouns in speaking of one's recent dates—and other manipulations of impressions. It may not be enough to avoid dress or demeanor associated with gay or lesbian stereotypes, but it may be necessary (or felt to be necessary) to present a convincing image of heterosexuality in various social contexts. Stories of lesbians and gay men enlisting each other's assistance as "dates" as well as entering into marriages of convenience with each other are part of the repertoire of passing, and many of us have our own versions of such subterfuge to relate. Of course, gay people are always aided by the "heterosexual assumption," the tendency of heterosexuals to regard heterosexuality as axiomatic, but when the stakes are high, it may not feel safe to rely too much on this (D'Emilio 1983; Ponse 1978; Warren 1974).

That secrecy and passing tend to have a painful effect on the individual's self-esteem is by now a truism; the personal history that includes a period of concealing one's orientation from oneself makes clear how painful it can be to realize that one belongs to a despised category. Like those Jews who pass as Gentile or blacks who pass as white, the strategy may involve complicated statements about the self, sometimes paradoxically combining self-deprecation and pride (Goffman 1963). Besides the family, work and professional involvements are contexts in which the consequences of revealing homosexuality are likely to be severe. Whether the much feared rejection or job loss actually will result is hardly the point; the gay man or lesbian carefully managing each dimension of the impression he or she makes fears the worst.

The centrality of coming out or revealing one's homosexuality to some segment of the social world (including at one level, oneself) in the cultural lives of gay people is indicative of the stress such revelations generate. Coming out stories have a number of classic elements and are part of the standard way in which gay people get acquainted (Weston 1991; Zimmerman 1984, 1990). Not only is it is common for a gay man or lesbian getting to know another gay man or lesbian to ask "who knows," particularly with respect to the family of origin and employers, but coming out stories, as Weston has shown, have also become cultural performances that help us elaborate and understand notions of commitment, loyalty, and identity.

This kind of constant, and conscious, identity management is something that needs to be organized in order to survive in a remote field setting as well as in "real life." What personal narratives of gay men and lesbians reveal consistently is the urgency of identity management in the course of ordinary activities. We must consider on a daily basis how much of our personal lives to reveal, how to create a "role" for ourselves that will lessen the likelihood of ostracism or other hostile treatment, and how to coordinate our homosexuality, however we perceive it, with other dimensions of our identities. It doesn't matter whether we gravitate personally toward an essentialist position on sexuality, a constructionist theory, or some position in between (Duberman, Vicinus, and Chauncey, eds. 1989; Fuss 1989; Plummer 1992; Vance 1989). Whether we believe that sexual orientation is a biologically driven propensity or a negotiated identity, whether we wish we could change or are defiantly proud, whether we believe that our sexual orientation is "who we are" or only a minor theme in our larger identities—the management of information about our homosexuality is still a central theme in how we move around in the world.

In graduate school and professional settings, this has generally meant being discreet about one's "personal life," probably concealing its details to some or all of one's colleagues and superiors. At the heart of these daily strategies is the knowledge that even under apparently accepting circumstances same-sex partners will never be regarded as the equivalent of husbands or wives and that gay and lesbian sexuality will always be seen as problematic in a way heterosexuality never is. A friendly heterosexual colleague might try to show openness by asking a lesbian or gay man to relate her or his coming out story, for example. Such a request has the trappings of acceptance and shows a certain amount of in-group knowledge about the cultural centrality of the coming out story, but it also suggests that there is more of a story to be told here than would be the case for a heterosexual life history. Certainly it is widely assumed that even when homosexuality is accepted to some degree at home, it will be a liability in the field, where sexual matters are, in any case, fraught with stress (Bell, Caplan, and Karim, eds. 1994; Whitehead and Conaway, eds. 1986).

Homosexuality, Fieldwork, and Representation

This book addresses two contexts in which the anthropologist's homosexual identity may emerge as an issue from a professional perspective—fieldwork and ethnographic representation. Although conduct in the field is profoundly influenced by personal attributes and by particular historical and social circumstances, fieldwork and writing ethnography are not isomorphic. Questions of identity management emerge not only in traditional—putatively heterosexual—settings but also can be problematic in "homosexual" field sites as well.

Some chapters in the volume—those by Geoffrey Burkhart, Liz Goodman, and Delores Walters in particular—address the question of what it is like for a lesbian or gay anthropologist to go to the field under the kinds of circumstances probably most typical for those beginning their careers. The stories are simple and direct, raising questions that have been raised elsewhere about how their authors faced loneliness, anxiety over how to undertake their research, and confusion about how the people in their research site perceived them. What is important about these stories is that the voices of gay and lesbian fieldworkers have not until now been part of the wider discussion of the mechanics and ethics of fieldwork; earlier works have carefully elided mention of sexuality of any sort (Vance 1991), and specific problems that might preoccupy gay and lesbian anthropologists have also been omitted almost entirely from the earlier literature (Blackwood 1986). The chapters show that many of the issues these authors raise—for example, identity management and fear of loneliness—differ little from those experienced by putatively heterosexual anthropologists. In some cases, after long bouts of self-examination, the authors are amazed by how very ordinary their field experience turned out to be and how their homosexuality neither marks them as different from others nor sours their ability to achieve rapport and complete their research successfully. In other cases, the authors reflect on how the ease with which they moved within the cultures they studied contrasts with the tension and animosity that attaches to homosexual identity in the United States, a striking commentary on relativity of sexual orientation as a central determinant of identity and behavior.

But despite the apparent banality of these stories, they need to be told. Each cohort of young gay and lesbian anthropologists sets off for the field with no idea of how others who share their sexuality have managed such experience in the past (Dickemann 1990). The fact that problems may arise and that they also may be solved, and that some problems may prove to be less significant in the field than they are at home, must be part of the preparation of younger scholars for their fieldwork. Some younger researchers may be encouraged to undertake fieldwork in sites they would otherwise have hesitated to enter, whereas others may learn that the pitfalls in an area they had considered may be more significant than they had anticipated. These stories give a voice to the fears of young anthropologists in particular and allow those whose experience is longer and more diverse to rethink past work. They also, perhaps most importantly, strip the experience of gay or lesbian anthropologists of its uniqueness even while acknowledging the special problems we may face. In many contexts it is being an anthropologist that defines experience and identity even more than particular characteristics such as race, gender, or, for that matter, sexual orientation.

Thus, the chapters that open this volume focus on what is probably the most common dilemma that lesbian and gay anthropologists face: doing fieldwork in "traditional" settings. Here the lesbian or gay researcher is not working on a "gay" topic; the question she or he faces centers on the presentation of self and on establishing an identity that will facilitate the research project at hand. Geoffrey Burkhart reviews the experiences he had over a twenty-year period, tying the kinds of questions he was drawn to study to the process of his own development as a gay man. In particular, he reconsiders the emotional caution he felt he exercised in the field, viewing it as a strategy for preventing his exposure as gay, and reassesses it in terms of its effects on his relations with Indian villagers. Burkhart's hesitancy to acknowledge the interaction between his homosexuality and his fieldwork experience is basic to the style of his piece. He comes to a new understanding of himself and his career, but as tentatively and with much of the uncertainty that marked the original experiences themselves. Just as self-revelation came hard to him during the various fieldwork trips he describes, so he discloses his reconsideration of these times with some continuing trepidation. Burkhart's chapter is a reminder of the uneven process that coming out can be, and of the constant reevaluation and reinvention of experience that is characteristic of intense self-disclosure.

Liz Goodman, who went to the field alone and feared exposure as a lesbian, found that her field experience offered the only context in which she could easily pass as a heterosexual. She learned what it was like to fit in where she had expected to feel lonely and estranged and thus gained a perspective on the stigma she experienced at home. Although she had been open about her lesbianism since her teenage years, being gay had often meant that she felt unwelcome in both professional and personal arenas, and she had assumed that this alienation would be much worse in another culture. But villagers in the North Yorkshire dale where she worked were far more concerned with fitting her into their extended kin networks than with considering whether she met conventional standards of femininity. Once they found a way to link her with a local family, she was accepted as a member of the community as a matter of course. At the same time, she found that her struggle to communicate with villagers, to cope with the harsh climate, and to complete the research needed for her dissertation were far more absorbing than wondering about whether people knew she was gay. The characteristic self-consciousness that stigma had imposed on her at home (Goffman 1963) slipped into irrelevance in the dales.

In a different scenario, Delores Walters describes her trepidation about bringing her partner to the field with her. But she found that having a woman companion, particularly one older than herself, facilitated participation in the local culture. Rather than stigmatizing her as a lesbian, the obvious intimacy between herself and her lover established the lover as an appropriate chaperone and guaranteed her respectability. Not only did villagers not stigmatize her relationship with her lover but they also failed to note the racial difference between them because their age difference loomed much larger in the local view and led to an early assumption that Walters's lover was her mother. Walters's experience, then, relativized her understanding of how intimacy between women might be perceived and dramatized the specificity of the American understanding of race as a core marker of identity.

These commentaries on fieldwork experiences share a common concern with identity management and exposure based on categories brought from the researchers' cultures. Their time in the field showed them that homosexuality may be perceived and evaluated differently in other cultures and that self-consciousness as lesbian or gay researchers shapes the conduct of their research, including the substantive questions they are inspired to ask and the cultural settings they choose.

Other contributions focus on doing fieldwork in a gay or lesbian cultural context. Walter Williams and Sabine Lang, for example, both approach the question of whether the gay or lesbian researcher finds greater acceptance when doing this sort of work and more easily establishes rapport with informants. Williams, who has conducted research on gay topics in a variety of settings from Native North America to Indonesia, reports that revealing that he is gay has eased his entry into other cultures by overcoming the social distance that otherwise undermines trust. In contrast, Lang focuses on the difficulties she experienced doing research with Native American lesbians, difficulties she attributes to the greater salience of being white and European compared to being lesbian. These chapters suggest possible gender differences, of course, but more provocatively remind us that establishing an identity as a gay person is not a simple matter of demographics. Operating in a gay or lesbian context as a lesbian or gay person may require as much negotiation and interpretation as entering a heterosexual domain. The question of whether being lesbian or gay spans cultural boundaries must be answered anew in each situation; there is no answer that will hold in all settings (see D'Emilio and Freedman 1988; Padgug 1989; Vance 1989; and Weeks 1977 on social constructionist views of sexuality). Identity management is not only an issue when lesbian or gay anthropologists work in a straight environment; it continues to be salient in gay contexts as well.

To the extent that studying "one's own" has been somewhat valorized by ongoing discussions in the discipline, such studies pose particularly difficult questions for gay and lesbian anthropologists.[9] Are gay and lesbian people "our tribe"? Is there such a thing as a gay or lesbian person or culture outside Western society? How do these affiliations intersect with others—ethnic group, neighborhood, or gender? Do gay and lesbian anthropologists move through the professional transitions associated with either traditional or nontraditional fieldwork in a manner distinct from that of other fieldworkers, and what are the implications of this for the way we construct ethnographic interpretations?

A biography of Ruth Benedict raises some of these very questions, suggesting that Benedict's lesbianism may have increased her interest in marginality and the experience of "outsiders" (Caffrey 1989). But the book also describes Benedict's deafness, an affliction that often left her feeling marginalized and alone. Without more precise information, is there any way to know whether Benedict's deafness or her lesbianism helped shape the specific questions that she put at the center of her career? Is such an archaeology of the intellect ever convincing or unassailable?

So what does it mean to put oneself in the ethnographic picture? The writing culture school and proponents of greater reflexivity have urged anthropologists to be more explicit about motives, expectations, and personal history, but can one always successfully determine how these factors have their influence? It is very different for anthropologists to put themselves in the picture when they share something with the people under study than when they do not, but what it means to have something in common continues to be a vexing question that, as Spiro (1992) has pointed out, challenges the limits of cultural relativism. Anthropology's raison d'être is drawn in large part from confidence that anthropologists and their informants share basic human qualities, but which these are and to what extent their perception is drawn from individual cultural assumptions remain unresolved (Rosaldo 1989).

Many of the essays in this volume take up the matter of representation of lesbian and gay cultures in one way or another. For some authors, the focus is on the questions to be asked in the conduct of the research and how to arrive at these questions. In what ways does earlier "non-gay" work offer a useful model, and how must old assumptions be revised in order to move into gay and lesbian research? Can anthropologists operate as they have elsewhere when they begin to do research on a population toward whom they have feelings of loyalty? Are the stakes higher? What expectations do the people being studied have for anthropologists? How can the stigma associated with working on a homosexual topic be negotiated? Like Limón, gay or lesbian anthropologists must consider how candidly to tell the "truth." Might they inadvertently reinforce stereotypes that have harmful consequences not only for the gay people with whom they worked but that also might revisit the anthropologists personally in an unpleasant form? How will the community needed for support regard the anthropologist once he or she has uncovered its myths and explained its secrets?

Ellen Lewin, William Leap, and Ralph Bolton all address the transition from "traditional" research to doing research on lesbian and gay populations. For Lewin, getting financial support to do her work on lesbian mothers meant conforming to methodological requirements imposed by the funding agency, including cloaking her topic under the label of "single motherhood." Meeting these expectations helped her to feel that her work was legitimate, but her coming of age as a lesbian researcher demanded overturning the paradigms they imposed on her work and returning to her original focus on lesbian mothers. While her "obedience" to funding agency demands allowed her to launch her project, achieving maturity as a researcher required letting go of her front, a process that freed her to help define the emerging field of gay and lesbian anthropology (Weston 1993) but, ironically, exposed her to discrimination as a lesbian scholar.

Leap describes the work he has done over some twenty years as an anthropological linguist and the growing significance of gay research in his career. He links his move into gay research to the urgency of the AIDS pandemic and his dissatisfaction with life in the academic closet; questions of commitment shape his methods and force him to confront his fears about professional exposure. But working in the gay community also presents methodological and theoretical challenges that reflect back on his work in American Indian languages. Working in a community that he views as his own also raises questions of intimacy and privacy that he has not had to confront in his work on Indian languages.

Ralph Bolton, like Leap, addresses the question of how his emerging gay identity intersected with his development as an anthropologist over his entire career. Although attending to the pressing questions presented by AIDS has shaped his recent work, his commitment to applied research and his focus on work that makes a direct contribution to the solution of a problem both have deep roots in his training and earlier professional activities. Bolton sees the changes in direction that coming out has spelled for him as dramatic in terms of the specific problems he now studies and as simply continuous with principles that have always told him what he should do as an anthropologist. What is different now is the personal stake that being a gay man gives him in the AIDS epidemic; his concerns with human welfare are no longer either altruistic or abstract.

Other chapters take the complexities of research in a gay or lesbian setting in a different direction. Esther Newton raises the question of erotic attraction in the field, ultimately a question of responsibility and commitment that all anthropologists need to consider. What inspires anthropologists to do their research? What does loyalty to their "people" actually consist of? How does this affect what they will write about them? Are the attractions that gay or lesbian anthropologists feel toward informants comparable to attractions they experience in non-research ("real") lives, or is their intensity an artifact of the fieldwork setting?

From a slightly different perspective, Elizabeth Kennedy delves into the problems of doing research in the community in which she lived. Although her work was ethnohistorical and focused on older members of the community as informants, ethical questions dominated the design of the study. What sort of involvement would the community have not only in data-gathering but also in shaping the emergent interpretation? How did this affect decisions about representation of "good" and "bad" aspects of the community's history? What responsibility did Kennedy, and her co-worker Madeline Davis, have toward the women who had shared their lives and to those others in the community whose views of themselves would be influenced by the book to be written? How would the interpretations they published affect their own standing in the community?

Will Roscoe, whose work has concerned two-spirited people ("berdache") in various American Indian groups, directly confronts the question of avoiding objectification of his informants by devising ways for them to collaborate in the conduct of the research.[10] He recommends emphasizing the historical dimensions of the research and other strategies that he believes may reduce the distance between researcher and informant and, in particular, promote a sense of sharing and thereby undermine the hierarchy implicit in a research relationship. Although this approach is surely reactive to the poor reputation anthropology has gained among American Indians, it leaves intact problems of insider-outsider communication.

Stephen Murray's chapter on sex in the field returns readers to the question raised earlier by Williams and Lang of whether the homosexuality of the anthropologists is the same, so to speak, as the homosexuality of people they encounter in the field. While Murray shows that encountering homosexual *behavior* in settings far from home is hardly difficult, assuming that the intent of such behavior is transparent and that the actors are therefore "gay" from the standpoint of personal *identity* may be unwarranted. In the final analysis, such experiences speak only of themselves; it is generalization about homosexuality (or any other behavior) in the field that may be risky at all levels.

Raising a different sort of question, Jim Wafer considers how to imagine a "gay ethnography." He points out that conventions of keeping one's sexual orientation private comply with traditional demands that separate personal and the professional dimensions of a researcher's life and pretend that his or her identity has no impact on the outcome of the work, in the case of anthropology, the ethnography. But Wafer's sexuality was not incidental to his work on an Afro-Brazilian religion, many of whose practitioners have been described as being homosexual. His solution, what he calls an "experiential" ethnography, actively incorporates his gay identity as an integral part of the text. Distinguishing this approach from what one might call a confessional ethnography, Wafer sees this textual strategy as a way to acknowledge the impact of his sexual orientation on all levels of his activities in the field and more broadly as a way of confronting the attempt of professional conventions to compartmentalize the personal and professional in the anthropological venture.

Kath Weston's chapter addresses a different aspect of connection with those being studied and the implications of loyalty to members of individual communities. By focusing on her complicated connection to a young woman in the community she studied, the person to whom she ultimately dedicated her book, Weston points to the ironies and ambiguities faced by lesbian and gay writers who hope to keep firm the connections between the work they do and the larger issues facing their communities and themselves. By choosing to dedicate her book to a person who never benefited from the illusive gifts of community, she reminds herself, and us, that an analysis of how lesbian and gay people survive must also include a recognition of those who do not. If being "insiders" allows lesbian and gay anthropologists any special knowledge, it is that no explanation can take all variations into account and that systems that work also fail. A longer commitment to communities can perhaps prevent us being too readily convinced by neat models and personal descriptive powers.

Sue-Ellen Jacobs's Afterword puts all of these approaches into the historical context that has surrounded the rise of lesbian and gay anthropology. Beginning with her experiences during the 1960s of intense self-consciousness as she attempted to negotiate an acceptable identity in graduate school, Jacobs describes how her efforts to cope with stigma shaped her development as an anthropologist and determined decisions she would make about research topics and the interpersonal style she would adopt in the field. At the same time, however, her awareness of how the ambiguities of sex and gender can be performed moved her toward the study of gender variance and to pioneering work in the development of feminist anthropology, the field with which she is most closely associated.

Implications: Toward a Lesbian and Gay Ethnography

The volume offers lesbian and gay anthropologists an opportunity to consider their relationships to these dilemmas and suggest further implications that their sexuality might have for their conduct as fieldworkers and ethnographers. Significantly, it also performs a crucial function for future generations of gay men and lesbians in the profession by making clear that the kind of self-examination and self-disclosure engaged in here is part of stripping stigma from personal as well as scholarly experience. Although not everything authors have to say here is totally unique or new—much reflects earlier ventures into reflexivity by other writers—what is new is our willingness to identify ourselves as lesbian or gay and our commitment to adding this aspect of our experience to growing debates about the nature of the ethnographic enterprise. Breaking our silence doesn't mean that all we choose to say is original; what is fresh and new is the understanding that lesbian and gay anthropologists have both mundane and strikingly different encounters in the field, that we struggle with the same ethical and representation dilemmas as our presumably heterosexual colleagues and can draw on the specific features of our experience to suggest new answers to old questions.

But the volume also raises questions that bear on the heart of the anthropological enterprise in the last years of the century—the growing need, of straight researchers as well as gay, to specify and understand their motivations, an insistence that anthropologists recognize how positionality affects processes by which they construct understandings of cultural phenomena. While these chapters attempt to define the ways in which lesbian and gay identity may intersect with the authors' objectives as writers and fieldworkers, they do not specify a fixed relationship between identities and activities. Lesbian and gay identities, like all identities, are contested and shifting, both within particular research and interpretive endeavors and as they resonate with the other identities that shape the authors' work. The increasing visibility of the lesbian and gay rights movement has provided us with the ability to use our particular circumstances to shed light on questions of identity, personhood, and commitment throughout the academy and, perhaps, beyond.

Notes

1   Anthropologists have frequently been criticized for their failure to record data on sexual behavior of all types accurately and for their particular reticence about reporting on observations of homosexual behavior. Because of these omissions, cross-cultural data on sexuality tend to be incomplete and idiosyncratic. See, for example, Blackwood (1986).

2   The rarity of such candor, and the use of pseudonyms in some of the few instances where it occurs, underscores the hesitation most anthropologists feel about revealing such experiences or feelings anywhere in writing.

3   The first explicit discussion of this notion may be as recent as Williams (1986).

4   For a personal account of how homophobia adversely affects academic careers, see Newton (1987).

5   For Ellen Lewin, it was Hortense Powdermaker's *Stranger and Friend* (1966) that provided a vivid image of what it would be like to do fieldwork as a solitary woman in a remote location. The necessity to manage significant physical duress and loneliness was offset, in the image she carried away from that book, by the rewards of achieving intimacy with the members of a distant culture. Along with this image was one of transgression—this was not the sort of thing educated, urban people normally did. Powdermaker's description of participating in a dance with village women and the sense of belonging she achieved in doing this contrasted with the way she imagined her family reacting to her "dancing with savages"!

6   When Ellen Lewin carried out her doctoral fieldwork among Latin American immigrants in San Francisco, she was criticized for working "too close" to home; although she is not Latina, she was a resident of San Francisco and lived less than a mile from the neighborhood where she planned to carry out her research. Once the fieldwork had been completed and she was beginning work on her dissertation, one of her professors jokingly suggested that she fly somewhere—perhaps to Los Angeles—and then return so that students and faculty could meet her at the airport and welcome her home. Instead, she marked the transition in her status from fieldworker to analyst by moving to a new apartment.

7   Unfortunately, the introduction to Clifford and Marcus (1986) retains a particularly obnoxious version of this credo. But see Behar and Gordon (1995) for a detailed critique of their position.

8   Being labeled as gay or lesbian is likely, as well, to result in professional discrimination at various levels. See Newton (1987) for one instance of what is anecdotally known to be a widespread pattern.

9   These preferences have not, it seems, penetrated the status system of the profession that still prefers to hire anthropologists who have worked in exotic locales and who have their "credentials."

10 The term *berdache* is derived from a French term that means "catamite" or "boy kept for immoral purposes." Long used in the anthropological literature to refer to gender and sexual diversity found among Native Amer-

icans, the term is now viewed by many as an outdated and demeaning vestige of colonial discourse. The term preferred by Native Americans and anthropologists who work in the area of gender diversity and sexuality among Native Americans is *two-spirit*, which can be used to refer to "individuals who are lesbian, gay, transgendered (cross-dressers, transvestites, and transsexuals), or otherwise 'marked' within bands, tribes and nations where multiple gender concepts occur" (Jacobs and Thomas 1994:7). Although many of those who favor adoption of the term *two-spirit* signal their displeasure with the outdated "berdache" by following every occurrence with the Latin [*sic*], for the sake of editorial simplicity we will use "two-spirit" throughout the text that follows except where "berdache" is called for in specific contexts.

References Cited

Abu-Lughod, Lila. 1991. "Writing against Culture." In *Recapturing Anthropology: Working in the Present*, ed. Richard G. Fox, 137–62. Santa Fe: School of American Research Press.

Agar, Michael H. 1980. *The Professional Stranger: An Informal Introduction to Ethnography*. New York: Academic Press.

Aguilar, John L. 1981. "Insider Research: An Ethnography of a Debate." In *Anthropologists at Home in North America: Methods and Issues in the Study of One's Own Society*, ed. Donald A. Messerschmidt, 15–28. Cambridge: Cambridge University Press.

Altorki, Soraya, and Camillia Fawzi El-Solh, eds. 1988. *Arab Women in the Field: Studying Your Own Society*. Syracuse: Syracuse University Press.

Ardener, Edward. 1975. "Belief and the Problem of Women." In *Perceiving Women*, ed. Shirley Ardener, 1–27. London: Malaby Press.

Beals, Alan R. 1980. *Gopalpur: A South Indian Village*. New York: Holt, Rinehart and Winston.

Behar, Ruth, and Deborah Gordon. 1995. *Women Writing Culture*. Berkeley: University of California Press.

Bell, Diane, Pat Caplan, and Wazir Jahan Karim, eds. 1993. *Gendered Fields: Women, Men, and Ethnography*. London: Routledge.

Blackwood, Evelyn. 1986. "Breaking the Mirror: The Construction of Lesbianism and the Anthropological Discourse on Homosexuality." In *Anthropology and Homosexual Behavior*, ed. Evelyn Blackwood, 1–17. New York: Haworth Press.

Briggs, Jean. 1970. "Kapluna Daughter." In *Women in the Field: Anthropological Experiences*, ed. Peggy Golde, 19–44. Chicago: Aldine.

Caffrey, Margaret M. 1989. *Ruth Benedict: Stranger in This Land*. Austin: University of Texas Press.

Cesara, Manda [Karla O. Poewe]. 1982. *Reflections of a Woman Anthropologist: No Hiding Place*. New York: Academic Press.

Chagnon, Napoleon. 1983. *Yanomamo: The Fierce People*. 3d ed. New York: Holt, Rinehart and Winston.

Clifford, James, and George E. Marcus, eds. 1986. *Writing Culture: The Poetics and Politics of Ethnography.* Berkeley: University of California Press.

Conklin, Harold C. 1960. "Maling, a Hanunoo Girl from the Philippines." In *In the Company of Man: Twenty Portraits of Anthropological Informants,* ed. Joseph A. Casagrande, 101–18. New York: Harper and Row.

Dickemann, Mildred. 1990. "The Imperative of Ethnography: Impact on Non-Heterosexual Fieldworkers." Paper presented at annual meeting of American Anthropological Association, New Orleans.

D'Emilio, John. 1983. *Sexual Politics, Sexual Communities: The Making of the Homosexual Minority in the United States, 1940–1970.* Chicago: University of Chicago Press.

D'Emilio, John, and Estelle Freedman. 1988. *Intimate Matters: A Social History of Sexuality in America.* New York: Harper and Row.

Duberman, Martin Bauml, Martha Vicinus, and George Chauncey, Jr., eds., 1989. *Hidden from History: Reclaiming the Gay and Lesbian Past.* New York: New American Library.

DuBois, Barbara. 1983. "Passionate Scholarship: Notes on Values, Knowing and Method in Feminist Social Science." In *Theories of Women's Studies,* ed. G. Bowles and R. D. Klein, 105–16. London: Routledge and Kegan Paul.

Fonow, Mary Margaret, and Judith A. Cook, eds. 1991. *Beyond Methodology: Feminist Scholarship as Lived Research.* Bloomington: Indiana University Press.

Foster, George M., Thayer Scudder, Elizabeth Colson, and Robert V. Kemper, eds. 1979. *Long-term Field Research in Social Anthropology.* New York: Academic Press.

Frake, Charles. 1962. "The Diagnosis of Disease among the Subanun of Mindanao." *American Anthropologist* 64:340–50.

Fuss, Diana. 1989. *Essentially Speaking: Feminism, Nature and Difference.* New York: Routledge.

Geertz, Clifford. 1988. *Works and Lives: The Anthropologist as Author.* Stanford: Stanford University Press.

Goffman, Erving. 1963. *Stigma: Notes on the Management of Spoiled Identity.* New York: Simon and Schuster.

Golde, Peggy, ed. 1970. *Women in the Field.* Chicago: Aldine.

Goodale, Jane C. 1971. *Tiwi Wives: A Study of the Women of Melville Island, North Australia.* Seattle: University of Washington Press.

Gwaltney, John L. 1981. "Common Sense and Science: Urban Core Black Observations." In *Anthropologists at Home in North America: Methods and Issues in the Study of One's Own Society,* ed. Donald A. Messerschmidt, 46–61. Cambridge: Cambridge University Press.

Harding, Sandra, ed. 1987. *Feminism and Methodology.* Bloomington: Indiana University Press.

Harvey, Penelope. 1992. "Bilingualism in the Andes." In *Researching Language: Issues of Power and Method,* ed. Deborah Cameron, Elizabeth Frazer, Penelope Harvey, M. B. H. Rampton, and Kay Richardson, 65–89. London: Routledge.

Hymes, Dell, ed. 1972. *Reinventing Anthropology*. New York: Random House.

Jacobs, Sue-Ellen, and Wesley Thomas. 1994. "Native American Two-Spirits." *Anthropology Newsletter* 35(8):7.

Jones, Delmos J. 1970. "Toward a Native Anthropology." *Human Organization* 29:251–59.

Kimball, Solon, and William L. Partridge. 1979. *The Craft of Community Study: Fieldwork Dialogues*. Gainesville: University Presses of Florida.

Kirshenblatt-Gimblett, Barbara. 1992. "Foreword." In *Remembered Lives: The Work of Ritual, Storytelling, and Growing Older*, ed. Marc Kaminsky, ix–xiv. Ann Arbor: University of Michigan Press.

Leap, William. 1981. "Roles for the Non-Indian Linguist in American Indian Bilingual Education." In *American Indian Language Renewal*, ed. Robert St. Clair and William Leap, 19–30. Rosslyn, Va.: National Clearinghouse for Bilingual Education.

Limón, José. 1991. "Representation, Ethnicity, and the Precursory Ethnography: Notes of a Native Anthropologist." In *Recapturing Anthropology: Working in the Present*, ed. Richard G. Fox, 115–35. Santa Fe: School of American Research Press.

Malinowski, Bronislaw. 1989 [1967]. *A Diary in the Strict Sense of the Term*. Stanford: Stanford University Press.

Marcus, George E., and Michael M. J. Fischer. 1986. *Anthropology as Cultural Critique*. Chicago: University of Chicago Press.

Mascia-Lees, Frances, E., Patricia Sharpe, and Colleen Ballerino Cohen. 1989. "The Postmodernist Turn in Anthropology: Cautions from a Feminist Perspective." *Signs* 15(11):7–33.

Myerhoff, Barbara, and Jay Ruby. 1992 [1982]. "A Crack in the Mirror: Reflexive Perspectives in Anthropology." In *Remembered Lives: The Work of Ritual, Storytelling, and Growing Older*, ed. Marc Kaminsky, 307–40. Ann Arbor: University of Michigan Press.

Nader, Laura. 1972. "Up the Anthropologist: Perspectives Gained from Studying Up." In *Reinventing Anthropology*, ed. Dell Hymes, 284–311. New York: Pantheon.

Nayarin, Kirin. 1993. "How Native Is a 'Native' Anthropologist?" *American Anthropologist* 95:671–86.

Newton, Esther. 1987. "Academe's Homophobia: It Damages Careers and Ruins Lives." *Chronicle of Higher Education*, March 11, 104.

Nielsen, Joyce McCarl, ed. 1990. *Feminist Research Methods: Exemplary Readings in the Social Sciences*. Boulder: Westview Press.

Oakley, Ann. 1981. "Interviewing Women: A Contradiction in Terms." In *Doing Feminist Research*, ed. Helen Roberts, 30–61. London: Routledge and Kegan Paul.

Ohnuki-Tierney, Emiko. 1984. "'Native' Anthropologists." *American Ethnologist* 11(3):584–86.

Padgug, Robert. 1989. "Sexual Matters: Rethinking Sexuality in History." In *Hidden from History: Reclaiming the Gay and Lesbian Past*, ed. Martin

Bauml Duberman, Martha Vicinus, and George Chauncey, Jr., 54–64. New York: New American Library.

Personal Narratives Group, ed. 1989. *Interpreting Women's Lives: Feminist Theory and Personal Narratives.* Bloomington: Indiana University Press.

Plummer, Ken. 1992. "Speaking Its Name: Inventing a Lesbian and Gay Studies." In *Modern Homosexualities: Fragments of Lesbian and Gay Experience,* ed. Ken Plummer, 3–25. London: Routledge.

Ponse, Barbara. 1978. *Identities in the Lesbian World.* Westport: Greenwood Press.

Powdermaker, Hortense. 1966. *Stranger and Friend: The Way of an Anthropologist.* New York: W. W. Norton.

Rabinow, Paul. 1977. *Reflections on Fieldwork in Morocco.* Berkeley: University of California Press.

Reiter, Rayna R., ed. 1975. *Toward an Anthropology of Women.* New York: Monthly Review Press.

Roberts, Helen, ed. 1981. *Doing Feminist Research.* London: Routledge and Kegan Paul.

Rosaldo, Michelle Z., and Louise Lamphere, eds. 1974. *Woman, Culture, and Society.* Stanford: Stanford University Press.

Rosaldo, Renato. 1989. *Culture and Truth: The Remaking of Social Analysis.* Boston: Beacon Press.

Said, Edward W. 1978. *Orientalism.* New York: Random House.

Samarin, William. 1967. *Field Linguistics: A Guide to Linguistic Field Work.* New York: Random House.

Sanjek, Roger. 1991. "The Ethnographic Present." *Man* (n.s.) 26:609–28.

Seligman, Brenda Z., ed. 1951. *Notes and Queries in Anthropology.* 6th ed. London: Routledge and Kegan Paul.

Spiro, Melford E. 1992. "Cultural Relativism and the Future of Anthropology." In *Rereading Cultural Anthropology,* ed. George E. Marcus, 124–51. Durham: Duke University Press.

Stocking, George W., Jr. 1987. *Victorian Anthropology.* New York: Free Press.

Tedlock, Barbara. 1991. "From Participant Observation to the Observation of Participation: The Emergence of Narrative Ethnography." *Journal of Anthropological Research* 47:69–94.

Trinh T. Minh-ha. 1989. *Woman, Native, Other.* Bloomington: Indiana University Press.

Vance, Carole S. 1989. "Social Construction Theory: Problems in the History of Sexuality." In *Homosexuality: Which Homosexuality?* ed. Dennis Altman et al., 13–34. Amsterdam: Schorer Press.

———. 1991. "Anthropology Rediscovers Sexuality: A Theoretical Comment." *Social Science and Medicine* 33(8):875–84.

Warren, Carol A. B. 1974. *Identity and Community in the Gay World.* New York: Wiley.

Weeks, Jeffrey. 1977. *Coming Out: Homosexual Politics in Britain from the Nineteenth Century to the Present.* London: Quartet Books.

Weiner, Annette. 1976. *Women of Value, Men of Renown: New Perspectives in Trobriand Exchange.* Austin: University of Texas Press.

Weston, Kath. 1991. *Families We Choose: Lesbians, Gays, Kinship.* New York: Columbia University Press.

———. 1993. "Lesbian/Gay Studies in the House of Anthropology." *Annual Review of Anthropology* 22:339–67.

Whitehead, Tony Larry, and Mary Ellen Conaway, eds. 1986. *Self, Sex, and Gender in Cross-Cultural Fieldwork.* Urbana: University of Illinois Press.

Williams, Walter. 1986. *The Spirit and the Flesh: Sexual Diversity in American Indian Culture.* Boston: Beacon Press.

Wulf, Robert, and Shirley Fiske, eds. 1986. *Anthropological Praxis.* Boulder: Westview Press.

Zimmerman, Bonnie. 1984. "The Politics of Transliteration: Lesbian First-Person Narratives." *Signs* 9(4):663–82.

———. 1990. *The Safe Sea of Women: Lesbian Fiction 1969–1989.* Boston: Beacon Press.

IDENTITY MANAGEMENT
IN THE FIELD

1. Not Given to Personal Disclosure
Geoffrey Burkhart

One morning in December 1965, quite early in my first fieldwork in a village in southern India, my landlord's son called attention to some people gathered in the street on which my house faced. Looking out the door, I was pleased to see a group of villagers aligned in such a way that I could suppose correctly, having studied many ethnographies, that a traditional dispute-settling process was displayed before me. After a troublesome first few days in the village, this recognizable, expectable event seemed a sign that my work was going to go now as it should.

Leaving my house, I approached the gathering quickly and positioned myself at the edge of the onlookers where I could see and hear all that was going on. Immediately, one elder, a member of this council of men hearing what was revealed to be a divorce case, summoned me to sit next to him at the center of the proceedings. As I moved to the seat offered me, I felt thrown into a spotlight, agitated and awkward at having interrupted the judicial process. I sat and listened quietly and, I hoped, unobtrusively to the lively arguments, helped by an English-speaking former serviceman who had come early to my aid. After some time, however, I was startled when I understood that the elders were asking for my opinion on the case. I was now certain that I had done wrong to allow myself to be drawn in these ways to the center of the proceedings. In response I sputtered my foreignness, my newness to the village, and my lack of understanding of local custom and procedure, all the while fussing inwardly about losing my objective stance so soon and worrying about the implications of that loss for the rest of my fieldwork. The council members listened patiently to me. When I had finished speaking about my difference, one elder said simply, "We know that. We just want to know what you think."

The juxtaposition of the elders' realism and my grandiose view of my place in this setting, and by extension in the village as a whole, contained a fortunate, critical lesson, one that has continued to signal for me complexities in a cluster of confusions and anxieties that I had brought to the field with me. After that morning, I began to become aware that I could relax a bit, because villagers were going to take me largely on their terms and only partially on my own. My simplistic misreading of the elders' relocation of me spatially from the edge to the center of the council's deliberations and the jarring comment, "We know that," suggested the necessity of seeing my place as places, my stance as stances. To claim, as I had begun to do with villagers, that I was a humble student of Tamil customs and practices was in some senses true but also ingenuous and naively unmindful of negotiated relations built upon contingencies of constraint and choice.

This experience raises questions about the ways in which self-knowledge is implicated in the delineation of a proper and effective role in the field. Aspects of personal character formation become linked, largely insidiously, I think, with constructions of 'fieldworker' that, in turn, are considered appropriate to operationalizing theoretical perspectives. The attempt to implement any fieldworker mode in a particular field setting is directly affected by the perceptions of "the fieldworker" held by those with whom the fieldwork ultimately unfolds. My aim in this chapter is to explore connections in a triad of issues: my adoption of a professional persona, shifts in my research interests, and my changing understanding of my sexual orientation. I will comment briefly on my continuing attraction to research in India in regard to changes in the relation of my personal and professional lives.

Numerous anthropologists, of course, have already paid considerable attention to conceptions of sex and gender in relation to those of people with whom they lived (Golde, ed. 1986; Panini, ed. 1991; Whitehead and Conaway, eds. 1986; Warren 1988). In something of the same way, but turning to a largely overlooked dimension, Pilling (1988) distinguishes elusive threads of lesbian and gay orientation in the larger knot of sexuality, gender, and other aspects of identity in his review of Stocking's *Malinowski, Rivers, Benedict and Others: Essays on Culture and Personality* (1986). Pilling's discussion draws attention to neglected aspects of the anthropological practice of major figures in the discipline. His review opens larger questions about what is silenced or muted in accounts of the shaping of the discipline and in the handing down of anthropological method.[1]

Field Settings

From 1965 to 1967 my doctoral research focused on social structure, with particular attention to caste, kinship, descent, and marriage in a village in Tamil Nadu, India. The villagers viewed me as not yet married. In 1972 my wife and I visited the village briefly. In 1976, after my wife and I had separated, I returned again for follow-up fieldwork of a few months. During the summers of 1977 and 1979, I undertook an exploratory study of adults at a cerebral palsy camp in the United States in the hope of weaning my interest away from the too-distant India. At camp, many staff members knew I was gay; campers did not. Unable to let go of the pull of India, however, in 1983 I began a study of a Lutheran congregation in a town in northern Tamil Nadu. There I was known as a divorced stepparent. I made return visits in 1987 and 1991. In the summer of 1985 in Copenhagen, I interviewed retired Danish women missionaries who had worked with the Indian Lutherans I had studied. I think these women understood me to be single; at least one knew I had stepchildren.

In the pages that follow, my discussion of practicing fieldwork refers only to what I did as an outcome of my perception of what an anthropologist was "supposed to do" in the field. Thus, the limitations I note were—and are—mine and are not to be understood as those of my teachers, who, I now suppose, might have welcomed a less conventional apprentice. To put it differently, I write about what I learned and attempted to practice and not necessarily about what others had hoped to teach me.

A SOUTH INDIAN VILLAGE

The story with which I opened this account characterizes my initial approach in Nallur, where I carried out dissertation research for thirteen months, from 1965 to 1967. My fieldworker persona included a now much-commented-upon convention, for males particularly: a pose of emotional neutrality. This stance was marked, among other things, by extreme caution in forming emotional connections in general. This is best represented by a taboo, a prescriptive avoidance of sexual relations, epitomizing the threats to "observer neutrality" and the fear of distortion that entangling affective ties might have brought. Similarly, it was important to me to hide frustration and anger for fear of alienating prospective informants. My aim was to laugh and cry, but only as I might come to understand that villagers did so, thus only as participant-observer. The emotional toll of these constraints, familiar to many anthropologists, for me resulted in spells of inertia and depression that I treated with escapes to town to visit friends and read.

However, in an odd juxtaposition to my professional distance, I was greatly struck by the emotional resourcefulness of Indians and by their sensitivity to and willingness to identify, identify with, and participate in emotional states of those close to them. I was impressed by (and continue to value) their presumption of continuity in personal relations. In particular I was struck by the emotional warmth of friendship among men in Nallur and by the physical closeness it often entailed. I was pleased with the easy warmth with which men, especially of my age then, mid-twenties and younger, accepted me.[2] It was only toward the end of my work in Nallur that I began to look on some villagers as friends, but even then our relationship was constrained. Although I welcomed the demonstration of friendship toward me by men and women, my stance restricted coming to grips with the confusion over emotional ties with informants. It also contributed to my defenses against developing self-understanding of my attraction to men. Only some years later did I understand how problematic for villagers was the fitful way in which I reciprocated their friendship.

As these comments suggest, many villagers were kinder to me than I was to myself. In regard to allowing the expression of personal style and feeling, most were surprisingly unconstraining. For example, after going regularly back and forth to a neighboring village for several days and nights to observe the festival of its deity, I was surprised and confused to hear a few men ask me in a matter-of-fact way what lover I had taken there. Their question was conventional, its spoken tone accepting and serious, but it also tweaked my assumption of a *brahmachari*-like status, the bachelor-student stage of life preceding that of householder in the Hindu life-cycle.[3] I sometimes took refuge in this status to deflect what I considered to be tangential conversations about my marital prospects, including offers of help in finding a bride locally; about divorce in America; and, on only two occasions that I can recall, my defenses being so sturdy, offers of aid in arranging a sexual tryst.

The costly stance of emotional neutrality, fed by my less-than-conscious confusion about sexual orientation and bulwarked by my casting of objectivity, prevented me from accepting fully those offers of leeway in placing myself in various areas of social life, even though I became expert in taking advantage of the flexibility allowed me due to my apprentice status. As my daybook makes clear, both by its entries and perhaps especially its gaps, attempts at maintaining emotional neutrality led me often to relations in which I was dependent, rather than a party to reciprocity. Of course, this led me to those good people of Nallur, whose compassion, understanding, and generosity encompassed and supported me. It also resulted in an extremely uncomfortable association with a few people who saw me merely as an amusement or a means to some private gain.

My emotional neutrality also included a conceit of gender innocence. I felt that gender made no important difference in my work beyond such conventional notions that women might not talk to me about personal subjects. My attempt to erase sexuality and my stance of gender innocence did not particularly interfere with the collection of conventional sets of data—household censuses, genealogies, and migration histories— nor with uncovering regularities of social life in norm and action that gave form to descent organization, household division, and marriage alliance. However, my stance did not encourage me to see as interesting or problematical, for example, the life of a man I will call Govindan, who was in his thirties yet unmarried and living alone on the edge of the village, outside his caste neighborhood and among households of several castes. His clothing was androgynous, and he was treated with a mixture of kindly yet sometimes whimsical remarks and slight smiles. Whatever Govindan's story, the idea that his situation might throw light on subjects of central concern to me the dynamics of household growth and division, the relation of household to descent orderings, and patterns of expectations regarding marriages among kin—escaped me. I did not view conceptions of gender as interestingly problematic despite the symbolic significance of gender representations—for example, transvestism—in some village festivals. Similarly, although I was struck by the prescriptive, highly affective relation of same-sex cross-cousins, I did not find a way to explore it and link it to my central focus on the structure of marriage alliance. My stance contributed to my reticence in raising questions about sexuality in general and sexual behavior in particular and about related subjects such as fertility and birth control. I barely allowed myself the dim perception of hints of sexual activity between male youths, and in this regard I learned nothing at all about women.

In 1972, now married, I returned to Nallur for a few days with my wife. For some people there, the progression of my life-cycle was clear: I had finished my studies by obtaining a Ph.D. and then moved on appropriately from studenthood to the stage of householder. Yet here some villagers perceived anomalies. How was it that my wife was slightly older than I? What did it mean that I now had three stepchildren, that I should think of them as my own children, and that I disavowed any interest in further progeny? And how could my class and marital status be properly validated in the photographs I was taking when I had given my wife so very little jewelry? (Friends obligingly lent her gold chains.)

In 1976 I returned alone to Nallur for three months of fieldwork. My wife and I had separated by then, and I was grappling with a new understanding of myself as a gay man. I felt, in part defensively, that these personal issues had no relevance to my study, an extension of my interest in local marriage alliances to regional marriage networks and to the use of caste titles and other customs as markers of caste boundaries. I tried to avoid answering questions about my marriage, at times rudely obfuscating, it shames me now to say, in response to the genuine concerns of villagers and friends in a nearby town. I failed to allow related questions—such as how, because I was understood to be separated or divorced, I could continue to think of myself as a stepparent—to bridge my life and research. I succeeded in compartmentalizing my professional and personal interests, in distinguishing villagers' kinship practices and notions from their personal interests in me, particularly those concerning my kinship practices and notions.

It is obvious that my ideas about the ranges of data that were pertinent to kinship studies in Nallur tended to follow well-worn tracks. I did not anticipate, for example, some present concerns with connecting data on sexuality and gender to kinship issues (Collier and Yanagisako 1987; Weston 1991). Neither could I move beyond a concern with standardized sentiment to explore wider issues of emotion (Trawick 1990).

During these periods of research, however, I was struck by the tendency of some South-Asianist anthropologists to understand southern India as made up of several core cultural areas and to consider an ethnographic case in regard to its typicality in fitting into its region. Nallur was not geographically central in this sense, but "marginal" or on a "frontier" (not belonging fully to either of the neighboring cultural regions of Kongunadu and Cholamandalam). I argued that rather than sort ethnographic cases into "central" and "peripheral" (in which case other anthropologists would have seen Nallur as peripheral)—with a tendency to understand these as an opposition between "standard form" and "mutation"—each case should be taken as having equal weight in understanding concomitant variation of forms of kinship and marriage institutions.[4] This allowed me, for example, to avoid falsely concretizing (and misapplying) a notion of lineage developed in classic African ethnographies yet still to examine processes of familial aggregation and displacement as related to the internal order of caste. (This general concern parallels some issues that have been reworked and developed as "polyvocality" and "voice.") The strength of my feeling about these issues mirrored, in a displaced and abstract way, my personal unrest as out of step with others' assumptions about diversity. It foreshadowed convictions about the misunderstandings that follow from the imposition of certain notions of normality. This concern led me next to research among a stigmatized group in the United States.

AN AMERICAN SUMMER CAMP

During the summers of 1977 and 1979 I volunteered as a counselor at a summer camp for adults with cerebral palsy. I came to treat this experience as exploratory fieldwork, with the hope of defining new lines of research in the United States. What interested me most about the camp as a field situation was that it united in a communal setting (if temporarily so) persons who are often stigmatized and that the camp was guided by a progressive, supportive ethos. In a curious reversal of common experience, one camp administrator, before camp began, expressed concern to me about my being gay but in practice was totally unrestrictive and entirely supportive of me.

As I began later to think about my experience at camp, I became interested in understanding the force of cultural constructs, for example, "handicapped," as they operated inexorably through a series of camp customs to reimpose a clear boundary between "handicapped" and "nonhandicapped" people regardless of efforts to deemphasize the cleavage. To put it differently, I was struck by the enormous difficulties of even the best intentioned, thoughtful people to escape the discriminatory implications of certain cultural categories. I also became interested in trying to understand how campers perceived themselves. For example, one man, who spoke with great difficulty, said to me, "When I talk I think I sound just like you do." Questions about how campers perceived patronizing and discriminatory acts and how they chose to deal with them became central.

Although I did not follow this experience at camp with further research on the handling of disabilities, it brought together three issues.

First was the great contrast between doing fieldwork in India and fieldwork at home. A major issue here was the difference between my attempts to maintain a "cool" mode of research in India and the demands of work in an emotionally charged setting like the camp. (It was at this point, for example, that the ardent anthropology of Jules Henry, as in his *Culture Against Man* [1963], first interested me.) Second, I became interested in connections between perspectives in ethnicity and personhood (especially as developed by Fortes 1971, 1983). Third, my concern with numerous categories of people marked by stigma was increased. Although I did not spell out specific comparative issues connecting what I learned at camp to my research in India (where I had largely focused on the study of a high caste), the resonance of ritual pollution, caste discrimination, and the management of low-caste identity certainly conditioned my interests. More obviously, the necessity of beginning to come to terms with identity, stigma, and community in claiming my sexual orientation guided both my topical focus and approach.

A SOUTH INDIAN TOWN

Despite the fascinating issues the camp setting provided and the rewards of working with adults in its emotionally engaged setting, the pull of India continued to be strong. Thus, in 1983 I returned to southern India, where I undertook a study of a Lutheran congregation in a town I call Arulur, then of twenty-three thousand people, about eighty miles from Nallur. The town and its region were both new to me. There I was understood by many people as a divorced man with adult stepchildren. Frequent letters from my male partner of several years were understood as coming from my best friend, whom my host families accepted with the same warmth they accorded me when he visited in 1983 and again in 1987 and 1991, when we returned to Arulur for short visits.

Not at first intending to study Christians, I chose Arulur, a *taluk* headquarters (something like a county seat) as a suitable place to investigate cooperative activity based on relationships other than those of caste and kinship. I had in mind groups such as temple committees, bank boards, teachers' associations, and sports clubs. However, on a chance invitation to a church festival, I was struck by qualities of family relations on this semipublic occasion, especially by the modulation of tones of authority in husband-wife and parent-child relations. These seemed different, in a possibly inappropriate comparison, than those among the middle- and high-caste Hindu families I had known best in Nallur.

I was drawn to these Lutheran families also because many of their forebears, although certainly not all, had converted from castes of low rank. I was curious about the shedding of caste-associated stigma in the context of the evangelistic, educational, and medical work of the Danish Mission Society, which had begun work in Arulur early in this century, and in the complementary work of its successor-church institutions. I became interested in individual and family histories and also in how Lutherans, numbering about two hundred, talked about themselves in relation to the larger religious setting that included some Pentecostal and several hundred Roman Catholic Christians, Hindus (the majority), a few thousand Muslims, and several families of Jains.[5] I investigated Lutherans' perceptions of changes in their lives as their families had become Christian and were able to take advantage of the opportunities provided by mission and church. I became especially interested in women's lives in this regard.

Although I tried to investigate various aspects of the larger town setting of Lutheran life—and despite an underlying interest in stigmatized groups—I did not allow myself to contact the *hijras*, people who claim to be neither men nor women (Nanda 1990), who frequently stayed in Arulur as they moved from town to town along the railway line. I was aware of their presence quite early in my work, yet, not knowing how they were thought of, I feared disapproval and jeopardizing my growing contacts with Lutheran families if I pursued my interest in them, and I did not want to become distracted from my focus on Protestants. I mentioned *hijras* to people in Arulur only once or twice, failing to elicit much comment on them, and no one ever mentioned them to me.

Similarly, after passing some months in Arulur, I began to discern suggestions of homosexual interests in the behavior of a few young men (to my knowledge not associated with *hijras*), whom I knew only in passing and who were not Lutherans. I began to have an impression of their mutual friendships as well as the vague sense that their interests outside of family life provoked a hint of dissatisfaction with them on the part of some others. But I did not pursue acquaintance with them because my recognition of them came quite late in my stay, and I did not know whether attempting to learn more about them would interfere with completion of my work in the little time I had left.

Townspeople and the pastor generously allowed me access to many Lutheran families and church activities. I was assumed categorically as a "European" to be a Christian. Despite my lack of church affiliation in the United States (or perhaps because of it) I was welcomed at nearly all church activities. Although at first some people assumed that I was some sort of missionary, I was allowed to distinguish between a role of scholar and of religious personage. The contact that many Lutherans, especially those over thirty, had with Danish and other foreign missionaries led many to welcome me into their homes, to treat me with much respect, and to encourage my interest in their lives. (The general willingness to understand my aims as academic also allowed others who were quite critical of the colonialist and missionary enterprise to present their views to me.) Within a matter of months, a much shorter time than had been the case in Nallur, I felt the beginnings of a personal connection—as well as a successful professional relation—with certain families.

It was then, after little more than three months of work, that searing personal tragedy struck, the death of my stepdaughter in Washington. I left for the United States immediately. When I returned to Arulur about two months later, I stepped into a circle of families whose warm interest in the circumstances of Carol's death acknowledged the rawness of my pain. Their numerous questions brought me closer to them, in time permitting me to understand their difficulties as well as mine.[6] With a few families, a kind of inclusion had come about quite differently than the one I had begun to build initially on a conventional anthropological plan for "rapport-building." On the one hand, this turn of events opened a grounding of relations not previously so fully available to me. On the other hand, it has raised acute questions about privileged grounds of ethnographic knowledge and appropriate ways to write about information gained through friendship. These are questions that my research stance in Nallur had allowed me largely to evade.

DENMARK

As I thought about the way that Arulur Lutherans, especially women, talked about how missionaries had influenced them, my interest in that relationship grew. In the summer of 1985 I was able to go to Copenhagen to speak with retired women missionaries about their work in northern Tamil Nadu. In the 1960s I had tended to avoid missionaries in India, falling too easily into what I implicitly understood to be an anthropological prejudice against them. I did not want my work to be associated with theirs in the minds of Nallur villagers. Yet by the 1970s I found missionaries, their lives, and their aims curious, their experiences an important chapter in the centuries-long contact between Indians and Westerners. By

the mid-1980s I was intrigued with how missionaries thought of themselves; how they understood cultural differences; and how they acted to
express, deny, or mystify their own and others' understandings.

The focus of my research became the working relationship among
foreign women and Tamil women in evangelism, teaching, and medical
work. In part I was interested in missionaries' accounts of changes among
women, many of whose families had once been oppressed and stigmatized due to their caste rank, and many of whom, at least in the early
days of mission activity, continued to experience added discrimination
due to their conversion to Christianity.[7] Given a limited time for my work
in Copenhagen and the fact that my research was largely confined to
somewhat formal interviews, I based conversations on what I shared with
these women, that is, a knowledge of the mission and church and of
Tamil family life in village and town. I did not directly raise questions
about the missionaries' personal lives or about the circumstances that led
them to mission work and to India. They, in turn, asked me little about
my personal life, and I volunteered little information.[8]

My analysis of the interviews and documents I gathered centered on
notions of identity that the Danes used to talk about self-respect as a
condition for inclusive identification with Indian women. Their accounts
strikingly referred to feelings of joy and fellowship as the means and
evidence of secure, close relations with Indians. These idioms tend to
be not of place, with associated notions of borders and boundaries, but
of process, engagement, and collective emotional participation. These
comprise a set of notions appropriate to a field method that finds ways
to incorporate involvement, advocacy, and the honoring of dissident
voices within the ethnographic enterprise.

Discussion

In reviewing aspects of my work of more than two decades, I have attempted to develop associations among three issues: the adoption of a fieldworker
persona, shifts in my topical interests, and the growing awareness of my
sexual orientation. A sub-theme has been the tenacious hold of India on
me. What may rescue my discussion from a charge of simple self-indul-
gence is to draw attention to the burgeoning production of fieldwork
accounts that suggest that biographical narratives are important in their
own right because they fill in information on the practice of anthropology that otherwise tends to be consigned to hallway talk and the anecdotal

aside of classroom lecture. More public telling of the mutual reflection of personal and professional interests of all kinds raises issues about what attracts people to the discipline. For lesbian and gay people in particular, anthropology, with its commitment to positive sanctioning of interest in others, its habit of attentive listening to diverse views, its taking of common sense as problematical, and its concern with humanistic problems of implication in the lives of others, may provide valuable space for examination of the mutual elaboration of self and discipline.

The connections I have drawn between the sequence of my anthropological interests (including choices of field settings and guiding questions for research) and the progression of my understanding of my sexual orientation may be interpreted as a displacement of self-discovery onto research interests. To state that such processes are surely inescapable (and likely desirable) may be a truism (cf. Devereux 1967; Whitehead and Conaway, eds. 1986:12), as may be the conventional wisdom that people become anthropologists in part out of a dissatisfaction with the way of life their culture offers them. Yet a rhetorical marking of anthropologists in general, and of lesbian and gay anthropologists in particular, as alienated or marginal is counterproductive. Such psychologistic notions frame collective issues as idiosyncratic, personal conflicts. Thus, they serve to dissipate critiques of the profession as tied problematically to the larger society (cf. Marcus 1992:180). The resonance between the form of relating particular biographies, of which gay and lesbian accounts are one example, and the unfolding and elaboration of disciplinary concerns merits further attention.

Looking back at the variety of topics that have interested me, a certain progression is discernible. First, in the mid-1960s, came a commitment to a social structural paradigm—a search for rules and regularities expressed or symbolized in myriad forms of custom. A concern with mutual interdependencies is followed by the issue of how the obligatory is made desirable, in Turner's memorable phrasing of social anthropology's long-standing attention to the standardization of sentiment (Bateson 1936; Lutz 1988; Turner 1967:30). My later interests were tied to notions of marginality, adding concerns about stigmatized groups: Americans with cerebral palsy, South Indians formerly of very low caste and class status, and women missionaries.[9] Building on a social structural foundation, my present interests are in how individuals construe their experience and how social identities are constructed and represented.

This set of concerns—the location of normative orders, concern with concomitant variation, questions of choice, the decentering of authority through life stories, and the relation of experience as thought and feeling— seem to me interpretable as an expectable sequence of someone trained, as I was, in a social anthropological perspective strongly rooted in an interpretation of Durkheim. Thus my account may be read to a certain extent as an expected response to disciplinary training as well as the working out of a sense of self. This suggests that the challenge is to understand the personal as an aspect of the collective. It surprises me, therefore, that many fieldwork accounts written by North Americans depict the idiosyncratic "I" simply meeting the "other." Although this may be accounted for in part by the fact that until fairly recently such accounts have been treated as peripheral to the serious anthropologist's work (and many may also have been written with an audience of individualist American college students in mind), the neglect of presenting an anthropological discipline's influence on shaping the fieldworker's persona seems oddly short-sighted. Privileging the self and personal recollection tends to nudge disciplinary matters from the line of exposition (cf. Marcus 1992:179). Among other outcomes, such a presentation encourages the charge of inconsequentiality of such accounts to be renewed continually.

Some aspects of personal and professional interests have been important through the several contexts of Indian life I have been privileged to know. On the whole, I have found Indians, in village, town, and city, in India and in the United States, to be complexly attuned to nuance, to shifts in scene, and to changing circumstance (Du Bois 1986:236; Moffatt 1979:xxxii). The readiness of Indians (and other South Asians) to recognize and accept others' idiosyncrasies, and also their general willingness to find a place for personal difference, deserves much further study.[10] Much of the subtlety in Indians' personal relations seems to me to be related to an ability to participate emotionally (as opposed to primarily intellectually and instrumentally) with others, an issue I hope to explore in future research.[11]

At the beginning of my professional work I opted, less than consciously, to interpret anthropology as offering me a fit between a model of dispassionate research and the inarticulated, closeted, self. The emotional neutrality with which I attempted to guide my research and, as is now clear, protect myself derives from the now familiar place where Western conceptions of gender and a dominant scientific conception of objectivity meet (Keller 1985; Nandy 1983). Once in the field, however, the open-endedness of fieldwork called for a less constrained approach, leading to the emergence of new fieldworker personae and the necessity of realizing a more harmonious relationship between my personal and professional lives. Along with other influences, my path to this recognition owes much to the ways in which Indians implicate emotion in social relationships. I cannot know how my fieldwork might have been different or perhaps better if I had knowledge of the experience of gay and lesbian fieldworkers before me, but I join with those who think that making stories such as mine public may encourage a more inventive and sounder practice and a more responsible discipline.

Notes

While writing this chapter I have often been urged on by thoughts of the engaged personal and professional life of Michael Walsh (1957–90). Grateful for his example, I offer this account in his memory.

I am indebted to the editors for much encouragement and several critical readings, beginning with an early version of this chapter that was read at a panel, "Lesbian/Gay Identity in Fieldwork," at the American Anthropological Association meetings in 1990. In addition, I thank Lynne Burkhart and Brett Williams for their informed guidance.

Several periods of fieldwork in India (in 1965–67, 1976, and 1983) were financed by generous grants from the American Institute of Indian Studies, to which I remain most grateful. Awards of both time and money also have come from various bodies of the American University, to which I am indebted. On the collegial, moral, and emotional sides, I wish especially to acknowledge the many kindnesses shown me by friends, both faculty and students, in the Department of Anthropology of the University of Madras, where I have been affiliated at various times, and particularly to mention N. Subba Reddy (now at the Centre for Economic and Social Studies, Hyderabad), M. A. Kalam, and V. Sudarsen. Elsewhere in Tamil Nadu, my debt to K. Pappamma and K. Sundaram is deep and long-standing.

1   Caffrey's biography of Ruth Benedict similarly provides new understandings of Benedict's work in relation to her sexual orientation (Caffrey 1989). Leach makes the general point: "Unless we pay much closer attention than has been customary to the personal background of the authors of anthropological works, we shall miss out on most of what these texts are capable of telling us about the history of anthropology" (1984:22).

2   Relations with older men and with many men and women who ranked low in the village hierarchy tended at least initially to be governed by notions glossed by the Tamil *durai* (master) and *vellaikkaaran* (white man), reflecting the colonial legacy and imputing high status, wealth, and power to European males (Berreman 1962; Khare 1978:240–41; Moffatt 1979:xli; Varadachar 1979:133; Warren 1988:24–27).

3   Srinivas reports having made the same appeal during his fieldwork in Ram-
pura (1976). I am struck by similarities in the accounts of Western and
Indian anthropologists in discussing issues of self-presentation in the field
(Kumar 1992:3–7).

4   I first learned this methodological caution in reading Fortes's treatment of
Talis and Namoos and of "so-called tribes" in northern Ghana (Fortes 1945).
Leach states this issue succinctly: "I have also tried to avoid the common ethnographic device of representing cultural variation as aberrant deviation from
an orthodox central norm" (1954:292; cf. Marcus 1992:171).

5   This paralleled my teaching a class on anthropological biographies (dislik-
ing certain psychological implications of the term *life history*), in which I
struggled to suggest to undergraduates that lives need not necessarily be told
or conceived of chronologically, that a coherent biography could center
around contradiction and inconsistency, and that "selves" may be understood more appropriately as socially ordered than as naturally given.

6   My experience has been something like that of Rosaldo's (1984) and Hitchcock's (1987) coming to terms with grief in the field.

7   It is perhaps worth mentioning that it was at this time that I considered seriously the possibility of fieldwork among Anglo-Indians, people treated as
not quite European and not quite Indian, who have been given only slight
attention by anthropologists.

8   I now think that parallels between anthropologists' and missionaries' projects
are well worth serious attention (Van der Geest 1990).

9   This sequence of concerns is exemplified in a sample of my papers: 1976,
1978, 1992, 1987, and 1989.

10   Roland's insightful treatment of Indian and Japanese notions of self (1988)
is an important contribution to such work, as is Angell's thoughtful analysis of affect, person, and self among Bengalis in North America, Bangladesh,
and India (Angell 1986; Rutherford 1984). The valuable recent study by
Nanda of *hijras* (1990) implicates notions of sexuality and gender with
concerns about idiosyncracy.

11   Studies by Lutz of Ifaluk (1988) and by Wikan of Bali (1990) offer similar
notions of thought-feeling for the analysis of social relations. A mirror on
the separation of thought and feeling is the Indian anthropologist Sinha's
comment on the "dehydration of personal sentiments" in the midwestern
town in the United States that he studied (Sinha 1966).

References Cited

Angell, Dorothy. 1986. "Bengalis in the United States: Patterns of Participation
and Identity." In *Tradition and Transformation: Asian Indians in America,* ed. Richard Harvey Brown and George V. Coelho, 95–113. Studies in
Third World Societies no. 38. Williamsburg: Department of Anthropology, College of William and Mary.
Bateson, Gregory. 1936. *Naven.* Cambridge: Cambridge University Press.
Berreman, Gerald D. 1962. *Behind Many Masks: Ethnography and Impression*

Management in a Himalayan Village. The Society for Applied Anthropology Monograph no. 4.

Burkhart, Geoffrey. 1976. "On the Absence of Descent Groups among Some Udayars of South India." *Contributions to Indian Sociology* 10:30–61.

———. 1978. "Marriage Alliance and the Local Circle among Some Udayars of South India." In *American Studies in the Anthropology of India*, ed. Sylvia Vatuk, 171–210. New Delhi: Manohar.

———. 1987. "Family Deity Temples and Spatial Variance among Udayars of Northern Tamil Nadu." In *Religion and Society in South India: In Honor of Professor N. Subba Reddy*, ed. S. P. Reddy, M. Suryanarayana, and V. Sudarsen, 3–20. Delhi: B. K. Agencies.

———. 1989. "Danish Women Missionaries: Personal Accounts of Work with South Indian Women." In *Women's Work for Women: Missionaries and Social Change in Asia*, ed. Leslie A. Flemming, 59–85. Boulder: Westview Press.

———. 1992. "Managing Ascriptive Categories at an American Cerebral Palsy Camp." *Ethnos* 57(1–2):61–76.

Caffrey, Margaret. 1989. *Ruth Benedict: Stranger in This Land.* Austin: University of Texas Press.

Collier, Jane Fishburne, and Sylvia Junko Yanagisako, eds. 1987. *Gender and Kinship: Essays toward a Unified Analysis.* Stanford: Stanford University Press.

Devereux, George. 1967. *From Anxiety to Method in the Behavioral Sciences.* The Hague: Mouton.

DuBois, Cora. 1986. "Studies in an Indian Town." In *Women in the Field,* ed. Peggy Golde, 221–36. 2d ed. Berkeley: University of California Press.

Fortes, Meyer. 1945. *The Dynamics of Clanship among the Tallensi.* London: Oxford University Press.

———. 1971. "On the Concept of the Person among the Tallensi." In *La notion de personne en Afrique Noire,* ed. G. Dieterlen, 283–319. Paris: Editions du Centre National de la Recherche Scientifique.

———. 1983. "Problems of Identity and Person." In *Identity: Personal and Socio-Cultural,* ed. Anita Jacobson-Widding, 389–401. Stockholm: Almqvist and Wiksell.

Golde, Peggy, ed. 1986. *Women in the Field: Anthropological Experiences.* 2d ed. Berkeley: University of California Press.

Henry, Jules. 1963. *Culture against Man.* New York: Random House.

Hitchcock, Patricia. 1987. "Our Ulleri Child." In *Children in the Field: Anthropological Experiences,* ed. Joan Cassell, 173–83. Philadelphia: Temple University Press.

Keller, Evelyn Fox. 1985. *Reflections on Gender and Science.* New Haven: Yale University Press.

Khare, R. S. 1978. "Anthropological Fieldwork: Some Experiences and Observations among the Urban Kanya-Kubja Brahmans." In *Field Studies on the People of India: Methods and Perspectives in Memory of Professor Tarak Chandra Das,* ed. Surajit Sinha, 235–52. Calcutta: Indian Anthropological Society.

Kumar, Nita. 1992. *Friends, Brothers and Informants: Fieldwork Memoirs of Banaras.* Berkeley: University of California Press.

Leach, E. R. 1954. *Political Systems of Highland Burma: A Study of Kachin Social Structure.* Cambridge: Harvard University Press.

————. 1984. "Glimpses of the Unmentionable in the History of British Social Anthropology." *Annual Review of Anthropology* 13:1–23.

Lutz, Catherine. 1988. *Unnatural Emotions: Everyday Sentiments on a Micronesian Atoll and Their Challenge to Western Theory.* Chicago: University of Chicago Press.

Marcus, George E., with Peter Dobkin Hall. 1992. *Lives in Trust: The Fortunes of Dynastic Families in Late Twentieth-Century America.* Boulder: Westview Press.

Moffatt, Michael. 1979. *An Untouchable Community in South India: Structure and Consensus.* Princeton: Princeton University Press.

Nanda, Serena. 1990. *Neither Man Nor Woman: The Hijras of India.* Belmont: Wadsworth.

Nandy, Ashis. 1983. *The Intimate Enemy: Loss and Recovery of Self under Colonialism.* Delhi: Oxford University Press.

Panini, M. N., ed. 1991. *From the Female Eye: Accounts of Women Fieldworkers Studying Their Own Communities.* New Delhi: Hindustan Publishing.

Pilling, Arnold R. 1988. "Anthropology's Culture and Personality School and Homosexuality: A Review of *Malinowski, Rivers, Benedict and Others: Essays on Culture and Personality,* George W. Stocking, Jr., ed." *Society of Lesbian and Gay Anthropologists Newsletter* 11(1):19–22.

Roland, Alan. 1988. *In Search of Self in India and Japan: Toward a Cross-Cultural Psychology.* Princeton: Princeton University Press.

Rosaldo, Renato. 1984. "Grief and a Headhunter's Rage: On the Cultural Force of Emotions." In *Text, Play, and Story: The Construction and Reconstruction of Self and Society,* ed. Edward M. Bruner, 178–95. Washington D.C.: American Ethnological Society.

Rutherford, Dorothy Angell. 1984. "Bengalis in America: Relationship, Affect, Person, and Self." Ph.D. dissertation, Anthropology Department, American University.

Sinha, Surajit. 1966. "Religion in an Affluent Society." *Current Anthropology* 7:189–95.

Srinivas, M. N. 1976. *The Remembered Village.* Berkeley: University of California Press.

Stocking, George W. Jr., ed. 1986. *Malinowski, Rivers, Benedict and Others: Essays on Culture and Personality.* History of Anthropology, vol. 4. Madison: University of Wisconsin Press.

Trawick, Margaret. 1990. *Notes on Love in a Tamil Family.* Berkeley: University of California Press.

Turner, Victor. 1967. *The Forest of Symbols: Aspects of Ndembu Ritual.* Ithaca: Cornell University Press.

Van der Geest, Sjaak. 1990. "Anthropologists and Missionaries: Brothers under the Skin." *Man* 25:588–601.

Varadachar, Beba D. 1979. "The Bottom Up: Some Cognitive Categories. Slums in Madras." In *The Fieldworker and the Field: Problems and Challenges in Sociological Investigation,* ed. M. N. Srinivas, A. M. Shah, and E. A. Ramaswamy, 127–40. Delhi: Oxford University Press.

Warren, Carol A. B. 1988. *Gender Issues in Field Research.* Newbury Park: Sage Publications.

Weston, Kath. 1991. *Families We Choose: Lesbians, Gays, Kinship.* New York: Columbia University Press.

Whitehead, Tony Larry, and Mary Ellen Conaway, eds. 1986. *Self, Sex, and Gender in Cross-Cultural Fieldwork.* Urbana: University of Illinois Press.

Wikan, Unni. 1990. *Managing Turbulent Hearts: A Balinese Formula for Living.* Chicago: University of Chicago Press.

2. Rites of Passing
Liz Goodman

As graduate students we are told that "anthropology equals experience"; you are not an anthropologist until you have the experience of doing it.—Rabinow 1977:4

F ieldwork has traditionally been the hallmark of social and cultural anthropology, the research technique that distinguishes it from the other social sciences (Stocking 1983). In disciplines such as sociology, ethnographic fieldwork is only one of an array of research methods, one means among many of doing research, with no special aura attaching to those who choose fieldwork as their chief method. But while other disciplines may make use of fieldwork simply as a means of doing research, one selected for its suitability to a particular research problem, traditional anthropological fieldwork is not only the means to an end—the gathering of ethnographic data—but also an end in itself. Anthropology differs from other fields of inquiry in that one cannot be an anthropologist without first being a fieldworker, or so anthropologists are told. Fieldwork is the essential anthropological rite of passage, legitimating the status of the neophyte as full-fledged member of the discipline (Wengle 1988).

Fieldwork, as it is expected to be experienced by the would-be anthropologist, shares many of the same traits associated with the classic rite of passage as described by Turner (1969, 1977), especially separation and physical hardship. The special knowledge and insight that is hinted at by those who have experienced fieldwork have little to do with the data collected in the field or with wisdom imparted by the wise elders of the clan, but with having survived the experience in the first place. The work one does in the field, as documented in the near-sacred writings known as field notes, becomes not so much a context for demonstrating one's knowledge and theoretical prowess but an occasion for revealing one's calling to the profession (Sanjek 1990).

Separation, as an integral part of the rite of passage and fieldwork, severs the ties to all of the cultural supports that we as anthropologists are accustomed to rely upon. We are forced to depend upon ourselves and develop relationships with the people we are studying. Total immersion in the host society, with an occasional respite provided by mystery novels and other "foreign" material, is supposed to allow us to learn the host culture from the native's perspective while preserving our objectivity because the culture is in fact alien and new to us. We are to learn and live the culture as the natives do, for it is only by learning to see through native eyes that we can gain insight into the culture. The goal is both to be the person peering through the microscope and one of the organisms on the slide. Of course, this is a nearly impossible goal that the discipline sets for itself, but we anthropologists try to arrange the situation so we can approach the goal as best we can. By cutting ourselves off from our own culture, our families and friends, and from the conveniences of home, we leap into the foreign culture of the host community and hope to be able to swim instead of sink. The psychological and emotional shifts this requires by the researcher may be harder than any physical difficulties that she or he has to undergo.

Most fieldworkers expect that this experience will offer their first real taste of being an outsider, of not fitting in but wanting to, and of intense loneliness and alienation. They also anticipate that rather ordinary aspects of who they are may become something that must be kept secret or not presented in a completely open manner for fear of losing their precarious place in the community. Paul Rabinow, for example, when working with Moroccan villagers, said that the villagers never questioned his claim that he was a "Christian" even though he knew that an identity as a Christian led to fears that he was there as a missionary (1977:90–91).

Marital status can also be problematic for researchers, whether they arrive in the field with a spouse or without. Regina Oboler (1986) took her husband with her when she went to do fieldwork in western Kenya but found that she had to conceal their household division of labor as well as the fact she was heading the research and not he. For lesbian and gay fieldworkers, however, the expectation that subterfuge and negotiation will be needed is perhaps more intense. Even in this post-Stone-wall era, being gay or lesbian may be problematic at home, and traditional field settings are widely perceived as likely to be, if anything, more conservative than the urban United States or university communities. Gay and lesbian anthropologists anticipating fieldwork cannot help but worry about how people will handle information about their sexual orientation. A negative response, like a hostile reaction to any other personal characteristic the research brings to the field, may have significant consequences for the research, jeopardizing not only the immediate completion of a research project but also the anthropologist's long-term career objectives. The stakes are particularly high for the graduate student embarking on a first fieldwork project. If successful completion of fieldwork will mark the student's entrance into the ranks of professional anthropologists, then a fieldwork failure will dash her or his hopes of ever establishing a career.

Preparing for the Field

As a graduate student I never questioned the importance of fieldwork to my training. But when the time came for me to decide on where to do my fieldwork, I had a series of concerns that constrained the choice I would eventually make. Some of these were rather prosaic. After many years in Southern California, where 90–degree days during the winter were not unusual, I felt that I wanted to go somewhere where it wasn't hot and that had "real" weather. Beyond this, I had not had great success in studying foreign languages in the past and feared that I would be unable to achieve adequate fluency in a new language in time to complete a fieldwork project. My decision to design a project that could be undertaken in a place where English was spoken seemed to resolve the language problem. But complicating these concerns was my recognition, based on advice from my professors, that fieldwork abroad was an essential part of the rite of passage. A field site closer to home was likely not to be viewed as sufficiently exotic or remote to meet the requirements for separation, physical hardship, and otherness demanded if the fieldwork was to function as a rite of passage into the profession.

With these constraints in mind, and considering my interests in kinship and agriculture, I decided to do my fieldwork in England with family farmers. Specifically, I settled on the Yorkshire Dales because of work that had been done in Northern England thirty and forty years earlier that would provide a solid comparative base for examining land tenure, inheritance, and succession patterns, the principal focuses of my research project.

But these practical matters were not my only concern. I was also worried about how I would actually do the research and tried to design a set of questions for interviews with farmers I would meet. I worried about what kinds of clothes to take with me and where I would live. Most important, because we did not have the money for my lover of six years to accompany me, I worried about what would happen to our relationship after almost a year's separation. Leaving her behind would resolve the problem of revealing my homosexuality in the field but would deprive me of her support and might undermine the stability of the relationship. In the end, I did all I could before I left the United States to deal with these things while realizing that I would just have to let things take care of themselves.

Although planning for the conduct of the fieldwork left me feeling uncertain and tentative, and I was anxious about how I would manage so far from my lover, I was most concerned about how I should handle my presentation of self in the field. As someone who had been out as a lesbian to family, friends, and teachers since I was sixteen, I had not given serious thought to concealing my sexual orientation for many years. But I knew that going to do fieldwork with farmers and other rural folk who were likely to have conservative expectations of appropriate behavior for a young woman and presenting myself as an out lesbian probably would not smooth the research process along. It seemed clear that the closet would be the only practical alternative to acting like "myself." This could take one of two forms: I could go for the old boyfriend-at-home routine or I could represent myself as an asexual (and, of course, eccentric) academic type. By the time I was ready to embark for England, I had still not decided which of these ruses I would adopt, although it seemed clear that whatever approach would enable me to pass successfully as straight in the field would have to be considered seriously.

At the same time that I was preparing to go to the field, there were big preparations underway in my family for another important event. My sister was going to be married, and the wedding was being planned for a date close to my scheduled departure for England. This impending event accentuated for me the extent to which I was something of an outsider in the family and the wider society. Although my family expressed considerable interest in my research and travel plans, their curiosity could hardly compare with the intense excitement that surrounded the wedding preparations. As the wedding approached, the focus of conversations with my family was increasingly directed toward the complexities of planning the ceremony, reception, guest list, flowers, and so on. With some regret, I realized that I would never do anything that would garner as much positive attention as this wedding would. To make matters worse, the final plans for the wedding scheduled it for after my departure for the field. I was unable to change my travel plans and had to reconcile myself to not being present when the big event took place. I knew that my marginality, always clear because of my lesbianism, would be expressed even more dramatically by my absence from the ceremony. The wedding, an elaborate affair for my southern family, had eclipsed my impending fieldwork, overshadowing the significance of the accomplishment for which I had hoped to be recognized within the family circle.

Arrival in England

In November 1986 I arrived in North Yorkshire. By a set of lucky coincidences I found a place to live in a small village in Swaledale, which was just where my background reading had suggested I should try to be. But despite my expectations that going to England would ease the stress of difference typical of fieldwork, it turned out to be a much stranger and more difficult experience than I had anticipated.

For one thing, when I first arrived I could not understand a word that was said to me. I knew, or at least suspected, that people were speaking English, but it sure didn't sound that way to me. I was embarrassed by how many times I had to ask people to repeat themselves, especially since my mild southern accent was quite familiar to them from watching American television shows ("Dallas" was especially popular during this period), and they could all understand me.

Conducting research also proved to be more difficult than I had anticipated. Beyond the problems I was having with the local dialect, I struggled with shyness. Just setting up the interviews through an introduction by my landlady or a member of her family scared me, although once I found myself in a farmer's house things weren't nearly as awkward or embarrassing as I feared they would be. But on most occasions, it took more courage than I could muster to arrange to visit and interview anyone, and the pace of data collection suffered accordingly.

I also spent a lot of time trying to stay warm. The house I was renting had no heat to speak of. A coal fireplace, a few electric heaters, and high ceilings did not make for a cozy environment. I was much warmer when I was out walking than I was inside and found myself constantly preoccupied with this aspect of my physical comfort, again to the detriment of my efforts to write field notes, read, and plan for future interviews.

One place where I did manage to find some warmth was the village pub. I went there in the evenings with my landlady's daughter, who was about my age. But the pub was not as good a place to meet people as one would imagine. Most of the patrons were men who seemed afraid to talk to me, not because I was a stranger but because I was female. Most seemed very uncomfortable with the idea of talking to a woman to whom they were not related and either avoided my efforts to strike up conversations or mumbled so indistinctly that I was dissuaded from pursuing responses.

There was one man who came over to introduce himself to me, however. Robert was an electrician who had lived all of his thirty-five years in the village but had worked all over the country and the Continent and traveled to the United States. He was one of the few people in the village who knew that there was life outside the Dales and was the one person who had some concept of how different my life had been before I arrived in the village.

Robert and I quickly became close friends. We talked about music, movies, spicy food, and America. He also became my best informant. Like everyone else in the village, he was related to most of the people there and knew all of the really juicy stories about the residents that no one else would tell me. As an electrician, he had worked at one time or another on many of the farms in the area, doing everything from fixing small appliances to installing new milking parlors.

Robert and I took to spending every evening together. At first I would go down to his house to watch color television and, most important, enjoy his central heating. After a few weeks, I could be seen walking across the village commons with a small bag and returning to my house later in the evening in different clothes. I knew what the villagers thought, but they would have been surprised to learn that I was partaking of the pleasures of a hot shower rather than of Robert's bed. When it was time for my holiday cottage to be rented to tourists again, I moved in with Robert.

Even though Robert and I had become close quickly, I agonized for what seemed a long time (actually, about two months) about telling him that I was a lesbian. By the time I finally got around to telling him, he had figured it out from the fact that we were so close but I had never shown any sexual interest in him. He was not in any way put off by my sexual orientation and, I think, glad that I trusted him enough to confide in him. It was such a relief to share my secret with someone. Being able to discuss how much I missed my lover and how much I missed acting as a gay person made my situation more bearable.

Village Perceptions

All of the time that Robert and I were spending together did not go unnoticed by people in the village and Dale. One Friday night, he and I were standing at the bar waiting to order beer when one of the old farmers who spoke with a particularly thick accent made a remark to Robert about a pullet (a young hen). Although *pullet* was the only word that I understood, I did recognize the somewhat salacious tone of the comments and understood that he was making a reference to the sexual relationship he assumed Robert and I shared.

I also began to notice that whenever I did an interview or would simply visit with one of the locals people would tell me stories about Robert's family or explain how they were related to him. I heard on several occasions about Robert's father's prowess as a cricket player and stories about Robert's grandfather, who was a local builder and quite a character. Although I had never said anything to encourage the assumptions about my relationship with Robert that seemed to fuel the stories, I was being treated like I had married into the local kinship network. I didn't need to figure out a way to hide my identity, they were doing it for me.

Late in the spring, my parents canceled a planned visit to England because they believed that the wedding of my second sister was "imminent." It was a terrible blow to me that they decided to stay at home for something that wasn't even certain, but another reminder that marriage was the most significant accomplishment they could imagine any of their daughters attaining. I felt cut off from my family, unacceptable despite my efforts to achieve professional status. The contrast with what I was experiencing in the village was ironic. In the village I was regularly asked by one of the young men with whom Robert and I sometimes drank in the pub when we were going to be married. I was experiencing something that I had rarely known before—what it felt like to live as a heterosexual and have approval I had never found, and knew I never would find, at home.

Becoming accepted by the people of the Dale made doing interviews easier even though I never completely overcame my shyness. But sitting in a farmhouse with an older farmer and his wife was much less awkward when they could start the conversation by telling me about their connection with Robert and thus remove my outsider status by bringing me into their world. In this small, endogamous community, being an insider meant that you were related to everyone. Although marrying into the community was not quite the same thing as being born to a local family, it was one way to be treated as something other than a tourist or other interloper. Because I was living with Robert and participating in the daily life of the Dale, it was as if I had married him. They knew where to place me and treated me as if I belonged. I had never before felt that I could claim full membership in a mainstream community; I had never before experienced the comfort of having my right to insider status assumed and understood.

As the time approached for me to return to the United States, I began to feel reluctant about leaving the Dales. It was hard to contemplate giving up a place where I had felt so at home on many levels. Without having to try, I had passed as a respectable member of the community and found out what it was like to be ordinary. In contrast, the home to which I was returning was a place where I only sporadically felt like everyone else. My first sister had by now had her wedding and settled down into married respectability, and my second sister was contemplating marriage with the son of a prestigious local family. It was difficult to contemplate leaving respectability, however temporary, behind and returning to a condition I imagined as marginal and remote from the central concerns of my family and community. Having been separated from my lover for the better part of a year also made me anxious about how easily I would be able to step back into that relationship.

Fieldwork in Perspective

The traditional view of fieldwork is one in which the anthropologist is totally immersed in an alien culture with a loss of familiar supports and comforts. I certainly heard plenty of stories like that from my professors and from other graduate students who had recently returned from the field. In the books I read about fieldwork and the war stories told in Friday afternoon drinking sessions, there was always the assumption that to experience fieldwork is to experience the status of outsider and that the mark of the "good" fieldworker is to become an insider, to be called by some kinship term.

But if one's status is that of outsider in one's own society, how is fieldwork to be experienced? As a lesbian, fieldwork was as much a rite of reversal as a rite of passage. I was able to take off the costume of the queer and put on the clothes of respectability. For me as an out lesbian, the field offered me a first taste of living at the heart of a community's values, of feeling like a normal and accepted person. I entered this community without a past and with no stake in people knowing that I was a lesbian. Once I learned to cope with practical aspects of living in the Dale, I was able to enjoy the status of normality that was such a sharp contrast to the sometimes painful outsiderness that I knew awaited me back home. The significance of becoming a part of the kinship network was greater for me as a lesbian than as an anthropologist because I was able to glimpse the world as it is seen by most people for the first time in my adult life. The trial by fire or rite of passage that is the first fieldwork experience became for me a rite of passing.

References Cited

Oboler, Regina Smith. 1986. "For Better or Worse: Anthropologists and Husbands in the Field." In *Self, Sex, and Gender in Cross-Cultural Fieldwork*, ed. Tony Larry Whitehead and Mary Ellen Conaway, 240–62. Urbana: University of Illinois Press.

Rabinow, Paul. 1977. *Reflections on Fieldwork in Morocco*. Berkeley: University of California Press.

Sanjek, Roger, ed. 1990. *Fieldnotes: The Making of Anthropology*. Ithaca: Cornell University Press.

Stocking, George W., Jr. 1983. "History of Anthropology: Whence/Whither?" In *Observers Observed: Essays on Ethnographic Fieldwork*, ed. George W. Stocking Jr., 3–12. Madison: University of Wisconsin Press.

Turner, Victor. 1969. *The Ritual Process: Structure and Anti-Structure*. Chicago: Aldine.

———. 1977. "Variations on a Theme of Liminality." In *Secular Ritual*, ed. Sally F. Moore and Barbara G. Meyerhoff, 36–52, Assen, The Netherlands: Van Gorcum.

Wengle, John L. 1988. *Ethnographers in the Field*. Tuscaloosa: University of Alabama Press.

3. Cast among Outcastes: Interpreting Sexual Orientation, Racial, and Gender Identity in the Yemen Arab Republic
Delores M. Walters

In the summer of 1982, my partner at the time and I left the United States for nearly two years, most of which was devoted to conducting fieldwork in what was then known as the Yemen Arabic Republic. The two Yemens, which are located on the Arabian Peninsula south of Saudi Arabia, were united as the Republic of Yemen in May 1990.

My objective in doing fieldwork in a country that had officially abolished its hierarchical social categories, including slavery, only in 1962 after a revolution and a civil war, was to assess whether social mobility was possible for members of the lowest social categories as a result of new economic opportunities. How much had a very rigid social hierarchy based on birth and occupation been transformed in twenty years?

I knew that my intention to study the lowest members of Yemeni society meant challenging views usually provided by members of elite and respected groups who claimed tribal status. Virtually no one had discussed tribal identity from the point of view of those at the bottom of the social scale and for whom tribal membership was usually denied. Similarly, the role of women was just beginning to be elaborated by anthropologists whose entry into the country had only been allowed since the middle to late 1970s. Thus, when I went to Yemen in the early 1980s to study a lowly group of menial laborers reputed to have Ethiopian origins dating back to the sixth century and whose women were reported to be engaged in prostitution, I was challenging the dominant insider and outsider views of Yemeni society. I was proposing that these silent viewpoints now be heard.

One of the pressing questions for those about to embark on fieldwork is how to conduct or maintain one's personal life. To a group of graduate students who inquired how I managed, I remarked that I had taken my personal life with me. These students, whom I encountered at an American Anthropological Association meeting on my return from the field in 1984, were somewhat in awe at such a novel idea. I am not sure whether it was the public statement about having a same-sex partner in the field that was mildly shocking or the fact itself, because I knew that among my sympathetic listeners there were other lesbians.

Anyone planning an extended stay in Yemen is required to pass a stringent security clearance. The question was how to get my partner, Lee, into the country, not if, once she decided that she was ready to endure the hardships of living in a country that had almost none of the amenities that most Americans are used to. Thus, one of my objectives when I visited Yemen the year before I began fieldwork was to determine whether a companion would be permitted to accompany me. Clearance through the proper Yemeni authorities might be facilitated by a few options, according to my British and American colleagues then resident in the country. Couldn't I claim that Lee was my mother? they asked. To which I replied, "Right age, wrong color" because she is white and old enough to be my mother. Little did I know that when they met us Yemeni women all over the country would immediately assume that Lee was my mother because they observed an appropriate age difference for this to be possible and ignored the fact that she is fair-skinned and blue-eyed while I, especially in the sunny climate of Yemen, am very brown. Apparently age difference was more important than skin color to Yemenis in guessing our relationship.

Adoption was another option, but it would take too long and, besides, my own mother would be eagerly awaiting my return from the land of the unknown. Finally, after exhausting all the possibilities, my colleagues and I simply inquired at the research center that gives official permission for foreigners to study in the country. Would I be allowed to have a companion? we asked. I was assured that permission would easily be granted. Once we arrived in the country, I had only to write Lee into my project for their records. The way was clear for the two of us to work together as a team. Granting permission for a companion made sense in terms of Yemeni culture, as I will explain.

Perhaps the central question for me on the topic of identity management in a cultural context very different from that of the United States is how I view my various selves and how these selves were viewed. It is critical to recognize that I do not experience the various aspects of my being separately. I do not prioritize being a woman over being African American, over having grown up in New York City public housing, over having acquired the professional status of an anthropologist, over being a lesbian. This is not to say that certain aspects of my self may not be more important in specific contexts than others. Different aspects of my identity were experienced, constructed, and negotiated in conjunction with one another during my fieldwork. All my selves were intertwined.

Clues to understanding my multifaceted being, including my interest in cultural differences, are evident in contemporary black feminist literature. Audre Lorde in particular incorporates sexuality in her description of multiple consciousness: "As a Black lesbian feminist comfortable with the many different ingredients of my identity, and a woman committed to racial and sexual freedom from oppression, I find I am constantly being encouraged to pluck out some one aspect of myself and present this as the meaningful whole, eclipsing or denying the other parts of self" (1984:120). Clearly, Lorde rejects the fragmenting of her race, class, gender, or sexual orientation into separate categories. Such partitioning interferes not only with her perceptions of self but also with her ability to perform the work she has chosen to do: "My fullest concentration of energy is available to me only when I integrate all the parts of who I am, openly, allowing power from particular sources of my living to flow back and forth freely through all my different selves, without the restrictions of externally imposed definition. Only then can I bring myself and my energies as a whole to the service of those struggles which I embrace as part of my living" (120–21).[1]

Like Lorde, I believe that all aspects of my identity are inextricably linked. My ability to carry out an extended period of field research was contingent on the full expression of those multiple identities. I also agree with Lorde that dissecting one's being into separate parts may seem harmful to one's creativity, especially when handled by outsiders. Nevertheless, what I attempt here is an objective interpretation of my multicultural encounters that necessitates disentangling my own overlapping identities.

Not surprisingly, the approaches that explicate individual lives as emerging from particular cultural histories provide the most insight into the multiple sources of social identities, including my own. This approach, of course, is used by anthropologists to study members of other societies. Irma McClaurin-Allen applies this perspective to her analysis of race, class, and gender integration in our society. Drawing on black feminist traditions, this anthropologist believes that the significance of a culturally and historically specific model is that at any given time in the creation of self, various aspects of one's identity may seem contradictory or incongruous: "I argue for an approach to the study of gender as a dynamic creation, always historically and culturally specific—and dialectically constituted together with other aspects of social stratification, including race and class" (1990:316). This approach resonates with my own experience. For many children growing up in New York City (the Bronx) public housing during the 1950s, aspirations and options seemed extremely narrow. Because of my grandmother, my childhood was culturally rich. On her modest earnings as a domestic, she introduced the city to me as a creative place. In addition, my commitment to earning a college degree was influenced by my grandmother and her siblings, whose dreams of advanced learning were never realized. Thus the foundation was laid for a curiosity about worlds that extended beyond my own. Further, my experience of living in public housing during the 1950s and 1960s was different from the bleak social and economic environment often depicted currently in the media. Rather than today's bleak picture, the lives of my family and neighbors were closer to Carol Stack's (1974) description of collectively shared resources among blacks in a midwestern urban ghetto during the 1960s.

I experienced the struggles for racial and gender equality during the 1960s and 1970s, even though celebration of my identity as an African American woman came later. My duties as a nurse both here and abroad, rather than the formal training I received, taught me the importance of social scientific inquiry for determining individual health needs. When I sought further study of largely unfamiliar cultures, I was aware of the exclusivity of graduate school.

It was not expected that a black child growing up in a city housing project, even one having the positive influences on her socialization that I did, would assume the role of social scientist. Preparation for this role, however, entailed a process of self-validation. This process was only partially underway when I embarked on my field research. First, I needed to recognize that certain aspects of my identity—race, gender, working class, sexual orientation—are devalued in American society. Second, I needed to reclaim those identities that were rejected or denied and integrate contradictory self-definitions. Certain aspects of my personal identity seemed relevant to the study of other African-identified peoples who were marginalized in their community. However, I could not immediately apply all of my prior experience, including the contradictory messages I had received regarding my identity, to the present research. Once I understood the interaction among my personal, political, and cultural identities as a researcher, I was able to analyze my fieldwork encounter in a different light.[2] I could more readily discern various intersecting social categories in myself and others.

Eventually, I recognized similarities between Yemeni village women, who were the primary focus of my field study, and women I had known as a child. In Yemen, as in my earlier neighborhood, women's coping strategies were crucial to their community's survival. Another commonality I observed was "woman-bonding," which according to Lorde has been a respectable tradition within African and African American communities (1984:121). In Middle Eastern locations such as Yemen, women's work groups are central to daily village life. Yet Yemeni women's groupings, even when they were composed of members of different social categories, often appeared more comfortable working together than did same-sex groupings in the United States. Lorde attributes the division between African American women to homophobia within the black community.[3] As a result of my observations among rural Yemeni women, I acquired a more global perspective from which to assess women's activities and to reaffirm my commitment to working in culturally diverse communities. Undoubtedly, the success of my study would have been adversely affected had I been limited in defining explicit areas of self-interest—social, sexual, and intellectual.

It would seem that my engagement in various stages of self-preparation, including formal training, would make me ideally suited to study and teach about diverse cultural identities. Yet I am presented with further contradictions when I seek to interpret my experience in Yemen as integral to academic teaching and scholarly responsibilities. From a theoretical standpoint, the experiential and intellectual realities of African American women have been marginalized in academia. Patricia Hill Collins (1990), for example, discusses not only the exclusion of black women as subjects but also as scholars in academia. From a practical standpoint, African American women and other women of color are nonetheless enabling students to have a more inclusive outlook. Elsa Barkley Brown, a historian who teaches about the experiences of African American women, believes that "all people can learn to center in another experience, validate it, and judge it by its own standards without need of comparison or need to adopt that framework as their own.

Thus, one has no need to 'decenter' anyone in order to center someone else; one has only to constantly, appropriately, 'pivot the center'" (1989:922).[4] Through pivoting the center, white or male students can learn to feel what it is like to be a black woman.[5] I welcome such practical and theoretical discussion, especially because they rely on black feminist academics and nonacademics.[6]

Anthropology, even those branches concerned with gendered social realities (feminist anthropology) and the personal experiences of the ethnographer (reflexive anthropology), has yet to find an appropriate way of centering the differences of race, ethnicity, gender, class, and sexual orientation as the object of inquiry. Especially in recognizing lesbian identity, feminist approaches outside of anthropology seem more beneficial. Henrietta Moore (1988:11), however, asserts that feminist anthropology is beyond the stage of merely providing a litany of activities and experiences engaged in by women worldwide, that feminist anthropologists are now involved in a search for real differences among women. If she is correct, the contributions made by lesbians of color, particularly as activists, will gain the visibility they deserve. Indeed, I envision an anthropology that is more "feminist" in that the personal identities of ethnographer and individuals or groups in the fieldwork interaction would be more fully elaborated in relation to particular social structures.

I gradually came to understand how my identities were negotiated in Yemen, using approaches both within and outside of anthropology.[7] If I looked at Yemeni society from the point of view of those who are devalued in it, how would I also recognize the dominant Arab, Muslim, tribal, male, and heterosexual character of Yemeni society? The approach called "world traveling" provided by Maria Lugones, a lesbian feminist philosopher who brings an Argentinean, upper-class background to her analysis, is useful. She describes (1990) having the capacity to be in different worlds simultaneously. World travelers, in her analysis, recognize the duality of their position wherever they find themselves. This ability to negotiate in different worlds is essential for the survival of women whose differences of race, ethnicity, class, and sexual orientation make them invisible members of society.

The advantage of the two perspectives—centering in another person's experience and world traveling—is that each accommodates both the visitor and the visited, the observer and the observed, at the same time. A Yemeni woman in the lowest strata of society who is seen only as a prostitute by other Yemenis would thus be capable of constructing her own position in the society using the stereotype to advantage, whether or not it is a true statement about her. For instance, I asked one woman why she, unlike most others in her status group, used the derogatory label *khadima* (feminine singular for "servant") to identity herself. It was clear from her answer that she knew that accepting the label allowed her to be the recipient of alms given by fellow Muslims, who, because they were in a better financial position, were also able to fulfill a religious obligation. Similarly, this indigent group's exclusive assignment to the role of street sweeping could also provide an advantage. In modern-day Yemen, such work translates into a lucrative employment opportunity as a sanitation engineer. Acceptance of the stigmatized label allows one to acquire improved economic status. Yet no matter how dignified a title is given to collecting garbage, this is a job that is shunned by all but those who accept, at least to some extent, both the positive and negative connotations implied in the label.[8]

Yemenis also demonstrated their ability to acknowledge a world different from their own. A similarity in racial features existed between myself and the members of the two groups having known or reputed African ancestry—former slaves (*'abid*) on the one hand, and menial laborers (*akhdam*), who were considered even lower than slaves on the other. Yet Yemenis, regardless of their background or ancestry, had no problem distinguishing between those they assigned to inferior status and myself. It was clear that race was not the main criterion in establishing social status in the Yemeni context.

My job, then, was to center on stigmatized communities while not decentering mainstream social views held in that society. Although many Yemenis expressed a preference for lighter as opposed to darker skin and for straighter, less woolly hair types, racial features were not the main issue in maintaining the social hierarchy. Similarly, just as race would have to be discussed in the context of birth status and occupation, which Yemenis do use to define social position, sexuality and homosexuality would also have to be considered in the context of a strong heterosexual bias.

In general, Yemeni men and women constructed or construed my identity in their own cultural terms. Basic concepts of honor, morality, kinship, and family informed their perceptions of me. In other words, I was expected to act like an insider—to show the same kind of decorum as a single woman, which is how Yemenis viewed me. A single woman would ideally be accompanied by a male relative, or at least a responsible older female. Yemen is a sex-segregated society where a woman's reputation is based on her ability to avoid contacts with unrelated males, thereby helping to uphold the family's honor. Lila Abu-Lughod provides the appropriate model for describing my position in Yemen. In her case, her father knew that his daughter's reputation would be at stake if she ventured into Egyptian bedouin society traveling alone "on uncertain business." He therefore went himself to introduce her to the people among whom she would be living (1988:141).

Abu-Lughod, who is half Arab and considered her identity as a Muslim to be tentative, was taken as a partial insider. She became, in her estimation, a "dutiful daughter." My situation in the Yemeni context was somewhat similar. It was acceptable, even necessary, that I as a "single" woman would have someone along who was responsible for protecting my reputation. The Yemeni women we encountered on travels around the country viewed Lee as my protector (*rafiqa*, which I find appropriate to translate as "bodyguard"). Even more significant for conducting fieldwork in which I intended to view the society from the bottom was the fact that having a companion allowed me to live semiautonomously within the village I was studying. I could, therefore, traverse among different social groups, including the lowest-status group, and still allow the elite family to fulfill their obligation to extend hospitality to us as village guests.

Women in the village took on the role of our protectors. In one instance, Lee and I had gone to the nearby city of Ta'izz. We always told villagers when we would be away, although on such a short trip we were sure to return by sundown. In our absence, an immigration official from Ta'izz arrived at the home of one of our neighbors to ask where we were. Knowing that we were only about fifteen minutes away, we were later told that 'Umm Nuria (a fictitious name), in her characteristically high-pitched, loud voice and wearing a black patch over one eye, informed him that we had returned to our country. Needless to say, the man never appeared again; there was actually no need for his visit, because our stay in Yemen had been cleared through the immigration office in Sana'a', the capital. This occurrence signaled to us that village women were prepared to protect us from outsiders, a customary gesture of Middle Eastern hospitality whereby hosts assume responsibility for strangers in their community. "Protection" by the village women not only enabled us to interact freely with other villagers of both sexes and from different social categories, but it also helped us maintain our intimate partnership—both essential for the fieldwork endeavor.

In Yemen, decorum regarding sexual behavior is more important than the behavior itself. Because we lived in a small village shack that afforded us little privacy, our lesbian relationship was probably not a total secret. As in other situations of nonconformity to sexual mores—adultery, for example—a woman's friends and neighbors will protect the participants if the illicit relationship is carried out with discretion. On the other hand, it was possible that some people easily avoided acknowledging the reality of my lesbian partnership. Physical closeness between members of the same sex is not a problem in Yemen or other Middle Eastern societies. Same-sex bonds are often the strongest bonds that Yemeni men form with other men and that Yemeni women form with other women. But they do not confuse same-sex friendships with homosexual relationships. In terms of their views of homosexuality, children of various ages and both sexes in our village talked about a sixteen-year-old neighbor as the passive partner for other young adult males. Ahmad (not his real name) was effeminate and always wore the *futa* (skirt) typical of male garb in Yemen, declining to wear pants, at least to school as did other adolescent males. He appeared to be ambivalent about his sexuality because he deemed my partner, Lee, to be an appropriate sex partner for himself and made advances to her. I suspect that no matter what sexual preference Ahmad ultimately settles upon he will still be expected to conform to societal rules that require that he get married. But his society will also permit him to engage with discretion in other choices for his sexual expression.

Yemenis held contradictory but overlapping views of my various identities. Although my Yemeni neighbors in the two places that we stayed came to believe in my nationality, it almost never occurred to any other Yemenis that I could be American. Those who inevitably asked assumed that I was Ethiopian, Sudanese, or Somalian. Persons from these countries commonly work as professionals and technicians in Yemen, whereas Yemeni contact with American blacks was much more limited. African Americans were rarely seen on television in the early 1980s.[9] As representatives of America, African Americans were mainly to be found in the "blaxploitation" films that were then showing, especially in the Yemeni capital. Although distortions of black African identities were previously available to Arab audiences, mainly from literary sources, exploitative images now were being popularized on a wider scale by American film exports to developing countries. Especially insidious was the fact that these films featured sex and violence against African American women. Perhaps these images accounted in part for the ease with which women of African descent may be viewed as sex objects in Yemen as elsewhere. Some Yemeni males categorized me as they would any other foreign, non-Muslim female coming from Western or African societies, where, they believed, sexual expression was more liberal and thus more accessible to exploitation or solicitation. In either case, I was perceived in this instance as an outsider. One's nationality and, to some extent, race and even gender were irrelevant to males in search of acceptable outlets for sexual expression.[10] Clearly, however, Yemenis included both race and gender in their perceptions of my social and sexual status.

My identity as an African American woman was not only challenged in Yemen but also confirmed in a way that contributed to the process of self-integration. Overall, we were the recipients of the Yemeni version of generous Middle Eastern hospitality from men as well as women. Furthermore, because they assumed that I was educated (I told them that I was a teacher and researcher), Yemenis treated me with the respect accorded to scholarly guests of privileged status. In fact, the preferential treatment I received in Yemen, particularly from men in official positions, heightened my awareness of how routinely women of color are disregarded in my country. Such easy acceptance of my achievements by Yemenis facilitated my progress toward self-recognition. To most Yemenis (even those living as migrant workers back in my neighborhood in New York City), because I spoke Arabic and was black I couldn't be American. This phenomenon is the result of the racist attitudes of Americans, not those of Yemenis. Discrimination in education and employment in my country reduces the possibility that African Americans will be viewed as respected representatives of the United States by individuals in host countries. Ironically, Yemeni conclusions that I was an educated African female entailed their rejection of my nationality as American. The greater irony perhaps is that their attitudes provided positive self-confirmations that were only partially available to me before my encounters in Yemen.

Like Middle-Easterners elsewhere, Yemenis apply informal social and sexual codes in certain situations. Being able to center in an experience different from mine was especially important in matters related to sexuality. Looking at my various selves through the vantage of Yemeni society allowed me to understand that my village neighbors operated in many different worlds at once. Centering on divergent experiences permits a fuller expression of diversity in explaining a complex society like Yemen than I have found in more readily accepted anthropological views. My hope is that anthropology will begin to provide a more lucid framework for discussing various aspects of diversity.

Notes

I acknowledge with appreciation the editorial insights and comments provided by Ellen Lewin and Liz Goodman. My thanks also to the organizers of the Society of Lesbian and Gay Anthropologists (SOLGA) panel who invited me to present an earlier version of this chapter at the 1990 American Anthropological Association meeting. I also wish to thank various colleagues for their comments and support during the revision of this chapter, especially Deborah Rubin and Harvey Williams at the University of the Pacific, as well as Beth Vanfossen and Fran Rothstein at the Institute for Teaching and Research on Women, Towson State University. I am also grateful to Lee Maher, Shelagh Weir, Margo Okaza-wa-Rey, Daniel Varisco, Najwa Adra, Dale Eickelman, Fran Kostarelos, Huda Seif, and Paula Johnson for their generous support and encouragement. Finally, I celebrate the life and writings of Audre Lorde, who died in 1992 but whose creative self-definitions of her multiple identities provide an ongoing lesson for all of us.

1   Andrea Canaan's (1983:234) description of overcoming restricted views of her femaleness and her brownness is also very useful.

2   See Deborah D'Amico-Samuels (1991:68), who challenges the notion that the fieldwork experience is separate from the life of the anthropologist in its entirety.

3   In particular, there is fear of guilt by association among heterosexual women (independent females are still perceived as lesbians) and fear that lesbian-identified behaviors will scare off the scarce number of available black men (Lorde 1984:121). Of course, the ultimate fear Lorde identifies is that social relationships will need to be redefined once independent, woman-identified black women's voices are really validated (121).

4   The words "pivot the center" are provided by Bettina Aptheker (1989).

5   Following Angela P. Harris (1990), who also contends that race and gender are linked inextricably, I am using "black" instead of "Black" in this essay. In her words, "to capitalize 'Black' and not 'Woman' would imply a privileging of race with which I do not agree" (Harris 1990:586n). I use "African American" to designate the origins and nationality of some people of color who identify themselves as black.

6   Neither Brown nor Hill is concerned directly with the marginality of black lesbians in academia.

7   Among my most recent multidisciplinary guides is the spectacular film *Daughters of the Dust* by Julie Dash.

8   For further discussion of a different political framework with which to analyze these and various other *akhdam* behaviors see Walters (1987).

9 Yemenis had seen the television version of "Roots," and men in particular asked whether I was the sister of boxing champion Muhammad Ali.

10 Inappropriate sexual advances from Yemeni males were usually deflected by appealing to the man's sense of honor (*sharaf*).

References Cited

Abu-Lughod, Lila. 1988. "Fieldwork of a Dutiful Daughter." In *Arab Women in the Field: Studying Your Own Society,* ed. Soraya Altorki and Camillia Fawzi El-Solh. New York: Syracuse University Press.

Aptheker, Bettina. 1989. *Tapestries of Life: Women's Work, Women's Consciousness and the Meaning of Daily Life.* Amherst: University of Massachusetts Press.

Brown, Elsa Barkley. 1989. "African-American Women's Quilting: A Framework for Conceptualizing and Teaching African-American Women's History." *Signs: Journal of Women in Culture and Society* 14, no. 4.

Canaan, Andrea. 1983 [1981]. "Brownness." In *This Bridge Called My Back: Writings by Radical Women of Color,* ed. Cherríe Moraga and Gloria Anzaldúa. New York: Kitchen Table, Women of Color Press.

Collins, Patricia Hill. 1990. *Black Feminist Thought: Knowledge, Consciousness and the Politics of Empowerment.* London: HarperCollins Academic.

D'Amico-Samuels, Deborah. 1991. "Undoing Fieldwork: Personal, Political, Theoretical and Methodological Implications." In *Decolonizing Anthropology: Moving Further toward an Anthropology for Liberation,* ed. Faye V. Harrison. Washington, D.C.: American Anthropological Association.

Harris, Angela P. 1990. "Race and Essentialism in Feminist Legal Theory." *Stanford Law Review* 42, 581–615.

Lorde, Audre. 1984. "Age, Race, Class and Sex: Women Defining Difference." In *Sister Outsider,* 114–23. Trumansburg: Crossing Press.

Lugones, Maria. 1990. "Playfulness, 'World'-Traveling, and Loving Perception." In *Making Face, Making Soul: Haciendo Caras,* ed. Gloria Anzaldúa. San Francisco: Aunt Lute Foundation.

McClaurin-Allen, Irma. 1990. "Incongruities: Dissonance and Contradiction in the Life of a Black Middle-Class Woman." In *Uncertain Terms: Negotiating Gender in American Culture,* ed. Faye Ginsburg and Anna Lowenhaupt Tsing. Boston: Beacon Press.

Moore, Henrietta. 1988. *Feminism and Anthropology.* Minneapolis: University of Minnesota Press.

Stack, Carol B. 1974. *All Our Kin: Strategies for Survival in a Black Community.* New York: Harper and Row Publishers.

Walters, Delores M. 1987. "Perceptions of Social Inequality in the Yemen Arab Republic." Unpublished Ph.D. dissertation, New York University.

4. Being Gay and Doing Fieldwork
Walter L. Williams

While writing this essay I am in Rarotonga, in the South Pacific, and the problems of doing fieldwork are immediately apparent. As I type these words I have to shoo away the chickens, which seem attracted to the peck-peck-peck sound of my portable laptop computer. This is the first time I have brought a computer along on fieldwork, and the manual does not explain how to keep insects out of it. Sometimes I think I have inserted a misplaced comma, only to realize it is a tiny ant on the screen. At night the huge roaches here insist on crawling all over everything. They are not shy at all and seem to realize that I will not smush them as they wander across the keyboard. I hope none will be inside my portable printer as I try to print out the finished product. Last night I was reluctantly forced to do battle with the biggest spider I have ever seen, which had settled on my bed.

The point of this introduction is to say that being gay is only one potential issue involved in living in a fieldwork setting. In my experience doing fieldwork on numerous Indian reservations, in a Maya village in Yucatan, among Native Alaskans, in Java, and most recently among Polynesians, I have found that my gayness is much less of a problem than the common obstacles facing most fieldworkers. Sanitation, deciding what local foods and drinks I can safely consume, money transfers, diarrhea, snarling dogs, allergies, finding a suitable place to live, arranging to keep in touch with my parents (who worry about me constantly, even though I assure them I am much safer in these villages than I am back home in Los Angeles)—these are the kind of daily issues to which one has to adjust when arriving at a new locale. They must be attended to before one can even begin to think about one's interactions with the local people.

In terms of personal interactions, the most immediate issues are being misunderstood and possibly offending someone while trying to speak a foreign language (or even in English), violating some cultural style that makes one appear foolish or uncouth, and deciding what to share or hoard among the few (and usually absolutely necessary) material possessions one brings along to the field. In addition to all this, I now have to worry about voltage regulators, finding a dependable source of electricity, and what to do if my computer malfunctions.

Yet despite these petty problems of day-to-day living, I would not once think of trading my experiences as a fieldworker with those of any other profession. I consider my times doing fieldwork to be among the happiest years of my life. I do not think I would have had the fascinating experiences that I feel blessed to have had if I had not gone out to live among people of quite different cultures. One gains daily insight in the continuing education that is lived experience and feels enriched by the wealth of experiences one would not have in one's native society.

Because some of the other essays in this book cogently address some of the problems facing lesbian and gay anthropologists in the field, I want to focus on the advantages gained by being open about one's affectional orientation. While just being uncloseted is no guarantee that doors are automatically opened in every research situation, it can provide positive benefits. I would like to use my personal history of research to show how I happened upon my research topics. From the beginnings of my academic career, I structured my research around questions that are important to me. Many anthropologists do this, of course, but it strikes me as odd that some ethnographers don't seem to have any particular personal motivation for doing what they do. My suspicion is that those anthropologists who have personal motivations make better ethnographers.

In my case, my initial fieldwork, among the Eastern Cherokees, was partly motivated by my desire to learn about my family heritage due to childhood memories of my Cherokee great-great grandmother, who died when I was six. That research led to my first book (Williams 1979). My next books, although based more on library research than on fieldwork, were a result of my personal involvement in (and political commitment to) the 1960s' Pan-African black pride movement and the 1970s' American Indian activism (Williams 1982, 1984).

It was in terms of my gayness, however, that I was led to my next experience with fieldwork. The late 1970s was when I began coming to terms with my homosexuality, and a turning point for my personal development was reading Jonathan Katz's *Gay American History* (1976). A whole section of that book consisted of documents relating to the Native American two-spirit alternative gender role and to the attempts of European imperialists to wipe out culturally accepted "sodomy" among Native Americans. In all of the anthropology classes I had taken, I had never once heard mention of such traditions. My anger at this denial of knowledge—information I desperately needed at that stage in my life—helped me determine to publicize this subject so that gays and lesbians in the future would not feel the isolation I had felt.

Even before I was openly gay at my university, I began to incorporate mention of the two-spirit roles into the class I was teaching on American Indian ethnohistory. In 1980 I received a Woodrow Wilson Foundation grant to do research at the UCLA American Indian Studies Center on ways to improve Indian legal status. After quickly writing a couple of essays on that topic I devoted the bulk of my grant time to research on two-spirit traditions.

I had decided that, having devoted years of my life to helping racial minorities overcome prejudice and mistreatment, it was time for me to devote my energies to helping my own gay minority. I clearly would not have undertaken this research had I not by that time developed a positive gay identity. Yet this was a case where my interests would not be in conflict, because I felt that by doing research on two-spirit traditions, I would also be helping contemporary Native Americans recapture part of their cultural heritage. I dedicated my energies especially to those young gay and lesbian native people, on reservations or in urban areas, who might never have heard of the two-spirit idea. The 1970s had been a time of cultural renaissance among Indian people, and I felt that gay and lesbian Indians deserved to participate in this renaissance of their heritage as well.

Because I was lucky enough to be in Los Angeles, I had access to the library of ONE Institute of Homophile Studies and to the International Gay and Lesbian Archives. Dorr Legg, Harry Hay, and Jim Kepner, truly pioneering heroes of the homophile movement of the 1950s, encouraged me and kindly provided additional sources. The most valuable anthropological writing they gave me was the path-breaking essay by Sue-Ellen Jacobs (1968). Armed with these leads, I began traveling to different archives, scouring obscure sources to see if I could find other mention of "berdaches" or "sodomy." My coming out in the profession consisted of a paper I presented on two-spirited people at the 1980 American Society for Ethnohistory annual meeting.

By 1982 I decided that, to pursue this topic, fieldwork with Native American traditionalists who were still following their aboriginal religions needed to be done. I was not confident of my ability to do such fieldwork because I did not have any prior experience among Western Indians, where knowledge of two-spirit roles was most likely to be remembered. Nevertheless, Sue-Ellen Jacobs and Harry Hay encouraged me to go ahead. I decided that if I did not pursue this fieldwork, it would not likely get done. After all, I at least had a background in American Indian studies and had fieldwork experience living as part of an Indian community. I realized I could probably not get a grant to do research on homosexuality, but I had a sabbatical due me, and I could choose whatever subject I wanted. Having the advantage of being tenured at my university due to my previous publications, I realized I was at that time one of a very few uncloseted gay scholars who had enough income and job security to conduct this research.

I felt lucky to know that the cultures that were my research specialty had a heritage of acceptance of same-sex eroticism. Still, I surmised that the impact of a century or more of Westernization and Christianity could not have failed to make such subjects sensitive. I hoped that, as I traveled to the Plains, I could locate a reservation where traditionalist elders might agree to talk to me about two-spirited people they remembered from their youth. The first reservation I went to in 1982 was the Omaha reservation. I had read century-old written documents about androgynous "mex-oga" being highly respected. When I asked local people for someone who could talk to me about the old Omaha traditions, I was referred to the tribal historian. He was a kindly gentleman who seemed to take an immediate liking to me. Yet, after long discussions on Omaha history, when I finally got up nerve enough to ask about the term *mex-oga*, his demeanor suddenly changed. His eyes narrowed, and he took on a hostile look as he demanded abruptly, "Why do you want to know about that?"

My heart raced as I nervously thought about how to respond. In near panic I visualized this man making sure I was immediately kicked off the reservation—or worse. Finally, not knowing what else to say, I decided to be honest. I summoned every bit of out-of-the-closet gay pride that I had picked up from gay activist political activities over the past few years and responded. Although my interests were about Omaha traditions in general, I explained, I had a personal interest in this particular subject because I am homosexual and wanted to see if the mex-oga tradition had anything to do with homosexuality as the written documents suggested.

As soon as I said this, the man relaxed and smiled warmly. I will never forget his next words: "We don't talk about me-xo-ga [which I had mispronounced] to outsiders, but I appreciate your honesty. I'll tell you. Me-xo-ga is the same thing as gay; it's just like in California." After that, we relaxed and began an even closer interaction. It was as if, knowing something deeply personal about me, this man found it easier to reveal his sacred tribal traditions. This was to be my first experience in coming out as openly gay to informants. I can say that in virtually all such experiences during the last ten years I have received a positive (or at the least, neutral) response. In my opinion, many lesbian and gay ethnographers have been unnecessarily closeted and overly cautious during their fieldwork, and I am dismayed that even some of those who are open about themselves at their university have so little self-esteem that they will lie to their informants. This statement, of course, ignores the fact that being openly gay or lesbian might have negative consequences in some situations, but in most instances an attempt to hide or deny one's sexuality results in a less trusting and information-sharing relationship with informants.

My experience on the Omaha reservation was also the first time I noticed that elderly Indian traditionalists prefer to use the term *gay* rather than *homosexual*. To them, focus on the sexual inclinations of the person is less important than what they call the person's "spirit." It took me a long time to realize, in many conversations with traditionalist Indians, that what they mean by spirit is close to what Westerners might call a person's basic character. Because of my informants' emphasis, my initial focus on homosexual behavior shifted to the spiritual and religious aspects of two-spirit traditions. That is why I ultimately titled my book *The Spirit and the Flesh* (1986).

When the Omaha historian became satisfied that I did not intend to approach his tribal traditions in a disrespectful manner, he did something even more surprising. He took me to meet a sixty-two-year-old male who is identified by his reservation community, and who identifies himself, as me-xo-ga. After I identified myself as gay, that man agreed to talk with me about his life. He said he would not have opened up if I had been the typical heterosexual anthropologist. He was the first two-spirited person I interviewed. In that experience, as with numerous others since then, I feel that I have had an enormous advantage in doing my fieldwork by being openly gay. Of course, a shared sexual orientation is not enough by itself to guarantee continued good relations with others (either cross-culturally or among persons of similar cultural backgrounds), but it does help open many doors that might otherwise remain closed.

What I have said certainly depends on my choice of subject matter and fieldwork locations. I have consciously searched out cultures that have a tradition of acceptance of same-sex eroticism. Since 1982 I have resolved to do a different kind of fieldwork. Rather than living on one Indian reservation for a year and doing the usual community study that ethnographers regularly do, I decided that my community of study would be two-spirited people themselves. Although an intensive community study focusing on such persons' interactions within that community is without doubt of value, the notion that two-spirit traditions have completely disappeared is so widespread among anthropologists that I decided it was more important for me to do a comparative study of these unique individuals on several reservations. I also think my prowess for exploring new locales and subjects is my strongest talent, whereas other ethnographers are more skilled in doing intensive analysis of one locale over a longer period. Both kinds of researchers are necessary to gain greater cross-cultural understanding.

After staying for a time with my initial Omaha informant, he sent his nephew to accompany me to the Rosebud Sioux reservation and to introduce me to *winkte*, two-spirits among the Lakota. After more experiences living at Rosebud and doing life history interviews and additional interviews with their relatives and neighbors, they referred me to other *winktes* on the Pine Ridge Sioux reservation. And from there, those *winktes* referred me to others they knew on the Crow and Northern Cheyenne reservations. And so it went, as I worked my way across the Plains.

I ended up observing, and eventually participating in, traditional religious ceremonies to which I am sure I would never have been invited had I not established a personal gay-to-gay (or two-spirit to two-spirit) relationship with my native informants. I was warned by whites in South Dakota that a white man would not be safe living on a reservation, especially in Pine Ridge, yet I never experienced hostility. I believe my acceptance in the community was because of my association with *winktes*. Traditionalist Lakotas are somewhat afraid of the spiritual power of *winktes*, which provides them and their consorts with a convenient form of protection. Being openly gay thus provided me an advantage in this fieldwork situation.

Although personal involvement was not my motivation for undertaking this research, one of my informants and I became very close as he went with me in doing my interviewing and I accompanied him in his Lakota religion ceremonial activities. We went everywhere together, and his religious intensity opened up a whole new realm of spiritual concern in my personal life. He is without a doubt the most spiritual person I have ever met, and I consider my interaction with him to be a turning point in my life. Shortly before I was scheduled to leave his reservation, he surprised me by proposing that I become his husband and live with him on his reservation. I had known of his sexual attraction to me because I had previously gently deflected his initiatives for sexual involvement, yet I considered him more as my teacher than as my husband.

I explained that I had to return to my teaching job after my sabbatical year was over. He responded that I could quit my job and he would support me. He said that I would not have to worry about anything, because I could move into his house and he would provide us a good living. I could, he said, focus on my writing and would not have to worry about teaching at a university. I thanked him for the offer but told him I could not give up my academic career. Besides, I needed to pursue research on two-spirited people among other groups of Native Americans beyond the Plains.

By the end of 1982 I traveled down to the Navajo reservation and did additional research and interviewing. I was amazed to find that Navajo traditionalists were even more respectful of "nadleh" than the Plains tribes had been of their two-spirits. But I found the Arizona winter unexpectedly harsh and decided I could depend on several excellent published sources on the Navajo nadleh. So, in the spirit of Joseph Campbell, who said the highest life course is to be attained by following your own personal bliss, in January 1983 I took off for Mexico. In my library research I had run across a few sixteenth-century sources by Spanish conquistadores complaining about how the Mayas in particular were "addicted to sodomy," and another later letter claiming that the Catholic missionaries and Spanish government officials had successfully wiped out such vices among the Indians (quoted in Williams 1986:135–40). My previous research led me to distrust that claim.

Armed with nothing more than those few four-hundred-year-old references, and knowing no one, I headed for Mayan villages in Yucatan. Although I had not one personal contact, my positive experiences on the Plains during my 1982 fieldwork led me to approach the task with anticipation. I spent my first weeks in Yucatan touring through the magnificent Mayan archaeological sites of Uxmal, Chichen Itza, Tulum, and other ruins. Whenever I asked my Mayan tour guides about homosexuality, they uniformly replied in a noncondemnatory, accepting way. Within a couple of weeks I had not only made contact with a group of Maya "homosexuales" but also was developing a circle of friends.

I found the Mayas to be among the most friendly and attractive people I have ever met. One, whose nickname was "El Sexy," took a particular liking to me. He lived with his mother, who took me under her wing and was soon cooking delicious meals for me. They both became committed to the importance of a book being written on this topic. El Sexy helped me meet other "homosexuales" to interview and was a joyful companion as I did my study. He felt pleased that his and other homosexuals' lives and viewpoints were going to be included in a book. He also used me as a status symbol in his pueblo. One day, as we were riding in my automobile, he got great enjoyment from the fact that a boy publicly called out to him, "El Sexy, I see you have found your husband!" This humorous reference to me was not in any way derogatory, but merely a relaxed kidding that reflected the general knowledge of his attraction to men (Williams 1986:143–44).

While I feel positively about all my fieldwork locations, and each group of people has left its own unique imprint on my education and personal life, I left Yucatan very reluctantly. I think the Mayas are my favorite people of all. Their friendly and open demeanor, as well as their whole joyful approach to life, impressed me deeply.

Again, I want to emphasize that being openly gay is not by itself sufficient to ensure a good fieldwork experience. What is most necessary is to treat people with respect, caring, and earnestness and to interact with them on a human-to-human basis. Without this, no amount of fieldwork training or sophisticated research methodology will allow one to establish and maintain a positive relationship of any kind. Being open about oneself is necessary before one can establish a genuinely trusting and sharing interaction with people. As Stephen O. Murray and others in this volume rightly point out, we still cannot assume from personal experiences that what we are told or observe is the kind of behavior that actually occurs among people of the studied culture. But we cannot gain much valid knowledge without these conversations and observations.

After returning from Yucatan, going back to teaching and staying busy writing my fieldnotes and publishing my research, my next fieldwork was in 1987 and 1988. I had written a number of grant proposals to do research on homosexuality cross-culturally, but all of them had been re-jected. Finally I managed to get funding by—once again—writing a grant for a different topic. This time I won a Fulbright Scholar Award to In-donesia. My Fulbright research proposal was to do life history interview-ing of Javanese elders, with a special focus on gender. On the way to Indonesia, I took the opportunity to stop over in Bangkok and did some interviewing of Thai gay activists (Williams 1990). My experience has been that I have managed to do fieldwork on gay topics by getting grants on other subjects, and then doing my gay research in addition to the research I did for my grant. The only time I have received a grant spe-cifically on homosexuality research was in 1989, when I won a small travel grant from the Institute for the Study of Women and Men at my uni-versity to go to Alaska to do research on homosexuality among Aleuts and Yupiks. In the case of my Indonesian work, I published a book of Javanese life histories (Williams 1991) and am still working on other publications specifically focused on homosexuality in Java (see, for ex-ample, Williams 1992a).

This process is not something I complain about; lesbian and gay eth-nographers just have to work twice as hard to get more research done while in the field. In addition, although I think it is important for openly gay and lesbian scholars to publish articles and books on homosexuali-ty, it is also important for us to publish general ethnographies that in-clude homosexuality as just one among many socially accepted aspects of particular cultures. This is what I tried to do in my *Javanese Lives* (1991:180–90, 210, 230n2).

Anthropologists can perform valuable documentation for the effort to overcome homophobia by pointing out to readers that same-sex eroti-cism is a fact of life in human societies around the world. It is thus dou-bly important that we focus upon cultures that are not inflicted with antihomosexual prejudices. We need to highlight the benefits that soci-eties gain by not harboring such prejudices. This cross-cultural perspec-tive can become an important part of the effort to reduce homophobia in American society (Williams 1992b).

I have written elsewhere (Williams 1990:126) about the great need for openly gay and lesbian ethnographers to investigate nonhomophobic cul-tures before their accepting values are destroyed by rampaging Western-ization. In every area of the world in which I have traveled I have found it alarming the extent to which fundamentalist Christian groups are ex-porting homophobia. Barraged with American missionaries, movies, television, literature, and outdated psychoanalytic theories of sexual deviance (that are still being propounded by many Western-educated teachers), many cultures are rapidly changing their attitudes toward sexuality. If we do not gather this research soon, it will be too late to learn about the vast array of differing institutionalized forms of same-sex eroticism.

We desperately need a more complete database for a broader understanding of human sexuality. Given the almost complete ignorance of female-female sexuality in non-Western cultures, I think the highest research priority is for lesbian scholars to undertake this work. As a male interviewer, I was painfully aware of my inability to get women to open up on this issue, and even my male informants usually knew very little on the subject. In *The Spirit and the Flesh,* I could only depend on the few historical documents and few publications on the subject by women scholars. In Java, I was not able to locate even one lesbian who would agree to be anonymously interviewed. I anxiously await the publication of more studies like Jennifer Robertson's (1992) fascinating ethnography of a female theater troupe in Japan.

It is not that sensitive heterosexuals lack the ability to do research on homosexuality; indeed, non-gay anthropologists such as Serena Nanda (1990) have made important contributions to the study of sexual variance. But it is still clear that openly lesbian ethnographers have an advantage in doing field research on female sexuality and openly gay ethnographers have an advantage in doing research on male-male eroticism. Peter Jackson (1989) suggested that gay people have a significant advantage over other foreigners in being able to integrate themselves quickly into a local culture. Because native homosexuals often see themselves as different, sometimes as outsiders in their own culture, they are likely to feel an immediate identity with others they perceive to be "like themselves"—even if those persons are from a different culture. I have certainly found that to be the case in my research.

Jim Wafer, an openly gay ethnographer in Brazil, pointed out several advantages to his being open about his sexuality among his informants. In the first place, his native lover provided many contacts and opened many doors. Because he had a personal relationship with the ethnographer and was committed to the project, this lover had additional motivation to make sure that what was written was accurate. Beyond that, Wafer pointed out, because their relationship was known and accepted in the community, it gave Wafer a "quasi-insider status. . . . It meant, for example, that I was regarded as 'accounted for' within the kinship system . . . [which] meant that I was less a threat than I might otherwise have been" (1990).

Anthropologists often verbalize an expectation that single fieldworkers who go into the field should refrain from any sexual activity in their fieldwork community. This expectation appears rather strange to the people of sexually free cultures, with anthropologists being pitied for denying themselves one of the basic necessities of life. Beyond the question of one's personal happiness, sexual involvement might also yield important research findings. For example, one gay male ethnographer (who shall remain nameless for purposes of this essay) has verbally spoken informally of his experience in a non-Western fieldwork setting where he lived for over a year as an openly gay man. It was not hard for him to come out to people because soon after meeting they would often ask him if he were married. When he replied that he was not married, they frequently asked "Why not?" He then simply responded that he preferred loving men. That response was greeted with an accepting understanding of his sexual inclinations, but many local people still could not understand why he did not marry a woman and continue his sexual activities with males as well.

Later, when word got around the community that he enjoyed sex with males, a number of local men (mid-teen to late-thirties) made sexual advances toward him. Not wishing to remain celibate for a year, he responded positively. Yet because he did not wish to impose his foreign sexual styles, he always let them take the initiative in bed. After several encounters he saw the pattern: erotic interaction between males in that culture involved only interfemoral friction. That is, one partner would lie down on his back or front, rub spit or lotion between his legs at the crotch, and cross his legs at the ankle. The other would lubricate his penis and stick it between the legs of the other. According to this anthropologist, "having his legs crossed at the ankle made all the difference, and it felt great—just like intercourse." Yet this was not intercourse, but "outercourse," a method of sexual interaction that does not lend itself to the transmission of most sexually transmitted diseases (including HIV). If he had not actually experienced the feeling of this type of interfemoral friction, with legs crossed at the ankle, he would not have thought to ask about the particulars of male-male sexual interaction and would have missed its safe-sex implications.

Prompted by this testimony of direct experience, I began to reexamine the literature and found mention of such interfemoral sexual methods being the standard form of male-male sexuality in many societies (ancient Greece, southern Africa, Morocco, some areas of Polynesia). With that anthropologist's encouragement, I hope to publish this data later as a contribution to safe-sex literature. By gathering information about varieties of sexual practices around the world, anthropologists in the age of AIDS can make important contributions in helping people expand their range of sexual practices to less dangerous noninsertive forms of expression. What more valuable application of applied anthropology could be more evident, if we will only drop our Western antisexual prudery? As Ralph Bolton (1991) has rightly pointed out, this is a high-priority, even "urgent," agenda for ethnographic research in the 1990s.

In nonhomophobic cultures a researcher can, by being open about his or her sexuality, be accepted by the local community and can gain access to people for interviewing. Over and over in my research, from Alaska to Java, informants have told me that they would never discuss such topics with a heterosexual. Native Americans in particular have reported feeling violated many times when things they told to white researchers were made fun of and written about in a disrespectful manner. By being personally involved in this subject, a researcher is better able to understand the issues facing informants and is more likely to be able to put data in their proper social context.

Yet it is not enough that a person simply be lesbian or gay and expect instant acceptance. I recognize that informants would not have continued to talk and interact with me had they not felt comfortable with me on an individual level. We must critically examine reports of nonacceptance by white anthropologists who feel that native people are summarily excluding them because of their race. Individual factors of personal interaction may more likely be the cause of such native nonacceptance. For example, in 1992 I was invited to speak at the annual gathering of the Two-Spirited People of the First Nations, which was held in an isolated rural area of British Columbia. A number of non-Indian gays and lesbians attended this gathering, which was organized by lesbian and gay American Indians and Arctic natives. Native people in attendance reacted to the non-Indians quite differently. Those non-Indians who came on their own as single persons were treated rather coolly by the native people in attendance. However, those non-Indians who were there as lovers and partners of natives were treated warmly, like they were "part of the family."

Native American gay people, like many other people I have encountered in Asia and the Pacific, seem to trust the judgment of their native friends. If a non-native outsider is a good enough person for a native person to enjoy being in a relationship with, then the others will accept that person's conclusion that such an outsider should be brought into the group. Otherwise, many of them will keep their distance. Given this situation, involvement of a fieldworker in an emotional personal relationship with a local native person can (besides its reward of personal happiness) also contribute to more effective interaction with the community within which one is living. I am not advocating that lesbian and gay anthropologists go out into the field with a cynical plan to locate a local mate in order to accomplish their fieldwork; such a plot would be exploitative in the extreme. What I am suggesting is that a prohibition on genuinely loving relationships is unrealistic and hypocritical. If a fieldworker and a local person are attracted to each other and the local person understands the realities of the fieldworker's situation (the anthropologist is honest about how long she or he will be resident there, and that the information gathered will likely be published), then such a genuinely felt emotional bond can be a positive experience for all concerned.

A fieldworker with a personal involvement in the subject of study, moreover, has an added incentive to persevere when problems arise (like a lack of funding). A lesbian or gay fieldworker can more easily avoid false information, which might be given to a heterosexual researcher because informants are well aware of Western anti-gay prejudices. As I found from the help I received from gay archival organizations, an openly gay researcher is also able to draw upon specialized sources and unpublished documents which might be withheld from a non-gay researcher.

Conversely, another factor to consider is the disadvantage of lesbian and gay ethnographers trying to remain closeted. Frank Proschan reported the difficulties in his fieldwork with a Cambodian community in trying to hide his homosexuality. His informants could not account for his asexuality: "As a result of my own evasiveness and their sensitive avoidance of potentially embarrassing questions, I remained a riddle to the people with whom I worked" (1990:59). He realized that he came across to his informants as a naive, asexual, childlike eunuch (61). Moreover (he learned years later) his informants had not told him of certain things about Cambodian sexual variance, simply because they were uncertain how he would react to them: "As long as I presented myself as a riddle, leaving any sexual identity undefined and unsaid, my Cambodian friends consistently left anything with explicit sexual content unsaid in my presence—silence begetting silence" (62–63).

Anthropologists are beginning to write about the intersubjective relations connecting fieldworkers to informants, yet the subject of sexuality—certainly one of the most important aspects of human behavior—remains practically unanalyzed in print. Anthropologists have incorporated the worst aspects of Victorian prudery in avoiding an honest assessment of their sexual behaviors in the field. Gay and lesbian anthropologists, by questioning sexual boundaries and social roles, seem ideally positioned to lead anthropologists into a new honesty and openness about sexual interactions in the field, just as they freely write about other forms of daily interaction. Bolton (1991:138) has pointed out that after sexual intimacy people often open up and speak honestly and profoundly about their lives.

By living as part of a community as openly gay people, if that community is not inflicted with the kind of rampant homophobia seen in the West (and all too often reflected in anthropologists' writings), then we can truly offer an honest account of our participant-observation in that community. This is not by any means to suggest sexual irresponsibility on the part of the fieldworker (especially in this age of AIDS), which will exploit or harm informants. Just as there is a difference between an intimate union and a rape, fieldworkers must learn to assess sexual interactions in a more realistic and sophisticated manner.

What is most important, I have found, is that being an effective fieldworker requires honesty with my informants as well as with my readers. If I wish to remain credible, I must inform my informants exactly what kind of information I am interested in, and that my intention is to publish a book on the information gathered. When doing interviews with informants, if at all possible I try to conduct the interview with no one else present. I assure them that I will protect their privacy by not using their real name in order to get them to speak frankly and candidly about their experiences. I emphasize the need for us to know more about the lives of gay people (or using whatever term is locally appropriate) in different cultures around the world, and then after the interview is completed I may tell them about my findings in other cultures if they are interested.

My research entails interviewing informants about their most intimate experiences and feelings. What I find is that if a person reveals a particularly personal detail, it helps for me to throw in some intimate detail about my own experiences. This simple act makes the interview less of a one-sided probing of informant by researcher and more of an exchange of information among equals. That, ultimately, is what anthropology really is all about: to establish an appreciation for human diversity and an empathy with other individuals across the boundaries of culture.

I certainly recognize my weaknesses as an ethnographer, but I also see that I have been able to get data in interviews that others have not. I do not exactly know what I do that seems to get people to open up about themselves. There is something intangible involved, something no amount of training in field-methods classes can impart, that promotes a deep person-to-person interaction between the interviewer and the interviewee. My experience convinces me that the most important factor in successful fieldwork is the ability to empathize with others on a soul-to-soul level. Given the paucity of unbiased data on homosexuality in non-Western cultures and the demonstrated incompetence of most heterosexual anthropologists in gathering such data, I want to do everything I can to encourage more lesbian and gay male researchers to go out into the field and gather information about the subject before it disappears.

Other chapters in this volume have focused on the problems that might be encountered in fieldwork. Although lesbian and gay fieldworkers should certainly be aware of such problems, I agreed to write this essay to provide an example that might help to inspire young anthropologists to embark on additional such research. My general approach to life is to accentuate the positive, and I find many academics so overwhelmingly pessimistic and critical that they unwittingly discourage others. I think ethnographic knowledge is important, and I take my role seriously as a mentor in encouraging other researchers. I have presented my experiences here not to glorify myself but in the hope that such knowledge may be of help to encourage others to accomplish better ethnography in the future.

References Cited

Bolton, Ralph. 1991. "Mapping Terra Incognita: Sex Research for AIDS Prevention: An Urgent Agenda for the 1990s." In *The Time of AIDS*, ed. G. Herdt and S. Lindenbaum, 124–58. Newbury Park: Sage.

Jackson, Peter. 1989. *Male Homosexuality in Thailand*. Elmhurst: Global.

Jacobs, Sue-Ellen. 1968. "Berdache: A Brief Review of the Literature." *Colorado Anthropologist* 1(1): 25–40.

Katz, Jonathan. 1976. *Gay American History*. New York: Crowell.

Nanda, Serena. 1990. *Neither Man nor Woman: The Hijra of India*. Belmont, Calif.: Wadsworth.

Proschan, Frank. 1990. "How Is a Folklorist Like a Riddle?" *Southern Folklore* 47(1): 57–66.

Robertson, Jennifer. 1992. "The Politics of Androgyny in Japan: Sexuality and Subversion in the Theater and Beyond." *American Ethnologist* 19(3): 419–42.

Wafer, Jim. 1990. "Identity Management in the Textual Field." Paper presented at the annual meeting of the American Anthropological Association, New Orleans.

Williams, Walter L. 1979. *Southeastern Indians since the Removal Era*. Athens: University of Georgia Press.

———. 1982. *Black Americans and the Evangelization of Africa*. Madison: University of Wisconsin Press.

———. 1984 *Indian Leadership*. Manhattan, Kans.: Sunflower University Press.

———. 1986. *The Spirit and the Flesh: Sexual Diversity in American Indian Culture*. Boston: Beacon Press. 2d ed. 1992.

———. 1990. "Male Homosexuality in Thailand." *Journal of Homosexuality* 19(4): 126–38.

———. 1991. *Javanese Lives: Women and Men in Modern Indonesian Society*. New Brunswick, N.J.: Rutgers University Press.

———. 1992a. "Gay Self-Respect in Indonesia: The Life History of a Chinese Man from Central Java." In *Oceanic Homosexualities*, ed. Stephen O. Murray et al. New York: Garland Publishing.

———. 1992b. "Benefits for Nonhomophobic Societies: An Anthropological Perspective." In *Homophobia: How We All Pay the Price*, ed. W. Blumenfeld, 258–74. Boston: Beacon Press.

5. Traveling Woman: Conducting a Fieldwork Project on Gender Variance and Homosexuality among North American Indians
Sabine Lang

From March 1992 until the end of February 1993 I conducted a fieldwork project on gender variance and homosexuality among North American Indians. My work was sponsored by a postdoctoral grant from the German Research Society (Deutsche Forschungsgemeinschaft). I had been working on these topics for several years for my doctoral thesis; I had also been active in lesbian events in Germany for many years, which was one of the reasons why my advisor at the University of Hamburg suggested that I should choose the "North American berdache" as the subject of my dissertation. While compiling the material, I was struck by the scarcity of sources on female gender variance. Thus, when I finally had received my Ph.D. (and could not find a job) I decided to apply for a grant that would enable me to do fieldwork on "manly females."

I received my Ph.D. in anthropology from the University of Hamburg, Germany, after having submitted a dissertation titled "Männer als Frauen—Frauen als Männer" (Men as Women—Women as Men) (Lang 1990). Its focus was on gender variance in North American Indian cultures, that is, on the cultural construction of more than two genders, allowing individuals to partly or completely take up the gender role of the opposite sex as defined by their respective culture.[1]

Native American males who live as women and females who live the lives of men are usually referred to as "berdaches" in anthropological literature.[2] Apart from discussing gender variance, I also analyzed alternative gender roles for women who were not classified as being of an alternative gender, such as the Piegan manly-hearted women (Lewis 1941) or the "warrior women" of the Plains (Medicine 1983). Finally, I looked at homosexual relationships, that is, sexual relationships between two individuals of the same sex that do not involve a two-spirited person. For the differences between homosexual relationships and relationships entered by two-spirited people with partners of the same sex but not of the same gender, see Callender and Kochems (1983, 1986), Williams (1986), Jacobs and Cromwell (1992), and Lang (1990).

Soon after I had started my research in 1987 my files were filled with sources referring to male "berdaches." Reports on females living in the role of a man as defined by their culture turned out to be comparatively scarce, however, and most writers who had analyzed gender variance among North American Indians had likewise paid little attention to manly females.[3] At the time, I did not consider Native American female gender variance as a potential research topic for a fieldwork project because I planned to apply for positions immediately after the completion of my Ph.D., eager to exchange my part-time job as a typist for the respectable status of an anthropologist employed by some anthropology department or museum. When I started my job hunt, however, few positions were open. I also had to realize that my lack of fieldwork experience might prove to be a serious impediment when my competitors for a position could well have extensive records of fieldwork projects. My dissertation was based entirely on library research, which is common in anthropology departments in Germany, and my fieldwork experiences consisted of six weeks spent in a village in Oaxaca, Mexico, during the course of a fieldwork training program offered by the Arbeitsbereich Altamerikanische Sprachen und Kulturen at the University of Hamburg. Moreover, dissertations on gender issues—to say nothing of gender variance and homosexuality—are still far from commonplace in German anthropology.

Thus, apart from feeling frustrated because I could not find employment, I began to feel increasingly isolated as far as my field of research was concerned. Finally, I took courage and wrote a long letter to Walter Williams, whose book *The Spirit and the Flesh* (1986) had been an important reference for me and who is an openly gay scholar conducting research on gay-related topics. I wrote about my current situation, explained my research, and admitted that writing my dissertation had been a lonely task and that I was at a loss for ideas on how to further my academic career. A lively correspondence followed, and Williams finally suggested that I apply for a grant that would enable me to do a fieldwork project on gender variance among Native American women. Realizing that the pressure of having to write a dissertation was gone—I could risk embarking on a difficult fieldwork project that might not yield all the data I hoped to obtain—I applied to the German Research Society for a two-year postdoctoral grant. I got the grant, but it would cover only twelve months instead of two years, a decision that was not explained to me but that might have had to do with the fact that I was over the official age limit (which is thirty for DFG postdoctoral grants) as well as with recent budget cuts.

Because Walter Williams, who teaches at the University of Southern California, was to be my advisor during my stay in the United States, I bought an airplane ticket to Los Angeles.[4] On March 1, 1992, I was on my way to my baptism by fire as a field researcher.

Getting on My Way: Where Are All the "Female Berdaches"?

According to Williams, it had not been difficult for him to establish contact with male "berdaches" on those Indian reservations he visited while doing fieldwork for *The Spirit and the Flesh* in the early 1980s (Williams 1986:6–7), and he anticipated no problems as far as my project was concerned. He suggested that I should buy a small motor home and travel from one reservation to the next, which would also save me money because I would not have to rent a room in Los Angeles for the time of my stay in the United States. An alternative would be to travel and visit various Indian reservations for most of the time and then rent a room in order to write a book based on the results of my fieldwork. Williams also emphasized the importance of openly gay and lesbian researchers doing fieldwork on gay and lesbian and related topics. I hoped that being openly lesbian might make it easier for me to gain the confidence of Native American lesbians. The fact that I have sexual relationships with women and that I exhibit a certain degree of "gender blending" might also help me approach females living in the tradition of female gender variance.[5]

A more adventurous soul would probably have embraced the idea of traveling in a camping van for a year, but I could not warm to it. I knew, for one thing, that anthropologists are by no means welcome on many reservations (as one of my friends at a reservation in Idaho later once put it, "People here have been anthroed to death"), and my research ethics would not allow me to be dishonest about my profession and intentions. Thus, I anticipated hostility if I just arrived at an Indian reservation without having been explicitly invited by some member of the tribe who lived there. And how was I supposed to introduce myself and my research project? I had read and heard enough to know that at many places I might encounter an attitude toward all kinds of same-sex behavior, whether between two men or two women or between a "berdache" and a person of the same sex, that would mirror Western society's homophobia. I could not just park my camping van on some reservation, hang out at the local trading post or grocery store, and ask people who entered or left the store, "Excuse me, do you have any women living like men on your reservation?" News about the white woman, possibly a lesbian looking for some "butch" of color to share the cot in her van, would soon spread, but I felt extremely uncomfortable about such an approach. Finally, having read recent writings by both heterosexual and lesbian women of color (e.g., Allen 1983; Brant 1985, 1991; Chrystos 1988, 1991; Moraga and Anzaldúa, eds. 1981; Silvera, ed. 1991), I expected women both off and on the reservations to be aware of issues of racism and to see me as a white woman first, regardless of my sexual orientation. In short, I expected my research project to be very difficult.

For all these reasons I decided that I did not want to live in a camping van for twelve months. I did not want to save money, and with the generous grant from the DFG I did not need to. I wanted some kind of a home, even though I knew I would be traveling most of the time. Thus, I rented a room in Hawthorne just south of Los Angeles International Airport and spent the first part of my stay thinking about the best strategy to get my project started and consulting a number of colleagues on the matter.

From reading such publications as *Living the Spirit* (Roscoe, ed. 1988), I knew that Native American gays and lesbians have come to see traditional two-spirits as role models who can help them find an identity in an atmosphere that more often than not is homophobic, both on and off reservations. Even though two-spirited people, classified as belonging to separate genders as "men-women" and "women-men" within culturally constructed systems of multiple genders, cannot be compared to gays and lesbians in Western culture, they are examples of individuals who engage in same-sex relationships and also are freely accepted and often held in high esteem by their respective tribes or local communities. Thus, they offer a precedent for present-day gay and lesbian Indians that helps them find self-identities and fight homophobia on reservations as well as in urban Indian communities (Lang 1992, 1993). I assumed, therefore, that urban

Native American gays and lesbians would likely have contacts to both homosexual and two-spirited individuals on reservations.

I decided to get my project started by driving up to San Francisco and calling two highly visible members of the organization Gay American Indians (GAI), Randy Burns (Northern Paiute) and Erna Pahe (Navajo). If I introduced myself to them, explained my research project and ethics, and was found to be trustworthy, I might have the opportunity to meet and interview other members of GAI, some of whom might even identify as being of an alternative gender rather than as gay or lesbian. Eventually, I hoped that on some reservations I would be referred to females who lived in a man's role. Besides, lacking addresses or telephone numbers of potential informants or people on Indian reservations who otherwise could help me, Randy Burns's and Erna Pahe's telephone numbers were all I had to go on.

Facing the Realities: Changing the Research Outline

My initial travels took me first to San Francisco, where I attended GAI events and taped conversations with a number of members of that organization. Four male members of GAI then invited me to join them for a trip to Portland, Oregon, where, at a conference on Native Americans and AIDS/HIV, I would possibly meet other two-spirits. In Portland, Randy Burns, one of the founding members of GAI, introduced me to a friend of his from one of the Shoshone reservations. The friend shared part of his vast knowledge about gender variance in his culture and invited me to visit his reservation, where I might be able to talk to females living the ways of an alternative gender.

From Portland I traveled on to Seattle, where Sue-Ellen Jacobs introduced me to Wesley Thomas, a member of the Navajo Nation. Thomas is conducting research primarily on male gender variance in that tribe. Henceforth, I no longer had to travel alone all the time because Wesley and I teamed up for several visits to the Navajo reservation, where we tried to locate examples of modern gender variance. I will not dwell on my travel schedule during those twelve months, but I drove tens of thousands of miles in nine states. Apart from spending time on the Navajo and Shoshone reservations, I attended, among other events, a women's sun dance in southern Arizona, an international gathering of Native gays and lesbians in British Columbia, several pow-wows, readings by gay and lesbian Native American authors, and fund-raisers for two-spirit groups.

Soon I realized that my project would differ widely from the long-term fieldwork projects usually done by anthropologists who decide on a topic and a suitable place, settle down for months at some village or city, slowly come to know the place and its people, and increasingly engage in interviewing informants and in participant observation. I must admit that I sometimes envied them, and I would jokingly tell friends that for my next fieldwork project I would choose the most boring and remote village I could find and spend a year there. I also realized that it would be almost impossible to locate the females I sought. With the exception of my friend at Fort Hall, no one I talked to had ever met a modern-day manly female, even though I heard scattered accounts of individuals who had lived years ago; for example, one or two women had competed with men at rodeos in New Mexico during the 1940s and 1950s.

It seemed wise to consider some changes in my original research outline. Instead of stubbornly sticking to an objective that might turn my project into a failure, I decided to broaden the scope of my research to include males living in the tradition of gender variance, as well as both urban and rural Indian gays and lesbians. Apart from continuing to search for females living in a man's role, I would interview gays and lesbians about their life histories and experiences as well as about any general first- or secondhand information they had concerning the situation of gays and lesbians on reservations. I would also ask them to tell me whatever they know about the persistence of male and female gender variance within their own tribes and in other tribes with which they might be familiar. I could also participate in gay and lesbian Native American events, gathering information informally.

Establishing Contact with Potential Informants

Establishing contact was always easiest when I approached long-time activists of the Native American gay and lesbian movement who were used to dealing with the media and to being interviewed by anthropologists or historians researching gay and lesbian topics. Both Randy Burns and Erna Pahe readily agreed when I asked them, shortly after my arrival in San Francisco, whether I might conduct and tape conversations with them.

I usually introduced myself as a lesbian anthropologist from Germany interested in learning more about Native American gays and lesbians as well as two-spirited people living on and off the reservations. One of the first things I learned was that almost all Native Americans to whom I spoke strongly resented the term "berdache," which derives, after all, from an Arab term for male prostitutes (Angelino and Shedd 1955). Thus, I soon tried to stop using it, substituting it with "males (or men) who live like women" and "females (or women) who live like men." As noted earlier, many urban Indians have come to refer to both gays and lesbians as well as individuals of an alternative gender as "two-spirited people," so I sometimes used that term, too.

Whenever I approached a person for an interview, I explained my research ethics: I would send a transcript of the taped conversation to the interviewee so she or he would have some influence on the way she or he would be quoted once I started publishing the results of my research. I also stressed matters of anonymity because a number of individuals I interviewed were rightfully concerned about the possibility that I might "out" them. If a consultant-informant wanted to remain anonymous, I would ask her or him to choose a pseudonym that would be used whenever I quoted him or her in my writing. Because I did not have enough time to transcribe many tapes while I was in the United States, I sent copies of the taped conversations to everyone I interviewed. I wanted to be honest about my intentions. For example, I did not approach lesbians or manly females under the pretense of being sexually interested in them in the hope of eliciting information while doing a very intimate kind of "participant observation."

As far as interviews were concerned, I usually approached people whom I had met before—for example, at GAI meetings or, later, at events in Seattle—and who had seemed to respond positively to my introduction. Establishing contact with two-spirited men and women was more difficult, even though, with one exception, everyone I approached agreed to be interviewed after I explained my research more thoroughly. Still, I always felt awkward when calling complete strangers, even though I usually could refer to a third person who had provided me with the telephone number and who was a friend of the person I called. During one of my earlier visits to the United States, a colleague had given me the number of a Native American woman who was an acquaintance of his and who, as he told me, at some occasion had come out to him as a lesbian. He suggested that I should call her and try to interest her in getting together with me for an interview. I called her and introduced myself and my research topic. When I mentioned that I had been referred to her because she was a Native American lesbian, there was a long silence at the other end of the line. Finally she replied, "But I do not identify that way." It turned out that she was living with a man even though she had lived with women earlier, and she resented the label "lesbian" because she identified as an Indian rather than in terms of her sexual orientation. It was a highly embarrassing situation, but it taught me an important lesson about different priorities in establishing one's own identity and involuntary ethnocentrism. Thereafter, whenever I called someone I had never met, I made no assumptions about that person's sexual orientation. Instead, I mentioned that the person who had referred me had thought that she or he might help me learn more about gender variance or, as I put it, "people living like persons of the opposite sex," "men living like women," and "women living like men."

A number of people I approached questioned my motivation. Sometimes, such as in the case of the only Shoshone manly woman with whom I had the chance to speak, they seemed to wonder why I had come to the United States to interview them. In other cases involving urban gays and lesbians, there was some suspicion, more implicit than explicit, that I might "use" the people I interviewed and the information they shared for my personal gain. My usual reply to questions concerning my motivation was to say that I was interested in learning more about Native American two-spirits because I was fascinated by the cultural construction of multiple genders in North American Indian cultures and that maybe the results of my research might help me and others challenge my own culture's concepts of gender and sexual behavior. To my ears this sounded selfish, and it was difficult to give back something immediately to those who so generously shared their time and insights. I did eventually receive a book contract, however, and the results of my research will be available to the Native American two-spirit community (Lang, in press).

Even though, with only one exception, the women and men I approached agreed to get together with me for a conversation, which was usually taped,[6] I felt that a number of people with whom I interacted were neither completely sure about my ethics, nor interested in my academic record or in my advisor's identity. I sometimes wondered why they let me interview them at all. In some instances, informants probably decided that I was trustworthy because of the references I could present, such as the name of some well-known and trusted Indian two-spirit activist. Eventually, however, I had to prove my trustworthiness through the way I interacted with those two-spirited people I met. Without my first being aware of it, they "tested" me all along the way, communicating on the telephone with one another on the impression I had left. News about my work activities at the women's sun dance reached San Francisco in no time, and the same happened when one of the GAI members and I, at the Portland AIDS/HIV conference, had too much to drink during a late-night conversation that was accompanied by the consumption of beer. Still, over the months I became more and more accepted, even though my Portland drinking companion jokingly referred to me as his "party girl" and there was some good-humored teasing whenever I went back to San Francisco.

At one time Wesley Thomas and I realized that gay and lesbian bars are also places where contacts might be established. Therefore, we visited two places in Albuquerque that are known to be popular among local Native American gays and lesbians and transsexuals. Even though we managed to talk to people, we finally dropped the "bar project" for a number of reasons. Due to a slight hearing defect, I can barely communicate in bars in the face of the noise of music and voices. More important, however, bars are places where people come to socialize and look for partners. It might be difficult to get them interested in participating in an anthropological project, and it would be unethical to pose as a potential sexual partner in order to elicit information.

Native American Lesbians: Sexual Orientation versus Ethnic Identity

I had hoped that my identity as a lesbian would facilitate contacts with Native American lesbians. This was usually not the case, however, for reasons that have to do with priorities in defining personal identity. As was emphasized by almost every Native American gay or lesbian with whom I talked, gay and lesbian Native Americans usually see themselves as Indian—or as a member of a specific tribe—first and as gay or lesbian second. The part of their identity that is most important to themselves is their ethnic background as Native Americans as opposed to white society, not their sexual orientation. A Navajo friend, for example, when reading the first draft of this chapter, commented that he identifies first as a Diné, second as a Native American, third as a person of alternative gender, and fourth as an American. Therefore, I was seen as a white woman first. It also became increasingly apparent during my conversations with gay and lesbian Native Americans that they do not necessarily see themselves as "gay" or "lesbian" the way white homosexual women and men do. Instead of striving for a "white" lesbian or gay identity and life-style, Native Americans, especially those in urban areas, are looking for an identity that is specifically Indian in the broadest sense of the term, referring to *winkte, heemaneh,* and *nádleehe* as their predecessors in tribal societies rather than identifying with Western gay and lesbian roles. Thus, not even my identity as far as sexual orientation was concerned was exactly the same as theirs.

Usually, gay men or males who identified as being of an alternative gender were more accessible and more interested in socializing with me than were lesbians. Part of the explanation for this lies in the fact that Native American lesbians are exposed to even more discrimination by white society than are gay Indian men. They are discriminated against by whites of both sexes as Indians, women, and lesbians. Therefore, the fact that I am white seemed more important to a number of women than the fact that I am also a lesbian, and my sexual orientation did not necessarily help me be accepted. The patterns of interaction among Native American gay men and white male gay researchers may be different. A gay German colleague who did research with two-spirited people in Canada told me that Indian men he met often tended to relate to him on a sexual level regardless of the fact that he is white, and that some, apparently for reasons that have to do with self-esteem, even consider it somehow prestigious to have a white lover. This was clearly not the case with most of the women I met, some of whom were conscious of issues of racism to such a degree that they would not even date white women.

I became aware of the implications of an emphasis on ethnic background rather than on sexual orientation when I arrived in southern Arizona early in July 1992 to participate in a women's sun dance. I had made sure beforehand that white women were not excluded from the ceremony, because a flyer announcing the event stated that "only native sisters and wimmin of color may dance after attending the ceremony for several years. . . . It is also the only [sun dance] ever held for native Lesbians" (Littlethunder 1992). I learned that although white women could not be sun dancers, they still could attend the ceremony. Soon after I had arrived, I discovered that—with the exception of a Jewish woman from San Francisco—I would be the only white woman attending the ceremony who had not for years been friends with one or more of the women of color who were present. Again I introduced myself as a lesbian anthropologist from Germany who wanted to learn more about Native American lesbians in general and the sun dance in particular. I also made clear that I was not going to disrupt the ceremony in any respect and that I was more than willing to accept responsibility as far as work chores were concerned. Even though none of the women voiced any concerns, their behavior showed that they did not trust me. The only way I could learn about the sun dance and its participants was by joining the work force—food had to be cooked, the sacred fire in front of the sweat lodge had to be watched constantly, and the arbor where the sun dance was to take place had to be weeded—and by carrying out instructions without asking questions that went beyond practical considerations. A taped conversation was completely out of the question.

The manner I was treated by the women of color varied from a reserved friendliness to unconcealed hostility. The friendly ones constituted a minority, as did the hostile ones. Most of the women seemed more or less indifferent. I made friends with a Métis woman from Canada who also attended the ceremony for the first time and whom I had met before at an event in Vancouver, British Columbia. I also made friends with the Jewish woman who was the other outsider. The leader of the sun dance and one of the other sun dancers welcomed me, the latter delighting in teaching me—and others—the right ways of behavior during the ceremony. The women present had come to the sun dance because they wished to gain spiritual strength together with other women of color. Most of them had varying degrees of North American or Mexican Indian heritage, but two women were African American. The white women present had come to support their sisters of color both spiritually and practically, for example, by providing water and firewood. Women of color would engage in brief conversation with me, which another woman of color would usually join. The two women would then continue the conversation, and I would gradually become excluded from it.

Still, I was treated politely, if indifferently. One of the sun dancers interacted an a very friendly and relaxed way with the other women of color, but she would go out of her way to treat the Jewish woman and me coldly and even rudely. At the end of the ceremony, however, after I had been working hard for eight days, proving that I was genuinely willing to fit in and learn and that I respected the rules pertaining to behavior during the sun dance, the general attitude toward me changed. Even the hitherto hostile woman was basically friendly when I bid her good-bye. Yet there was a time during the ceremony when I got into my car, drove to a remote place down the road, and cried for half an hour because I felt completely isolated and humiliated despite the fact that I did not act the role of the nosy anthropologist but was instead eager to learn and worked as hard as any other woman did. Here, as in other contexts I encountered during the course of my research project, ethnic background outweighed sexual orientation. I was seen as part of white society first, and my identity as a lesbian was not of primary importance to the women with whom I interacted and who, moreover, all were extremely aware of issues of racism.

Another, less traumatic, experience of this kind occurred when I attended the 1992 annual gathering of Two-Spirited First Nations, a gathering of lesbian and gay Native Americans from all over the United States and Canada. This time I did not travel alone, but was accompanied by a friend who is a central—and highly respected—figure within the two-spirit community. I hoped that his respectability would rub off on me and make it easier to establish contact with some of the people who would be present. One of the organizers of the gathering had also suggested that I should give a presentation of my work on Native American lesbians and female gender variance. This, too, would hopefully pave the way for a discussion that might help me to learn more.

Both women and men treated me cordially, but again men were more inclined to socialize and talk with me than were women. A number of women hung out with other lesbians, and it seemed to me that they did not want to be bothered by questions by a German anthropologist, but rather wanted to get together with other Indian lesbians or with the gay men. I could not bring myself to walk up to any of those women, introduce myself, and engage her in a conversation. Moreover, the woman who had suggested that I should give a presentation told me that "some women" felt uncomfortable at the thought of a white woman delivering a presentation on Native American lesbians. After thinking the situation over, I canceled my presentation, telling the women of the organizing team that I did not want to give any kind of presentation as long as any Indian women felt uncomfortable about my doing so. My friend and I also pointed out, however, that no one apparently had objected to Walter Williams giving a presentation at the same gathering and that a number of lesbians had attended his lecture earlier that day. In this case, fame outweighed ethnic identity and sexual orientation. Because *The Spirit and the Flesh* has been widely read by gay and lesbian Native Americans, it seemed proper to have Walter Williams talk about gay male issues. Because no one knew me—or had read my dissertation, which was published in German—my presentation seemed inappropriate.

I eventually learned that "some women" had by no means objected to my presentation; two women had just said that they would not attend it. Anxious not to offend any of the Native lesbians, the organizer had overreacted and given me a distorted and misleading message. As had been the case at the women's sun dance, I ended up with numerous pages of notes based on casual conversations and participant observation but with no taped interviews. Also as at the sun dance, toward the end of the gathering some women came up to me and started a conversation.

I began to realize why the kind of postdoctoral grant for which I had applied usually enables anthropologists to spend two years in the field. It took me a year of various encounters to gain the confidence of those to whom I wanted to talk. A second year would have enabled me to reap the fruit of my efforts to a much greater extent. It would also have probably involved twelve more months of traveling from one place to the next, a way of life that is exciting on the one hand but extremely strenuous on the other.

On the Road Again: Traveling to Where the Two-Spirits Are

Whereas my research project, as any anthropological fieldwork project, was directed at studying a specific topic—in my case, originally female gender variance—it differed from more "classical" fieldwork projects in a number of respects. Not too many anthropologists have ever visited any native society with the explicit purpose of studying gender variance or homosexuality.[7] Information obtained by anthropologists on these topics is usually a byproduct of a prolonged stay with one and the same community where the anthropologist is studying other aspects of culture or where she or he is compiling material for a general ethnography of the respective village or local community.[8] He or she will come to be acquainted with and accepted by a number of members of the community who, during the course of any conversation or if asked specifically, eventually volunteer information about gender variance or homosexual behavior. In some cases, such as Lurie's consultants (1953:708), it is difficult to obtain that kind of information because consultants either do not readily share what might be offensive to the anthropologist or because they have adopted negative Western attitudes toward gender variance or homosexual behavior. In other words, while I was preparing for my research, I became increasingly aware that it would be much easier to arrive at an Indian reservation with the objective of conducting research on child education, water rights, or general ethnography.

Another difference with other anthropological fieldwork projects lay in the fact that I knew what I wanted to study but had no idea where to find it. Of course I knew in which tribes female gender variance had been reported. But there was no way I could drop in at nearly forty Indian reservations and ask, "Excuse me, are there still some women living like men here?" I decided to proceed by means of a "snowball system," beginning in the cities, that hopefully would bring me into contact with individuals on some reservations. I came close to Walter Williams's suggestion concerning a motor home, but instead traveled first in an old station wagon that finally gave up the ghost and then in a small car, my tent and sleeping bag always in the back. I also did not just arrive on Indian reservations. I was handed up and down the western part of the United States by an increasing number of new Native American friends, traveling from a pow-wow in Washington to another one in California, from a sun dance to a two-spirit gathering, and from the Navajo reservation to Idaho. I slept in motel rooms, in my tent, and in the homes of various Indian friends—and now and then in my own bed at the house in Los Angeles I shared with an exceptionally nice lesbian truck driver and her three dogs.

What an anthropologist doing a traditional, long-term study at some community has to do only once, I had to do over and over. Wherever I went for the first time, I had to introduce myself and my project and urge people to cooperate. Yet I did not have several weeks to accomplish this; I usually only had a few days because my objective was not to compile an in-depth study of one community but to gather all the material on gender variance I could obtain. This meant that I had to follow the events scheduled with the two-spirit community (such as the women's sun dance and the two-spirit gathering in Canada) while at the same time repeatedly spending time on the Shoshone and Navajo reservations trying to locate the manly females I originally was supposed to interview. I greatly enjoyed my stays on both reservations. Because I came visiting as a friend of a member of the family, my host families welcomed me warmly, and I would comfortably just act as another family member, joining chats and joking and cooking a "German chicken soup" that fortunately was met with great approval. Usually it took me at least two days to get from one place to the next, where I would stay from several days to nearly two or three weeks before heading for my next destination. Strenuous as it may have been, this research strategy eventually yielded a considerable amount of data, ranging from taped interviews and fieldnotes to all kinds of brochures and flyers. Whenever I stopped at my home base in Los Angeles, however, I would be completely exhausted and spend two or three days on the sofa in the living room, sipping sodas and watching whatever was on television.

Every once in awhile I would panic because the females I was paid to interview were more than evasive. During one of my visits to the Shoshone-Bannock reservation I finally poured out my heart to my friend there at whose home I was staying. He had more or less arranged for me to talk to one of the manly females living on the reservation. As I, once again, lamented my failure to locate females living in the tradition of female gender variance, he asked me whether it had ever occurred to me that I did not find those females simply because there are hardly any left. I think he was right, and I also knew that two other women anthropologists, one of them familiar with the reservation on which she worked, had also been looking in vain for manly females. Moreover, I had learned that the majority of manly females and womanly males are concealed from outsiders and sometimes even from other Native Americans due to the homophobia that has, at many places, replaced the once-favorable attitude toward gender variance.

During the course of my travels I also began to realize that, in spite of the difficulties in locating modern examples of gender variance, I had been collecting a huge amount of data on the life situation and identities of Native American gays and lesbians. Even though a number of anthropologists and historians had been conducting research on the historical two-spirited people in recent years, none of them had paid too much attention to the present-day interconnections between traditional gender variance and the development of specifically Native American gay and lesbian identities. Yet their life experiences and their search for identity as two-spirited people today were the topics my informants seemed to be most eager to discuss. As I skimmed my notes and other materials toward the end of my stay in the United States, it dawned on me that writing about modern-day two-spirited people's lives instead of about roles that in many cases no longer exist apparently would be the result of my fieldwork endeavors.

Conclusions

When Walter Williams conducted his fieldwork on "berdaches" on some Indian reservations in 1982, the "effort was much easier than I had thought it would be. The first reservation I visited . . . was the Omaha. Shortly after my arrival, I was introduced to an elderly person who fulfills this role. From his family I made other contacts on a Lakota reservation, where I stayed with another berdache. This person put me in touch with berdaches on two other nearby reservations" (Williams 1986:6). Because I did not follow Williams's advice, I do not know whether I would have been equally lucky had I just boldly gone to an Indian reservation in order to learn more about female gender variance. When I asked my Indian friends whether they thought it might be a good idea to do so, they invariably answered in the negative, telling me I would not get very far if I arrived uninvited at a reservation. In the end, however, my overall research strategies were somewhat similar to Williams's. We both were handed from one place to the next by means of some kind of a "snowball system," even though he started his research directly on one of the Indian reservations whereas I started with Gay American Indians in San Francisco. I was lucky to be befriended by two males who still, in different ways, carry on the tradition of gender variance in their tribes and who invited me to stay with them and their families on their respective reservations. I was also lucky to finally make friends with a manly female on one of the reservations.

I have often used the word *lucky*, because I am convinced that getting in touch with Native Americans who are of an alternative gender has at least as much to do with luck as it has with fieldwork techniques. For example, if some of those persons whom I first contacted in San Francisco and Seattle had not found me trustworthy or had disliked me, I would not have gotten much further. Yet I was unable to interest the first manly female I approached in talking to me. If an anthropologist goes to an Indian reservation and ends up with a host family that turns out to be homophobic, he or she will encounter a wall of silence instead of being referred to manly females or womanly males. Homophobia is, as I learned, much more common on reservations than some earlier publications might suggest. I heard stories about young Indian gays who were ostracized by their families and threatened to commit suicide and about a womanly youth on a small reservation in the Southwest who was being beaten, first by his father, then by his peers. Gender variance clearly is not just any research topic, it is a very delicate subject.

The sort of itinerant fieldwork I did is one way to locate manly females and womanly males. I usually did not have too much time, however, to overcome barriers that made it difficult to gain confidence. In many cases, it took me a year of repeated visits to gain the confidence of those with whom I wanted to talk. In order to gather a considerable amount of firsthand data I would have had to live in the household of a manly female for some time, but I was not invited to do so.

There certainly is more than one way to get in touch with manly females and womanly males on the Indian reservations. A snowball system worked for both Walter Williams and me, and we were both able to spend some time with males of an alternative gender and their families. I think, however, that the most promising way to gather a large amount of data is by becoming casually acquainted with persons of an alternative gender during the course of a long-term fieldwork project on a topic that has nothing to do with gender variance. As time goes by, the anthropologist usually gains the confidence of numerous members of the community. He or she will get acquainted with two-spirited people just as with others in the community, and, most important, will witness interactions between womanly males and manly females and other community members not as abstract gender categories, but as individuals.

On many Indian reservations the once-favorable attitude toward gender variance has changed due to the massive impact of Western morals and ideas. From my conversations with two-spirited people I also got the impression that those manly females and womanly males who still hold onto their traditional roles are extremely protected by their families and local communities, which makes them almost unapproachable for outsiders. Conducting research on gender variance during the course of long-term community-based fieldwork also has the advantage of providing a certain depth of time. The anthropologist would not be just catching a glimpse of manly females and womanly males at some point of their lives, but would be able to view them within the changing contexts of their cultures over a period of years. For example, the status and life circumstances of a hypothetical womanly male visited by an also hypothetical anthropologist in 1985 may have changed dramatically by now due to the fact HIV/AIDS is spreading on his reservation. The roles and status of womanly males and manly females are no more static than are Native American cultures themselves. To obtain a correct picture of gender variance, it seems wise to look at individuals of an alternative gender over a period of time instead of just once.

During the course of my fieldwork, I had to revise my assumption that the fact that I am openly lesbian would make it easier for me to be accepted among two-spirited Native Americans. Quite obviously, there is no "universal gay community," at least as far as North American Indians are concerned. Maybe there was a time when Native Americans tried to merge with Western urban gay communities, but for a number of years they have looked for specifically Indian gay and lesbian identities, referring to traditional two-spirits as role models rather than gay and lesbian identities and life-styles that are the result of Western history and culture. Thus, their gay or lesbian identity differed from mine. Moreover, the gay and lesbian Native Americans with whom I talked viewed their Indian identity as far more important than their sexual orientation. These priorities were also applied to me, and I was seen as a white woman first, not as a lesbian. Native American two-spirits generally did not see the fact that I am a lesbian as being of primary importance. I was first of all the German anthropologist, a member of white society who had to prove her integrity and trustworthiness, and I was happy and proud when people finally did accept me. Gay American Indians, for example, hosted a potluck dinner for me toward the end of my stay, an event that gave me the opportunity to thank all those who so generously had helped me. The parting presents I gave people were well received, even though I was teased that in the old days people used to give away horses instead of just necklaces and key chains.

I returned to the United States for ten more weeks in the summer of 1993 to continue with my project, again supported by a grant from the Deutsche Forschungsgemeinschaft. It still was next to impossible to locate examples of gender variance, but it also became apparent how much my status had changed since I first appeared at two-spirit events. Because people now knew me, instead of being seen as part of some category like "lesbian" or "anthropologist" I was seen, and approved of, as a person— which is just the way Native Americans want anthropologists to see them.

Notes

I wish to thank all those who so generously shared their time, insights, and suggestions with me. Walter L. Williams encouraged me to do my research project and helped me receive a postdoctoral grant by writing a letter of recommendation and by volunteering to be my advisor at the University of Southern California. He also arranged for me to be an affiliated scholar at USC, first during a six-week stay in 1991 and then during the time of my stay in 1992 and 1993. My research was made possible by a postdoctoral grant from the Deutsche Forschungsgemeinschaft. Hans Fischer at the University of Hamburg has been my advisor both for my dissertation and for my postdoctoral project. He has always motivated me, and I especially appreciated his constant reminders that kept me from sacrificing scholarly integrity to any political agenda. Sue-Ellen Jacobs and Wesley Thomas, my "unofficial advisory team," supported me as colleagues and friends with advice, suggestions, and, when I was in my darker moods, with the constant reassurance that I was doing my project the way it should be done. Wesley Thomas (Navajo) and Clyde Hall (Shoshone) invited me to their reservations and helped in my search for informants and consultants. Randy Burns and Erna Pahe warmly welcomed me when I came to San Francisco and contacted GAI; they have not only helped me in many respects but have also become friends. Thanks also go to Mildred Dickemann, Evelyn Blackwood, Will Roscoe, all those who agreed to share some of their experiences in being two-spirited, and the women who were at the Wimmin's Sun Dance and allowed me to become a part of it. Finally, I thank my mother, Ruth Lang, for loving and supporting a daughter who in many respects has not chosen to walk a straight way.

1   I am following Jacobs and Cromwell's definition of gender variance as the "cultural expressions of multiple genders (i.e., more than two) and the opportunity for individuals to change gender roles and identities over the course of their lifetimes" (1992:63). Concerning multiple genders see also Callender and Kochems (1983), Kessler and McKenna (1977), Martin and Voorhies (1975), and Nanda (1990).
2   The most comprehensive publications on the "berdache" are Blackwood (1984), Callender and Kochems (1983), Jacobs (1968), Lang (1990), Roscoe, ed. (1988), Roscoe (1991), Whitehead (1981), and Williams (1986). Sources on "berdache" have been compiled exhaustively by Roscoe, ed. (1987) in his bibliography on the subject.

Both a number of anthropologists and many Native Americans have come to feel increasingly uncomfortable about the term "berdache." During two conferences on "The 'North American Berdache' Revisited Empirically and Theoretically" held in Washington, D.C., in 1993 and Chicago in 1994, the participants—Native American and non-native scholars and activists—reached a consensus to replace the term "berdache" with "two-spirit," a term in current use by a number of self-identified alternative sex and gendered Natives as a contested compromise to move forward the debate in eliminating the culturally inappropriate usage of "berdache." It was further resolved to indicate the cultural inappropriateness of that term by adding [sic] whenever still using it, for example, in quotations from earlier sources.

For editorial simplicity in this chapter "two-spirit" will be used wherever possible. When referring to traditional two-spirit roles such as the Lakota *winkte,* the Shoshone *tainna wa'ippe,* or the Navajo *nádleehe,* I will also use the term *womanly male* to refer to males partially or completely living in the gender role of a woman as defined by their culture and who other members of their culture classify as being of an alternative gender, as being neither man nor woman. Likewise, *manly female* will refer to a female who has taken up partly or completely the role of a man as defined by her culture and who is classified as being of an alternative gender.

3   Exceptions to this are Blackwood (1984), Callender and Kochems (1983), Whitehead (1981), and Williams (1986).

4   The Deutsche Forschungsgemeinschaft requires candidates for postdoctoral grants to name two advisors who have to be university professors, one in Germany and the other in the country where the research will be conducted.

5   "Still other people [other than hermaphrodites, transsexuals, and transvestites, S.L.] indisputably belong to one sex and identify themselves as belonging to the corresponding gender while exhibiting a complex mixture of characteristics from each of the two standard gender roles" (Devor 1989:vii).

6   Two women I interviewed did not want our conversations to be taped. I therefore memorized the content of the conversations and wrote it down as soon as the conversations were over.

7   As far as Native American cultures are concerned, Walter Williams went to Indian reservations to conduct fieldwork for *The Spirit and the Flesh*. Will Roscoe went to Zuni when researching *The Zuni Man-Woman* (1991). Wesley Thomas has been conducting research on mostly male gender variance and gender categories on the Navajo reservation, as has Carolyn Epple, who has presented a paper on Navajo *nádleehe* at an American Anthropological Association meeting (Epple 1991). Annie Lorrie Anderson (Stanford University) conducted fieldwork on the same topic on the Navajo reservation in the summer of 1992. We had an interesting conversation early in December 1992 and reflected on our experiences in doing research on female gender variance in Native American communities, one of us being a white lesbian, the other a straight woman of color.

8   Examples for this are Devereux's account of gender variance among the Mohave (1937); Ruth Landes's accounts of gender variance contained in her ethnographies of the Mystic Lake Sioux (1968) and the Potawatomi (1970); Stevenson's ethnography of Zuni containing data on the *Ihamana* (1904); the information about *heemaneh* contained in Grinnell's ethnography of the Cheyenne (1962); or the data on gender variance obtained by a number of ethnographers compiling cultural inventories for the Anthropological Records (e.g., Stewart 1941, 1942; Steward 1941, 1943; Voegelin 1942).

References Cited

Allen, Paula Gunn. 1983. *The Woman Who Owned the Shadows*. San Francisco: Spinsters/Aunt Lute.

Angelino, H., and C. L. Shedd. 1955. "A Note on Berdache." *American Anthropologist* n.s. 57(1): 121–26.

Blackwood, Evelyn. 1984. "Sexuality and Gender in Certain Native American Tribes: The Case of Cross-Gender Females." *Signs* 10:1–42.

Brant, Beth. 1985. *Mohawk Trail.* Ithaca, N.Y.: Firebrand Books.

———. 1991. *Food and Spirits.* Ithaca, N.Y.: Firebrand Books.

Callender, C., and L. Kochems. 1983. "The North American Berdache." *Current Anthropology* 24:443–70.

———. 1986. "Men and Not-Men: Male Gender Mixing Statuses and Homosexuality." In *The Many Faces of Homosexuality,* ed. Evelyn Blackwood, 165–78. New York: Harrington Park Press.

Chrystos. 1988. *Not Vanishing.* Vancouver: Press Gang Publishers.

———. 1991. *Dream On.* Vancouver: Press Gang Publishers.

Devereux, George. 1937. "Homosexuality among the Mohave Indians." *Human Biology* 9:498–527.

Devor, Holly. 1989. *Gender Blending.* Bloomington: Indiana University Press.

Epple, Carolyn. 1991. "Beyond Berdache: Navajo Nádleeh as Becoming Again." Paper presented at the 90th meeting of the American Anthropological Association, Chicago.

Grinnell, George Bird. 1962. *The Cheyenne Indians.* 2 vols. New York: Cooper Square.

Jacobs, Sue-Ellen. 1968. "Berdache: A Brief Review of the Literature." *Colorado Anthropologist* 1:25–40.

Jacobs, Sue-Ellen, and Jason Cromwell. 1992. "Visions and Revisions of Reality: Reflections on Sex, Sexuality, Gender, and Gender Variance." *Journal of Homosexuality* 23(4): 43–69.

Kessler, Suzanne, and Wendy McKenna. 1977. *Gender: An Ethnomethodological Approach.* New York: Wiley.

Landes, Ruth. 1968. *The Mystic Lake Sioux.* Madison: University of Wisconsin Press.

———. 1970. *The Prairie Potawatomi.* Madison: University of Wisconsin Press.

Lang, Sabine. 1990. *Männer als Frauen—Frauen als Männer: Geschlechtsrollenwechsel bei den Indianern Nordamerikas.* Hamburg: Wayasbah-Verlag.

———. 1992. "Two-Spirited People: Gender Variance and Homosexuality Among North American Indians Today." Paper presented at the 91st meeting of the American Anthropological Association, San Francisco.

———. 1993. "Masculine Women, Feminine Men: Gender Variance and the Creation of Gay Identities among Contemporary North American Indians." Paper presented at the conference "The North American Berdache Revisited Empirically and Theoretically," Washington D.C., November 17, 1993, organized by Sue-Ellen Jacobs, Wesley Thomas, and Sabine Lang.

———. In press. *The Other Way: Gender Variance and Homosexuality among Contemporary Native Americans.* Austin: University of Texas Press.

Lewis, Oscar. 1941. "Manly-Hearted Women among the Northern Piegan." *American Anthropologist* (n.s.) 43:173–87.

Littlethunder, Beverly. 1992. "Wimmins Sundance July 12–19 Bisbee, Arizona." (Flyer announcing the sun dance.)

Lurie, Nancy O. 1953. "Winnebago Berdache." *American Anthropologist* (n.s.) 55(5): 708–12.

Martin, M. Kay, and Barbara Voorhies. 1975. *Female of the Species*. New York: Columbia University Press.

Medicine, Beatrice. 1983. "'Warrior Women': Sex-Role Alternatives for Plains Indian Women." In *The Hidden Half: Studies of Plains Indian Women*, ed. Patricia Albers and Beatrice Medicine, 267–80. Washington: University Press of America.

Moraga, Cherríe, and Gloria Anzaldúa, eds. 1983. *This Bridge Called My Back: Writings by Radical Women of Color*. New York: Kitchen Table, Women of Color Press.

Nanda, Serena. 1990. *Neither Man nor Woman: The Hijras of India*. Belmont: Wadsworth.

Roscoe, Will, ed. 1987. "Bibliography of Berdache and Alternative Gender Roles among North American Indians." *Journal of Homosexuality* 14(3–4).

———, ed. 1988. *Living the Spirit: A Gay American Indian Anthology*. New York: St. Martin's Press.

———. 1991. *The Zuni Man-Woman*. Albuquerque: University of New Mexico Press.

Silvera, Makeda, ed. 1991. *Piece of My Heart: A Lesbian of Colour Anthology*. Toronto: Sister Vision Black Women and Women of Color Press.

Stevenson, Mathilda Coxe. 1904. *The Zuni Indians: Their Mythology, Esoteric Societies, and Ceremonies*. 23d Annual Report, Bureau of American Ethnology. Washington, D.C.

Steward, Julian H. 1941. "Culture Element Distributions 13: Nevada Shoshone." *Anthropological Records* 4(2).

———. 1943. "Culture Element Distributions 23: Northern and Gosiute Shoshoni." *Anthropological Records* 8(3).

Stewart, Omer C. 1941. "Culture Element Distributions 14: Northern Paiute." *Anthropological Records* 4(3).

———. 1942. "Culture Element Distributions 18: Ute—Southern Paiute." *Anthropological Records* 6(4).

Voegelin, Erminie W. 1942. "Culture Element Distributions 20: Northwest California." *Anthropological Records* 7(2).

Whitehead, Harriet. 1981. "The Bow and the Burden-Strap: A New Look at Institutionalized Homosexuality in Native America." In *Sexual Meanings: The Cultural Construction of Gender and Sexuality*, ed. Sherry Ortner and Harriet Whitehead, 80–115. London: Cambridge University Press.

Williams, Walter L. 1986. *The Spirit and the Flesh: Sexual Diversity in American Indian Culture*. Boston: Beacon Press.

2

TRANSITIONS

6. Confessions of a Reformed Grant Hustler
Ellen Lewin

In the fall of 1976, when I first began background research for a study of lesbian mothers, I had only tangential experience with women in this situation. I was neither a mother myself nor had I ever wished to become one. I had no mothers in my immediate circle of close friends. The previous year, I had seen a dramatic photograph published in the *San Francisco Chronicle* of Mary Jo Risher, a lesbian mother in Dallas, Texas, who lost custody of her nine-year-old son after her older, teenaged son gave testimony against her before a jury (Gibson 1977). The Risher case was one of a number that were being covered in the lesbian community media with some frequency at the time, and no one active in the community could fail to know that lesbian mothers were vulnerable in custody cases.

By the time I saw this picture, I had become acquainted with a number of lesbian mothers. Those I knew at the time had all been married before coming out as lesbians, and for most the possibility of losing custody of their children was a significant and persistent fear. The most dramatic story I knew of concerned a woman who was the mother of one of my neighbors. She had three children and had lost custody of all of them in the early 1950s after her former husband called the police to report that she was sleeping with a woman. The police demanded entry, arrested both the mother and her partner, and removed the children to foster care, where they remained for several years. Only after the death of her ex-husband was she able to regain custody, and this only after convincing the court that her lesbian activity had represented a "phase" from which she was now recovered.

This was the context within which I launched a study of lesbian mothers which got underway in 1977. At the time I began this work, lesbian mothers and their families were not commonly discussed when the topic of the "changing American family" was raised. Most of my colleagues were confused when I described my new research goals. Where would I find such people? How could a lesbian be a mother? they asked. Wasn't that a contradiction in terms?[1]

The first phase of the project—during which the proposal was formulated, the research designed, funding obtained, interviews conducted, and preliminary analysis completed—was informed by an emphasis in the emerging field of feminist anthropology and in feminism generally on universal female oppression and on describing or naming the nature of that oppression. It was also inspired by my desire to offer substantial assistance to lesbian mothers, particularly with regard to custody litigation or other legal problems. This phase of the project was largely defined by descriptive goals, partly determined by feminist and anthropological theory of the period, as well as by community service aims and by the exigencies of applying for and receiving federal research funds.

The second phase of the research, which gradually emerged as I wrote about my findings, has had a very different emphasis. As I tried to transform my interview data into an ethnographic study of lesbian mothers, I found that I could not assume that lesbian motherhood was a unitary phenomenon or that I could "describe" it in purely behavioral terms. Pervasive similarities between the narratives of lesbian mothers and the heterosexual single mothers who served as a comparison group, as well as clear discontinuities between the content of narratives and other evidence of informants' experience, led me to focus my attention on a broader construction of maternal identity.

This shift had important consequences for my approach to what would ultimately emerge as my central finding: that lesbian mothers, like heterosexual single mothers, frame accounts of their maternal experience in substantially the same language, emphasizing the same core values and offering strikingly similar descriptions of their lives as mothers. During the first phase, I saw these results as representing similarities in the actual experience of the two groups, thus indicating that neither group was "better" than the other. By the second phase, however, I came to interpret them differently. It is beyond dispute that lesbian mothers share an array of quite concrete material difficulties with other unmarried mothers—economic stresses deriving from the sex-segregated labor market and from the erratic enforcement of child support awards, as well as well-documented problems with child care, housing, and health care. Although the surrounding structural constraints remain substantially the same, however, I now would argue that the similarities in the narratives of lesbian and heterosexual mothers point to the appropriation of similar cultural resources by both groups, and probably by many mothers in American culture.

In this chapter I will trace the evolution of my views on lesbian mothers, focusing on the extent to which the research design I chose at the beginning of the project shaped, and to some extent confused, my analytical progress. The choices I made throughout the course of the research reflected not only prevailing theoretical trends but also my changing understanding of myself as a lesbian anthropologist studying lesbians from my community. By the time I completed a book on the research (Lewin 1993), I not only had to rethink my views of lesbian mothers but also to revise my view of how similar I was to the women I studied.

Getting Started in the Late 1970s

My early effort to gain a rightful place for lesbian mothers in the feminist reexamination of the family was only one example of a growing concern with carving out a place for lesbians in the expanding literature on gender and the family. Like other topics in the emerging field of women's studies, cross-fertilization between academic and popular publications was extensive during the 1970s. Scholars often took their inspiration from current political controversy or public concern over pressing social problems, while popular writers tended to draw upon scholarly literature to support their positions. In both cases, writers and scholars were opportunistic in their interactions with the other domain, pulling what they needed and using it however it would most conveniently support an argument or line of research.[2]

This was also a period characterized by the continuing feminist academic project (both in anthropology and other disciplines) of describing the nature of women's oppression across cultural boundaries and thereby legitimizing "women" as a domain for research. If sex oppression was to be overcome, these early scholars reasoned, women would have to be viewed as a group, defined by universal, cross-culturally valid features (de Beauvoir 1952; Mitchell 1971; Rosaldo and Lamphere, eds. 1974).

What establishing the legitimacy and reality of lesbian mothers seemed to mean in 1976, when I first began to think about the issue, was describing them and showing that they were not different from other mothers or that lesbians were at least *ordinary* mothers and therefore likely to be "as good as" non-lesbian mothers in comparable social and economic circumstances. It seemed to me that the basis on which custody cases were argued needed to be challenged, that the focus should be on the ways in which lesbian-mother families, like other families, met the basic needs of their children rather than on the mother's affectional preferences. This also meant to me that research needed to be more sociological and structural than psychological, shifting concern from how the mother's sexuality or the absence of a father would affect the children's development to the ways in which the daily lives of lesbian and heterosexual female-headed families would tend to coincide.

But beginning this project raised other, more personal, concerns for me as well. At the point when I began to contemplate writing a research proposal on lesbian mothers, I was engaged in a personal struggle over defining the kind of career I would have as an anthropologist. I had a history of sporadic political activism during high school and college, but in 1969—midway through my career in graduate school—feminism emerged as a force in my life. More than any of my previous political commitments the women's movement came not only to shape my personal life but also to define my academic interests. This meant that my progress in graduate school became increasingly tied to the development of an anthropology of women. My coming out as a lesbian overlapped with these political and intellectual developments. By the time I had completed a dissertation on motherhood as an economic strategy among Latina immigrants in San Francisco (Lewin 1974), a research venture I saw as firmly connected to my feminist objectives, my identity as a lesbian had solidified, along with my loyalty and commitment to what I defined as a lesbian community.[3]

Studying lesbian mothers seemed to meet all the criteria I had for making a research endeavor into a meaningful social contribution and for devising a way to maintain an explicitly feminist, and preferably lesbian feminist, agenda in my research. There was an obvious need to generate knowledge about this highly stigmatized population, first, to make its existence visible, and second, to help dispel the stereotypes that prevailed in custody challenges and could be considered responsible for injustices in the resolution of these cases. As a lesbian, I felt I would not only be equipped to ask more meaningful, culturally informed, questions about the lives of lesbian mothers, but I would also have obvious advantages gaining access and acceptance among those I sought to study.

Planning the Project

When I first began working on a research proposal on lesbian mothers, however, I found myself being rather secretive about what I was up to. The first glimmerings of a project had occurred to me during discussions with another lesbian anthropologist, a friend then completing her doctoral dissertation. We brainstormed for many hours, finally identifying research on "lesbian mothers" as the next obvious step in my career following my dissertation research on motherhood. But my affiliation at that time (my first job out of graduate school) was in a department where I held a minor research position, and when I first tentatively mentioned my new interests to a senior colleague I had the distinct impression that the topic created some discomfort.

Convinced that I could not possibly conduct such marginal research in the relatively respectable domain of a regular university department, I was alerted to the existence of a private research organization in San Francisco that was known for sponsoring a range of unconventional, and sometimes relatively radical, research projects. I began working with their development office on the project, and for many months I assumed that this would be the site where I would work on the study.

During this stage of the grant writing, I had moved to a different department for a year of postdoctoral training. A senior colleague there, not coincidentally a lesbian, showed great interest in my work, and after some delays we finally got together to discuss the proposal I was working on. She was impressed with the work I had done so far and immediately offered me access to the resources of the department, along with the opportunity to be the principal investigator (PI) on the grant. This was a significant offer because junior researchers in my position often had to content themselves with subordinate status on their own projects while senior faculty members served as PIs, sometimes enhancing their reputations with work done by the younger researchers. The offer also carried with it, at least at that time, the possibility of a future academic affiliation because other faculty had tended to be offered line appointments on this campus only after serving an apprenticeship of sorts during several years of "grant-hustling." With this offer in hand, I extricated my project from the private research organization and began to prepare a final revision of the proposal.

My senior colleague, now acting as my mentor, also advised me about how to apply for a grant. She demystified the process, advised me about the specific agencies I should target, how to get assistance from their staffs, and recommended that I think about doing a project far larger and more ambitious than what I had originally contemplated, offering me examples of successful grant proposals from our department to use as models. Nearly all of the members of the department were full-time researchers or grant hustlers; she viewed my project as one that could add to the department's reputation as a productive grant machine.

Her encouragement, and that of other colleagues, made me feel that I had come of age as a scholar and researcher. I was thirty years old and less than two years out of graduate school, and my ideas were being taken seriously and being received enthusiastically by an audience of seasoned, and well-funded, researchers. A department research seminar took up my sampling design, various colleagues offered suggestions and amendments, and it was clear that no one thought my topic was too hot to handle or threatening to the respectability of the department. Although I never discussed my personal stake in a topic concerning lesbians, it seemed clear to me that my colleagues understood that I was a lesbian researcher working on a lesbian topic and that they found nothing wrong with that. The mere fact that the project could be developed as a conventional research grant proposal endowed it with legitimacy; once I took this path, I began to see my work as bringing together good politics and good research, a possibility I had not thought achievable in the academic world.

It is clear to me now that the exigencies of applying for, and receiving, federal research funds were probably the most powerful factors in shaping the research, aside from the political climate I described earlier. I applied to the National Institute of Mental Health (NIMH) during a time when the institute was regularly supporting controversial social research. My application was considered by a committee at NIMH charged with supporting research on something loosely labeled "social problems." This funding pattern depended on a broad construction of "mental health" as including the ordinary round of social behavior, particularly with reference to populations at risk for some kind of discrimination or economic deprivation.[4]

Scholars on the review committee were known to be primarily sociologists, social psychologists, and psychiatrists; their preference was for highly quantified hypothesis-testing projects, with standardized research instruments producing data amenable to statistical manipulation. Because lesbian mothers, as members of a stigmatized population, could not be sampled randomly, I devised a comparative design based on theoretical sampling. Lesbian mothers would be matched with a control group of heterosexual single mothers who resembled them in terms of socioeconomic status, children's age, and household composition, that is, whether the mother lived with a "domestic partner" or was "single" in the demographic sense. In addition, two separate samples were to be drawn (corresponding to the two stages in which research funding was obtained): one comprising women whose children had been born, conceived, or adopted in a marital context (who I called "formerly married") and the other women who became mothers outside of marriage, whether by conventional means, donor insemination, or adoption (who I called "never-married").

All of these categories were bifurcated into lesbian and heterosexual comparison groups, with sexual orientation to be determined by self-attribution. All data were to be collected in semistructured interviews with informants who met the criteria mandated by the sampling strategy. Here my concern was with generating data that would be easily amenable to comparative, and hopefully statistical, analysis. In order to make my claim to an objective, well-controlled study plausible, I eliminated references to standard anthropological techniques like participant observation and rejected the possibility of conducting a traditional community study.

This design was intended to produce comparative data that would meet my broader goal of generating findings that might benefit lesbian mothers defending themselves in custody actions. In supporting this design in the proposal, I made much of the likelihood that lesbian mothers and heterosexual single mothers would face many of the same economic and social problems by virtue of not having their children's fathers in residence. At this point, however, I still thought of the aims of the study in terms of an ethnographic description of lesbian mothers.

After some consultation by telephone, I submitted a preliminary proposal to a senior staff member of the institute. Among his suggestions was the advice that I change the title of the proposal so that the "L-word" would not appear in either the title or the abstract. His concern was that Senator William Proxmire or a member of his staff, then on the lookout for projects that could be ridiculed with the notorious Golden Fleece Award, would be less likely to notice the proposal if its title was sufficiently bland. The title became "Single Mothers: Adaptive Strategies."

What I want to emphasize here is how my desire to demonstrate the lack of significant differences between lesbian mothers and others was easily transformed into framing lesbian mothers as "single mothers." Once lesbian mothers were "just" single mothers, a deviant but relatively benign category, I could more easily make my case for tolerance. It was as though the composite label "lesbian mother" was conceptually bifurcated into the still-abnormal, stigmatized "lesbian" and the relatively acceptable "mother."

Framing lesbian mothers as single mothers was already a congenial perspective in that it conformed to my underlying notion that women, regardless of situational variations, share fundamental common features and that these lead to, or somehow are implicated in, their predicament in patriarchal society. My thinking was that lesbian mothers, insofar as they share with single mothers particular material circumstances, most of which are related to the absence of an adult male from the domestic unit, also are likely to experience similar problems such as low incomes, difficulty obtaining adequate housing and child care, feelings of being overwhelmed by responsibility for the children, and low prestige in the community. I did anticipate some differences as well, reasoning that lesbian mothers would be more vulnerable to custody litigation or threats of such litigation, and that lesbian mothers' access to traditional, kin-based, systems of social support would be impaired.

Discovering "Single Mothers"

What were the consequences of this strategy for the findings generated by the research? There can be little doubt that the final design of the project—comparative, framed in a quantitative mode, and ultimately tied to the notion that lesbian mothers could be best understood with reference to other (heterosexual) single mothers—had a significant impact on the subsequent conduct of the inquiry and on the kinds of results the research generated. Despite the fact that the focus on "single motherhood" as a unifying theme was primarily a strategy intended to make the study workable within the federal grant context, the terminology started to take on a life of its own as the study progressed. Single mothers began to seem like a bounded group, like an ethnic group or a tribe, rather than the reification of a label I had chosen to use for reasons of convenience. Questions framed from this standpoint made it seem that "lesbian" was something to be added to "single," the source of additional oppression but easily thought of as categories that did not overlap.[5]

I knew from the beginning that "single mother" was not necessarily the way that either lesbian or heterosexual mothers designated themselves—that is, not a "native category"—but reminded myself that the term was just "shorthand" for the general civil status of the mothers I was studying. From a purely legal point of view, they were not married to the fathers of their children, a fact that influenced, or sometimes even determined, their economic status, their position in the judicial system, and nature of daily dilemmas they faced as parents, particularly with respect to the problem of bearing the primary responsibility for the survival and well-being of their children. Viewing both lesbian mothers and the controls as "single mothers" made possible the comparative, hypothesis-testing design the federal grant structure mandated.

Starting from the goal of destigmatizing lesbian mothers, of proving that they were just as worthy of custody as non-lesbian mothers facing comparable material challenges, I was gratified (though also a bit perplexed) to find that, with one exception, there were no statistically significant differences between lesbian and heterosexual mothers on any of the hundreds of variables we analyzed. The exception had to do with the likelihood that mothers had experienced either an actual custody problem or been threatened with a custody challenge. The lesbians reported such problems about twice as often as heterosexual mothers.

Because none of our statistical operations produced meaningful findings, after lengthy coding and repeated processing of the quantitative data I began to study the narratives of both lesbian and heterosexual mothers as fieldnotes, reading them over and over in search of patterns, consistencies, or incongruities.[6] That is, despite the carefully crafted quantitative design I had devised, the nature of the material I gathered threw me back to my training as a cultural anthropologist. At the same time, however, I continued to search for behavioral patterns and thus focused on the women's reports of very similar experiences in heading their families. For example, despite my early expectations that lesbian mothers would tend to substitute friendship for kinship ties in constituting support networks, my interviews showed something very different. Lesbian mothers, no less than heterosexuals, regarded family members, particularly their parents, as the most reliable source of support and as their most appropriate resource when times were hard. This pattern did not seem to be seriously altered by the strains in family relationships that the revelation of lesbianism often engendered. Mothers I interviewed explained that family ties were simply too profound to be broken permanently, sounding much like heterosexual mothers who had disagreements of other sorts with their families.

Similarities among the accounts of lesbian and heterosexual mothers were not limited to the domain of kinship. Mothers from both groups also reported that they went to great lengths to encourage their children's relationships with their fathers, even with considerable contrary provocation; that they tended to seek out other "single mothers," regardless of sexual orientation, as friends; that their friendships with non-parents became attenuated and fraught with mistrust over time; and that they expected relatively little support from sexual partners, whether they were women or men. For those who experienced concrete or threatened custody challenges, very similar strategies of avoidance and appeasement were mounted, whether the women were lesbian or not.

Similarly, lesbian mothers framed discussions of what it meant to them to be mothers in language that resonated dramatically with that offered by non-lesbian mothers. The association of being a mother with access to "goodness" was striking, as was pervasive imagery of motherhood superseding and overwhelming other sources of identity. Women of both sexual orientations spoke with similar intensity of the ways in which motherhood formed the focus of their identities, both materially and spiritually, and of the ways in which they felt it gave value and significance to their lives.

Seeking identity through motherhood was a quest that lesbians seemed to share with unmarried heterosexual women. In a number of cases, women described motherhood as making them live more productive, worthwhile lives. They described non-mothers as having significantly different (and less worthy) interests and goals and spoke with some intensity of how motherhood was a more crucial determinant of their identities than their lesbianism, a more compelling indicator of loyalties and affiliations. Such usages alerted me to the need to examine motherhood not only as a practical condition but also as a moral domain, one that enables mothers of all kinds to demand public recognition and make claims to cultural, if not material, benefits.

Rediscovering Lesbian Mothers: Negotiating Identity

But did this mean that something about being a single mother was a shared experience for both lesbian and heterosexual women? And what about the varied realities of being a lesbian—did they just evaporate under the pressure of heading a household and raising a family? These are questions that became insistent after completion of data collection, as I began to formulate a plan for a book on the research. But as I tried to write a book, which I originally called *The Contours of Single Motherhood,* I found myself hopelessly blocked. I thought my data would enable me to describe the ways in which lesbian and heterosexual single mothers managed their social networks, but I found myself going around and around about what the apparent "similarities" meant when neither categories like sexual orientation and socioeconomic status nor any of the other variables I had used to organize my data-gathering activities produced any discernible patterns in the women's accounts of themselves. Most acutely, I became bored with the symmetries of my findings, with the sense that I was condemned to report blandly repetitive comments that seemed, as I read and reread them, trite and conventional.

The shift to my current focus on motherhood as a negotiated identity first grew out of my increasing recognition of the contingent nature of my data, drawn as they were exclusively from interviews. At first I worried about how little information my interviews provided about "real" behavior. How could I defend lesbian mothers under attack if I couldn't say something concretely descriptive about how they lived? And what would it mean to say I had studied lesbian mothers if there were no apparent behavioral features (other than sexuality) associated with the label? Would my only other choice be to produce a book that would be little more than an enlarged version of the comparative psychological studies I had found so mechanical, studies that asserted the nonpathology of homosexuality?[7] Were the 135 women I had interviewed at such great length to be reduced to cases, or examples, stacked up against each other comparatively?[8] Would my description of their strategies strip their accounts of the passion and pain they related to me, making them significant only in terms of a set of hypotheses that might form the basis for publications and perhaps generate yet another grant?

My growing understanding that these accounts would be best interpreted as having cultural, rather than descriptive, significance pointed to the problematic nature of the "single mother" label as a way to think about these women. Lesbian and heterosexual mothers framed their narratives similarly and selected particular experiences as meaningful and worth describing as instances of "being mothers." But strong feelings about the burdens associated with motherhood, combined with a thematic focus on motherhood as the core of identity, tended to eclipse substantive differences in the routine life experiences of lesbian and heterosexual mothers—differences that often emerged indirectly. Further, information gleaned from interviews with others in informants' social networks sometimes yielded contradictory accounts of relationships and events. I began to consider the possibility that the narratives of lesbian and heterosexual mothers were similar in spite of the fact that their experiences may not have been comparable.

From this perspective, lesbian and heterosexual mothers, despite concrete differences in their daily lives, use narratives to construct their experience as mothers and, by extension, as women, from shared cultural elements. Their narratives are shaped, among other concerns, by the need to achieve a satisfying individual identity, particularly to demonstrate some measure of independence. They are heavily influenced by relatively conventional gender expectations centered on women's special vocation for nurturance and altruism and men's disinterest in parental responsibilities. They are further influenced by notions about the essential impact of motherhood on identity; more than other aspects of identity, motherhood is seen as being driven by elemental, probably biological, forces not readily controlled by the individual. These forces make mothers and non-mothers different in fundamental ways and work to undermine desires they may have to understand and support each other. Finally, the narratives reveal a strong acceptance of the specialness of kinship as a source of support and continuity. Although mothers often express frustration with particular dimensions of their relationships with blood relatives, they also demonstrate a commitment to transcend these difficulties and thus strengthen their own kinship bonds with their children.

These shifts in my thinking paralleled changes in anthropological theory that were in process during the years that I worked on this project, as ethnographers' concerns moved from an emphasis on positivistic description to an interest in the more relative, and explicitly negotiated, aspects of the production of ethnographic knowledge.[9] On one level, incongruities between mothers' accounts of themselves and what I could discern of their material circumstances forced me to rethink my grounding in the early feminist commitment to the authenticity of personal experience (DuBois et al. 1987; Eichler 1982; Harding, ed. 1987; Roberts, ed. 1981) along with the rigors of the methodology to which my research design had committed me. I could no longer take either the women's accounts literally or accept the significance of the demographic indicators I had used to define my "sample." If lesbian and heterosexual mothers talked about motherhood in the same way regardless of their differences, then other variables had to be seen as equally arbitrary. But once I no longer thought I could know what women did based on what they told me, then other assumptions also had to be discarded, most importantly the certainty I had at the outset that this study enabled me, as a lesbian, to work in and for my own community. I began to understand that the women say what they do, or what they did, as a way of constructing key notions of self and in the process go on to construct gender. By focusing on the personal narratives of lesbian and heterosexual mothers, I saw how they made sense of their situations and designated themselves in relation to others—how they, in fact, negotiated their identities in collaboration with or in opposition to prevailing cultural expectations.[10] But this process was not just meaningful in the abstract; it was demonstrated most powerfully by its emergence from interviews conducted by non-mothers.[11] Mothers constructed their narratives in a specific context—the interview—in which presenting the meaning of their situations as mothers would have particular salience.

In becoming mothers, lesbians join heterosexual women in a particular organization of identity that partakes of mainstream gender ideology. The notion that motherhood (or womanhood, by extension) supersedes other dimensions of identity is shared both by lesbian and heterosexual mothers. Lesbian mothers encounter not only the same material conditions as other mothers but also demand access to the same cultural and symbolic resources available to non-lesbian mothers. This suggests that the resistance to conventional gender ideology implied by the oxymoronic status of the lesbian mother can be compromised by its resolution of the "problem" of lesbian identity. Although I do not wish to argue that lesbians become mothers purposefully in order to regularize their status, as a direct response to stigma, I would contend that motherhood indirectly enables women (whether lesbian or heterosexual) to claim a specific location in the gender system.

In order to be able to make this sort of argument in the book I wrote about my lesbian mother project (Lewin 1993), I had to overcome the forces that had led me to design my study along the quantitative, hypothesis-testing lines that had been demanded of me by the federal grant-making structure. I had to allow myself to view the mothers I wrote about in terms of what they said rather than who they were (lesbian or heterosexual or single) or what they did (something I could never really know). That shift further demanded that I be able to accept the legitimacy of my goals as a lesbian anthropologist and, more specifically, as a lesbian *non-mother* anthropologist studying a segment of her own community. I not only revised my views of my informants, overcoming the tendency promoted by the research design to view them as inhabitants of cells in my theoretical sample, but I also came more critically to revise my view of the interaction that had occurred between myself and the mothers I interviewed. If personal narratives have to do with making cultural sense of one's situation in a specific interactional context, then the data I gathered had everything to do with who I was as well as with who my informants were. Being a lesbian, then, didn't necessarily mean that lesbian mothers saw me as like them; as a non-mother my difference very likely shaped the way they constructed themselves as mothers for my project.

I had feared at the outset that others would view my project as merely politics, an effort to promote a positive image of a population to whom I had personal feelings of loyalty. This concern had become transformed into a fear that others would see my work as unscientific. Thus, I had eagerly adopted the cumbersome constraints of the recommended sampling design, not only, I realized, in order to achieve the practical goal of getting a grant, but also to prove to myself and members of my profession that my interest was suitably disinterested. Once I came to understand that my relationship to my informants, like their relationship to their narratives, is negotiated, mediated, and imbued with immediate and personal meanings, I could finally allow the mothers to tell their stories, unencumbered by requirements of consistency or demands of facticity.

These observations do not really change the fundamental finding of my research: Lesbian mothers are not systematically different from other mothers who share some similar concrete problems. But the stance to which I came during the writing of the book, and which now informs my analysis, returns to a fundamental cultural question about the construction of the self, including that of the ethnographer. It is now clear that not only the underlying validity of the lesbian mothers' stories was hidden by the original design. By thinking only in terms of responding to accusations (including those which might be directed at me as an openly lesbian researcher), by allowing the need to defend the mothers and defend myself to frame the terms of the investigation, I also let the point of the study get away from me. Returning to the question of the cultural process whereby individuals construct notions of the self and thereby negotiate gender not only leads to more sensitive, reflexive ethnography. It also reminds us that ethnography produced by a committed researcher need not repudiate its origins or purify its motives; negotiating meanings is what we all do in the field, whether we be ethnographers or natives.

Notes

An earlier version of this chapter was presented at the Fourth Annual Lesbian, Bisexual and Gay Studies Conference, Harvard University, 1990. Portions also appear in Lewin (1993). I want to thank Liz Goodman, Bill Leap, and Kath Weston for comments on various versions of this paper.

1   Judges hearing custody cases involving lesbians tend to make the same assumptions. Because they implicitly define lesbianism as purely sexual, they conclude that lesbians cannot be adequate mothers. The pursuit of sexual gratification, following this reasoning, is antithetical to the kind of altruism expected of mothers, a view that also can affect the outcome of custody cases of non-lesbians who are sexually active (Lewin 1981).

2   See Davis (1971), Firestone (1970), Millett (1970), and Morgan, ed. (1970) for some examples of the popularization of scholarship in the service of various feminist agendas.

3   *Community* is a term that often has been used with relatively little precision in studies of gay men and lesbians. Deborah Wolf's (1979) usage, for example, rests on the implicit assumption that the "lesbian feminist community" of San Francisco she studied in the early 1970s is a closed and self-sustaining collectivity, the boundaries of which are not only firm but also mutually agreed upon by "community members." Although I was already critical of the monolithic fiction this usage tends to encourage, I still retained some notion, when I began the study, that there was such a thing as a lesbian "community" and that I was a member of it.

4   Support for this kind of research might be viewed as a surviving element of the policies of the 1960s and 1970s, which also brought the war on poverty, Project Headstart, and a host of other social programs stimulated, in part, by Michael Harrington's influential book *The Other America* (1962). These research priorities suffered the same fate as housing subsidies, food programs for the poor, and other programs eliminated or weakened after the 1980 election of Ronald Reagan (Ehrenreich 1989; Harrison and Bluestone 1988).

5   Similar problems arise in studying multiple sources of oppression in other contexts, for example, when race is added to gender in looking at the situation of black women (King 1988).

6   See Sanjek, ed. (1990) for varied accounts of what fieldnotes are and how anthropologists use them.

7   Virtually all scholarship before my work involved studies by psychologists of the children of lesbians and matched groups of single mothers. Most were concerned with the effects of lesbianism under circumstances of "father absence" on children's mental health or adjustment as measured through performance on various standardized tests. The overriding concern in these studies was on the children rather than on the mother herself. See, for example, Kirkpatrick, Smith and Roy (1981).

8   Interviews lasted between three and seven hours, nearly all conducted in informants' homes, often involving two or more sessions for completion. Written transcripts of the complete taped interviews ran an average of a hundred double-spaced pages.

9   This literature is concerned with the conditions under which field data are produced and particularly speaks to ambiguities in the relationship of the fieldworker to the nature of her or his findings. See, for example, Clifford and Marcus (1986), Fabian (1983), Rabinow (1977), Rosaldo (1989), and Wolf (1992).

10 For related efforts to show how narratives may be viewed not as literal accounts of events, but as occasions that facilitate making particular kinds of cultural points, see Ginsburg (1989), Personal Narratives Group, ed. (1989), Rosaldo (1989), and Steedman (1987).

11 My research associate, who conducted about half of the interviews, was also a lesbian non-mother.

References Cited

Clifford, James, and George E. Marcus. 1986. *Writing Culture: The Poetics and Politics of Ethnography.* Berkeley: University of California Press.

Davis, Elizabeth Gould. 1971. *The First Sex.* Baltimore: Penguin.

de Beauvoir, Simone. 1952. *The Second Sex.* New York: Knopf.

DuBois, Ellen Carol, et al. 1987. *Feminist Scholarship: Kindling in the Groves of Academe.* Urbana: University of Illinois Press.

Ehrenreich, Barbara. 1989. *Fear of Falling: The Inner Life of the Middle Class.* New York: Pantheon.

Eichler, Margrit. 1982. *Nonsexist Research Methods: A Practical Guide.* Boston: Allen and Unwin.

Fabian, Johannes. 1983. *Time and the Other: How Anthropology Makes Its Object.* New York: Columbia University Press.

Firestone, Shulamith. 1970. *The Dialectic of Sex: The Case for Feminist Revolution.* New York: William Morrow.

Gibson, Gifford Guy. 1977. *By Her Own Admission: A Lesbian Mother's Fight to Keep Her Son.* Garden City: Doubleday.

Ginsburg, Faye D. 1989. *Contested Lives: The Abortion Debate in an American Community.* Berkeley: University of California Press.

Harding, Sandra, ed. 1987. *Feminism and Methodology.* Bloomington: Indiana University Press.

Harrington, Michael. 1962. *The Other America: Poverty in the United States.* New York: Macmillan.

Harrison, Bennett, and Barry Bluestone. 1988. *The Great U-Turn: Corporate Restructuring and the Polarizing of America.* New York: Basic Books.

King, Deborah. 1988. "Multiple Jeopardy, Multiple Consciousness: The Context of a Black Feminist Ideology." *Signs* 14(1): 42–72.

Kirkpatrick, Martha, Katherine Smith, and Ron Roy. 1981. "Lesbian Mothers and Their Children: A Comparative Study." *American Journal of Orthopsychiatry* 51(3): 545–51.

Lewin, Ellen. 1974. "Mothers and Children: Latin American Immigrants in San Francisco." Ph.D. dissertation, Stanford University.

————. 1981. "Lesbianism and Motherhood: Implications for Child Custody." *Human Organization* 40(1): 6–14.

————. 1993. *Lesbian Mothers: Accounts of Gender in American Culture.* Ithaca: Cornell University Press.

Millett, Kate. 1970. *Sexual Politics.* Garden City: Doubleday.

Mitchell, Juliet. 1971. *Women's Estate.* New York: Pantheon.

Morgan, Robin, ed. 1970. *Sisterhood Is Powerful: An Anthology of Writings from the Women's Liberation Movement.* New York: Vintage.

Personal Narratives Group, ed. 1989. *Interpreting Women's Lives: Feminist Theory and Personal Narratives.* Bloomington: Indiana University Press.

Rabinow, Paul. 1977. *Reflections on Fieldwork in Morocco.* Berkeley: University of California Press.

Roberts, Helen, ed. 1981. *Doing Feminist Research.* London: Routledge and Kegan Paul.

Rosaldo, Michelle Z., and Louise Lamphere, eds. 1974. *Women, Culture and Society.* Stanford: Stanford University Press.

Rosaldo, Renato. 1989. *Culture and Truth.* Boston: Beacon.

Sanjek, Roger, ed. 1990. *Fieldnotes: The Making of Anthropology.* Ithaca: Cornell University Press.

Steedman, Carolyn Kay. 1987. *Landscape for a Good Woman.* New Brunswick: Rutgers University Press.

Wolf, Deborah Goleman. 1979. *The Lesbian Community.* Berkeley: University of California Press.

Wolf, Margery. 1992. *A Thrice-Told Tale: Feminism, Postmodernism, and Ethnographic Responsibility.* Stanford: Stanford University Press.

7. Studying Gay English: How I Got Here from There
William L. Leap

My interests in lesbian and gay ethnography are language-centered: I study the rules of sentence formation, principles of narrative conversational structure, assumptions about cooperative and competitive discourse, turn-taking strategies, and other points of grammar and discourse that enable English-speaking gay men in the United States to communicate as gay men.[1]

The gay-centered knowledge of language at issue here is shared knowledge, and one of my research goals is to understand how gay men come to acquire—and share—these language skills. I suspect that the processes of (second) language-learning at issue coincide with coming-out experiences and other elements affecting the success (or limitations) of the speaker's gay "career."

Shared language knowledge does not mean homogeneous discourse, however. Any number of situational and personal variables (e.g., conversation topic, context, and event structure, and speaker age, ethnic background, social class, and erotic interests) have prompted different groups of gay men to create their own gender-specific speaking styles. In current sociolinguistic theory, these could be called varieties or codes of a more inclusive gay English language, and this is the usage I follow in my research and writing. Similar to the case for other American English varieties and codes, the characteristics of these topic- or context-oriented gay English fluencies contribute to the distinctiveness of, for example, B&D (bondage and dominance) enthusiasts, drag queens, postmodernist queer intellectuals, and other segments within gay social structure as a whole. And just as there are some non-gays (lesbians and heterosexual persons) who are fluent speakers of these codes, there are also gay men in the United States who, while certainly proficient in "mainstream" English, are not fluent in any of the conventions of gay English usage.

So while I am studying gay English as a shared linguistic phenomenon, I am also exploring the factors promoting gay English diversity and
the implications of such diversity for the construction and maintenance
of gay community and culture in the United States. In this sense, my
studies of gay men's English are closely linked to my long-standing professional interests in American Indian languages and in American Indian varieties of English. Indian language research has given me a useful
point of departure for gay English ethnography, but other concerns have
been equally influential.

Background: Studying Indian Languages and Indian English

I decided I wanted to be an anthropologist during my first year (1964–
65) of undergraduate study at Florida State University (Tallahassee). A
career in anthropology would let me explore topics and issues quite different from those open to me through a career in mathematics, history,
and secondary school education (areas of study also vying for my attention at that time). Linguistics was one of those topics of anthropological interest, and it became my area of specialization quite by accident: I
enrolled in an introductory course, liked the material, and made an A
on the final examination. So I enrolled in a second course, then a third,
and soon began taking reading courses and specialized tutorials in structural analysis and its cultural implications.

The language base for these courses was solidly Indo-European. I did
not become interested in American Indian languages until I entered the
graduate program in anthropology at Southern Methodist University in
Dallas. My mentor there, George L. Trager, was a specialist in native
languages and cultures of the U.S. Southwest, and working with Trager
meant that I would become a Southwest Indian specialist, too. Through
field-based studies of the languages of the Rio Grande Pueblos (from
1967 to 1970) I learned how to elicit linguistic information from cooperative informants, how to prepare phonetic transcriptions and carry
out morphemic analysis of elicited data, and how to locate text-based
indicators of connections between language and culture.

Working in these settings also taught me how to wrap my linguistic
research in a cloak of secrecy. Pueblo communities are not enthusiastic
about outsiders attempting to gain access to cultural tradition. Finding
cooperative informants was difficult and convincing them that "scientific"
studies of their languages might have some merit was even more so.
Persons willing to be informants demanded that I conceal their identi-

ties at all times. Their need for caution limited our in-community inter-action; frequent contacts with outsiders could raise questions about the nature of that association and jeopardize the informants' community credibility in other ways. I could not talk openly about my work, or about my interests in Pueblo languages, when I did arrange to visit in some-one's home. And I had to meet fluent informants individually, in loca-tions far away from their homes, each time I wanted to gather more data or recheck materials I had already collected.

These conditions made it difficult to study Pueblo language use in "natural" speech settings. So I had to develop informal, nonobvious techniques for descriptive note-taking when I was able to observe such usage—for example, in the general store, the post office, or the offices of tribal government—because formal data-gathering or interviewing in those settings was completely out of the question.

Community-based (pueblo) English discourse was much less con-strained by puebloan rules of secrecy and, accordingly, much more ac-cessible to me. As time passed, I noticed a convergence between pueb-lo-based English usage and the rules of grammar and discourse from the speaker's ancestral languages, which gave speakers of Pueblo English a means of talking about the world in distinctively pueblo-centered terms even when speaking with outsiders. I used language data from on-site observations and from formal interviews to show that these English codes were as structurally well formed and functional as were the other variet-ies of English used in American society. I also showed how fluency in these "nonstandard codes" had serious consequences for schooling, employment, and other areas of speaker social experience.

Contacts with Indian language maintenance and renewal programs and on-reservation schools in Oklahoma, Washington state, Wisconsin, South Dakota, and Arizona helped me broaden my perspectives on these themes. An extended association (from 1978 to 1989) with the Tribal Division of Education on the Northern Ute reservation in northeastern Utah was particularly important in this regard. Frequent trips to the reservation throughout this period gave me many opportunities to watch how Ute people move between ancestral language tradition, varieties of Ute-cen-tered Indian English, and more mainstream English codes, as appropri-ate to setting, topic, and the co-participants in the speech event. Impor-tantly, the conditions of secrecy that had restricted my research and other in-field activities in the Southwest did not exist here. Ute people identi-fied me as the "man from D.C. who is helping us with our language." They talked with me in small group sessions and in one-on-one interviews about their interests in Ute language maintenance and the importance of Ute fluency in daily life. They answered my questions about the details of syntactic and lexical variation that characterize Ute discourse in all of its forms. And they teased me; for all the interest I showed in their language I still had not learned to speak Ute. I was pleased to have access to this information, but they were right. I consciously was not attempting to use my familiarity with Ute as a basis for building fluency: Ute was, after all, their language, and I was still an outsider.

Transition: Studying the Language of AIDS

I was not "openly gay" or sexually active while at FSU and SMU. I was in school to complete my doctoral work and begin my career in American Indian linguistics, and nothing was going to impede progress toward those goals. However, after I moved to Washington, D.C. and began full-time teaching at American University in the fall of 1970, my priorities began to change, and I began to participate in Washington's gay scene and started to explore similar social opportunities in other cities when Indian language research or other professional activities took me away from home.

"Gay life" in D.C. during these years was largely an after-work and often a late-night, after-hours construction; this meant that I kept my personal life completely independent of my teaching, my work with students or colleagues, or my research, a style of identity management that many gay men in academe have also employed (Tierney 1991). Just as I made no attempt to establish contact with lesbian or gay colleagues on our campus, I made no attempt to find lesbian or gay Indians in on-reservation or urban Indian settings. With very few exceptions, I avoided any interaction with them if we happened to meet in an unambiguously lesbian or gay domain. I did not ask questions about homosexual practices or gay life within the tribal settings where I was working because my research interests were language-based not gender-based. Once I settled into a long-term, one-on-one relationship and had to be away from home for a prolonged period, my partner and I arranged to meet for long weekends in urban areas near the research site. We kept a very low profile if he came onto the reservation or some other Indian-oriented research site, and we rarely entertained Indian friends (straight or gay) in our home when they came to Washington.

Certainly, many people (Indian and non-Indian) saw through this charade, but I am aware of only a handful of instances—in the field or in academe—where such insights had negative effects on my work in the field. Indian people rarely asked me questions about my private life other than to inquire if I were married or had any children, and I did not attempt to probe beyond my friends' voluntary comments about their personal interests and activities. This meant, among other things, that I spent many evenings in Indian country entirely on my own. But data analysis and other research tasks gave me plenty to do, and when all else failed I knew that the isolation was temporary and I would soon be going home to my partner.

This segregation of professional (Indian language/Indian English researcher, college professor) and personal (closeted, partnered gay man) experience ended with the coming of the AIDS pandemic. I watched as HIV illnesses began to appear in Indian country and as Indian people began to talk about these conditions. Sometimes they created new forms of discourse by borrowing words and phrases from English; other times they reworked frames of reference from tribal discourse to keep the discussion closely aligned with their cultural tradition.

I began to examine Indian and Indian English-based varieties of AIDS discourse—to the extent that my in-field activities gave me access to such usage. Unlike my earlier work with Indian languages and Indian English, AIDS language research hit very close to home. The AIDS issues under discussion in Indian country—negotiating "safe sex," distinguishing high- and low-risk activities, and demystifying biomedical jargon—were issues that many people in American society, myself included, were also trying to put into words. And that made it difficult to keep my own interests separated from this research agenda.

So I decided to shift my point of reference to include AIDS-related usage in (non-Indian) varieties of American English. I began focusing on discussions of these issues by friends and colleagues, students and faculty, gay and straight. Next, I started observing people's construction of discourse when they talked informally about AIDS (or consciously avoided doing so) and making notes on those conversations whether I knew the speakers or not. Then I broadened the research focus to include interviews with health-care workers, with PWAs, and with their family members and friends so I could examine AIDS-related language use within longer, uninterrupted narratives (Leap 1990, 1991).

The data-gathering skills developed during my Indian English research—particularly techniques for coping with secrecy and eliciting speaker-centered perspectives on problems and problem-solving—proved to be quite helpful to my AIDS-related research interests. But because I was now working in a language (non-Indian English) whose basic features were already familiar to me, I was able to ask questions, evaluate informant responses, and record insights with a level of detail not possible during any of my work in Indian country. This meant that I could now make greater demands on the quality of data I used to support or reject claims about AIDS discourse. I was no longer dependent on the informal, anecdotal, or secondhand observations that had contributed so greatly to my database on American Indian languages. Now that I had greater access to "natural" speech settings, I let the conversations I observed in those settings became the central element in my database and used interviews and group discussions to elicit reactions to my analysis of those conversations rather than to establish glimpses into linguistic features I hoped to explore at some later time.

New Directions: Studying the Language of Gay Experience

I did not expect that my studies of AIDS language would take on a "gay English" focus. But as I became more familiar with the content and organization of AIDS-related commentary in conversations and life-history narratives, I found that speaker use of rhetoric, imagery, person-reference, subject-verb relations, and other features of AIDS discourse varied considerably according to speaker gender; for example, women talked about AIDS quite differently from men, lesbians and gays quite differently from straights, and lesbians quite differently from gays. (The gender-related distinctions in AIDS discourse turn out to be even more detailed than these contrasts suggest, but I was not yet aware of such conditions at this stage in my research.)

I turned to the literature on language and gender to see what other scholars had to say about such contrasts. They had recognized, I found, broad differences between men's and women's uses of languages but had paid little attention to diversities of language use by particular groups of women or men and had ignored almost entirely how speaker age, economic status, erotic interests, and other factors prompted such diversity.

Published descriptions of lesbian and gay languages were especially disappointing. I found rich presentations of lesbian and gay-related terms of reference and other lexical details. Some scholars embellished these word lists with insights into the history of lesbian and gay terminology, which helped me understand how changes in social and cultural context prompt new configurations of word meanings in lesbian and gay cultures. And some scholars discussed the importance of these terms for lesbian and gay identity maintenance or otherwise explored relationships between specialized vocabulary, "secret code," and socially stigmatized groups. But scholars did not explore other areas of lesbian and gay language knowledge, nor did they present examples of lesbian and gay language-in-use or show how features of context (or speaker-specific background) prompted speakers to favor (or avoid) lesbian and gay-centered discourse in particular speaking domains.

The need for such situated perspectives on lesbian and gay language choice-making became quite apparent to me when, through the invitation of a good friend, I began a language-related ethnographic project in a District-area health club during the summer and fall of 1990. Club members had been complaining to management about increasing incidences of same-sex erotic activity in the men's locker room. Gay clients were particularly outspoken in this regard—which surprised me because I assumed that gay men would support the right of their colleagues to engage in erotic activities of their choice as long as participation was voluntary and the erotic activities were conducted safely and with suitable discretion.

I found out, first by talking to staff and clients and then through on-site observations, that gay clients were far from unanimous in their reactions to this situation. Some, as I had suspected, saw the all-male erotic activities as private and personal encounters. Others considered these activities to be instances of public exhibitionism, the sort of behavior that "gives gay men a bad name in the public's eye" (to cite one informant's assessment). Some were flattered when invited to participate in such activities. Others ignored the overtures and the activities that accompanied them. And still others used verbal (and sometimes physical) means to express their indignation. Some of the participants in these activities accepted the disinterested or indignant responses on face value; others read these statements as cautious expressions of enthusiasm for consensual sex and as invitations for participants to be more explicit and persistent in making their desires known. Straight clients' assessments of these events were equally diverse—so much so that some straight men were just as likely to become involved in on-site male erotics, or speak out in defense of those activities, as gay men were to oppose them.

I had only a limited period of time to carry out research at the site. Club management supported the inquiry, but administrators in the parent company opposed it, claiming that I was drawing attention to issues that they preferred not to acknowledge. I was not able to identify criteria that influenced individual clients' interpretations of these activities. I was convinced, however, that male-to-male communication in this context involved rules of grammar and discourse that were much more complex than the generic contrasts between gay and straight vocabulary and speaking styles explored in the literature. Interpreting these contrasts, I realized, was going to require a much broader perspective on gay men's English skills—and on the interface between grammar and gender in American English—than my preliminary data-gathering had allowed.

So I began discussing my observations about health club language use with lesbian and gay anthropologists, with students (lesbian, gay, and straight), and with gay friends. These were largely unstructured conversations: I described instances of gay and straight language use in locker room, steam room, showers, or workout area settings and explained the consequences of the usage as best I could reconstruct them. Then participants gave their own interpretation to each example, often offering additional anecdotes to illustrate their experiences with similar gay-related speech events in other settings. Everyone with whom I spoke seemed to have at least one such story that they wanted to tell. That enthusiasm led to a general discussion of all of the examples that participants had volunteered. I took notes on their comments and used my notes to construct a summary statement identifying the gay English issues that participants associated with the given examples; participants then reviewed the statement and revised its wording, as needed, to be certain that its claims accurately reflected the group consensus on each issue. These sessions were patterned after the group discussions of Indian language and AIDS language issues that I had conducted earlier. Now, of course, I could identify closely with the topics, and I frequently shifted from my traditional role as at-distance group facilitator to become an active participant in the dialogue.

Comments raised during these group discussions suggested facts about gay English grammar and discourse I had never thought of. Gay men in their forties and fifties, for example, report that they will assume someone is not gay, and constrain their conversation accordingly, until that person offers concrete evidence of male-oriented gender interests. Gay men in their late teens and twenties will assume that this individual is gay and consciously use gay English as the code of choice when talking with him until evidence proves otherwise.

Other comments from these interviews focused my attention on issues with which I had been struggling for some time. Particularly important were gay men's descriptions of the obstacles limiting their development of gay English skills discourse before and after they came out—obstacles that I had been trying to overcome throughout my gay career.

All of this made me eager to learn more about the linguistic and cultural significance of gay men's English. I continued to host focus group discussions and to study gay and straight erotic communication at several health clubs in the D.C. area. With my partner as my field assistant and colleague, I began observing, taking notes, and (when possible) making audio or video recordings of gay men's use of language in various speech settings in the D.C. area. I encouraged the students in my department interested in lesbian and gay gender issues to do the same.

I discussed my findings at lesbian and gay studies conferences in 1990 and 1991, at other scholarly meetings, and during guest lectures at my university and on other college campuses. I used all of these concerns as the focal point for research and writing during a twelve-month sabbatical leave from university teaching in 1991–92, and I plan to keep these issues at the top of my research agenda now that my sabbatical has come to an end.

Text-Centered Research Strategies

For me, linguistic research has always been a descriptive and data-driven activity. Theory is important because it orients research, but theory-building occurs only when context-centered inquiry establishes a foundation for such constructions.[2] This is why fieldwork was always an important component of Indian language and Indian English research, even though being "in the field" meant lengthy journeys to geographically and emotionally distant locales on long weekends or over other periods when my university and personal commitments could accommodate out-of-town travel.

Gay English research has substantially altered the need for such logistics. I can observe gay English usage and make judgments about its significance while interacting with friends and acquaintances in my home, during visits in the homes of others, while at the university, in department stores, bars, and restaurants, on airplane flights, and in any number of other locations. Gay-centered environments are important sources of data for my research but are not the only sources available to this end. In fact, some gay English discourse skills—the use of linguistic markers to confirm gay identity and overcome other risks that limit public interaction between gay strangers—can best be observed only in heterosexually dominated speech domains.

The following example records the conversation that occurred in one such public setting, a counter in the men's clothing section of a large department store in the D.C. suburbs (Leap 1993:56). My partner (speaker C2) and I (speaker C1) finished making our selections and moved to the counter to pay for them. The salesman (speaker S) began talking as we approached the counter.

1   S: May I help you?
2   C1: [presents items to be charged; says nothing]
3   S: [looks at merchandise] Was this on sale ? Let me check the
4   amount of the discount. [leaves counter, checks, returns, and
5   begins the transaction]
6   Do you need gift boxes for these?
7   C2: No. We don't believe in Santa Claus.
8   S: You didn't see that movie last night? With Kate Jackson?
9   About Santa Claus and orphans? That'd make you believe
10   in Santa Claus.
11   C1: Sounds thrilling.
12   S: Yes, I enjoyed watching it. But my room-mate fell asleep.
13   C1: [said to S, but half-directed at C2] Sounds like our house.
14   C2: We sit in front of the TV and I fall asleep.
15   S: Like at our house.
16   C2: That's why we always go to bed so early.
17   S: Old age is not for sissies, just like Bette Davis said.
18   [pause] Here's your purchases. I hope you'll come here
19   again.

A rapid scan of this passage may suggest nothing particularly "gay" about the speakers' word choices, phrasings, use of sentence constructions, or sequencing of statements. But that is one of the characteristics of gay English discourse that makes it an especially valuable mode of discourse in public settings. Listeners can easily identify gay-centered clues and linguistic constructions in this exchange if they have the knowledge of language and familiarity with gay culture appropriate to that end. In this case, such details include:

- S's offer to check on the customer's discount (lines 3–4), a form of personalized service uncommon in D.C.-area department stores and a signal that the salesman is willing to personalize the exchange in other ways.
- C2's rejection of the Santa Claus myth (line 7), a primary icon of the family-oriented, heterosexual life-style in the United States. The first-person plural pronoun in this statement anticipates comments about C1 and C2's domestic arrangement presented in lines 13, 14, and 16.
- S's enthusiasm for Kate Jackson, Santa Claus, and orphans (lines 8–10), which gives C2's earlier reference to Santa Claus a more explicitly gay flavor and introduces two other gay-centered themes into the conversation: the allure of glamorous gender-style (recall Kate Jackson's role in "Charlie's Angels") and the loneliness of orphans at Christmas (they, like some gay men, are unable to interact with parents or family members during the holiday season).
- S, C1, and C2's mutual confirmation of their domestic relationships (lines 12–16). Note how the use of overlapping ideas—television-watching, falling asleep in front of the television, and sleeping together—gradually leads these strangers to common ground. Once again, pronoun choice (lines 13, 15, and 16) is an important element in message exchange.
- S's homage to Bette Davis (an important source of inspiration within gay tradition) as the code for the speech event (line 17).

My partner and I did not go into the department store expecting to do fieldwork that afternoon. But once the exchange began and I realized that gay English discourse was afoot, I began to follow the content of the conversation quite carefully and recorded key words and phrases in each statement on the back of a shopping receipt. This is one reason why my partner (C2) was a more active participant in the conversation than was I. When we left the counter, I asked my partner to reconstruct the exchange as best he could remember it, and I made additional notes to preserve his comments once we returned to our car. What the example presents is not a verbatim transcript, but it is a close approximation of such a transcript, as confirmed (independently and jointly) by two of the event's participants.

Gathering context-centered language data is one component of gay English ethnography. Interpreting these data is another, equally important, component. Following de Certeau (1984:80–81), I do not believe the analysis of conversations like that in the example should focus on the underlying messages, implicit themes, or other notions that the text is *presumed* to express. The text itself is a meaningful construction, and the analysis can locate that meaning by focusing on the explicit forms of its signification—for example, on the text as practiced in its setting. Ethnographic observation of text construction provides powerful insights into such practice (Sherzer 1986), as does careful assessment of the evidence of choice-making that gives each segment of the text its particular form (Halliday 1978:109ff). As my comments on the example suggest, metaphors and other instances of verbal imagery, pronouns and other deictic markers, cooperative turn-taking, and other textual tactics offer useful clues to choice-making and often reveal additional connections between text and other products of social action unfolding at the site.

Adapting to Ethnography "at Home"

Once I began to gather texts and analyzed them in these terms, I realized that I have been "doing" gay English ethnography for quite some time (although admittedly in a less formalized or systematic fashion). Learning how to "talk gay" is an important part of gay socialization in the United States and (I suspect) in other contemporary settings as well. The language-learning process here is not regulated by institutional practice or established social norms as is otherwise the case for second-language or dialect learning. Experiences vary considerably from one gay man to the next (Leap 1994). I recall during my earliest days in Washington, D.C., when I tried to remember other gay men's carefully worded sentence constructions, clever metaphors, and compelling verbal images, and to practice using those linguistic items in solitary conversations until I became comfortable with their details. Then I introduced what I had learned at appropriate points in other gay conversations, hoping other participants would take notice of my verbal skill. Sometimes the "experiment" was successful; other times things became lost in the translation.

The unstructured, serendipitous data-gathering skills at issue were very similar to the techniques I had employed when studying Indian language discourse in the pueblos and at Northern Ute. As my discussion of the example has shown, they have become important elements in my gay English fieldwork. But now that I am developing a richer sense of gay English grammar and discourse, my data-gathering does not need to be completely undirected. On some occasions, I have decided to listen for particular usage patterns while in gay speech domains; on others, I have deliberately refocused conversations so co-participants are forced to use particular gay English constructions within the exchange.

Memory remains an important data-gathering device, but its reliability is limited, especially if the text in question is lengthy or richly detailed in other ways. Just as I did when studying Indian language and Indian English discourse in on-reservation speech settings, I now transcribe segments of gay English conversations while I observe them. I often use a pen and the back of a cocktail napkin, positioned carefully in my lap, or, as in the example, I sometimes find myself standing at a department store counter and doodling on a sales slip. I also ask co-participants in the given speech event to help me monitor a conversation or (again as in the example) reconstruct specific details when the event has ended.

Verbatim management of data is less of a problem in group discussions and one-on-one interviews. With participants' permission, I audio-tape the conversations and, as just explained, add a verbatim transcription of those tapes, as well as the ideas that come out of the discussions, to my database. This is also a research technique I first employed while working in Indian country.

There are components of gay English research that have no precedent in my Indian language and Indian English field experiences, however. Being a fluent speaker of the language variety I am studying raises particular problems in that regard, and so does being a co-participant in the speech events I am trying to understand. For years, as I have explained, I kept my fieldwork and other career-building and professional activities completely separate from my private life. Now that I am studying gay English grammar and discourse, the boundaries between scholarship and privacy are no longer sharply drawn. I do not want my research activities to ignore the unique ethnographic opportunities that gay social networks and familiarity with gay culture provide. At the same time, I cannot ignore the responsibilities and privileges that come with having an insider's access to the gay community.

I have developed some strategies to help me come to terms with the problem. For example, I do not disclose my status as language researcher or my interests in gay English while in large, public, relatively anonymous settings—gay restaurants and bars, book stores and other gay-oriented businesses, or contexts where gays and straights interact with patterned regularity. However, in smaller or more personal group settings (particularly when visiting friends or when guests are invited to our home), I am quite open about my interests in gay English. I talk about my research activities, the insights I have gleaned from data-gathering, and my publication plans. And I invite listeners to respond to the issues I raise, either at that point in the conversation or at some other time.

Being up front about research interests has its advantages. I find that gay men seem to enjoy talking about gay English, especially in small group settings, and the insights I gain from their reflections more than offset any opportunities to observe spontaneous and unbiased gay speech that I am being denied.[3]

Because the group discussions and one-on-one interviews are, by design, formalized, structured speech events, I do not try to ignore the rigor that these features impose on data-gathering. Instead, I deliberately use those features to help address my research goals. Participants come into the sessions aware of my research interests and, in some cases, familiar with my writing. They know that I am going to ask them questions about gay language and cultural experiences; often they have organized their own list of appropriate topics and suggest that we use that list as the guidepost for the dialogue. Together, we establish ground rules for discussion—how to indicate that my questions are confusing, that the discussion is becoming too personal, or that the tape-recorder needs to be turned off. The sessions end whenever participants are ready to end them. And once I transcribe the audio-tape of a session, I am happy to let participants review the transcripts and add follow-up comments to make certain that their point of view has been clearly summarized in my database.

Data-gathering in structured settings is important to my research, but so is data-gathering in unstructured and often anonymous public settings. I realize that transcribing such conversations can be seen as an invasion of privacy and that I must ensure that my analysis of these speech events does not create conditions of irreparable harm. This means, among other things, that the published accounts of these data cannot contain clues to speaker identity or other, unnecessary personal references. It also means that, where possible, I need to obtain speaker permission to include the observations in my database; some of my most productive one-on-one interviews have grown out of these after-the-fact negotiations.

Finally, I have also come to realize that I can build my gay English database through means other than firsthand observation and in-field interviewing. Language and gender and gay studies publications may not address these themes. However, short stories and novels by gay writers are filled with examples of gay men's conversations, passages outlining key events in gay lives and careers and other language-based glimpses into the world of gay experience. Ethan Mordan's collections of short stories depicting life in gay Manhattan during the days before the AIDS pandemic (Mordan 1985, 1986, 1988) have been especially useful in this regard. And gay men's poetry (Klein, ed. 1989) overflows with metaphor and trope, reflecting the range of images that individual speakers use to talk about key events in their lives. Very few straight writers have been able to replicate such perspectives in their descriptions of gay experience, and this makes the knowledge of language underlying the literary discourse of gay authors a worthwhile topic for study in its own right.

Addressing Self-Disclosure

Discussing the rules of grammar and discourse of any language variety forces the researcher to acknowledge some level of association with speakers of that code. As far as discussions of gay English grammar and discourse are concerned, admitting to such an association leads to additional questions and, ultimately, to the disclosure of the researcher's own gender interests, whether he or she intended this outcome or not. Avoiding self-disclosure under these circumstances withholds information about data quality, prevents others from making an honest appraisal of the research findings, and weakens the researcher's authority to present the analysis in the first place.

It took me a long time—from 1986 to 1989—to come to terms with this dimension of gay English ethnography. My identity management strategies in Indian country included everything from cloaked ambiguity (as among the pueblos) to an explicit stance as an outsider with useful skills (as at Northern Ute). But in no case did research topics and personal identity need to coincide. With gay English research, such convergence was unavoidable. I had not publicly confirmed my being gay within the context of my university or within the profession of anthropology when I began to work with gay English issues in 1986. My research made my gender commitment a matter of public record. To help me through this transition, I employed several strategies.

First, I started teaching an undergraduate course in sex, gender, and culture. I focused one-third of the course on lesbian and gay experiences in cross-cultural perspective and integrated comments about lesbian and gay life throughout the remainder of the course. Students were very enthusiastic about content and seemed not to notice when I stumbled over words and phrases that I had not used in a classroom setting before. I decided I would use the first-person plural pronoun—not the third-person plural pronoun—when talking about lesbians and gay men. If students were made uncomfortable by these personal statements, they did not indicate their displeasure through the university's course evaluation process or through other, formal channels.

Through associations with students in this course, I was asked to serve as one of the faculty sponsors for the university's lesbian and gay student group. Saying yes to the invitation was the next step in self-disclosure, and it was one of the wisest decisions I could have made. Group members have expressed great interest in my gay English research, they have participated enthusiastically in group discussions and one-on-one interview sessions, they have given me much-needed anecdotes to demonstrate differences between my generation's language skills and their own, and they have supported my work in many other ways. Under their sponsorship, I gave several public lectures on gay English themes on campus, which helped broaden university awareness of my research and its gender implications. And by using gay English research as the focus for sabbatical leave in 1991 and 1992—a proposal that had to be approved by my department's rank and tenure committee, by the dean of the College of Arts and Sciences, by the dean of faculties, and by the university provost—I was able to make these issues a matter of public record on campus.

Joining the Anthropology and AIDS Research Group (AARG), an affiliate of the American Anthropological Association's Society for Medical Anthropology, was my first step toward managing self-disclosure within the profession. Through AARG and a subsequent appointment to the AAA's Task Force on Anthropology and AIDS I became friends with a small cadre of lesbian and gay anthropologists who encouraged my interests in language and AIDS, prompted me to begin separating AIDS discourse, writ large, from the AIDS discourse of gay American men, and fully supported my decision to focus on gay English grammar and discourse as a research topic in its own right.

Because of my AARG/AATF ties, I decided in 1987 to join the Anthropology Research Group on Homosexuality (ARGOH) and became an active participant once the membership changed the group's name to the Society for Lesbian and Gay Anthropologists (SOLGA) and included advocacy as well as scholarly activities within the group's agenda. My contacts with lesbian and gay anthropologists expanded under SOLGA's auspices, particularly so when in 1989 I was elected SOLGA cochair for a two-year term. SOLGA officers have a certain amount of visibility within the anthropological profession and affiliated fields. Becoming SOLGA cochair upstaged additional concerns about self-disclosure and encouraged my application for a gay English-oriented sabbatical leave and my promotion of lesbian and gay studies on our campus once I returned to full-time teaching in 1992.[4]

Gay English Ethnography and Gender Theory

My work with gay English has drawn heavily on the approach to text analysis developed during my studies of American Indian English. Equally influential have been the theories of language and gender that I have incorporated into this inquiry.

The theory of language I am using in this research is highly situated and contextual; it emphasizes close relationships between language and human experience—the point of view outlined by Benjamin Lee Whorf when he observed that language and cultural norms "grow up together, mutually influencing each other" (1955:156). Of the two, he added, language is the least malleable given that certain regularities have to be maintained within linguistic structure so speakers can interact and communicate effectively with each other. Today, most linguists recast Whorf's remark, much as I have done throughout this chapter, to stress the dynamic interaction between knowledge of language and situated linguistic practice. But the point of the observation remains unchanged: The connections between language and experience need to be explained, not merely accepted on face value as self-evident truth.

By analyzing individual gay English texts in terms of such connections, I am also exploring the larger social discourse of which these texts are a part, and this inquiry also requires theoretical framing. Like most anthropologists, I share Ortner and Whitehead's concerns about "the bias that often underlies studies of both sex roles and male dominance—an assumption that we know what 'men' and 'women' are, an assumption that male and female are predominantly natural objects rather than predominantly cultural constructions" (1981:1). Linguistic-oriented gender research offers useful ways to move beyond such bias because speakers constantly demonstrate the "non-natural," constructed basis of their gendered identities through their linguistic practice. As the example suggests—and see other examples in Leap (1993; in press)—gay men regularly make use of a rich inventory of references and images when defining themselves as gendered persons, and the co-construction of such references is a recurring theme in gay English conversations, even if the results of those constructions yield conflicting messages when compared across textual sites. Unavoidably, I have to consider the gendered meanings in the texts in pluralistic terms, and I cannot make sense out of the pluralism if I submerge such details within a unified, totalizing category of male gender. Demonstrating the diversity of male genders in American society is one of the goals of gay English ethnography—and so is destabilizing America's monolithic notions of masculinity and male privilege.

Notes

My thanks to Geoff Burkhart, Liz Goodman, Gil Herdt, Sue-Ellen Jacobs, Ellen Lewin, Steve Murray, Karen Sacks, Kath Weston, and Brett Williams for their helpful comments on drafts of this manuscript.

1   I do not mean to devalue the cultural and social significance of lesbian English by focusing exclusively on the English of gay men. But by narrowing my focus in this way, I can study language-gender dynamics within my own speech community, and I can direct research findings toward language needs that I encounter every day of my life. After years of working with the languages of others, it is time for me to start working at home.

2   For a richer statement of this position, see Glaser and Strauss (1967) and Lincoln and Guba (1985).

3   Making such explicit statements is also likely to cause some gay men to monitor their use of English more carefully or make conscious changes in their discourse that could affect the quality of the ethnographic data obtained through that setting. I expect that the outcome here is no more serious than the changes in usage prompted by my presence as outsider in American Indian speech communities.

4   Serving with Esther Newton as cochair of the American Anthropological Association's Commission on Lesbian and Gay Concerns from 1994 to 1997 was the next step in this progression.

References Cited

de Certeau, Michel. 1984. *The Practice of Everyday Life*. Berkeley: University of California Press.

Glaser, Barney, and Anselm Strauss. 1967. *The Discovery of Grounded Theory.* Chicago: Aldine Press.

Halliday, M. A. K. 1978. "Language as Social Semiotic." In *Language as Social Semiotic,* 105–26. London: Edward Arnold.

Klein, Michael, ed. 1989. *Poets for Life: Seventy-six Poets Respond to AIDS.* New York: Crown Publishers.

Leap, William L. 1990. "Language and AIDS." In *Culture and AIDS,* ed. Douglas Feldman, 137–58. New York: Praeger.

———. 1991. "AIDS, Linguistics and the Study of Non-neutral Discourse." In *Anthropology, Sexuality and AIDS,* ed. Gilbert Herdt, William L. Leap, and Melanie Sovine. *Journal of Sex Research* 28(2): 275–88.

———. 1993. "Gay Men's English: Cooperative Discourse in a Language of Risk." In *Prejudice and Pride: Lesbian and Gay Traditions in America. New York Folklore* 19(1–2): 45–70.

———. 1994. "Learning Gay Culture in a 'Desert of Nothing': Language as a Resource in Gender Socialization." *High School Journal* 77 (1–2): 122–31.

———. In press. *Word Is Out: Gay Men's English.* Minneapolis: University of Minnesota Press.

Lincoln, Yvonna S., and Egon G. Guba. 1985. *Naturalistic Inquiry.* Newbury Park: Sage Publications.

Mordan, Ethan. 1985. *I've a Feeling We're Not in Kansas Anymore.* New York: NAL Penguin Inc.

———. 1986. *Buddies.* New York: St. Martin's Press.

———. 1988. *Everybody Loves You.* New York: St. Martin's Press.

Ortner, Sherry B., and Harriet Whitehead. 1981. "Introduction: Accounting for Sexual Meanings." In *Sexual Meanings: The Cultural Construction of Gender and Sexuality,* ed. Sherry B. Ortner and Harriet Whitehead, 1–27. Cambridge: Cambridge University Press.

Sherzer, Joel. 1986. "A Discourse-Centered Approach to Language and Culture." *American Anthropologist* 89:295–309.

Tierney, William G. 1991. "Building Academic Communities of Difference: Gays, Lesbians and Bisexuals on Campus." *Change* 24(2): 40–46.

Whorf, Benjamin Lee. 1955. "A Linguistic Consideration of Thinking in Primitive Communities." In *Language, Thought and Reality: Selected Writings of Benjamin Lee Whorf,* ed. John Carroll, 65–86. Cambridge: MIT Press.

8. Coming Home: The Journey of a Gay Ethnographer in the Years of the Plague
Ralph Bolton

T he following narrative is one gay man's uncensored, although incomplete, autobiographical account of a journey through life as an ethnographer, a journey which began before the plague and which took him to distant lands south of the equator in search of knowledge and adventure. Along the way, he encountered hostile natives whose hostility he converted to friendship and whose sorrows and joys he shared and about whom and from whom he learned many things. On his return to civilization, his discoveries were both lauded and maligned by his peers. During a sojourn to the frozen north, he embarked on his most difficult journey, a voyage in discovery of self and in search of his own tribe from which he had been separated since birth. His major accomplishment was to unearth his own true nature as a man. He arrived home just as his tribe was faced with a terrible tragedy, a plague which was spreading fear and death, and his elation at finally being united with his own was tempered by sadness and despair over the unfolding cataclysm. What follows is a chronicle of his travels and travails, from his earliest days in the mountains of Peru to the present.

Life Before the Plague

THE SIXTIES: LIFE AMONG THE QOLLA

My life as an anthropologist began on the shores of Lake Titicaca in the early 1960s, when, as a Peace Corps volunteer, I was asked to teach an anthropology course to Peruvian social work students in the Altiplano town of Puno.[1] Although my academic training was in international relations and political science, on the basis of my having taken two anthropology courses as an undergraduate I was selected as the most qualified person available to teach the subject. With such a deficient background and an almost total lack of teaching materials other than a Spanish edition of a book by Clyde Kluckhohn, despite my fears and misgivings, I tackled the assignment with the optimism and nerve that were so characteristic of that can-do era, the Kennedy years when idealism and service were going to lead to a better world.

Simultaneously, I was assigned to community development activities in rural villages along the lake. It was in my daily contacts while living alone in a Quechua-speaking Indian community, miles from other Americans, that my commitment to anthropology as a way of life was born. For three years I immersed myself deeply in village life, going to the city once a week to teach my class and spending the rest of my time working with the local community on the development of consumer cooperatives and craft enterprises and teaching literacy classes and Spanish to adult Qolla men and women (Bolton 1979). For me, as an outsider, life was idyllic and very romantic. I rode my horse around the countryside, danced at fiestas, joined in local soccer games, learned enough Quechua to get along, and contributed to community endeavors with the limited skills at my disposal.

It was in this initial "fieldwork" that I discovered the undesirability and the impossibility for me of keeping separate my professional and personal lives. My life was a seamless cloth. And while I would not claim that I ever became a full-fledged member of either of the two communities in which I resided during those three years, my integration into the social and political life of these communities was considerable by the standards of most ethnographers and particularly in view of the cultural differences between the Qolla, noted for being extremely suspicious of all outsiders, and middle-class North Americans.[2] Because I was raised on a farm in the Pennsylvania Dutch countryside, perhaps my rural roots facilitated my identification with Qolla life. I seriously entertained the idea of "going native" and remaining permanently in Peru to work in rural communities. After two years, I signed up for an additional year of Peace Corps service.

Perhaps it was the realization that at some level I would always be a foreigner in Peru, a gringo, that induced me eventually to abandon the plan to remain indefinitely. And so, reluctantly, I returned to the States to pursue an advanced degree in anthropology, my return ticket to the field. I chose the program at Cornell University because of its preeminence at the time as a center for training in applied anthropology and because of the presence there of Allan Holmberg, the distinguished Peruvianist whose work exemplified a humanistic dedication to using anthropology to find solutions to problems of poverty, inequality, and oppression. His work in Vicos, Peru, had served as a model for my own during my Peace Corps service.

From the outset of my career, I have considered myself an "applied anthropologist." I was never attracted to academic life by notions of abstract theorizing divorced from the problems of everyday life. As a child I had been taught by deeply religious kin that service to others, even at the expense of self, was a duty and having faced at close hand on a daily basis the pervasive poverty, disease, hunger, and violence in southern Peruvian highland villages that caused so much suffering in the lives of the people among whom I had worked, I could not imagine doing any other kind of anthropology.

So from the shores of Lake Titicaca I went to the shores of Lake Cayuga, and for three years I studied with an illustrious cadre of anthropologists. During this time, I fell madly in love with a woman who to this day remains a powerful source of support in my life. We got married.

As a dissertation topic, I chose to focus on social conflict among the Qolla. My work as a Peace Corps volunteer had convinced me that intravillage friction and interpersonal aggression were key impediments to economic development in Altiplano communities, and I investigated the patterning and etiology of aggression.

At first we were not welcome in Incawatana, the village we selected for fieldwork. The timing of our arrival was inauspicious, to say the least, the beginning of a period of drought that threatened villagers with crop loss and the specter of hunger. Famine is no stranger to the Altiplano. The villagers blamed us for driving away the rains, and for the first two months we lived under a barrage of death threats. We took turns sleeping at night, one of us remaining awake and armed in case of an attack. Stubborn and foolhardy, we refused to retreat. After all, I had come to study aggression, and there was no escaping it. Indeed, this was participant observation; we were not granted the luxury of being mere observers of the conflicts of others. We were initiated into the ways in which the Qolla so frequently treat each other.

Our tenacity paid off. After a few months, the threats diminished as the villagers got to know us, and by the end of two years there was genuine sorrow on the part of many over our departure. We had served as godparents to literally dozens of children, and by the end bonds of ritual kinship tied us to a majority of the inhabitants of Incawatana. The trust that we established eventually provided us with entré into the most secret domains of the culture, some of which had never been personally witnessed by Andean ethnographers, for example, sorcery sessions (Bolton 1974), and others that ethnographers had never even suspected of existing, such as the mate-swapping institution called *tawanku* (Bolton 1973b).

THE SEVENTIES: A CONVENTIONAL LIFE
ON THE ANTHROPOLOGICAL FRINGE

While life among the Qolla during the sixties had been exotic and exciting, in the seventies my personal life became solidly conventional. Jobs for anthropologists were easy to come by, and I chose to accept a visiting lectureship at my alma mater, Pomona College, where I have remained ever since. Except for a one-year return to Peru (1973–74) and a year in Norway (1978–79), the seventies were spent in California, teaching anthropology to undergraduates and analyzing and writing up the voluminous ethnographic material that Charlene and I had collected in the field. Our two sons were born in these years, bringing with them the delightful pleasures and enormous responsibilities of fatherhood. We constituted an ideal family, right out of the fifties except for my wife's part-time job that was necessary to enable us to purchase a house. We settled in for the long haul. It was a productive decade, with a steady flow of publications on a variety of topics.

Throughout this period, my research had no apparent connection to my sexuality, but appearances can be deceptive, and in retrospect I understand that my homosexuality, repressed as it was, had a powerful influence on my work. Quite obviously, the energy I poured into work was part of the processes of repression and sublimation that I employed to avoid dealing with homoerotic desire; on that issue at least, Freud (1961) is right. More subtle, however, is the fact that my understanding of my own condition made me more open to a theoretical perspective that called into question the dominant paradigms in the discipline. Aggression among the Qolla was not socially approved behavior despite its pervasiveness; cultural ideals and real behavior diverged. My own life illustrated this in the domain of sexuality, albeit in mirror image. My sexual behavior conformed to the heterosexist ideals of American culture; my desires were not acted upon, and I understood the price of this conflict between biology and culture.

In other ways as well, my repressed homosexuality influenced my work. My wife and I collected an enormous amount of data on human reproduction, including sexuality, and although she had no qualms about questioning her female informants about same-sex eroticism, I had largely refrained from raising this subject with men because it was too personally problematic and difficult for me to handle. We wrote a draft of a monograph on Qolla sexuality and reproduction that has languished in my files for two decades precisely because I am aware of the gaps that exist in it due to my inability while in the field to deal with the topic of sexual orientation in a frank and forthright manner.

Repression obviously had its rewards, and by most standards I should have been happy. I had an excellent job, a budding career, a wonderful family, and perhaps I could have sustained this path of denial. But the convergence of several events between 1976 and 1982 forced me to assess the life I was leading. The first of these was a series of sudden episodes of illness that despite extensive medical testing yielded no diagnosis other than "idiopathic." These episodes forced me to confront the issue of mortality and the possibility that I could die at any time without ever having lived according to my deepest desires. What was the point of all this? Was life just a bad joke?

A second incident provoked pessimism over the direction and possibilities of anthropology for having an impact on human well-being. The incident was an ill-informed critique of my hypoglycemia-aggression hypothesis (Bolton 1973a) that emerged not from a solid understanding of the issues but from a romantic vision of the Andes that during this period replaced the applied emphasis of Andeanists in preceding years (Lewellen 1981). This forced me to write a detailed rebuttal. Andean ethnology was on a Pollyanna-ish path of denial of the harsh realities of the world I had come to know in Peru. No one in anthropology took the hypoglycemia-aggression work seriously enough to replicate it, both because of the difficulty of doing such research and because it did not fit the dominant paradigms emerging in the discipline, away from science and from applied concerns. It was, and is, a discipline in the process of self-destruction. I could see that a decade of work was having no beneficial impact and was certainly much less gratifying than had been my direct involvement in efforts to improve people's lives that characterized my years as a Peace Corps volunteer.

At the end of this period, I participated in a summer seminar on psychoanalysis and culture led by Mel Spiro. The course offered me an opportunity to read widely and to reflect on my situation, providing further insights into my motivations and goals. And, finally, I met and fell in love with a man. The experience, of necessity wholly platonic in view of the heterosexuality of the man in question, was overpowering, and the implications unavoidable.

The Plague Years

THE EIGHTIES: COMING OUT AND COMING HOME

Although I was living a completely heterosexual life-style, monogamous marriage and all, I was an interloper, a participant observer who managed the identity well, but just as I finally realized among the Qolla that I would always be a foreigner and eventually relinquished my aspirations of "going native," so, too, I eventually abandoned the straight world to come home to my own. The process was agonizing and difficult, especially because it had a painful, disrupting, and complicating impact on the lives of loved ones, my wife and sons. But for the sake of personal survival and integrity, it was one I had to pursue. It is a decision I have never regretted, although I shall be forever sorry that it caused, in the initial stages, so much sorrow and distress to others.[3]

I had missed the turmoil in American life during the sixties by spending five of those years in Peru and by being fully devoted to work and family, I managed to be oblivious to the gay liberation movement in the seventies. All my life I had avoided information on and contact with gay society. This denial was overdetermined: my background in a rural, religious milieu, the repressive atmosphere of the fifties in general, my career ambitions, a recognition that being "deviant" would close off many options, and my acceptance of the belief that this was "just a phase" that marriage would resolve (a commonly held fallacy among gay men who marry). I never spoke to anyone about my inner self, and I never knew anyone who was openly gay. The "only" gay man in the small town where I grew up was the "village queer," despised and condemned by all, hardly a role to which I aspired.

The first person to whom I came out was the straight man I had fallen in love with. He was sympathetic and supportive; our friendship continued for awhile, then gradually diminished and eventually disappeared. This experience was largely responsible for a decision to re-make myself, inside and out, to prepare for coming out fully. My first sexual coming-out occurred in the early eighties in a bathhouse in Copenhagen during a sabbatical spent in Norway. It was incredible. After decades of repression, the impact was staggering. Several months later I met the Norwegian man who was to become my first lover. He was the first openly gay man with whom I ever spoke. I could now stop running away from myself; I had come home at last, and everything had to change. I had no idea, however, how greatly the decision to be myself would transform not only my personal life but also my professional life.

Once back in California, like any good ethnographer, I continued my exploration of a culture that was new to me by immersion in as many facets of it as I could, beginning with voracious reading of its literature. Gay men, I found, were as exotic as any tribe. And I began my "fieldwork" by participating in many aspects of gay life, learning about all of the rituals, language, and daily life of gay men in the area where I live as well as in distant lands during trips abroad. Exploring this new life was exhilarating and fulfilling. My "informants" were lovers, friends, tricks, fuckbuddies, and people I met in bars, baths, social gatherings, and other venues where gay men meet each other and socialize. The reception I received was warm beyond my wildest dreams. And over the years I discovered that, despite differences of dialect, the language of gay men in places I have been is the same; we are one tribe in diaspora, whether living in Trondheim or Zagreb, San Juan or Oaxaca, San Francisco or Atlanta, Las Vegas or Chicago. We are indeed everywhere and in all walks of life. We have subcommunities formed on the basis of stylistic preferences, from leather, Levi's, and s/m to preppy attire and vanilla sex, and on other attributes such as age, but we are one tribe.

There was only one problem. In the early eighties this was a tribe celebrating its increasing successes in the struggle for freedom and civil rights from an oppressive heterosexist society, but it was also a tribe on the edge of an unprecedented threat to its survival. I had finally achieved personal liberation just as the dam broke. It is said that everyone alive when President Kennedy was assassinated can recall where they were when they heard the news. Similarly, every gay man who was an adult in the early eighties no doubt remembers the moment when he first heard about the plague. I was on a date with my Norwegian lover. We were pausing in the middle of a cross-country skiing expedition in the forests above the city of Trondheim. While resting, he turned to me and asked if I had heard of the new disease that was striking down gay men in New York, San Francisco, and Los Angeles. I had not. This was January 1983, four months after my initiation into the mysteries of gay sexuality in

Copenhagen. It was a measure of both my isolation from gay life in America and the deficient manner in which the American press covered the epidemic that I was ignorant of this ominous development.

I often wonder what would have been the course of my life had I come out earlier. By now I would probably have departed this planet. Or if I had heard of the plague before I had the courage to explore myself, would I have dared to come out or would I have continued a life of quiet despair and alienation from my true self? Both my personal life and my work as an ethnographer might have taken an entirely different course.

Plague or no plague, there was no turning back once I had reached this point. Life had taken on new meaning, and I was determined to restructure it so as to achieve the fullest sense of personal, moral, and intellectual integrity possible. I came out to everyone—family, friends, and colleagues.[4] There was to be no more hiding from self or others.

I rather quickly incorporated my new perspectives into my teaching, first with a section on sexual orientation in the introductory social anthropology course that I taught regularly and second with the introduction of a major component on the plague in my course on medical anthropology. Eventually I shifted my teaching more completely to reflect my new identity, interests, and concerns. I taught a freshman seminar on epidemics and society and began a course devoted to the AIDS pandemic. My concern for the health and safety of my students as well as for the impact that the epidemic would have on sexual culture in the years ahead led me to begin to teach courses in human sexuality, first one on sex and culture and then a basic course that achieved the distinction of having the largest enrollments in the history of the college. This was applied anthropology at the local level, at home (Bolton 1986c, 1992c).

THE EIGHTIES: THE PERSONAL BECOMES PROFESSIONAL

When I returned to America after the year in Norway, given the potential personal implications for my life, I felt an urgent need to know more about the plague and to get involved. My initial involvement was as a volunteer at AIDS Project/Los Angeles, stuffing envelopes, photocopying, and doing other menial tasks. When a call went out for human guinea pigs for a prospective AIDS study, the Los Angeles Men's Study, part of a national, multicenter investigation, I volunteered despite my innate dislike of being poked with needles and having tube after tube of blood drawn at each biannual visit (a process that continues twelve years later). Eventually I realized that I might make a more important contribution by applying my anthropological training to the problem. But what could I do? What follows is an account of my efforts to zero in on research areas where I thought I might make a contribution.

I had a strong reluctance to do any research on people with AIDS, not because of fear of contagion but because of a reticence to intrude on the lives of individuals who were already being subjected to intense medical scrutiny and who were coping with a diagnosis then interpreted as a death sentence. At this time I was convinced that I was probably already infected; my first lover, we both discovered after the relationship had ended, was seropositive.

It was transparent by 1984 that American society was responding with indifference to the epidemic, and so my first investigation involved a study of how the plague was being handled in a culture where social values are quite different. I returned to Norway for the summer in 1985 to study the situation there. My activities included interviewing gay leaders, government officials, physicians, and gay men I met in bars and saunas as well as through the network of Norwegian gay friends. This study showed that in Norway the epidemic was being addressed much more seriously even at a stage when only twenty-six cases existed in the entire country (Bolton 1986b). This I attributed to a set of cultural values that emphasize social responsibility, respect for human rights and human life, legal protections for gays and lesbians, public health policies that are determined in large measure by professionals and politicians in consultation with the groups most heavily affected by the policies, and a tradition of engaging in long-range planning rather than waiting until a problem is out of control.

Back in the States, I began to seek other ways to study what was happening at home. I wrote a paper documenting the genocidal approach to the epidemic that characterized the Reagan years; the lack of action was clearly determined by the views of high administration officials on homosexuality and the Reagan government's desire to retain the support of the Religious Right (Bolton 1987).

Becoming interested in the responses of the gay community, in particular in efforts to reduce sexual risk-taking, I carried out a study of personal advertisements as an indirect measure of the extent to which gay men were changing their sexual practices in response to the health crisis, for example, mentions of health status and references to a desire for risky or safe sexual practices (Bolton 1986a). Data were drawn from several gay publications, and I looked at differences in disparate locations, epicenters of the epidemic versus less affected communities. The study was interesting at the theoretical level inasmuch as it showed that in response to the crisis behavioral change was occurring at the individual level before a change in gay culture and the onset of significant prevention campaigns.

But I was dissatisfied with doing these types of analysis because they seemed too remote from the urgent problem of stopping the epidemic; they might be theoretically fascinating and even have some relevance at some future time to help prevent a repetition of the type of disaster we were now witnessing. But I could not see how they might have an immediate impact on the present situation. As a result, increasingly I began to focus on prevention, an area where anthropology could prove useful. There was nothing in my training to enable me to do research that counted toward what mattered most, finding a cure, and I had little confidence that a cure or vaccine would be forthcoming soon, which meant that it was essential to halt HIV transmission in order to save as many lives as possible. I did a study of prevention messages used on AIDS posters that during the early years were a major medium of getting word out within gay communities. I also compared European and American posters and found the former much more erotic and sex-positive and the latter highly negative, focusing on risk, death, and scare tactics (Bolton 1988; Bolton and Good 1988).

At the same time, I saw the need to sound the alarm within the discipline, to encourage fellow anthropologists to become involved in this problem. For the first few years of the epidemic, only a handful of anthropologists were active in AIDS research (Bolton, Lewis, and Orozco 1991). I wrote a paper on incorporating AIDS issues into the medical anthropology curriculum (Bolton 1986c), and I became active from the outset in the AIDS and Anthropology Research Group, whose aim is to further anthropological research on the epidemic. With the assistance of Gail Orozco and Michelle Lewis, I generated bibliographies intended to facilitate entry into this research domain (e.g., Bolton, Lewis, and Orozco 1991; Bolton and Orozco 1991a, 1991b, 1992a, 1992b, 1994a, 1994b), and I pulled together the first issue of any anthropological journal wholly devoted to AIDS (Bolton 1989). During the 1980s, I organized and/ or chaired countless symposia and roundtable discussions on AIDS at regional, national, and international anthropology meetings in an effort to stimulate interest within the profession.

Although I gave numerous public presentations on my initial research efforts, the papers were never published because I was still floundering around trying to find a way to engage in research that would matter. I recognized that these studies, although intriguing, had no serious potential for making a difference. Increasingly I felt that to have any hope of reducing high-risk behaviors it was essential to gain a more profound understanding of gay male sexuality. In my personal life I was doing this experientially, and as a result I became convinced that the research being done on the subject was superficial (most of it surveys limited to a few questions about numbers of partners and participation in a small subset of sexual behaviors). It did not begin to reveal the complexity of sexual behavior and motivation.

Drawing on my background in cognitive anthropology and experimentation with this approach in several of my Peruvian studies (Thomas and Bolton 1979), I felt that an urgent task was to explore the cognitive domain of sexuality among gay men. I designed such a study and enlisted a gay student to carry out a pilot study in his network in San Francisco, while I tried, with no success, to find funding for a major study of the domain of gay male sexuality (Bolton and Jaramillo 1988).

But I did get lucky when I applied for a Fulbright grant for Belgium to study the "social and cultural dimensions of AIDS" in that country, a replication of the Norwegian study. I discovered later that the director of the program had a friend who was dying of AIDS, and I have no doubt that this influenced the favorable outcome of my application. When I got to Belgium I was free to pursue my research in any way I wished.

Assigned to the Belgian Ministry of Public Health and Hygiene, I was given free rein to pursue my interests, and I plunged into exploring the gay community, meeting people in bars, saunas, and through friends, and participating fully in the life of the community in Brussels, including intimate encounters with many men. When I arrived, I was surprised to read in the official literature on the epidemic the conclusion that gay men in Belgium had learned what behavior to avoid and that they had adopted safe sex, with the further suggestion that because this was the case, attention need not be paid to their situation but could be focused on other segments of Belgian society that might still be at risk. This was an astounding assertion in view of the fact that the epidemic was still in its infancy in Belgium, with not many men having died yet, and individual information on seropositivity was rarely shared with friends or family members. In view of results from studies in the United States that indicated that one of the major motivators of behavior change was precisely nearness to people known to be infected or to have died, it seemed unlikely that such massive behavior change could have occurred in Belgium already. After all, there had not even been a major prevention campaign in the weakly organized gay community of the country. Official conclusions sounded to me like wishful thinking or denial.

Throughout my stay in Belgium I took notes on my personal sexual encounters, because this was part of my process of learning about the lives of gay men, and I eventually concluded that Belgian gay men, for the most part, were in fact not playing safely; even though they knew that I was an American coming from an epicenter of the epidemic, they neither avoided me sexually nor did they show any inclination to request or insist on safe sex in our encounters. My methodology was to allow my partner in an encounter to take the lead and set the limits, although I never followed through on any high-risk behavior. It was the rare partner who mentioned condoms or limiting sex to safer techniques.[5]

At the end of my tenure at the Institute I conveyed this conclusion orally to the head of epidemiology. At that time I did not feel that my unorthodox methodology would permit me to take the bolder step of reporting it in writing. Although I have no knowledge that this report actually resulted in increased funding for prevention in the gay community in Belgium, I had done what I could as a researcher to make certain that the authorities were fully aware that their policy conclusions were faulty, and I tried to impress on them that if they wished to avoid an absolute disaster on the scale of what we were then seeing in metropolitan areas of the United States, they would have to take immediate action while the situation was still manageable.

Toward the end of my stay in Belgium I met a young Belgian sociologist who also was interested in HIV prevention among gay men. He immediately grasped the potential of the cognitive study I had designed and offered to enter into a collaborative effort to carry out the proposed research. Whereas I had failed to obtain funds for such research in the United States, within a few months he managed to generate funding in Belgium for a major project that was to include this type of investigation. That project has produced a series of publications and papers that help to clarify the psychological and social factors that have an impact on sexual risk-taking by Flemish gay men (Bolton, Vincke, Mak, and Dennehy 1992; Vincke and Bolton 1995; Vincke, Bolton, Mak, and Blank 1993; Vincke, Bolton, and Mak 1990, 1992; Vincke, Mak, and

Bolton 1991; Vincke, Mak, Bolton, and Jurica 1993) as well as to document seroprevalence rates, the incidence of sexual risk-taking in this
community, and the health-seeking behavior of Flemish gay men (Mak
et al. 1990; Mak, Vincke, and Bolton 1991). The analysis of data from
surveys conducted in 1989, 1993, and 1994 continues, with an emphasis on efforts to understand the cognitive domain of sexuality of these
men.

A major thrust of this set of publications has been a serious critique
of much of the prevention research done on gay men during the first
decade of the plague, research that has relied heavily on models drawn
from previous health behavior research on domains other than sexuality
(Bolton 1995a); it has emphasized psychological factors largely to the
exclusion of social factors and generally takes a negative and often homophobic stance toward sexuality, revictimizing and remedicalizing the
community. Space considerations prevent summarizing all of our findings, but our work on the role of alcohol as a risk factor can be cited as
an example.

Although much of the AIDS prevention literature places considerable
stress on alcohol as a facilitator of risky behavior and hence of HIV transmission, our research found no association between risky sex and alcohol consumption (Bolton, Vincke, Mak, and Dennehy 1992). A critical
review of the literature then revealed that this prevention recommendation was being made on the basis of very little evidence in support of a
link between alcohol and risky sex, with more studies disconfirming the
association than confirming it. What this illustrated quite clearly was that
despite the evidence, preconceived expectations based on inappropriate
models were having greater influence than were the findings of empirical studies. Indeed, authors often strained to discount their negative
findings in order to retain their belief in the hypothesized influence of
alcohol on risky sex.

I became more and more concerned about the content of prevention
messages (cf. Bolton and Singer 1992). In particular, because we have
known almost from the outset of the epidemic that specific behaviors
alone are responsible for transmission and that who one has sex with or
how many people one has sex with is irrelevant, I became interested in
the emphasis placed on the reduction of number of partners as a prevention strategy that has been stressed in most programs, the antipro-
miscuity message. As a result, I published an extensive critical analysis
of the role of "promiscuity" in HIV transmission (Bolton 1992a).

My interest in sexual orientation theories and problems of the gay community resulted in three other studies during this decade. The first, still unpublished, is an analysis of how homosexuality is understood by anthropologists. This study examined the treatment of this subject in introductory anthropology textbooks. A general conclusion of that analysis is that anthropologists usually ignore the topic entirely, and when they do discuss it they use it to illustrate some cultural concept rather than focus directly on it as a subject worthy of understanding in its own right. The second, undertaken with a sociology colleague, Peter Nardi, was a review of the scope of the problem of violence against gay men and lesbians (Nardi and Bolton 1991). This study was published in an edited volume of victims of violence, and what makes this unique is that it is the first time that a book by specialists on aggressive behavior has included a discussion of aggression directed against gays and lesbians. In the third study (Bolton 1994), presented as the Presidential Address to the Society for Cross-Cultural Research, I critically evaluated the few extant cross-cultural studies of same-sex eroticism, pointing out the pitfalls associated with such research and emphasizing the need to do basic ethnographic work on homosexualities worldwide.

THE NINETIES: THE PROFESSIONAL BECOMES POLITICAL

By the end of the 1980s I had arrived at several disturbing conclusions concerning the directions of AIDS research and possibilities for contributing directly to the most urgent task of reducing sexual risk-taking and HIV transmission. It is fairly evident that most risk reduction that has taken place in gay communities owes little or nothing to the prevention research that has been done, mostly by non-anthropologists, that is, by other behavioral scientists who have had greater access to funding. Given the kinds of research that have been done, this is not surprising because most of it is unsophisticated about sexuality and often quite ignorant of the target community. Furthermore, it has become clear that funding of serious sex research is unlikely in the future because of political opposition and because of the failure of social scientists to fight courageously for appropriate research.

Consequently, I have attempted to both promote the kinds of research that are needed, as well as to lay bare the deficiencies in the research that has been done (Bolton 1992b, 1995a; Carrier and Bolton 1991). The response to these efforts has been both expectable and disheartening. Some examples must suffice.

In 1990 I was invited to participate in a Wenner-Gren conference on AIDS and anthropology where I presented a paper outlining my proposals on methods for studying sexuality and in which I went public with my sexual participant observation, jokingly referred to by conference participants as the "Bolton method" (Bolton 1991). In discussions about publication plans for the conference papers, several participants voiced strong doubts about publishing my discussion on this matter. Subsequently the editors of the volume suggested a solution to the issue; they recommended presenting a discussion of the proposal to do such work but asked that I not acknowledge that I had personally done this kind of research. The comment was that "the discipline is not prepared for this." Truth, then, was to be sacrificed to the immaturity of the discipline. I was appalled and angry. Here in a nutshell was the main obstacle to successfully coping with this plague, dishonesty combined with cowardice.

When I discussed this work at another conference in Philadelphia, Renee Fox, a distinguished medical sociologist, stood up and branded my research as immoral. Ethicists have had a field day with AIDS, and, to be sure, there are serious ethical issues raised by this epidemic. Only rarely, however, are these issues tackled by ethical experts. But it is time to reconsider how we decide what is ethical and what is not. I reject the idea that research that harmed no one and may potentially save countless lives is immoral. My participant observation research that includes sexual encounters continues in the United States. Because such encounters often lead subsequently to discussions with my partners about safe sex and AIDS, I am confident that the research process itself has saved more lives than has much of the "ethical" research funded by millions of dollars. This research is applied anthropology that does have an impact.

The total financial support I have received for AIDS-related research over a decade has not exceeded $20,000, including the Fulbright award and numerous small grants from Pomona College. Gay anthropologists working on AIDS have had insurmountable difficulties in obtaining funds for ethnographic work. To date, there have been no funded general ethnographic studies of gay communities in the United States. Recognizing this problem, leaders of the AIDS and Anthropology Task Force, tired of hearing gay men complain, decided in 1991 that the Task Force would give priority to supporting efforts to obtain funding for ethnographic research on gay men. The results of this effort are instructive. Following a CDC-sponsored conference on AIDS and anthropology, Task Force leaders approached the CDC on this issue and reported back a willingness on the part of the CDC to fund such research. When the guidelines for applying came through, however, it was clear that gay ethnography was not to be taken seriously. The guidelines indicated that the CDC would consider research proposals on "unstudied small communities" and on "couples." (Does the CDC know something about "where the boys are" that gay men do not? Is the emphasis on studying couples a confession that the partner-reduction and monogamy strategies promoted by the government instead of sex-positive approaches are not working? Are they writing off those who have not adopted coupledom as the solution to HIV transmission?) The research areas delineated in the guidelines did not address the main problems in preventing transmission among gay men, and it is reasonable to suspect that they were never intended to include serious consideration of the real problems of doing work to prevent the continued spread of the plague among gay men in areas where the greatest number at the greatest risk are concentrated.

Furthermore, real ethnography was not to be tolerated; distance must be maintained through the use of data-collecting techniques that keep informants at bay, the worst of these the telephone sex interview (appropriate at best, I would argue, for studying phone sex). We were told that at most six months of ethnographic work could be incorporated as an adjunct to larger projects using quantitative methodologies. Worst of all, discussions with CDC personnel were to be handled through a project leader who is straight because of a fear that gay ethnographers might not be able to negotiate successfully with bureaucrats owing to our anger and "lack of objectivity." In short, as usual, gay men and the needs of the gay community were relegated to the back of the bus—if they were on the bus at all.

Under such conditions, gay men who happen to be ethnographers would serve their (our) communities better through militant action with ACT UP or Queer Nation than through efforts to contribute professional skills with the support of public institutions charged with safeguarding the nation's health. But this has always been the case: Prevention in the gay community has been done by the gay community with little assistance in the face of obstacle after obstacle raised by outsiders through legal means (e.g., the closing of bathhouses and prohibitions on explicit and effective safer-sex communications), delaying tactics, and subtle manipulations.

Political actions that go against both scientific justification and the culture of the gay community have yielded little protest from scholars, and in some cases have not even generated appropriate research (my proposal to the Wenner-Gren Foundation to do research on gay saunas was turned down in 1991). For instance, no ethnographer studied gay bathhouses in the 1980s; indeed, almost no research of any kind was done on the question of whether or not the baths contributed to the epidemic, even in the face of the closing of these institutions in some cities in the United States and restrictions placed on their operation in others. My colleagues and I have analyzed our Belgian data on this issue, the first study to compare men who go to baths with those who do not, and discovered that gay men who go to baths know more about AIDS, have changed their behavior toward lower riskiness proportionately more, and practice safer sex than do men who do not go to baths (Bolton, Vincke, and Mak 1994).

In the absence of financial support for ethnographic research, I have opted to use low-cost methodologies to continue my efforts to understand gay male sexuality. I continue to do participant observation in the hours I can spare while teaching full-time. And I have begun a computer-based content analysis of gay erotica in an effort to probe the language of gay male sexuality, the structure of sexual encounters, and the meanings of specific sexual acts (Bolton 1995b). At the same time, I am trying to determine how to write an account of my participant observation on sexuality that will document what I have learned in a way that will be useful to those on the front lines in trying to reduce HIV transmission.

We are still in the decade of the 1990s, and it is too soon to say where my research efforts will go in the years ahead other than finishing the projects I have discussed. Just as I think I know how to orient my work, I am hit with another development. As the epidemic unfolds and as we struggle to find where we can focus on what counts most, we are constantly buffeted by our personal experiences. While writing the first draft of this chapter, I had an encounter that has transformed my perceptions of what is important. On a nine-day visit to a close friend, I had the opportunity to observe how he was coping with the plague. Rejecting all biomedical approaches, he had chosen to seek out an idyllic environment in which to live a life as stress-free as possible, leaving behind all considerations of HIV, doctors, medications with poisonous side effects, and other paraphernalia of the culture of AIDS. Given my professional obsession with the plague, it was difficult for me to learn to accept the wisdom of his approach. It is the uncertainty of almost everything associated with this plague that makes it so difficult to act with any confidence that one is doing the right thing. His approach forced me to question all my assumptions about how to respond to the epidemic, a painful lesson indeed.

Will this encounter lead to new research directions for me? I do not know at this point. What I do know is that I am increasingly convinced that research during the first decade has largely failed. And my preoccupation with prevention lessens as my preoccupation with strategies for surviving with AIDS becomes more and more pressing as more and more of my loved ones face illness and possibly death. We are in a chess game with Death, and the stakes are disturbingly high—the lives of friends and lovers and the survival of a community (see Ingmar Bergman's film *The Seventh Seal*). Each false move brings the game closer to a disastrous conclusion. In this context, the research game itself seems trivial. Perhaps the best that can be done is to work with what is already known for prevention at the local level, while devoting energies to supporting friends who search for meaning and survival during these hard times, even if this entails abandoning "the field."

As I write these lines, a slip of paper comes in the mail, the latest report on my health from the prospective AIDS study in which I am a subject. It reads quite simply: "No changes were observed in your antibody status at your last visit." And I wonder how they would notify me if my test had turned out positive. This news should be a comfort; I have not yet been tapped to cross the great gulf that divides my community into positives and negatives. If it had turned out positive, would I have finished this manuscript? How would it have changed? Would I have told you about it, dear reader? And what impact would it have on my future work as an ethnographer? Each step along this journey during the epidemic potentiates a dramatic shift in consciousness with significant repercussions on the work we, as anthropologists, do. Yes, the personal is professional and the professional is political. There are no boundaries, only untraversed territories.

Notes

This chapter is a highly revised and expanded version of a paper entitled "Zeroing In: Reflections of an AIDS Researcher" presented at the annual meeting of the Society for Applied Anthropology, Charleston, South Carolina, March 1991.

I would like to thank William Leap for the invitation to participate in that session and for his subsequent support as I reworked this material. Thanks are also due to Ellen Lewin for superb editorial work in condensing the manuscript to an acceptable length, to Sue-Ellen Jacobs for her encouragement, and to Mildred Dickemann and Stephen Murray for helpful comments on a draft of the manuscript. This account is dedicated with deepest affection and gratitude to my friend David. "And his arm lay lightly around my breast—and that night I was happy." *Mahalo*. "Your seed of thought will bud, blossom, and bear fruit." *Aloha*.

1   I have segmented this journey by decades, but the periodization corresponds imprecisely with the actual dates. The "sixties" are really 1962–70 (five years of fieldwork in Peru and three years of graduate school); the "seventies" begin in 1971 and end in 1982 (a period of settling into teaching, publishing, and raising a family, with fieldwork in both Peru and Norway); the "eighties," from 1983 to 1990, saw my coming out, a shift to research on AIDS, and an expansion of my research interests to other parts of Europe and the United States; the "nineties" begin in 1991 with an intensification of my interest in research on gay male sexuality. Because of lags in publications, publication dates do not necessarily reflect the period in which either fieldwork or data analysis was done.

2   My life as a Peace Corps volunteer was described in a research report on Peru that examined the adaptation of volunteers, under the pseudonym of PT-5 (Dobyns, Doughty, and Holmberg 1964).

3   Out of consideration for the privacy of family members, I have deliberately omitted a discussion of some issues that might otherwise seem pertinent. It is for this reason that this account gives less attention to my family life than is warranted by the situation. Suffice it to say that through all the changes in our lives my former wife, my two sons, and I have constituted—and always will—a family in the truest sense of that concept, connected to each other by strong bonds of love, respect, and mutual support.

4   As many other gay men have found, I suspect that AIDS actually facilitated my process of coming out, first because the existential problems it posed placed all other difficulties in a different perspective and second because it provided an indirect way of raising issues of sexual orientation.

5   Discussions of many of the ethical and methodological issues surrounding my work on sexual behavior, including participant observation, are contained in Bolton (1991a, 1995c).

References Cited

Bolton, Ralph. 1973a. "Aggression and Hypoglycemia among the Qolla: A Study in Psychobiological Anthropology." *Ethnology* 12:227–57.

———. 1973b. "Tawanku: Intercouple Bonds in a Qolla Village." *Anthropos* 68:145–55.

———. 1974. "To Kill a Thief: A Kallawaya Sorcery Session in the Lake Titicaca Region of Peru." *Anthropos* 69:191–215.

166   Ralph Bolton

————. 1979. "Who Are the Qolla? A Note of Clarification." *El Dorado* 4(3): 49–58.

————. 1986a. "AIDS and Ads: Behavior Change among Gay Men in Response to the AIDS Epidemic." Paper presented at the annual meeting of the Kroeber Anthropological Society, Berkeley, March.

————. 1986b. "AIDS and Culture: The Case of Norway." Paper presented at the annual meeting of the American Anthropological Association, Philadelphia, December.

————. 1986c. "Teaching about AIDS: An Important Task for Medical Anthropologists." Paper presented at the annual meeting of the Southwestern Anthropological Association, Las Vegas, March.

————. 1987. "AIDS: The Final Solution?" Paper presented at the annual meeting of the American Anthropological Association, Chicago, November.

————. 1988. "AIDS Prevention Campaigns: A Comparative Study." Paper presented at the Twelfth International Congress of Anthropological and Ethnological Sciences, Zagreb, Yugoslavia.

————. 1989. "The AIDS Pandemic: A Global Emergency." *Medical Anthropology* 10(2–3): 93–104.

————. 1991. "Mapping Terra Incognita: Sex Research for AIDS Prevention— An Urgent Agenda for the Nineties." In *The Time of AIDS: Social Analysis, Theory, and Method,* ed. Gilbert Herdt and Shirley Lindenbaum, 124–58. Newbury Park, Calif.: Sage Publications.

————. 1992a. "AIDS and Promiscuity: Muddles in the Models of HIV Prevention." *Medical Anthropology* 14:145–223.

————. 1992b. "Under the Bed or in it? The Mating of 'Risky' Sex and 'Safe' Research in the Marriage from Hell." Paper presented at the annual meeting of the Society for Cross-Cultural Research, Santa Fe, February.

————. 1992c. "Sexual Orientation Issues in a Human Sexuality Course." *Society of Lesbian and Gay Anthropologists Newsletter* 14(3): 20–26.

————. 1994a. "Sex, Science, and Social Responsibility: Cross-Cultural Research on Same-Sex Eroticism and Sexual Intolerance." *Cross-Cultural Research* 28(2): 134–90.

————. 1995a. "Rethinking Anthropology: The Study of AIDS." In *Culture and Sexual Risk,* ed. H. T. Brummelhuis and G. Herdt, 285–313. New York: Gordon and Breach.

————. 1995b. "Sex Talk: Bodies and Behaviors in Gay Erotica." In *Beyond the Lavender Lexicon: Authenticity, Imagination and Appreciation in Gay Languages,* ed. William Leap. New York: Gordon and Breach.

————. 1995c. "Tricks, Friends, and Lovers: Erotic Encounters in the Field." In *Taboo: Sex, Violence, and Erotic Subjectivity in Anthropological Fieldwork,* ed. Don Kulick and Margaret Willson. London: Routledge.

Bolton, Ralph, and Julie Good. 1988. "Playing Safely: A Cross-Cultural Analysis of AIDS Posters." Paper presented in the Symposium on AIDS and the Anthropology of Risk at the annual meeting of the American Anthropological Association, Phoenix, November.

Bolton, Ralph, and David Jaramillo. 1988. "Gay Men, Gay Sex: A Behavioral

Space Analysis." Paper presented at the annual meeting of the American Anthropological Association, Phoenix, November.

Bolton, Ralph, with the assistance of Michelle Lewis and Gail Orozco. 1991. "AIDS Literature for Anthropologists: A Working Bibliography." *Journal of Sex Research* 28(2): 307–46.

Bolton, Ralph, and Gail Orozco. 1991a. "Recent Anthropological Publications on AIDS." *AIDS and Anthropology Bulletin* 3(2): 3–4.

———. 1991b. "AIDS and Anthropology Bibliography: September 1991 Update." *AIDS and Anthropology Bulletin* 3(3): supplement.

———. 1992a. "AIDS and Anthropology Bibliography: January 1992 Update." *AIDS and Anthropology Bulletin* 3(4): supplement.

———. 1992b. "AIDS and Anthropology Bibliography: May 1992 Update." *AIDS and Anthropology Bulletin* 4(1): supplement.

———. 1994a. "AIDS and Anthropology Bibliography: May 1994 Update." *AIDS and Anthropology Bulletin* 5(3): 12-page supplement.

———. 1994b. *The AIDS Bibliography: Studies from Anthropology and Related Fields.* Washington, D.C.: American Anthropological Association.

Bolton, Ralph, and Merrill Singer. 1992. "Introduction: Rethinking HIV Prevention: Critical Assessments of the Content and Delivery of AIDS Risk-Reduction Messages." *Medical Anthropology* 14:139–43.

Bolton, Ralph, John Vincke, and Rudolf Mak. 1994. "Gay Baths Revisited: An Empirical Analysis." *GLQ: A Journal of Gay and Lesbian Studies* 1(3): 255–73.

Bolton, Ralph, John Vincke, Rudolf Mak, and Ellen Dennehy. 1992. "Alcohol and Risky Sex: In Search of an Elusive Connection." *Medical Anthropology* 14:323–63.

Carrier, Joseph, and Ralph Bolton. 1991. "Anthropological Perspectives on Sexuality and HIV Prevention." *Annual Review of Sex Research* 2:49–75.

Dobyns, Henry F., Paul L. Doughty, and Allan R. Holmberg. 1964. *Peace Corps Program Impact in the Peruvian Andes: Final Report.* Peace Corps Contract No. PC-(W)-155. Ithaca: Cornell University, Department of Anthropology.

Freud, Sigmund. 1961 [1930]. *Civilization and Its Discontents.* Vienna: Internationaler Psychoanalytischer Verlag. Translated and edited by James Strachey. New York: W. W. Norton.

Lewellen, Ted C. 1981. "Aggression and Hypoglycemia in the Andes: Another Look at the Evidence." *Current Anthropology* 22(4): 347–61.

Mak, R., R. Bolton, J. Vincke, J. Plum, and L. Van Renterghem. 1990. "Prevalence of HIV and Other STD Infections and Risky Sexual Behavior among Gay Men in Belgium." *Archives of Public Health* 48:87–98.

Mak, R., J. Vincke, and R. Bolton. 1991. "Health Care for Homosexual Men in Belgium." Poster presented at the Seventh International Conference on AIDS, Florence, Italy.

Nardi, Peter M., and Ralph Bolton. 1991. "Gay-Bashing: Violence and Aggression against Gay Men and Lesbians." In *Targets of Violence and Aggression,* ed. Ronald Baenninger, 349–400. Advances in Psychology Series. Amsterdam: Elsevier–North Holland.

Thomas, Lynn, and Ralph Bolton. 1979. "Rote Learning and Semantic Clustering: Analysis of Free Recall Test Data from Peru." *Journal of Cross-Cultural Psychology* 10:23–39.

Vincke, John, and Ralph Bolton. 1995. "Social Stress and Risky Sex among Gay Men: An Additional Explanation for the Maintenance of Unsafe Sex." In *Culture and Sexual Risk,* ed. H. T. Brummelhuis and G. Herdt. New York: Gordon and Breach.

Vincke, John, Ralph Bolton, and Rudolf Mak. 1990. "Stress, Physical Complaints, Role Impairment and the Coming-Out Press." Paper presented at the annual meeting of the American Sociological Association, Atlanta, August.

———. 1992. "Minority Status: The Perception of Control and AIDS-Related Sexual Risk Behavior." Paper presented at the annual meeting of the American Sociological Association, Pittsburgh, August.

Vincke, John, Ralph Bolton, Rudolf Mak, and Susan Blank. 1993. "Coming Out and AIDS-Related High-Risk Sexual Behavior." *Archives of Sexual Behavior* 22(6): 559–86.

Vincke, John, Rudolf Mak, and Ralph Bolton, eds. 1991. *Mannen Met Mannen: Welzijn, Relaties & Seksualiteit.* Ghent, Belgium: C.G.S.O.

Vincke, John, Rudolf Mak, Ralph Bolton, and Paul Jurica. 1993. "Factors Affecting AIDS-Related Sexual Behavior Change among Flemish Gay Men." *Human Organization* 53(3): 260–68.

3

REPRESENTATION

9. Constructing an Ethnohistory of the Buffalo Lesbian Community: Reflexivity, Dialogue, and Politics
Elizabeth Lapovsky Kennedy, with Madeline Davis

When Madeline Davis and I started the research for *Boots of Leather, Slippers of Gold: The History of a Lesbian Community* in 1978, we did not consciously adopt a research methodology, other than the decision to use oral history for learning about Buffalo's mid-century butch-fem community.[1] Because we were attempting the first full-length historical study of a working-class lesbian, or for that matter gay male, bar community, the territory was uncharted.[2] The book's ethnohistorical approach emerged in response to our political perspectives, our training, and the material itself.

A key step in the development of the research and writing was the early decision to write an analysis of the community's history and culture, rather than compile a collection of reminiscences. In our minds, the juxtaposition of individual life stories had the effect of isolating lesbians, thereby playing into the dominant ideology that presents lesbians as victims. Not only individual lives and voices were missing from history, but also an understanding of common culture, concerted action, and consciousness of kind. We knew that old-timers followed rules of conduct and had a strategic sense for survival. We guessed from this that they shared some sort of common culture. We wanted to explore how, if at all, the culture of resistance that developed in working-class lesbian bars and house parties contributed to shaping twentieth-century gay and lesbian consciousness and politics.

Despite working with oral histories, nontraditional sources for anthropologists, in the process of research my training as an anthropologist began to surface. I intuitively found ways to construct an in-depth analysis of community structure and culture.[3] This allowed us to take readers inside butch-fem culture, to explore how social life, intimate relationships, and identity intermeshed in lesbian resistance before the women's and gay liberation movements of the late 1960s. But analysis of community culture and consciousness did not deflect us from our interest in knowing how the lesbian community was connected with larger political and economic forces and how lesbians' own activities shaped twentieth-century history. As a result, *Boots of Leather, Slippers of Gold* became an ethnohistory; it attempts to combine the methods of ethnography—the intensive study of the culture and identity of a single community—with history—the analysis of the forces that shaped how that community changed over time.

As lesbians doing research and writing about and for lesbians in the 1980s, Davis and I faced two related challenges. First, how would we negotiate the power relations between the researcher and the subject of research, in particular the hierarchy implicit in researching a black and white working-class lesbian community, which at the time was despised both by the dominant society and the developing feminist movement? We were concerned about this issue not only to design an ethical research program, but also to better understand the nature of the information we generated. Second, how would we establish reliability for an ethnohistory constructed primarily from oral narratives? The new directions of interpretive anthropology and feminist research supported us in finding solutions.[4] From different perspectives they both emphasized reflexivity and dialogue in the research process, while feminist scholarship also raised issues of politics, in particular questions about purpose and audience.[5]

Like many feminists beginning to study women in the 1970s, I started out with a naive belief that when women study women, power relations become muted. My first field experience with the Waunan, Native Americans in the rain forest of Colombia, while training to be an anthropologist in the 1960s, both impelled me toward this egalitarian hope and made me fundamentally suspicious of it. Fieldwork with the Waunan had been a personally transformative experience about which I found it extremely difficult to write. The traditional methods of the objective field report were not conducive to exposing the relations of imperialism or focusing on issues that were useful to the Waunan.[6]

Unable to imagine the transformation in the writing of ethnography that was to come in the next thirty years, I decided to quit doing fieldwork abroad and focus closer to home with the assumption that the issues of power relations and otherness were less daunting. In the context of a burgeoning feminist movement, the decision to study a lesbian community seemed to lessen the division between self and other, author and subject, and the academy and the community; and the research could become part of the community's struggles against oppression. Toward this end, I joined forces with Davis, a librarian, lesbian-feminist singer and songwriter, and activist. She was particularly clear on the political meaning of the work, and in fact undertook it as her political work for the gay and lesbian movement. She was drawn to the topic from her firsthand knowledge of some older lesbians. She wanted to give back to them some of what they had offered her when she was coming out in the 1960s. Not being an academic, she assumed that doing research meant doing something useful for lesbians. If not, why bother?

In the process of research and writing, Davis and I became progressively aware that the common bond of lesbianism and familiarity with the social context did not make positioning ourselves in relation to the complex and powerful forces of class, race, and gender oppression—not to mention homophobia—easy. How are black and white working-class butch voices heard when they are stereotyped as low-life alcoholics? How can fem confidence and satisfaction break through the dominant assumptions about femininity? How can African American lesbian agency in desegregating the bars be portrayed in an ideology that denies racial difference? How can feminism's fundamental ambivalence about working-class lesbian life and sexuality be challenged? There were some important ways in which having close ties with the subjects of research allowed us to struggle successfully with clearing a space for their perspectives on the world. But for the most part the way we could negotiate the divisions between researcher and subject of research was to be vigilantly reflective about our narrators and our location in the hierarchies of class, race, and gender and to be forthright about making working-class lesbians central to lesbian and women's history.

The power differential between working-class lesbians and middle-class academics that had marginalized the former made questions about the reliability, objectivity, or truth of the ethnography important to us. While giving priority to the perspectives of working-class lesbians, we were looking for the best way we could recount and interpret this period of lesbian history. One story would not necessarily be as good as another. History had indeed moved on. The same events would not occur in the same way in 1930 as in 1960, and how were we to understand that change?

Ironically, our concern for the historical record required us to develop a methodology that could respond to two kinds of challenges. On the one hand, traditional social scientists who were still wedded to the idea of an objectivity that transcends the particular location of inquirer and research subject were immediately suspicious of the validity of our analysis because it was based on oral histories. From this perspective, individual memories were too subjective to be taken seriously as the basis of a community study. Our methodology had to be able to withstand careful scrutiny when we argued that a community history based on oral history made a reliable contribution to the historical record. On the other hand, interpretive anthropology with the relativist bent of postmodern thinking implies that all interpretations are equally valid. The search for an "objective" report seems superfluous or dated. I, like many feminists, am skeptical of such a position. Recognizing the need to deconstruct the idea of masculine universality, feminists are also wary of having alternative perspectives of the world viewed as just one of many.[7] Having once found our voice we are hesitant to have it deconstructed before our views are heard. Drawing on the writings of feminist researchers, I came to understand that the greater degree of self-consciousness Davis and I could convey about our social position as scholars, and about the social positions of the narrators, the more helpful that would be for revealing the limitations of the work and therefore its usefulness as history.[8]

In this chapter I will explore what reflexivity, dialogue, and politics meant to Davis and me as we confronted questions of ethics and "truth" (or historical reliability) in researching and writing *Boots of Leather, Slippers of Gold.* Although I envision this as a general contribution to ideas in interpretive anthropology and feminist methodology, I am particularly interested in questions of research and writing as they affect lesbians and, when applicable, gay men. After establishing the context for the relationship between the narrators and ourselves as researchers and authors, I will consider basic issues such as identifying narrators and protecting their identity. A major concern is with the negotiated relation between narrators and authors in the process of interviews and interpretation and in the writing of the text.

Establishing the Context for the Research: The Buffalo Women's Oral History Project

The social relations of the research were determined by both the similarities we shared with narrators and the differences. As a lesbian, my intention to minimize the power differential between inquirer and subject of research by doing research in the United States for and about other lesbians was partially successful. But the focus of the research on black and white working-class lesbians who were out in the 1940s and 1950s, people whose voices have not been heard or accorded respect in the academy or the society at large, meant inevitably that social hierarchies of race and class were at the core of the project. The shared lesbianism could not erase this.

Because our research was one of the first on working-class lesbian communities, Davis and I did not have a tradition that could help us question the dominant society's stereotype of working-class masculine lesbians as derelicts and pathetic imitators of men and feminine lesbians as dupes of their butches. The situation was aggravated because feminism, a framework that had been central to my developing a critical stance toward traditional male supremacist scholarship, had marginalized working-class lesbians. In the early 1970s lesbian feminism attempted to disassociate itself from the explicitly sexual butch-fem working-class communities of the past. On the surface this was a reaction to the gender-defined roles of that community, but it also down played sexuality between women, lessening the stigma of sexual deviance (Echols 1989:215–19). This trend became fully elaborated in the 1980s.[9] At the same time, a feminist sex radical position emerged that recognized sex as a source of pleasure as well as danger for women and recognized butch-fem roles as an erotic system that fostered and shaped women's desire.[10] The entire feminist movement became embroiled in the debates about women's sexuality and its practices.[11]

Unquestionably these debates affected our research—the questions we asked and the perspective we brought to interpretation. In reclaiming the history of a working-class butch-fem lesbian community, we were not simply going against the assumptions and stereotypes of the homophobic dominant society but also contradicting emotion-laden ideas about lesbians and women's sexuality within the feminist and lesbian feminist communities. At presentations during the mid-1980s we would grit our teeth and wait for the inevitable hostile comments from the audience or later in the feminist press about how we were antifeminist, antiwoman, and dangerous in our "glorification" of gender roles and the patriarchy. In private we also received thanks from many young lesbians for giving them a glimpse of what lesbian life had been like before gay liberation and from lesbians who had lived through that period for capturing and validating their experiences.

In this situation we found that being in our own nation, and having a connection to narrators in the sense that we were all lesbians, made it easier for us to engage in a political struggle against marginalization of working-class lesbians and sexuality within feminism. We were familiar with the complicated political issues and able to integrate activism in our daily lives without having to travel great distances. Now, at the end of the research project, we can have the satisfaction of knowing that most lesbian feminists have come to appreciate working-class lesbian history and develop perspectives that include and respect working-class lesbians' sexual experience, in part due to our small contribution to the debates within feminism.

Davis's and my ability to handle this complex political situation was helped by the fact that we had experience as activists in social movements, she in gay and lesbian liberation and I in antiwar activism and feminism. Having some awareness about the implications of the similarities and differences between ourselves and narrators, we began the research by founding the Buffalo Women's Oral History Project as a part of a grass-roots movement of gays and lesbians to learn their history. The project had three goals: to research the history of Buffalo's working-class community, to write a book on that history, and to return the research to the community. On many levels the project was a fiction. We never developed a community board with an independent power base in relation to our research. Narrators did not have interest in this degree of responsibility. Although our original intention was to have the project attract, train, and support a number of people interested in lesbian history, in fact it never grew very much. One factor limiting its growth was our concern for writing a book, which meant that we had to focus on analyzing the material rather than on perpetually gathering new and different material.

Despite these limitations the existence of the Buffalo Women's Oral History Project was significant in specifying and bringing to consciousness the power relations involved in research. We had to give priority, no matter how difficult it became, to giving that research back to the community. To give back was a general statement of responsibility to lesbian communities, the meaning of which we developed over the years. It meant that our research and writing was in some way always in dialogue with narrators and with a larger lesbian community in Buffalo and nationally. Once a year we did a local presentation of our research to which narrators and fifty to one hundred other Buffalo people came. We also went on the road to lecture about our research and engage in debate about its meaning. Although we never had a detailed discussion with any narrators about our commitment to give the research back to the lesbian community, our clear orientation conveyed this implicitly and anchored us in a perspective that was broader than our individual research interests.

The commitment to give back also oriented us toward sharing the rewards from the project, be they professional, financial, or ego-based. It encouraged us to think of spreading these rewards rather than garnering them only for ourselves. Concretely, this meant that professional advancement was only one consideration among many when making decisions about the development of the project. In addition, the existence of the Buffalo Women's Oral History Project allowed us a convenient vehicle for keeping a financial record of our earnings and expenses that could be open to public scrutiny. Because lesbian projects do not easily find support and we both had full-time jobs, we put all of our earnings from speaking engagements into such research expenses as transcriptions, trips to archives, and preparation of the final manuscript—and even that did not cover all our expenditures. We also decided to divide the royalties of the project between ourselves (in recognition of the years of hard work of research and writing) and the Buffalo Women's Oral History Project (to be used for projects that better the lives of older lesbians) in recognition of the debt the book owes to the larger lesbian communities that narrators helped to build.[12] These decisions meant that narrators and the lesbian community in general could have a realistic sense of how much is earned from a book, avoiding destructive speculation. They also affirmed the seriousness of our desire not to exploit narrators.

Although we did not participate in the lesbian community during the 1940s and 1950s, we do participate in the same general community in which narrators now function, and our paths variably interconnect, depending on age, friendship groups, class, race, ethnicity, and culture. Unquestionably this connection helped us and allowed us to bridge some of the hierarchy implicit in research. When we approached narrators, one of the things we said to interest them in participating in the project was that we wanted to know more about our history, and to record that history for future generations. This immediately established a bond that we think continued throughout the interviews. On our part, the work was a labor of love that gave us the patience and stamina necessary to face the problems that emerged over the years. For their part, most narrators felt they were doing something worthwhile for other, particularly younger, lesbians. They gave it good energy and allowed us to come back over the years for further interviews or to ask questions of clarification over the telephone. It is our guess that if someone who was not a lesbian had approached them with this same research interest narrators would not have taken the request as seriously. The importance of being a lesbian or, more precisely, a known lesbian is underlined by the fact that we had greater luck finding narrators who moved in social circles that overlapped ours. Even with introductions it was very hard to convince narrators who were completely unfamiliar with us to participate in the project.

Although we were aware of our special connection with narrators, we did not attempt to intensify it to pursue the research.[13] Rather than attempting to break down boundaries between narrators and ourselves by becoming emotionally involved in narrators' lives, we developed an operating style that respected the divisions between us. We felt this was the best check on the hierarchical relationships of research. Because gossip about what people have or have not done to one another is rampant in the lesbian community, we tried to avoid fueling such situations. In addition, we knew realistically that we couldn't become genuine friends with everyone. If we were friendly with a narrator before the research, we consciously tried not to let the research affect the relationship. We followed all the same rules as with other narrators. If we did not know them, we were careful not to use the interview to build the friendship. Sometimes we wanted to respond to a narrator beyond the confines of the interview. Our policy was to hold off involvement until a set of interviews was finished; then, if we wished, we could establish an ongoing relationship.

In all cases we guaranteed confidentiality to narrators, which was sometimes hard to maintain because we did function in the same community.[14] We felt—rightly or wrongly—the need to be models of respectability and sensitivity in order to convince people that we were trustworthy and that the project was worthy of their participation. We also had to manage our personal lives carefully so that we did not inadvertently become involved in community tensions and rifts, thereby limiting our access to those who might help us find narrators. We think the respect and care paid off. Over a period of fifteen years, we did not get caught in any major community problems. During the research process the major complaint from narrators and other members of the lesbian community was our slowness. Because we both worked full-time jobs, it often took us a long time to follow up with people on interviews, and it took us fourteen years to complete the book.

Finding Narrators

Lesbian communities are rarely, if ever, demarcated by clear boundaries such as residence or work. Rather, the community is a network of overlapping people who socialize in the same places over time. Therefore, who we interviewed was particularly significant in delineating the shape of the community and had a significant relation to the results. Because we knew from the beginning that we wanted to study the working-class public bar community, we looked for narrators primarily from that group. Research in newspapers and some interviews led us toward a more upper-middle-class group that we consciously did not pursue because they had few if any connections with working-class lesbians.[15]

The first women we interviewed were friends of ours. After these initial oral histories, we began to map out who we needed to interview for a full understanding of the lesbian community in the 1940s and 1950s. Some narrators made suggestions about key people and helped us locate them. The oral histories themselves also gave us clues. When we began, we assumed that we were studying one racially mixed community, but as we listened to narrators we came to suspect that the public lesbian community during this period consisted of two subcommunities, African American and European American, and that desegregation began to take place only in the middle 1950s and did so without undermining the separate identity of each. (Native American women socialized in either community, but usually in the primarily European American community, and we know of no Latina or Asian American women in the pre-1960 Buffalo lesbian community.)[16] We also learned that the working-class lesbian community of the 1950s began to divide internally into the more upwardly mobile and the more rough and tough. In addition, it became apparent narrators paid little attention to ethnic divisions in the European American community.[17]

As we came to understand the dynamics of lesbian community, we desired to interview a relatively equal number of African American and European American lesbians, of butches and fems, and of upwardly mobile and rough and tough lesbians. We were particularly conscious to achieve a diversity of racial/ethnic voices because we felt the historical record has been predominantly white. But we were unable to achieve our goals for a variety of reasons rooted in the history of the community and our own position as researchers. European American and Native American tough butches who had been leaders in challenging the double life were quite easy to contact and interest in the project, as were the African Americans who had taken leadership in desegregating the bars. Perhaps because discretion had never been central to their lives, they felt relaxed about sharing their views. But all others were very difficult to locate or convince to participate. I could not help but be struck by the irony of the fact that we could not establish even minimal contact—not to mention trust—with some members of our own society, and yet I had spent two harmonious years with Native Americans in the rain forest of Colombia.

African American butches who traveled primarily in the African American community of the 1950s were hard to recruit as narrators for two different kinds of reasons. Racism in society made them suspicious of us as outsiders.[18] To what end were we picking their memories? The recession in Buffalo also aggravated the situation. A lot of African American women had lost their jobs and were scrambling for survival, making it hard to give a priority to a history project. European American and African American butches who came out in the 1940s had been leaders in forming a public lesbian community; nevertheless, they were quite circumspect after a lifetime of caution and took a great deal of persuading to participate in the project. Upwardly mobile butches, who had a lot invested in camouflaging their lesbianism, had developed elaborate strategies for discretion and were even more difficult to convince. Fems of all groups were more difficult to find than butches and usually more hesitant about participating. Part of the problem was that when we started the project we were steeped in the ideology of gay liberation and made a sharp distinction between lesbians and heterosexuals. This led us to interview only those people who were still lesbians, thereby eliminating many fems who were no longer lesbians. We only decided to track them down late in the project and to no avail.

After years of patient pursuit, we collected oral histories from forty-five people.[19] Ten of them entered the bar community in the 1930s and 1940s. Of these, nine were European American and one African American; seven were butch and three fem. Twenty-three of the narrators entered the public lesbian community in the 1950s. Of these, sixteen were European American, five African American, and two Native American; nineteen were from the rough and tough crowd, and three from the more upwardly mobile crowd; and seventeen were butch and five fem. The remaining twelve did not participate in the public lesbian community of the period but provided information about or perspectives on it.

Protecting Narrators' Identities

In doing lesbian and gay research—finding narrators, archiving oral histories, or writing a book—issues of anonymity take on a political meaning that they do not have for other groups because pressure to hide and lead a double life has been at the core of gay oppression. We were caught in a contradictory situation. Unless we could guarantee anonymity to some people as we approached them, there was no chance of us interviewing them or of their introducing us to others. At the same time, most of the people we interviewed who came out in the 1950s had been leaders in challenging the double life and did not want to be anonymous. They had spent their lives defying the need to hide, but they too were concerned that we respect others' wishes.

To solve this situation we separated the issue of identity in the oral history archive from identity in the book. Everyone could identify herself as she wanted and either take a pseudonym or use her own first name in her oral history. We limited the choice to first names because given the active anti-gay stance of the radical right we were not willing to have a file with peoples' full names.[20] Perhaps we were overcautious, but we didn't want people to be hounded or denied social services because of this research project. Narrators were completely satisfied with their use of first names, at least to the extent that no one challenged it. In fact, some expressed a distinct preference for only using their first names in order to avoid causing trouble for their families, something they had been careful about throughout their lives. We also committed ourselves to changing the name of any person who was referred to by a narrator on the tape unless we had express permission to use the name.

In the actual writing of the book we were scrupulous about concealing the identities of narrators and their friends. Although the statements by narrators offer insight into the life experience, character, and philosophy of particular people, we have been careful to subtly disguise individuals. We used pseudonyms for everybody. In addition, all identifying features of a particular person—distinctive physical features, city of birth or place of work, or activism in a particular organization—were altered.

Even nicknames were recast. This is standard research protocol for most social sciences, including ethnography, and we decided to follow it despite the political meaning that camouflage has for lesbians and gay men. We were concerned about the problems that might surface during the writing of a book that camouflaged the identities of some but not all narrators. But more important, because the book deals with the full range of life issues, social life, sexuality, relationships, and identity we were wary of how narrators might feel when they saw in print what they had said in an interview about friends or past lovers. What was to be gained by using the names of some narrators seemed to be countered by the inevitable censorship that would occur of some sensitive views. In order to recognize the importance of not hiding for some narrators, yet still use the research protocol of anonymity, in the Foreword we thanked by either first name or first and last name those who wanted to be known as lesbian contributors.

Perhaps the most controversial decision we took was to modify by computer the faces of those who were uncomfortable in having their photos in a book or those who we were unable to reach for permission to use their image. We did this to provide readers with multiple photographs that included details of clothing, hairstyle, and recreational environment, thereby expanding the record of lesbian history. The difficulty of this decision is heightened by the oppressive role of camouflage in lesbian history. Didn't the practice of camouflage fly in the face of the whole argument of the book? By taking the risk of being out publicly, narrators became leaders in developing lesbian communities and preparing the way for lesbian and gay liberation. But in our own minds such a position does not take into account the changing meaning of being out. Those who challenged the double life before gay liberation did so in situations that were completely within their control. They always knew the repercussions of their actions and could fight them. Appearance in a book has unknown repercussions. We therefore did not want to force a person to be identified as a lesbian through her photo. Many colleagues felt uncomfortable with our decision to camouflage faces for different kinds of reasons, querying whether a modified photo can be a document. We certainly understand this discomfort, but after careful consideration it seemed right to use modern technology to its maximum advantage. An abstract commitment to preserving all the details of an image seems to ignore the constructed nature of images to begin with and the constructed nature of ethnography and history.

Negotiating the Relations between Narrators and Ourselves in the Actual Interviews

In the actual interview the power differential between narrators and researcher are fluid. Theoretically, narrators are at the center of the interview, and their stories are of the utmost importance. This should give them substantial control. However, as many writers on oral history methods have pointed out, interviews do not always work that way.[21] An interview can be structured in such a way that the narrator in fact is not able to share her views; in addition the researcher for social, cultural, or personal reasons may have a hard time listening to what the narrator has to say. We consciously worked against these pitfalls.

Knowing from the beginning that we wanted to write a community history meant that in the interview process we had to balance our desire to give narrators control over the interview with our need for comparable information from narrators. We were faced with the challenge of asking detailed questions that would help us understand the social and cultural life of the Buffalo lesbian community without destroying the narrator's authority to set the direction of her story. To solve this contradictory situation, we opened our interviews with some variation on three questions. First, what is important for us to cover in a book about the lesbian community of the past and lesbian lives? Second, what do you see as turning points in the history of the lesbian community? Third, what do you see as the turning points in your own life? The first question allowed a narrator to say what was on her mind and let her know that we were interested in what she had to say. The next two questions helped us and the narrators to think historically. Together these questions supported the narrator to take charge of her story.

Beyond this opening, we did not have a set interview format. The interviews were organized by a combination of the flow of narrators' memories, the periods a narrator had delineated in her discussion of turning points, and the topics that concerned us: bars, relationships, socializing, coming out, family, motherhood, aging, butch-fem roles, racism, work, gay men, the gay and women's liberation movements, oppression and resistance, sexuality, and how these changed over time. Early in our work we had what we called "hunch sessions" on each topic to determine why a topic might be important to our study, what other people had said about it, and our own hunches about what we expected to find and why. We also did background research using newspapers, law cases, and so forth. We then developed a thorough list of questions that we needed answered. Before an interview we refreshed our memories on these topics and questions; during the interview we listened carefully to the narrator, developing particular questions from what she said. Only when there was a definite lull in an interview and a narrator had finished what she wanted to say might we interject one of our own questions.

We were struck by how, in this atmosphere of respect, narrators had clear agendas for their narratives. Frequently, we would interrupt them with a question that was important to us but not to them; they would pause to respond and then go back to their stories as they wanted to tell them. Many narrators had a flare for storytelling. We were surprised when by mistake we asked a narrator a similar question to one we had asked several years earlier and she told a story that resembled the one we had heard the first time, with similar embellishments. We came to understand that we were tapping into an oral tradition that had helped working-class lesbians survive in difficult conditions. Our experience suggests that black and white working-class lesbians who were out in the 1940s and 1950s did a lot of thinking about what it meant to be different or lesbian. They discussed these subjects together in the bars and at house parties and therefore have a lot to say to the world today. It is as if they were waiting to be asked.[22]

Equally important as the structure of the interview for empowering narrators was our ability to listen and to respond sensibly to what they were saying. Learning to listen was more difficult than we expected. To improve our listening skills we reviewed one another's tapes, pointing out our lapses, that is, our responses that came entirely from our own agendas and not from what had been mentioned by the narrator. Being from the same culture made us more and less sensitive as interviewers. Unquestionably, we were motivated to pay attention because we wanted to learn about ourselves and our history. We also knew some of the subtleties of lesbian culture, so we had a head start on ways to explore issues and problems. At the same time, this advance knowledge could also be problematic, leading us to gloss over things we thought we knew. In addition, the shared social oppression of lesbians sometimes created emotional blocks to thinking clearly about a particular topic, making it hard to explore that area openly in an interview. It was not easy, for example, to explore the fact that most narrators' relationships did not last more than eight years when we feared that our long-term love relationships were ending.

Attentive listening allowed narrators' words and ideas to challenge our preconceptions and shape the direction of our research and the final book in important ways. This happened during the interviews and every time we reread the transcriptions. The most dramatic example of this kind of reformulation is the way narrators educated us about the place of sexuality in lesbian life. Coming as we did from a lesbian and gay movement that was challenging the stereotypes of gays as being only interested in sex, we had not assigned sex an important part in our research agenda. In addition, the lack of developed historical material on sexuality, plus a general middle-class female modesty in talking about sex, had made questions about sex perfunctory. But when our most timidly asked questions elicited elaborate and enthusiastic responses we realized that we needed to change our perspective and make sex more central to our interviews and therefore our analytical framework.

Narrators seemed generally satisfied with the interview process, enough so that they were open to a second interview if we wanted it, and some allowed us to return again and again over the years. Two narrators who had been very hesitant to participate in the beginning had liked the interview so much that afterward they went to a bar for hours of reminiscing; they then shared these memories in the next interview. Only one person withdrew her tapes after the interviews; we think it was because she had disclosed some unpleasant aspects of her behavior. In fact, she did not reveal more about the seedier side of lesbian life in the 1950s than others, but for whatever reason she felt the stigma more severely.

For the most part we too are pleased with the interviews. Every time we reread—not to mention listen to—the narratives we question our decision to write a community history rather than present the complete individual narratives, which are breathtakingly beautiful documents. In their own words narrators convey a dignified and complex struggle against multiple oppression. Whether an analysis of community structure and culture can do them justice is difficult to judge.

Negotiating Matters of Interpretation between Narrators and Ourselves

Inevitably in the interpretation of the research and in writing the final ethnohistory the control of narrators diminishes and that of the researchers increases.[23] Power in matters of interpretation is at the core of the research hierarchy. In part this is because interpretation and writing in the Western tradition are predominantly individual quests. But in part this is due to the entrenched nature of the social hierarchies of race, gender, and class. In order for us to research and write an ethnohistory that made working-class lesbians central we had to make room for and validate their perspectives. Society is usually not interested in hearing the ideas of those who are not in power. This point has been amply made by Third World peoples' critiques of anthropology, people of color's critique of white social science, feminists' critique of patriarchal studies of women, and, of course, gay male and lesbian critiques of homophobic medical and social sciences. The excluded are validated only if they fit into the preconceptions of those in power.

This situation makes it critical for the researcher to have some commitment to the community and keep channels for communication open at all stages of the project, particularly in matters of interpretation. Our goal of giving this research back to the community helped us structure into the research ways for people to influence our interpretation. The process therefore was dialectical, encompassing our understanding of the material and the narrators' input about how we were doing.

Narrators were involved in all stages of the interpretations. Often when we were trying to develop an analysis we would call three or four narrators and ask them some questions that would help us determine whether we were on the right track. Our yearly public presentation brought us into dialogues with narrators and other members of the lesbian community. Rarely more than eight of the forty-five narrators came to the presentations, but those who did come always had a lot to say. In addition, some of those narrators who did not come to presentations provided feedback after reading portions of a chapter or listening to us give a summary of an argument. Thus when we were struggling with our analysis of relationships we gave a draft of our first paper to two narrators from different generations who were friends and asked them for feedback. We met together for a three-hour discussion afterward. Another narrator read the chapter on desegregating the bars to check how we were treating the agency of black lesbians. Two other narrators gave us feedback on almost all aspects of the book without reading any of it; they simply listened to our concerns and questions. Several narrators read the first draft of the entire book, and one read the first and second drafts.

Our interaction with narrators, although not as formally structured as we might have liked, was very helpful in orienting us to the perspectives of working-class lesbians in the mid-twentieth century. In time, we found ourselves imagining what narrators would say in response to what we had said. In the final stage of revisions, when space constraints required drastic cuts of the lengthy last chapter, I found myself arguing with narrators who talked to me from the computer screen, insisting that their stories were important and should not be cut. I did not feel that this kind of interaction in any way compromised my analysis. Because the purpose of the work was to understand the lives of this generation of lesbians, I assumed that they were the best authorities on the topic. No narrator ever attempted to censor our ideas, but I can't imagine even that experience being a problem. Davis and I would have integrated it into the text in the form of a dialogue between ourselves and a narrator.

An analysis that makes working-class lesbian experience central requires more than simply clearing space in society in general, and in the academic tradition in particular, for a working-class point of view. We needed a useful methodology and a relevant framework for interpreting information. A basic element was to be as aware of the social positions of narrators as well as of our own. Who we interviewed unquestionably influenced the final shape of the project. Although we are confident that our analysis of lesbian community history is revealing and reliable, we also recognize that it has definite limitations based on who agreed to be narrators. Our desire to understand how working-class communities were forerunners of gay liberation implicitly made a positive evaluation of these communities, leading us toward the survivors, those who felt good about their participation in and contributions to this community. In addition, our analysis privileges the views of white rough and rebellious butch lesbians, primarily because they were the easiest for us to contact and also because of the cultural baggage we brought with us to begin the study. As a result, the stories of African American lesbians and upwardly mobile white lesbians play second and third fiddle rather than emerge strongly on their own. A study that made either one of these other groups central would be somewhat different, as would one that was able to give the same weight to all three, which we had originally intended to do. Similarly, the story might have a different perspective if we had oral histories from an equal number of fems and butches.[24]

We developed our analyses from as deep and complete immersion in the oral narratives and supplementary written sources as possible, always taking into account the social position of those who generated the information. We would juxtapose all the information we had on a broadly defined topic and begin to interrogate what it meant for community history. From experience we learned that we needed to interview at least five people from any social group in order for our analysis not to change dramatically with each new narrator. This was true whether we were concerned with analyzing the history of bar life, emotional and sexual life, or identity.

From close work with the data, we reexamined our original hunches and developed new or more precise interpretive frameworks. Finding the best interpretive framework was a very exciting experience. The first time we realized that bar fights were rarely mentioned in the memories of bar life in the 1940s but predominated in the memories of the 1950s we had a major clue for revealing the processes of change. We then looked for other manifestations of change and the reasons for them. Suddenly, a mountain of disparate detail came to take on historical meaning. We could see how bar socializing in the 1940s was different from that in the 1950s and how the difference reflected new forms of lesbian culture and consciousness. The search for the best approach to butch-fem image and sexuality was equally exciting, although less confined to our data. Others like Joan Nestle were already exploring these issues and we worked in dialogue with them as well as with our narrators.[25]

Perhaps the clearest example of the need for an analytic framework that emerges from and illuminates the data is in our writing on relationships. For several years we assumed that we did not have enough information on relationships to write about them, despite the fact that we had many note cards on different aspects of relationships. All the material seemed disjointed and irrelevant. In time it became apparent that we were inadvertently approaching the topic with the model of heterosexual marriage. Although narrators had actively led us to rethink our assumptions about sexuality, they were unable to do this in regard to relationships, possibly because they themselves were not completely clear about how lesbian relationships were distinct from heterosexual relationships and what their experience had to offer younger lesbians. After several years of reflecting on the various stories of narrators and on internalizing the feminist critique of frameworks that view women, or in this case lesbians, as victims, we gradually came to conceptualize lesbians as having formed a distinct system, serial monogamy. Once we could articulate this new framework, the voluminous details on relationships began to make sense.

The search for the best interpretive framework is in some sense a search for and a belief in some kind of objectivity and "truth."[26] I don't mean this in the sense of a truth that surpasses all others, but one that takes into account the situated knowledge of all parties in order to contribute an analysis of community culture and structure to the historical record.[27] Given the social position of our narrators and that of Davis and myself, there is no question that some interpretations were better than others. From seemingly unrelated facts, they established cultural patterns and explained apparent contradictions. They revealed elegant themes and resonance among different aspects of culture. They "let the data sing."[28]

The push for the best interpretation came not only from Davis and myself but also from the narrators. As much as we might like to, we can't claim that we as researchers had an unwavering, noble search for the "truth." Rather often it was the narrators who pushed us in this direction. For instance, we put off writing about violence in relationships as long as we possibly could. We had presented two papers about relationships and never mentioned it. In fact, we might have avoided it forever had several of our narrators not told us that the picture we presented was too rosy. When we finally did write about violence, they were consistent in supporting us. When we presented a paper on relationships to a Buffalo audience, for example, some people who were not narrators said they were uncomfortable with the way we insisted on uncovering the violence in lesbian relationships in the 1950s. In response, one narrator rose and said, "But this is oral history. This is our lives; this is the truth." She was followed by a second: "What do you want them to do? Spend ten years working on a book and then have it cover up the truth? That would be a waste of time." Such expectations kept us on our toes.

This is a perfect example of how writing the ethnography we did and telling a story that included violence required that we listen to narrators and position ourselves in the variety of complex contradictions surrounding lesbians and feminists in the 1980s and 1990s. In our own minds, albeit unconsciously, the material on violence was displaced by pro-lesbian ideas. Like members of the audience, who had not participated in the 1950s bar community, we had wondered why we, as researchers, should contribute to the bad press that lesbians already received. Steeped in the feminist ideas of the 1970s, we perhaps didn't take women's potential for violence seriously.

A successful interpretive framework worked not only for ourselves but also for narrators. It articulated ideas that maybe no one narrator would have formulated on her own but, with the juxtaposition of all the data at hand, made sense. Over the years narrators indicated this to us in numerous ways. One particularly rewarding experience occurred at the presentation on relationships to the Buffalo community. We were concerned about the usefulness of our framework for analyzing the dynamics of butch-fem relationships as a fine balance between the mutuality and cooperation of butch and fem and the control of butches. The discussion with the audience completely ignored this aspect of our paper, but narrators grasped its importance. One of them before leaving that night came up to me, winked, and said, "I'm glad some of my exes weren't here. They always thought they did everything I said because they wanted to, they didn't know it was because I was bossy." I could not have asked for a more graceful way of letting Davis and me know that we were on the right track.

One issue that consistently concerned narrators was achieving the correct balance between the good times and the bad in lesbian life during the 1940s and 1950s. In public lectures or in private conversation we were frequently told that either we had not adequately conveyed the difficulty of the times or that we had not captured the good times. During the writing process we found ourselves pulled between the facile poles of romanticizing lesbian struggles or seeing lesbians as victims due to their defeats. It is interesting to us that we had such a hard time achieving this balance.[29] We are not sure whether this is a problem shared by studies of all oppressed people or whether it is particularly problematic for research about and for lesbians. Perhaps because we are not born into our culture and have not had it passed on since childhood we lack formalized ways of combining oppression and resistance. It is also possible that we had not yet developed adequately sophisticated concepts to talk about lesbian life because so little history of working-class lesbians was being written at the time we began.

Constructing the Final Text

One of the distinctive features about the text of *Boots of Leather, Slippers of Gold* is its extended quotations from narrators. In fact, in the search for a publisher this was one of the most controversial aspects of the book. At speaking engagements around the country, the long quotes were very effective when we read from the work in progress. We would take turns, one of us reading our analysis and the other the words of the narrators, so that the dialogue between narrators and ourselves was vivid. But it was difficult to transfer this process onto the written page. Most publishers responded to a prospectus for the manuscript and sample chapters by saying that our project made an interesting and worthwhile book but that the quotes were too long and that there wasn't a strong enough narrative line. Many of my colleagues in history and anthropology had a similar reaction.[30]

We wanted to use extended quotations for a variety of reasons. Above all, despite our confidence in our analytical techniques, we think they only work because we made long quotations central to the text. It seems impossible in a situation of social hierarchy to make working-class black and white lesbians central without including their views in their own words. This was the only way that genuine dialogue could be inserted into the text. To heighten the affect of dialogue we included narrators' comments and queries to us that were part of the actual interview.

The use of long quotations also allowed us to convey to readers that much of what appeared to be individual memories were in fact an oral tradition of stories that narrators had shared with one another over the years as part of the process of martialing energy and developing strategies for resistance. It is only in their entirety that the power of the stories emerges. Many such stories appear throughout the book; for example, the Robin Hood tale of a narrator who was tired of being harassed for her "obvious" and unruly behavior in a more upwardly mobile bar. After being thrown out, she and a friend returned to the bar and entered through the back window. They distributed—free—all the fried chicken in the kitchen refrigerator to the other rough and tough lesbians who congregated in the backroom away from the surveillance of the bartender. By the time the management caught on to what was happening, they had gone, taking all the cream pies from the refrigerator with them. Such stories enrich the text and convey the sense of narrators as active agents in shaping lesbian consciousness and culture.

Narrators' quotes were minimally edited. For smoother reading we eliminated repetitious phrases and diversions on extraneous ideas, and in a few cases we changed grammar at narrators' requests. We never changed the order of narrators' words or integrated pieces from disparate parts of a life history into an uninterrupted statement. We are not sure that we were right to be so rigid, particularly because extensive editing is a common process in other collections of individual oral histories.[31] But because we were concerned about the dialogue between narrators and ourselves and how it created an analysis of lesbian community history, we felt we had to stick fairly closely to what narrators had said and follow their lines of thinking. Besides holding us to a rigorous standard, doing so also allowed readers a better check on our analysis. We are aware, however, that there is some irony in the fact that we were willing to modify faces in photographs and change details about individual lives but not to extensively edit narrators' words. In our minds, for a historical analysis of a community, changes in personal details were cosmetic. They were also done in the final revisions after our interpretation was more or less complete.

Because we were, from the beginning, trying to write a community history, even though we wanted to use long quotations, we did not intend to use names for speakers, not even pseudonyms. We liked this format because it allowed us to guarantee the anonymity we felt essential. This approach had not been challenged in our oral presentations because our interpretive reading made narrators come alive. But several readers for our publisher felt that it was contradictory to use such long quotes and not develop a persona who was speaking them. We were hesitant to make the change but think it was essential that we did. Despite our attempt to camouflage individual details of people's lives, we still think the narrators come alive by the consistency of their thinking throughout a chapter and in some cases throughout the book. To facilitate this we created an index of narrators so someone could follow a person throughout the book.

In order for the dialogue between narrators and ourselves to be effective, it was not enough just to intersperse extended quotations with our analysis. We also tried to include the development of our thought processes as we progressed with the research. What did it mean to make working-class lesbians central in our thinking? How were we blocked and in what ways did we move ahead? How were we affected by the feminist sexuality debates? This kind of self-consciousness seemed necessary in order for us to negotiate the power differences of class and race and think creatively about the past.

The use of the term *lesbian* in the text presented problems we had not anticipated. We learned as the research progressed that the term freezes human sexuality into two dichotomous fixed practices—heterosexual and lesbian—that do not reflect historical reality. Although some narrators' identities were fixed throughout their lives, others were not. The meaning of woman-to-woman relationships also differed depending on culture, and it changed even in the short period covered by the book. We did not quite know how to deal with this problem.[32] When we began what we know now, we would have struggled with the issue more. We would be much more cautious about using the word *lesbian* as the general historical term. In hindsight we think that Jonathan Katz's suggestion that researchers should only use the terms that are specific to a particular time period and cultural group is a wise beginning point—no matter how awkward—for developing a language that better reflects the fluidity and potentiality of human sexuality (1983:13–18).

From our experience it is impossible to generalize about the best methodology for doing lesbian and gay fieldwork and writing. Sherna Berger Gluck and Daphne Patai's thoughts about feminist oral history seem applicable: "No blanket prescription will help us; we need, rather, to engage in self-critical examination of our practices and to go on to develop a range of models from which to select our procedures according to the needs of specific, and often unique, research situations" (1991:222). Although the specifics of our research on the Buffalo working-class lesbian community will not work for most projects, some general principles deserve attention. Although it is impossible to generate a completely ethical fieldwork project in the hierarchical world within which we live, it is still necessary for gay and lesbian studies to take ethics seriously. As the field develops, most research will need to negotiate the hierarchies of class and race, because communities of lesbians and gay men have crossed these social divisions throughout this century. It is a mistake to assume that the similarities generated by a shared sexual orientation can override the social hierarchies of the contemporary world. Attention to guidelines for not exploiting and objectifying subjects of research is essential in this situation.

Furthermore, we need research that is for and about lesbians and gay men, and by definition such a construct includes an ethical commitment. It not only promises original thinking but also implies a consciousness of purpose and audience and an interest in building a political movement. In the long run, ethical research has a better chance of empowering lesbians and gays to work in a movement to effect change.

One of the most successful aspects of our research was the way we encouraged feedback from narrators and involved them in the interpretive process. Although I would argue that all research endeavors could use more feedback from the subjects of research, our model might not work in all research settings. It is possible that a great deal of dialogue might not be required in studies of upper-class lesbians and gay men, some of whom might have had a hand in setting the culture's social values, in order to clear space for their views. Studies with communities decimated by AIDS might not afford opportunities for full feedback. In addition, it is my guess that our system worked well because working-class lesbians were conscious of themselves as agents in history. They had a story to tell and were concerned that it be accurate. That would not happen in all situations. The specific method of accomplishing dialogue between the inquirer and the subject of research is not as important as consciously developing a plan for how this will occur in the interviews, in matters of interpretation, and in how to convey the interaction in the final report.

Vigilant self-consciousness about the researcher/author's social position and that of the narrators is key for gay and lesbian studies. It helps in establishing a sound context for the research, in identifying narrators who represent the breadth of the gay and lesbian community, and in addressing issues of anonymity that are often central to gay lives. In addition, it is necessary for a sound interpretation as well as for ethics. It both helps in revealing the limits of an analysis and in evaluating the meaning and importance of the work. Placing oneself in the analysis, knowing one's location, moves the research/author toward understanding the larger forces at work in society, how they influenced gays and lesbians, and how gays and lesbians, in turn, have shaped their own history.

Notes

This chapter covers some of the same material as the introduction to *Boots of Leather, Slippers of Gold*. It is written as a supplement to that chapter, with an audience of anthropologists in mind. I am grateful to my writing group—Claire Kahane, Carolyn Korsmeyer, Isabel Marcus, and Carol Zemel—for feedback on earlier drafts.

1   Before the 1970s, butch-fem roles were unmistakable in all working-class lesbian communities; the butch projected the masculine image of her particular time period—at least regarding dress and mannerisms—and the fem, the feminine image. Almost all members were exclusively one or the other.
2   Two studies of the contemporary lesbian community were published shortly after we began work: Wolf (1979) and Krieger (1983). Newton's historical study of Fire Island and Chauncey's study of gay male communities in New York City during the twentieth century were published shortly after we finished.
3   I am indebted to my colleague Ellen DuBois for bringing to consciousness how much our work was shaped by the anthropological tradition.
4   Although the concerns of feminist scholars and interpretive anthropologists

are parallel and might mutually benefit one another, they have had very little interaction. This lack of dialogue has been noted by several scholars; see, for example, Mascia-Lees, Sharpe, and Cohen (1989) and Strathern (1987). The division is also noted in Stacey (1991). For a helpful overview of interpretive anthropology see Marcus and Fischer (1986). For an early discussion of feminist method see Bowles and Klein (1983). Helpful contemporary statements include Harding (1987) and Gluck and Patai (1991).

5 Mascia-Lees, Sharpe, and Cohen (1989) comment cogently on the lack of a political perspective in postmodernist anthropology.

6 Having practiced ethnography, unlike Judith Stacey, I did not have illusions about its feminist potential (Stacey 1991:114–15).

7 For a discussion of this dilemma, see Harding (1986).

8 See, for example, Rich (1986) and Haraway (1988).

9 In terms of historical writing see, for example, Rich (1989) and Faderman (1981).

10 See, for example, Nestle (1987).

11 For a helpful discussion of this debate, see Phelan (1989).

12 The actual division is 30 percent for us and 70 percent for the Buffalo Women's Oral History Project. We established these figures on an intuitive basis and are not sure that they are sensible and fair. We aimed to strike some balance between self-denial and self-aggrandizement. To the best of our knowledge there is no existing literature on the topic that could guide us. The results of this allocation of money are quite exciting. In May 1993 Viking Penguin bought the paperback rights, giving us more money than we had expected. This allowed us to establish Elder Action in a Lesbian and Gay Environment (EAGLES) with the help of a generous gift from a local donor, Julia Reinstein, to develop a multidimensional program for older lesbians and gays. Beginning January 1, 1994, the organization hired a full-time director, Laura Gottfried, for one year. Twelve narrators have become active in the project, meeting once every two months to serve as consultants to the director, and four of these sit on the advisory board. EAGLES raised its own money for 1995.

13 Early feminist research tried to overcome the hierarchy and objectifying aspects of patriarchal research by conceptualizing the interview as a two-way process, with the interviewee or narrator asking as many questions as the inquirer. See, for instance, Oakley (1981).

14 We were the only people who listened to the tapes. Narrators could get a copy of their own tape but no one else's. Although they could authorize a friend or a lover to hear their own tape, that never happened. The agreement with all narrators is that at some future date these tapes will be turned over to an archive where they will be available for educational purposes.

15 Kanes (1992) pursued the leads to this upper-middle-class, woman-identified community in the 1920s and 1930s.

16 The Latin community in Buffalo was very small at this time, and there was virtually no Asian American community.

17 In retrospect, I think we did not explore issues of white ethnicity adequately.

For instance, I am puzzled by why we did not give more thought to the fact that we had no Jewish narrators, yet both of us are Jewish.

18   Although Wanda Edwards, a young black woman hired on a small grant in 1981, stayed on as an advisor to the project, she was not at that time well known in the black lesbian community and therefore was not able to help us find more black narrators.

19   The majority of the interviews were conducted by the two authors. However, some were done by a class of Davis's, and Avra Michelson and Wanda Edwards did a few while associated with the project.

20   We did this research and writing primarily during the Reagan-Bush years, which were extremely homophobic. The Supreme Court's Hardwick decision (1986) upholding Georgia's state statute criminalizing sodomy typifies the dangerous tenor of the times (*United States Reports* 1989). The Clinton administration's stand on the civil rights of gay men and lesbians in the military during its first ten days in office suggested that the climate for gay men and lesbians might be improving in the United States and we might have been too cautious. But the ideas expressed at the 1992 Republican convention and the November 1992 anti-gay propositions in Oregon and Colorado suggest the opposite. The situation of gays and lesbians in the United States is in flux, and the future is hard to predict.

21   There is some debate in the feminist literature about whether giving undivided attention to a narrator is the best way to structure an interview. At least in early feminist writings on methodology (e.g., Oakley 1981) there is the idea that reciprocal discussion and questioning make for a more egalitarian interview and lessen the possibility of turning the narrator into an object. There is some truth to that; however, it does not take into account existing power relations in society and the general fact that many people in advanced capitalism do not listen to others. Therefore, reciprocity, if not carefully controlled and thought through, can easily reproduce the power relations of society. We felt that the focus on the narrator need not turn the narrator into an object of study but could give her the respect she deserved and didn't normally receive in this society. For further discussion of this issue see Patai (1991).

22   It is my guess that the experience of interviewing middle-class lesbians of this period might be very different. Because discretion was such a central part of their lives, middle-class lesbians were unlikely to have the experience of discussing "difference" or lesbianism with anyone other than intimate friends. Furthermore, rather than developing strategies for expanding the public presence of lesbians they focused on strategies that allowed them to comfortably lead a double life. The hiding was intrinsic to being lesbian, a situation that would not encourage sharing elaborate and eloquent stories about life as a lesbian.

23   For a useful discussion of the process of interpretation see Gluck and Patai (1991:59–102). It is also considered in other essays in the book.

24   Because the ethnography is about butch-fem culture, we are perhaps most vulnerable on the imbalance of butch and fem narrators. However, we in-

terviewed enough fem narrators that the research captures some of the sub-tleties of fem life. Furthermore fems' memories didn't radically contradict those of butches'. Only in the discussion of relationships did we notice a marked difference between butch and fem perspectives. Fems tended to claim that butches were too bossy, something that butches did not say about themselves. As a result, we organized chapter 8 around this distinction. Nevertheless, we wonder how different the community history would have been had fems been the majority of the narrators. Would the themes we identify as central have been the same? We simply do not know.

25 See, for example, Nestle (1987, 1992).

26 For a feminist discussion of objectivity see Keller (1982).

27 For discussions of the concept of situated knowledge see Rich (1986) and Haraway (1988).

28 This is a phrase that I coined to capture the "rightness" of some interpre-tive frameworks. The idea of "letting the data sing" closely resembles thoughts expressed by Barbara McClintock about the research process. Good research is more than a rational process. It requires a total immer-sion in the data, which generates a "feeling for the organism," from which comes analytical and theoretical insight (Keller 1983:197–207).

29 For an interesting discussion of this balancing act see Smith (1990:213–45).

30 Lillian Robinson was an important influence in convincing our publisher that the quotes should not be edited drastically and in giving us confidence in our intuition about their importance.

31 See, for instance, Frisch (1990: 81–146).

32 This problem of naming seems to be behind the revival of the term *queer* in the 1990s, as in queer nation and queer theory. Although the term aims to be inclusive of a variety of sexual identities and experiences, its inclusive-ness does not work for historical study. "Queer" was used by society for the extremely masculine butches of the 1950s, and sometimes they adopted this language for themselves. It was not applied to or used by fems of the 1950s or by butches and fems of the 1940s. To designate such people by the term would distort their history.

References Cited

Bowles, Gloria, and Renate Duelli Klein. 1983. *Theories of Women's Studies.* Berkeley: University of California Press.

Chauncey, George. 1994. *Gay New York: Gender, Urban Culture and the Mak-ing of the Gay Male World, 1890–1970.* New York: Basic Books.

Echols, Alice. 1989. *Daring to Be Bad: Radical Feminism in America, 1967–75.* Minneapolis: University of Minnesota Press.

Faderman, Lillian. 1981. *Surpassing the Love of Men.* New York: William Morrow.

Frisch, Michael. 1990. "Preparing Interview Transcripts for Documentary Pub-lication: A Line-by-Line Illustration of the Editing Process." In *A Shared Authority: Essays on the Craft and Meaning of Oral and Public History,* ed. Michael Frisch, 81–146. Albany: State University of New York Press.

Gluck, Sherna Berger, and Daphne Patai, eds. 1991. *Women's Words: The Feminist Practice of Oral History.* New York: Routledge.

Haraway, Donna. 1988. "Situated Knowledges: The Science Question in Feminism as a Site of Discourse on the Privilege of Partial Perspective." *Feminist Studies* 14 (Fall): 575–99.

Harding, Sandra. 1986. "The Instability of the Analytical Categories of Feminist Theory." *Signs* 11 (Summer): 645–64.

———. 1987. "Introduction: Is There a Feminist Method?" In *Feminism and Methodology,* ed. Sandra Harding, 6–10. Bloomington: Indiana Open University Press.

Kanes, Candace. 1992. "Swornest Chums: Buffalo Women in Business and the Arts, 1900–1935." Master's thesis, State University of New York at Buffalo.

Katz, Jonathan Ned. 1983. *Gay/Lesbian Almanac: A New Documentary.* New York: Harper and Row.

Keller, Evelyn Fox. 1982. "Feminism and Science." *Signs* 7 (Spring): 589–602.

———. 1983. *A Feeling for the Organism: The Life and Work of Barbara McClintock.* San Francisco: W. H. Freeman.

Kennedy, Elizabeth Lapovsky, with Madeline Davis. 1993. *Boots of Leather, Slippers of Gold: The History of a Lesbian Community.* New York: Routledge.

Krieger, Susan. 1983. *The Mirror Dance: Identity in a Women's Community.* Philadelphia: Temple University Press.

Marcus, George E., and Michael M. J. Fischer. 1986. *Anthropology as Cultural Critique: An Experimental Moment in the Human Sciences.* Chicago: University of Chicago Press.

Mascia-Lees, Frances E., Patricia Sharpe, and Colleen Ballerino Cohen. 1989. "The Postmodernist Turn in Anthropology: Cautions from a Feminist Perspective." *Signs* 15 (Autumn): 7–33.

Nestle, Joan. 1987. *A Restricted Country.* Ithaca: Firebrand Books.

———, ed. 1992. *The Persistent Desire: A Femme-Butch Reader.* Boston: Alyson Press.

Newton, Esther. 1993. *Cherry Grove, Fire Island: Sixty Years in America's First Gay and Lesbian Town.* Boston: Beacon Press.

Oakley, Ann. 1981. "Interviewing Women: A Contradiction in Terms." In *Doing Feminist Research,* ed. Helen Roberts, 30–61. London: Routledge and Kegan Paul.

Patai, Daphne. 1991. "U.S. Academics and Third World Women: Is Ethical Research Possible?" In *Women's Words: The Feminist Practice of Oral History,* ed. Sherna Berger Gluck and Daphne Patai, 142–45. New York: Routledge.

Phelan, Shane. 1989. *Identity Politics: Lesbian Feminism and the Limits of Community.* Philadelphia: Temple University Press.

Rich, Adrienne. 1986. "Notes Towards a Politics of Location." In *Blood, Bread and Poetry: Selected Prose, 1979–1985,* 210–31. New York: W. W. Norton.

———. 1989. "Compulsory Heterosexuality and Lesbian Existence." *Signs* 5:631–60.

Smith, Barbara. 1990. "The Truth That Never Hurts: Black Lesbians in Fiction in the 1980s." In *Wild Women in the Whirlwind: Afra-American Culture and the Contemporary Literary Renaissance,* ed. Joanne M. Braxton and Andree Nicola McLaughlin, 213–45. New Brunswick: Rutgers University Press.

Stacey, Judith. 1991. "Can There Be a Feminist Ethnography?" In *Women's Words: The Feminist Practice of Oral History,* ed. Sherna Berger Gluck and Daphne Patai, 111–19. New York: Routledge.

Strathern, Marilyn. 1987. "An Awkward Relationship: The Case of Feminism and Anthropology." *Signs* 12 (Winter): 276–92.

United States Reports. 1985. [U.S. Supreme Court October term.] 478:186–220. Washington, D.C.: Government Printing Office.

Wolf, Deborah Goleman. 1979. *The Lesbian Community.* Berkeley: University of California Press.

10. Writing Queer Cultures: An Impossible Possibility?
Will Roscoe

Kath Weston's landmark ethnography on lesbians, gay men, and families begins with a poignant yet enigmatic dedication: "In memory of Julie Cordell / 1960–1983 / who came looking for community" (1991b). Of course, dedications are often cryptic, referring to relationships and experiences that the author considers important yet has chosen to segregate from the larger work. Indeed, their very placement, as part of the miscellany that publishers refer to as frontmatter, marks them as marginal, interesting but incidental. But what appears marginal often stands for something that cannot be represented in any other way—yet cannot be left out either. Dedications have stories behind them, and the dedication of *Families We Choose* is no exception.

I might never have known the story of Julie Cordell, however, except for my good fortune in hearing Weston relate it on a panel at the 1991 OutWrite Conference (Weston 1991a). It was a dramatic and tragic story of a young woman who desperately needed a family to replace the one that had rejected her for being a lesbian. But in the fast-lane life-style of the lesbian and gay world of the early 1980s real support proved elusive, and, in the end, Julie committed suicide. As Weston explained, Julie's memory became central to the intellectual, political, and ethical gestalt of her research project because she represented a case where nontraditional families, which *Families We Choose* otherwise argues are viable alternatives to traditional families, failed. Weston described with refreshing honesty how the self-reflections that this triggered resulted, on the one hand, in a more critical attitude toward her own research and, on the other, a renewed commitment to tell the story of lesbian and gay families-of-choice in the hope that young lesbians in the future will not have to do without them.

While listening to Weston's moving account, the thought suddenly occurred to me: How many lesbian and gay anthropologists could read from the margins of their publications—from the dedications and acknowledgments and notes—whole narratives of lesbian and gay lives based on research experiences that they otherwise cannot or dare not write about? Reflecting on my conversations with other lesbian and gay anthropologists over the years, I am struck by how many them have had similarly profound experiences, related to their sexual identities, in the course of their research, experiences they rarely mention in their "official" writings.

If we accept anthropology's traditional ban on self-reference and personal reflection in ethnographic writing, then the exclusion of such experiences is unproblematic. But if these experiences, as I will argue here, are exemplary instances of the very thing that lesbian and gay studies is struggling to understand, then surely the rules of discourse that require their exclusion must be questioned. My point is not that lesbian and gay ethnography needs to be confessional or subjective, although some may choose to experiment in these ways. Rather, my argument is that the experiences self-acknowledged lesbians and gay men have while pursuing anthropological research, even when homosexuality is not their ostensible subject, provide revealing instances of what I would call gay *cultur-ing*—using the noun as a verb to refer to the negotiation and formulation of homosexual desire into cultural forms and social identities. If lesbian and gay ethnography is to advance, ethnographers must be able to draw on these experiences as valid sources of data and as integral elements of cross-cultural research. At the same time, powerful conventions and sanctions remain in place to prevent the inclusion of first-person accounts of lesbian and gay experience within academic discourse. As long as that is the case, the project of lesbian and gay ethnography will remain an impossible possibility.[1]

The umbrella term *cultural studies* covers a broad range of work being pursued by scholars employing interdisciplinary approaches to the study of culture with little regard for such traditional distinctions as "high" and "low," "fine" and "popular," and "advanced" versus "tribal." What these studies share is not so much an object of knowledge as a set of themes, one of the more common of these being a fascination with borders. Boundaries and borderlands have come to stand for the geographic, social, psychological, and discursive spaces in a multicultural world where identities and differences are mutually constituted. One finds these themes in works ranging from Anzaldúa's automythography (1987), in which the mixed-blood lesbian *mestiza* emerges as the vanguard feminist subject, to Haraway's speculations on epistemological boundaries in the age of the cyborg (1991), to Garber's exploration of boundary-transgression in her survey of transvestism and cross-dressing (1992).[2] As Anzaldúa writes, "A border is a dividing line, a narrow strip along a steep edge. A borderland is a vague and undetermined place created by the emotional residue of an unnatural boundary. It is in a constant state of transition. The prohibited and forbidden are its inhabitants" (1987:3).

Rosaldo (1989) has explored the relevance of these themes for anthropology. He argues that the traditional anthropological concept of cultures, as discrete, self-contained systems, is giving way to the recognition that even small, isolated societies encompass a diversity of beliefs, meanings, and behaviors. The negotiation of these differences, often highly contested, lies just below the surface of the institutions and customs that, for anthropologists, serve to characterize whole peoples. As Rosaldo observes, "By defining culture as a set of shared meanings classic norms of analysis make it difficult to study zones of difference within and between cultures" (1989:28). But human cultures are rarely coherent or homogeneous. "More often than we usually care to think, our everyday lives are crisscrossed by border zones, pockets, and eruptions of all kinds. . . . Such borderlands," Rosaldo concludes, "should be regarded not as analytically empty transitional zones but as sites of creative cultural production that require investigation" (1989:207–8).

Now it seems to me that lesbian and gay anthropologists know quite a bit about boundaries and border zones as well as the various ways of crossing, bridging, and transgressing them. Further, I think that viewing themselves in these terms, as specialists in crossing borders and managing ambiguity, can help lesbian and gay anthropologists identify both the obstacles and opportunities they face in developing ethnographies of sexual diversity.

To begin with, there is the border between self and other, between anthropologists and the subjects that they study. When lesbian and gay anthropologists identify strongly with their "subjects," which they are bound to do when the latter are also same-sex-oriented, this boundary is quickly blurred. The subject of lesbian and gay anthropology becomes both other *and* not-other. The result, depending on one's point of view, is either a violation of the "objectivity" that makes anthropology a "science" *or* the attainment of a dialogical relationship with the subject that is the goal of postcolonial anthropology (Tedlock 1992).

Yet another border that gay and lesbian anthropologists cross is the one between observation and participation. I'm not referring here to the participant-observer method as such, but to actual participation in making and/or changing a culture. Of course, non-interference is anthropology's official policy, but in fact anthropologists affect cultures all the time. Simply asking questions triggers changes in peoples' self-image, so that everywhere anthropologists go they leave behind forms of self-consciousness that have proven fertile ground for the growth of nationalism, tribal identity—and, in this case, sexual identity.[3]

At an even more fundamental level, anthropologists participate in shaping and making culture whenever they attempt to represent it. Culture is, in the perspective of cultural studies, in large measure representation, a system of symbols for patterning human thought, behavior, and events. If discourse constitutes its objects of knowledge, as Foucault has shown, then writing lesbian and gay culture cannot be disentangled from constructing it. Certainly this is the case where the very existence of lesbian and gay culture is politically and intellectually contested. Merely formulating a research project involving lesbian and gay cultures amounts to taking a stand in this debate.

And this points to yet another border occupied by lesbian and gay anthropology—the ever-shifting ground between the poles of constructionism and essentialism. I only mention these battle-scarred terms to state my belief that the tension of their opposition animates all modern gay texts.[4] The will to knowledge that has given rise to lesbian and gay studies, what Harry Hay, a key organizer of the early Mattachine movement, referred to in the 1950s as the "homosexual in search of historical contiguity," is grounded on the hypothesis of presence, that is, on the predication that forms of same-sex love are not absent in other times and places but rather that the record of them has been erased by the discursive imperatives of mainstream historiography.[5] To the extent that this hypothesis is implicit in the work of lesbian and gay anthropologists, they operate at the borders of essentialist and constructivist theories rather than their centers.

One more border is that which separates academic and popular audiences. Although many gay and lesbian anthropologists still struggle to convince academia of the validity of their research, a broad, community-based audience is eager to hear what they have to say and ready to buy their books. Because even academic publishers are sensitive to market demand, it is now much easier for lesbian and gay scholars to publish than it is to get a job or tenure. In any case, whether for political reasons or simply to find support, many queer anthropologists traverse another border when addressing themselves to the community as well as the academy.

Ultimately, I believe the gay affinity for borders derives from the fundamental experience of being outsiders. Gay men and lesbians are participant-observers in heterosexual culture, whether in the field or at home. They survive by being sensitive to all borders—whether social conventions or rules of discourse.[6] In short, the postmodern subject, whose identity is divided and dispersed, whose subject position is multiply determined and constituted, might very well be a lesbian or gay anthropologist writing lesbian and gay cultures.

The value of seeing themselves this way—as if they were guinea pigs in a postmodern experiment in split subjectivity—is that it focuses attention on precisely those marginal and borderline experiences that lesbian and gay anthropologists tend to leave out of their official reports. This includes all those encounters in which personal identity and, yes, sexual desires are hopelessly entangled with professional roles. These interactions trigger processes of identity formation and negotiation over sexual meanings that transform both anthropologist and subject. From the point of view of cultural studies, these are exactly the experiences that should be written about. Unfortunately, I believe a variety of constraints prevents lesbian and gay anthropologists from doing so. Two decades after Stonewall, writing lesbian and gay culture remains largely an impossible possibility.

Foremost among the constraints on queer discourse are the innumerable social conventions, proprieties, and sanctions against talking about homosexuality. We are still quite far from being able to discuss homosexuality freely, to speculate about it, and to attribute it to others without repercussions.[7] Lesbian and gay anthropologists discover the practical value of a bland, detached, objective mode of discourse when it comes to writing about homosexuality. Those who say, "By the way, I'm one of them," are quickly marked, categorized, and dismissed. All this is somewhat ironic because deconstruction shows that signification is always implicated with desire. But, of course, in the Western tradition this is always-already heterosexual desire. The naming and unleashing of homosexual desire in discourse remains socially explosive.

In short, lesbian and gay anthropologists face powerful social and professional pressures to suture their multiple subjectivity as outsider/ insiders, to downplay the ambiguities of their border crossings, to avoid above all first-person accounts of their sexuality and identity, and to adopt instead the traditional, unified voice of ethnographic authority when writing. *Being* lesbian or gay and *writing* about lesbian or gay subjects is radical enough, producing avant-garde texts would surely marginalize gay and lesbian anthropologists even further. As Paul Rabinow has observed, "Asking whether longer, dispersive, multi-authored texts would yield tenure might seem petty. But those are the dimensions of power relations to which Nietzsche exhorted us to be scrupulously attentive" (1986:253).

Perhaps I can make these risks clearer if I cite examples of authors who write lesbian and gay culture and do not hide the play of homosexual desire in their texts or their own gay will to knowledge. I have in mind Tobias Schneebaum (1970, 1988) and Judy Grahn (1984). Both writers acknowledge their desires quite openly without relinquishing claims to truth in what they report. As Grahn describes her research methods in the preface of *Another Mother Tongue*, "I read and read, filled boxes with notebooks of notes, thought and thought, wept, cried out to the phantoms of history, muttered to myself" (xiii)—not the kind of confession one usually finds in the introductions of ethnographies. Similarly, in Schneebaum the reader encounters ethnographic detail intermingled with accounts of sexual adventures with the natives. Not surprisingly, both authors have provoked sharp debates over whether their works "count" as anthropology and history or not. But I would argue that any experiment in this direction, no matter how valid the research, is going to provoke similar reactions and take the same risk of being disqualified as ethnography and consigned instead to the genre of travel writing, personal memoirs, or even erotica. Ensuring the advancement of lesbian and gay ethnography may require greater tolerance for works that occupy the borders of these genres and greater respect for the risks involved in representing homosexual desire in discourse.

And then, of course, there are the ethical and personal constraints that gay and lesbian ethnographers place on themselves because it is so often the case that they cannot write about those they encounter without the risk of exposing them. Even when individual anonymity is not an issue, members of the communities with which they work, especially heterosexuals, may try to co-opt lesbian and gay ethnographers into not discussing their culture's homosexuality. Although their reasons may be understandable, the net effect is, again, silence and erasure.

At the same time, the combined message of gay liberation and the postmodernist critique of ethnographic authority suggests that gay and lesbian anthropologists must not only discuss homosexuality, they must discuss their *own* homosexuality, or, at the very least, the personal dimension of their interactions with others relative to their sexual identities.[8] The issue is unavoidable, for the failure to project a sexual identity has just as much an impact on others as coming out does. By the same token, the ethnographies of heterosexual anthropologists, especially those by the many heterosexual couples who have been so prominent in American anthropology, require reexamination. How did the people they studied react to their performance of Western gender roles and sexuality? How might natives have adjusted their own behavior and statements based on the presence of this microcosm of Western culture in their midst?[9]

To answer questions like these we must find ways to circumvent the external and internal constraints on queer discourse. It may be that the best model for lesbian and gay anthropologists at the present time is something along the lines of biculturation—a survival strategy attributed to urban American Indians.[10] That is, gay anthropologists may have to produce one kind of work that counts for an academic career and another in which they give themselves freedom to explore the intersubjective experience of lesbian and gay anthropology. Gay media and the newsletters of lesbian and gay professional networks are examples of forums where they might be able to put at least some of their experiences of border-crossing into the record.

Certainly one of the more fascinating sidelines to the history of American anthropology is the number of its practitioners who have also been poets and writers. Often it has seemed to me that the best solution for the problems of anonymity and privacy would be to write a novel instead of an ethnography. It would not advance an academic career, but it would be a way of recording and sharing what lesbian and gay anthropologists learn about lesbian and gay cultures and lives.

As for the internal constraints on queer discourse, I think much of this is related to the fact that traditional models of anthropological inquiry just don't work when it comes to lesbian and gay studies. Coming from a community that has itself been the object of uninvited scrutiny, lesbian and gay anthropologists simply don't have the stomach to subject others of their kind to the invasive gaze of social science or to write about them in a detached or exoticizing style.

In my work, I have found alternative models of working relationships by looking to other professional identities and practices. Social workers, journalists, consultants, and therapists, for example, all form collaborative relationships and balance accountability to their clients or subjects with accountability to the standards of their profession and the institutions that employ them. (Journalists, for example, can at least be sued for what they write; only recently have I heard of a tribe suing an anthropologist.)

Learning to draw from a broader repertoire of professional practices can also help address the resistance many native peoples have to anthropology. The Zunis, for example, have learned that as a "primitive" people they have plenty of "culture," but that only Western societies have "history." Approaching them as a historian, therefore, made an enormous difference in how I was received (Roscoe 1991:xiv–xvi).[11] Cultural preservation and anthropological research may result in a similar end-product, but there is a world of difference in how these respective endeavors are perceived—the former is a widely shared priority of ethnic groups around the world, the latter is seen as an invasive mode of inquiry practiced by Western elites upon others.[12]

One of the shortcomings of the postmodern critique of anthropology is the way that it reinforces the notion that writing up field experiences is what anthropology is all about. The fact is, there are many ways to produce artifacts out of intercultural encounters that are multivoiced, dialogic, and collaborative without resorting to the affectation of avant-gardism—especially when other media besides writing are employed. In this regard, anthropologists deserve more credit. I'm thinking of the many ethnographic films, collections of native literature and art, bicultural educational materials, oral histories, museum displays, and other projects in which anthropologists have worked with direct input from the people being represented.

I think the most useful model for our purposes, however, is that of the anthropologist as culture-bearer and of lesbian and gay anthropology as a cultural exchange.[13] On one of my visits to Zuni, for example, I brought a set of snapshots taken at the Folsom Street Fair, an outdoor event held in the neighborhood of San Francisco's leather bars. In the conversation sparked by these pictures I began to learn the basics of a Zuni sexual vocabulary. An even better example is the approach taken by a friend of mine, Will Doherty, in contacting members of the third-gender *hijra* cult in India. Doherty's interest in *hijra* is basically anthropological, but he did not travel to India with the professional identity of an anthropologist. Instead, he put together a photo album documenting the gay men's spirituality movement in the United States, in which he has participated. When he was able to meet some *hijra*, he showed them his photo album as a way of sharing from his background and inviting them to share something of theirs—a self-conscious culture-bearer offering an exchange that affirms the other rather than disempowers them.

Openly embracing the role of an ethical culture-bearer and inaugurating contact by proposing a cultural exchange establishes the grounds for collaboration. It seems to me an approach like this would avoid many of the problems that arise when subjects do not feel they have control over what will be asked and what will be revealed.

If, following Bruno Latour (1987), traditional anthropology created knowledge along the lines of an industrial mode of production—"raw materials" in the form of observations of other cultures being extracted from remote locations and brought back to Western centers for processing into ethnographies—then perhaps anthropology in the future will reflect today's postindustrial, service-sector economy. If so, then anthropology's emphasis will shift from the extraction of cultural data to the processing and transmission of this information, something that can happen at the peripheries of the world order as well as its centers. Anthropologists of the future will be specialists in cultural exchange, experts in crossing borders who produce collaborative translations of culture addressed to audiences on both sides. To the extent that anthropologists come to understand their work as simultaneously involving the construction and the transgression of borders, they will become more like lesbian, gay, bisexual, and transgendered anthropologists today. They might come to better understand what it is that their colleagues need from their discipline—the support, the resources, the freedom of expression—to be able to produce the impossible possibility of queer ethnography.

Notes

1   The Society of Lesbian and Gay Anthropologists (1992) reports that only six Ph.D.s have been granted in anthropology for dissertation research on

homosexuality, transsexualism, or alternate genders since 1980. In the same period, only two articles on these subjects appeared in the major anthropological journals, the *American Anthropologist* and *Current Anthropology.* The report observes that "lesbian and gay individuals suffer from lack of support within anthropology departments from the time they are undergraduates. . . . These problems continue throughout the careers of lesbian and gay anthropologists, limiting our choice of research and publication topics, and in some cases our hiring, promotion and tenure" (1).

2 See Pratt (1992) for a discussion of "transculturation" and "contact zone."

3 The impact of anthropologists on tribal self-consciousness among the Zuni Indians, for example, is detailed in various articles by Pandey; see especially Pandey (1972).

4 Murray (1991), for example, points out how the preoccupation of many social constructionists with demonstrating the historical contingency of homosexuality results in other essentialist categories remaining unexamined—race, class, heterosexuality, sexuality, and personality among others.

5 Throughout the period in which he was active in Mattachine (1950–53) and through the remainder of that decade Hay pursued historical and cross-culture research on homosexuality. In 1957 he titled a paper based on this research "The Homophile in Search of an Historical Context and Cultural Contiguity: An Overt Provocation to Basic Inquiry and Further Investigation" (Hay 1996). On the founding hypotheses of lesbian and gay historiography see also Boswell (1983) and Chauncey, Jr., Duberman, and Vicinus (1989).

6 Grahn (1987) makes some interesting points along these lines.

7 See, for example, the various strategies—ranging from outright avoidance to painstaking rationalization—employed by the biographers of Margaret Mead and Ruth Benedict in naming, or not naming, the desire of their subjects: Howard (1984), Modell (1983), Caffrey (1989), and Bateson (1984).

8 See, in addition to Clifford and Marcus, eds. (1986), Tedlock (1983).

9 See, for example, Tedlock's description of how Zunis reacted to her and her husband as a married couple (1992:38). The Tedlocks refrained from making noise while having intercourse in their friends' home, leading one of the girls in the family to ask Barbara Tedlock, "Do you fuck?" Several of the children had apparently decided that because they had not heard sounds of love-making the couple was celibate.

10 See, for example, Spicer (1961) and Metcalf (1981).

11 Roscoe (1988, 1991). I hesitate to overgeneralize my experience at Zuni, in that at no time in the ten years that I have been visiting the village have I had the identity of an institutionally affiliated anthropologist. Having had extensive, largely negative, experiences with anthropologists, it took a while for my Zuni friends to understand why someone who was not an academic would be interested in their history and to believe that once I had completed my research I would not disappear from their lives. Both assessments, I think, were key in their willingness to speak with me.

12   My ten-year involvement with Gay American Indians has also been based on collaborative projects, in particular the GAI History Project, which produced *Living the Spirit* (Roscoe, ed. 1988b). See also Roscoe (1987).

13   In her comments on a version of this chapter presented at the 1991 American Anthropological Association annual meeting, Jennifer Robertson noted, "Implicit in the role of culture-bearer is the notion that anthropologists who are lesbian or gay are 'naturally' more open, sensitive, virtuous, likable, and persuasive than their straight counterparts . . . as if simply being a self-identified lesbian or gay male necessarily made one a better, more reflexive anthropologist." It mystifies me how such an interpretation of my comments can be made. My intention is merely to describe what seems to be common experiences among lesbian and gay anthropologists, whether they are pursuing gay-related research or not, in managing their sexual identity in the course of performing their professional role. Heterosexual anthropologists are culture-bearers, too. Nor am I saying whether anthropologists should or should not be culture-bearers, but simply that they *are* agents of cultural exchange whether they like it or not. Becoming aware of the impact that they have on those being studied at least makes it possible to submit their actions to ethical self-scrutiny.

References Cited

Anzaldúa, Gloria. 1987. *Borderlands/ La Frontera: The New Mestiza*. San Francisco: Spinsters/Aunt Lute.

Bateson, Mary C. 1984. *With a Daughter's Eye: A Memoir of Margaret Mead and Gregory Bateson*. New York: William Morrow.

Boswell, John. 1983. "Revolutions, Universals, and Sexual Categories." *Salmagundi* 58–59 (1982–83): 89–113.

Caffrey, Margaret M. 1989. *Ruth Benedict: Stranger in This Land*. Austin: University of Texas Press.

Chauncey, George, Jr., Martin B. Duberman, and Martha Vicinus. 1989. "Introduction." In *Hidden from History: Reclaiming the Gay and Lesbian Past*, 1–13. New York: New American Library.

Clifford, James, and George E. Marcus, eds. 1986. *Writing Culture: The Poetics and Politics of Ethnography*. Berkeley: University of California Press.

Garber, Marjorie. 1992. *Vested Interests: Cross-dressing and Cultural Anxiety*. New York: Routledge.

Grahn, Judy. 1984. *Another Mother Tongue: Gay Words, Gay Worlds*. Boston: Beacon Press.

———. 1987. "Some of the Roles of Gay People in Society." In *Gay Spirit: Myth and Meaning*, ed. Mark Thompson, 1–9. New York: St. Martin's Press.

Haraway, Donna J. 1992. *Simians, Cyborgs, and Women: The Reinvention of Nature*. New York: Routledge.

Hay, Harry. 1996. *Vision Quest: Selected Writings of Harry Hay*, ed. Will Roscoe. Boston: Beacon Press.

Howard, Jane. 1984. *Margaret Mead: A Life*. New York: Simon and Schuster.

Latour, Bruno. 1987. *Science in Action*. Boston: Harvard University Press.

Metcalf, Ann. 1981. "Indians in the San Francisco Bay Area." In *Proceedings of the Third Annual Conference on Problems and Issues Concerning American Indians Today*. Chicago: Newberry Library Center for the History of the American Indian Occasional Papers 4.

Modell, Judith S. 1983. *Ruth Benedict: Patterns of a Life*. Philadelphia: University of Pennsylvania Press.

Murray, Stephen O. 1991. "Social Constructionism and Ancient Greek Homosexualities: The State of the Art." *Society of Lesbian and Gay Anthropologists Newsletter* 13(1): 21–28.

Pandey, Triloki. 1972. "Anthropologists at Zuni." *Proceedings of the American Philosophical Society* 116(4): 321–37.

Pratt, Mary Louise. 1992. *Imperial Eyes: Travel Writing and Transculturation*. London: Routledge.

Rabinow, Paul. 1986. "Representations Are Social Facts: Modernity and Postmodernity in Anthropology." In *Writing Culture: The Poetics and Politics of Ethnography*, ed. James Clifford and George E. Marcus. Berkeley: University of California Press.

Rosaldo, Renato. 1989. *Culture and Truth: The Remaking of Social Analysis*. Boston: Beacon Press.

Roscoe, Will. 1987. "Bibliography of Berdache and Alternative Gender Roles among North American Indians." *Journal of Homosexuality* 14(3–4): 81–171.

———. 1988a. "The Zuni Man-Woman: A Traditional Philosophy of Gender." *Out/Look* 1 (June 1988): 56–67.

———, ed. 1988b. *Living the Spirit: A Gay American Indian Anthology*. New York: St. Martin's Press.

———. 1991. *The Zuni Man-Woman*. Albuquerque: University of New Mexico Press.

Schneebaum, Tobias. 1970. *Keep the River on Your Right*. New York: Grove Press.

———. 1988. *Where the Spirits Dwell: An Odyssey in the New Guinea Jungle*. New York: Grove Press.

Society of Lesbian and Gay Anthropologists. 1992. "Proposal to the American Anthropological Association for the Creation of a Task Force on Discrimination against Lesbians and Gay Men in Anthropology."

Spicer, Edward. 1961. "Types of Contact and Processes of Change." In *Perspectives in American Indian Culture Change*, ed. Edward H. Spicer, 517–44. Chicago: University of Chicago Press.

Tedlock, Barbara. 1992. *The Beautiful and the Dangerous: Encounters with the Zuni Indians*. New York: Viking.

Tedlock, Dennis. 1983. *The Spoken Word and the Work of Interpretation*. Philadelphia: University of Pennsylvania Press.

Weston, Kath. 1991a. "Requiem for a Street Fighter." Paper presented at Out/Write: National Gay and Lesbian Writers Conference, San Francisco.

———. 1991b. *Families We Choose: Lesbians, Gays, Kinship*. New York: Columbia University Press.

11. My Best Informant's Dress: The Erotic Equation in Fieldwork
Esther Newton

Malinowski's "Sex-Sickness"

Aren't there any anthropologist jokes?" asked a doctor friend of my mother's who had just entertained a table of lunch buddies at their retirement community with a series of doctor gags. To my mother's disappointment, I couldn't think of even one. I do have a poor memory for jokes, but a quick survey of my peers revealed that we are not given to either wit or thigh-slapping when it comes to the practice of our trade. The only anthropologist to deliver was my friend and former mentor David Schneider, who came up with this one: "A postmodern anthropologist and his informant are talking; finally the informant says, 'Okay, enough about you, now let's talk about me.'"[1]

Retelling this joke I realized one reason that it struck me as funny was its similarity to a recent television advertisement. A young man and woman, postmodern looking in their tight black clothes and spiked hair, are chatting at a party, and she says to him, "Okay, now let's talk about you; what do you think of my dress?"

Not only did Schneider's joke suggest a certain absurdity in the so-called reflexivity discourse, but its kinship with the suggestive commercial also inspired me to wonder why the postmodern scrutiny of the relation between informant, researcher, and text is limited to who is talking or even what is said. What else is going on between fieldworker and informant? Is "the romance of anthropology" only a manner of speaking?

In their germinal article contrasting postmodernism and feminism in anthropology, Mascia-Lees, Sharpe, and Cohen see "a romantic yearning to know the 'other'" behind the reflexive "turn" (1989: 25–26). But rather than leading on to the obvious erotic possibilities, they circle back within the metaphor: "Traditionally, this romantic component has been linked to the heroic quests, by the single anthropologist, for 'his soul' through confrontation with the exotic 'other' . . . in turning inward, making himself, his motives, and his experience the thing to be confronted, the postmodernist anthropologist locates the 'other' in himself."

Following Mascia-Lees, Sharpe, and Cohen's suggestion to be "suspicious of relationships with 'others' that do not include a close and honest scrutiny of the motivations for research" (1989:33), I am going to ask an embarrassing question. Is all this romance totally sublimated in fieldnotes and language learning only to emerge in texts as a metaphor for the "heroic quest by the single anthropologist," or does the erotic ever make a human gesture? If so, what might be the significance of the erotic equation in fieldwork and its representation or lack thereof in ethnographic texts?

Rarely is the erotic subjectivity or experience of the anthropologist discussed in public venues or written about for publication. If this omission is not due to any plot or conspiracy, neither is it incidental. In the dominant schematic that has set the terms of discourse the distanced neutral observer presented in traditional anthropological texts is at the opposite pole from the sexually aroused (repelled? ambivalent?) fieldworker. By not "problematizing" (dreadful word but none other works as well here) *his* own sexuality in his texts, the anthropologist makes *male* gender and *heterosexuality* the cultural givens, the unmarked categories. If straight men choose not to explore how their sexuality and gender may affect their perspective, privilege, and power in the field, women and gays, less credible by definition, are suspended between our urgent sense of difference and our justifiable fear of revealing it.

In graduate school during the early 1960s I learned—because it was never mentioned—that erotic interest between fieldworker and informant didn't exist, would be inappropriate, or couldn't be mentioned; I had no idea which. The anthropologist was pictured as a man who would ideally bring his wife to the field as company and helper. That she would absorb his sexual interests was, I suppose, understood. I knew that Margaret Mead and Ruth Benedict had done fieldwork, of course, but the former seemed to always be married to another anthropologist and the latter—whose "private" life was opaque—to have spent little time there.[2]

If single male fieldworkers were thought by our male professors to engage in, or even refrain from engaging in, sexual activities, these were
never discussed in front of me. This being the case, how could the sexuality of female fieldworkers ever emerge as an issue?

The black hole enveloping this non-subject in most anthropological
writing invites one of two conclusions. Either desire is to be firmly
squelched—even though many anthropologists are (or were) young, un-
attached, and living in lonely, isolated situations for months at a time—or
it should be satisfied away from the glare of the published account, cor-
doned off from legitimate ethnography. A comprehensive guide to conducting fieldwork (Ellen, ed. 1984) has no index heading under "sexuality." From Casagrande's groundbreaking collection *In the Company of Man*
(1960) to *In the Field* (Smith and Kornblum, eds. 1989), when a fieldworker writes in the first person, she or he thinks and sometimes feels
but never actually lusts or loves. Most guides ward off desire with vague
warnings against getting "too involved," hardly daring to admit that fieldworkers and informants do and must get involved emotionally.[3]

Between the lines lurk certain shadowy givens. The straight male
anthropologist's "best informants" are likely to be, or at least to be represented as, male, presumably minimizing the danger of these key relationships becoming eroticized.[4] On the other hand, a veil of professional silence covers the face of indulgence toward men's casual sex with
women in the field. For instance, the fieldwork guide mentioned earlier
with no index heading for "sex" may allude to it coyly in a discussion of
why anthropologists tend to "get so much more out of their first than
out of subsequent fieldwork." Among other factors is the suggestion that
"when anthropologists first go into the field they are often single" (Ellen,
ed. 1984:98).

Most reflexive anthropology, which explicitly spotlights how ethnographic knowledge is produced, has rendered sex and emotion between
ethnographers and informants more abstract than before. The exceptions
show a pattern: Briggs (1970) and Myerhoff (1978), who do make their
subjectivity gendered and grounded, are women; of three men who come
to mind, Murphy (1987) was disabled and Rosaldo (1989) is Chicano.
So far the only white, able-bodied, and, one is led to infer, heterosexual
male who writes as if he knows this affected his fieldwork is Michael
Moffatt (1989).[5]

Generally, practitioners of "new ethnography" have used metaphors
of emotion and sexuality to express their ethnographic angst. Vincent

Crapanzano (1980:134) likens his quest for knowledge of the Moroccans to a "belief in total sexual possession" and acknowledges that "passion" and "science" "are not in fact so easily separable" without grounding this observation in flesh.[6] And despite James Clifford's (1986:13–14) observation that "excessive pleasures" and "desire" have been absent from traditional ethnography, these topics remain equally absent from the chapters in *Writing Culture* (Clifford and Marcus, eds. 1986). Why are emotion and sexuality less important or less implicated in what Clifford calls the "relations of production" of ethnography (Clifford 1986:13) than are race or colonialism? And if the absence of odor, which played a large part in travel writing (Clifford 1986:11), leaves ethnography at best stale and at worst deodorized, what does the absence of an erotic dimension do?

Historian John Boswell (1992) has advocated the contemplation of social margins both for their own beauty—he invoked the medieval manuscript page—and to advance our knowledge of the text. In anthropology, only the margins—marginal texts, the margins of more legitimate texts, or the work of socially marginal members of the profession—can tell us why we signify or squelch the erotics of fieldwork. By looking at who has written about sexuality in the field and how they have written about it, I will ask why the erotic dimension is absent from the anthropological canon and, after offering an example from my fieldwork, I will argue for its future inclusion.

As far as I know, only two white heterosexual men belonging to what Geertz (1988:73–101) termed the "I-Witnessing" literary genre of ethnography have problematized themselves as "positioned [sexual] subjects" by writing about sexual encounters with women in the field.[7] The revered ethnographer Bronislaw Malinowski was one of the few anthropologists to write about the sexuality of a non-Western people (1955), and in his private diary, in Polish (1967), he detailed his *own* sexual subjectivity, a persistent and painful struggle against "lewd" and "impure" fantasies about Trobriand and missionary women, whom he "pawed" and perhaps more (the *Diary* was censored by Malinowski's widow before publication).

Not only was an exemplary "competent and experienced ethnographer" (Geertz 1988:79) caught with his pants down, so to speak, but if anthropology's historic political agenda has been "to secure a recognition that the non-Western is as crucial an element of the human as the

Western" (Mascia-Lees, Sharpe, and Cohen 1989:8), why was Malinowski thinking of Trobrianders, including objects of his ambivalent lust, as "niggers"?

The anthropological honchos who reviewed the *Diary* defended, dismissed, or gloated over it within a common and familiar frame of reference: "These diaries do not add in any significant way to our knowledge of Malinowski as a social scientist. They do, however, tell us a good deal about Malinowski as a person" (Gorer 1967:311).[8] Malinowski's sexuality, his physical health, his bigotry toward the Trobrianders, and his insecurity as a fieldworker were private matters subsumed in the concept "person," which had—or should have had—nothing to do with Malinowski the public social scientist. Underlying all the reviews is the belief that human beings can be sorted into "lower" and "higher" parts corresponding to self-consciousness and consciousness, emotions and intellect, body and soul. Of course Malinowski shared these same assumptions. Geertz (1967) noticed a resemblance between the *Diary* and a "Puritan tract," and Geoffrey Gorer (1967:311) compared Malinowski to "the desert Fathers, [who are] tempted by devils" and likened the *Diary* to "spiritual confessions, with the same person being both the penitent and the priest." The hostile and dismissive reaction of the reviewers suggests even less tolerance in scientific dualism for the "lower" aspects of human experience than there had been in its Christian version. Ian Hogbin (1968) fumed that the *Diary* was concerned with nothing but "trivia" and should never have been published.

At the time, only Clifford Geertz realized the profound significance of the *Diary* for the anthropological enterprise.[9] The gap between Malinowski the "person" and Malinowski the "social scientist" revealed by the *Diary* was indeed "shattering" to the "self-congratulatory" image of anthropology (1967:12). But for Geertz, Malinowski was all the more admirable because "through a mysterious transformation wrought by science" (13) he had heroically transcended his bad attitude and lack of empathy toward the Trobrianders to become a "great ethnographer."

Twenty years later Geertz looked backward and saw in the publication of this "backstage masterpiece" the first signs of the profound disquiet revealed in "new ethnography" and "the breakdown of epistemological (and moral) confidence" (1988:75, 22) in postmodern anthropology. While Malinowski had turned his cultural pockets inside out in a diary he could bring himself neither to publish nor destroy, the postmodernists have made I-Witnessing central to their legitimate texts.

But the unpleasantly corporeal body in Malinowski's diary has become, in deconstructionist thought, a more comfortable "metaphor of the body" (Bordo 1990). Admitting that there is no objective location outside the body from which to transcend culture, postmodernists in and out of anthropology have conceived the body as a "trickster" of "*indeterminate sex and changeable gender*" (Smith-Rosenberg 1985:291, emphasis added) whose "unity has been shattered by the choreography of multiplicity. . . . Deconstructionist readings that enact this protean fantasy are continually 'slip-slidin' away'; through paradox, inversion, self-subversion, facile and intricate textual dance, they. . . *refuse to assume a shape for which they must take responsibility*" (Bordo 1990: 144, emphasis added).

Postmodern anthropologists are taking upon themselves one part of the white man's burden—the power to name the "other"—but they still do not want to shoulder the responsibility for their erotic and social power in the field, possibly, as Mascia-Lees, Sharpe, and Cohen (1989) have argued, because they are not enthusiastic about the insights of feminism. Paul Rabinow, who has explicitly rejected a feminist perspective (Mascia-Lees, Sharpe, and Cohen 1989:18) published—although not in his principal ethnography—an account of his one-night stand with a Moroccan woman thoughtfully provided by a male informant (1977:63–69). Most of Rabinow's description is disingenuously off-handed and is made to seem—despite the unexplored admission that this was "the best single day I was to spend in Morocco"—primarily about validating his manhood to male Moroccans while fending off "haunting super-ego images of my anthropologist persona" (1977:63–69).

Several women anthropologists have told me they read Rabinow's account as a boasting admission about what is really standard operating procedure for male fieldworkers. Very likely one of the models for the "haunting super-ego images" that interfered with Rabinow's pleasure was that of his mentor, Clifford Geertz. In his brilliant analysis of postmodern texts by (male) anthropologists Geertz specifically interprets the episode as part of Rabinow's literary strategy to show himself as a "pal, comrade, companion" type of fieldworker.[10] Just in case we might hope that Geertz's thinking had evolved beyond Malinowski's in the sexual department, he dismisses the woman involved as a "wanton" (1988:93).

Progressives who want to transform the cruel, oppressive Judeo-Christian sexual system and the correlated "objectivist" power grid that both entraps and privileges white heterosexual men should not condemn

Malinowski or Rabinow for writing explicitly about the sexual subjectivity they struggled against or indulged, because coercive silence regarding the unwritten rules of the sex and gender system makes changing them impossible. As the issues crystallize out of our history, anthropologists must begin to acknowledge eroticism, our own and that of others, if we are to reflect on its meaning for our work and perhaps help alter our cultural system for the better.

Changing the gender and/or sexual orientation and probably the race of either fieldworker or informant modifies the terms of the erotic equation.[11] The sexuality of heterosexual men—however much a puzzle or pain on a personal level—is the cultural "ego," the assumed subjectivity, and it is predictable that women and gays, for whom matters of sexuality and gender can never be unproblematic, have begun to address these issues for the discipline as a whole.[12]

Quite a few women anthropologists of undisclosed sexual orientation have written about *not* having sex with men where apparently even being seen as (hetero)sexual meant losing all credibility, risking personal danger and the catastrophic failure of their fieldwork projects. As Peggy Golde put it, women anthropologists have felt compelled to "surround [themselves] with symbolic 'chaperones'" (1970:7). Working in South America, Mary Ellen Conaway restricted her freedom of movement and wore "odd-looking, loose-fitting clothing, no makeup, and flat-soled shoes" to prevent local men from getting any wrong ideas (1986:59, 60). Maureen Giovannini warded off Sicilian men by "dressing conservatively and carrying a large notebook whenever I left the house" (1986:110).

"Manda Cesara" [Karla O. Poewe] (1982) is the only woman I know about who has written for publication, although under a pseudonym and not in an ethnographic text, about having sex with male informants. Unlike the male anthropologists, she neither retreated into abstraction nor narrated her erotic experience as a casual notch on the bedpost: "To lay hold of a culture through one's love of one individual may be an illusion, but there can be no doubt that love became a fundamental relation of my thoughts and perceptions to both, the world of the Lenda and myself" (59); "Douglas opened for me the gate to Lenda. I don't mean that he introduced me to his friends. I mean that he opened my heart and mind" (61).

The male Africans' so-called natural attitude toward heterosexual intercourse and extramarital affairs buttressed Cesara's doubts about the

Judeo-Christian system. And in the midst of a long reflection beginning with "sexuality is a cultural system" (146) but veering off into a discussion of what is wrong with Western culture as measured by the prevalence of male homosexuality, she adds, "The Lenda, thank heaven, and I am speaking selfishly, are beautifully heterosexual" (147). While Cesara's homophobia upset me enough to write her an open letter (Newton 1984)—straights are still holding gays accountable for the decline of the Roman Empire—I do hope to read more bold papers and books like hers in which the erotic dimension of power and knowledge is acknowledged openly.

For years the pages of *SOLGAN*, formerly the *ARGOH Newsletter*, the quarterly publication of the Society of Lesbian and Gay Anthropologists, has been enlivened by accounts of (mostly) male homosexuality in far-flung parts of the world. Many of these brief accounts include a note on the fieldworker's sexual orientation, and a few have implied participation.[13] Walter Williams, in *The Spirit and the Flesh* (1986), was clear that his being gay gave him access to Plains Indian "berdaches" (105) and suggests that intimate relations enabled his knowledge (see especially 93).[14]

The anthropologist who has most lyrically expressed eroticism toward the "other" is Kenneth Read in his work on the Gahuku-Gama of New Guinea.[15] In *Return to the High Valley* (1986), Read, in hot pursuit of honesty about fieldwork and that illusive emotional dimension to ethnographic texts, scales the barbed wire fence between emotion and ethnography: "I have the greatest affection for . . . [the Gahuku-Gama]," he writes, adding, "I have never known why this admission generates suspicion" (ix, x). That this attraction is or borders on homoerotic desire is signaled in code words that are understood by both gay and straight: "Lest anyone begin to feel uneasy at the possibility of being exposed to embarrassment, I assure the more sensitive members of my profession that I will not *flaunt this personal ingredient like a banner*" (x, emphasis added).[16]

Yet such is the intensity of Read's attachment, and so insistent, that he winds up doing a kind of literary striptease, first putting out disclaimers to alert the "more sensitive members of my profession" (x), then revealing what had just been hidden. Read's "best informant," and the man who "may be said to have invited me there," was Makis, "an influential man in the tribe" (11). Although Read reassures his readers that "propriety restrains me from revealing the full depth of my affective bond to him" (12), he throws propriety to the winds, it seems to me, in his subsequent description of remembering, thirty years after the fact, Makis coming into his (Read's) room, "emerging with a marvelous physical solidity into the circle of light cast by my lamp, all the planes of his chest, his face, his abdomen and thighs chiseled from black and shining marble, his lips lifted upward with the natural pride of an aristocracy owing nothing to the accidents of birth, and his eyes holding mine with the implications of at least a partial understanding neither of us could express in words" (75).[17]

Following in Read's footsteps (but with banners flying) I offer an account—perhaps the first to describe a relationship between a lesbian anthropologist and her female "best informant"—of the emotional and erotic equation in my recent fieldwork.[18]

Kay

My fieldwork experience has been fraught with sexual dangers and attractions that were much more like leitmotifs than light distractions. To begin with, the fact that I am a gay woman has disposed *me*—the great majority of gay anthropologists work with heterosexuals and avoid sexual topics—toward working with other gay people (a correspondence that heterosexuals observe more often than gays do, albeit with the unexamined privilege of the powerful).[19] I was not looking for sexual adventure in the field. Cultural, political, and psychological factors more than eroticism have determined my affinity for gays as research subjects—for one thing, I have worked more with gay men than women. Looking back, I used my first fieldwork among gay people, mostly male, to consolidate a fragile and imperiled gay identity. Prospective dissertation projects in East Africa and Fiji—again I stress I am not speaking *for* gay fieldworkers but *as* one—presented unknown dangers that scared me off. Most closeted gay people—as I then was—manage information and stress in America by retreating to private or secret "gay zones" where, alone and with other gays, we can "be ourselves." No African or Fijian village would offer such refuge, I figured, and what if they found me out? Bringing my then-lover to an exotic field locale was never imaginable, and the prospect of living for months without physical and emotional intimacy was too bleak.[20]

So by the "erotic dimension," I mean, first, that my gay informants and I shared a very important background assumption that our social arrangements reflected—that women are attracted to women and men

Kay at a Grove costume party in the 1950s. (Collection of Esther Newton)

to men. Second, the very fact that I have worked with other gays means that some of the people who were objects of my research were also potential sexual partners. Partly because of this, my key informants and sponsors have usually been more to me than an expedient way of getting information and something different than "just" friends. Information has always flowed to me in a medium of emotion, ranging from passionate—although never consummated—erotic attachment through profound affection to lively interest, that empowers me in my projects, and, when it is reciprocated, helps motivate informants to put up with my questions and intrusions.

I had thought of writing an ethnohistory of the gay and lesbian community of Cherry Grove several months before I met Kay, having become attached to the place—a summer resort on Fire Island about forty-five miles from New York City—during the previous summer. Career pressures and political commitment were behind the initial decision. I needed a second big field experience and book to advance professionally. From the outset I also intended to write for New York's huge gay communities in whose evolution Cherry Grove had, I suspected, played a starring role.[21]

Kay and the author on Kay's deck, 1988. (Photo by Diane Quero; collection of Esther Newton)

But not everyone who sets sail keeps afloat—or catches the wind. A great deal of the lift one needs in the field when one is becalmed or swamped came through my love for two elderly Grove women, and because of them the work was suffused with emotion and meaning. Two years after starting fieldwork I described them in my notes as "the sun and the moon of my love affair with Cherry Grove—without them there would be neither heat nor light in me to pursue and embrace my subject." Peter [Ruth] Worth became my Grove cicerone, my close friend, and my confidant; I was in love with Kay.[22]

Kay was an old-timer I should meet, Grovers said. After several weeks I matched the name with a dignified and classy-looking old woman who rode around the boardwalks in an electric cart. Like most able-bodied people, I had looked through her out of misplaced politeness and because of her advanced age. When I did introduce myself, I received more than I hoped—a warm and impulsive invitation for a drink at her cottage. That evening I wrote about my first encounter:

> Kay lives in a tiny charming white house, the deck full of potted flowers. I found her shuffling (she moves precariously by advancing each foot a few inches ahead of the other) to get me a drink of juice and complaining that her hair wasn't done—she hates that. Despite wrinkles and thinning hair, she still pulls off a look.
>
> She told me unsentimentally how infirm she was: the hearing aid, the contact lenses, the inability to read, a slipped disk she was too old to have fused, and how she hated to be one of those complaining elderly. . . . Emphysema makes her wheeze painfully with every movement. (She still smokes: "I don't inhale, dear. Please—it's my only vice, the only one I have left.")
>
> Was it because I liked her cottage which still had the diminutive charm of an earlier Cherry Grove, because I found her beautiful and her suffering poignant, or because her allusions to past vices intrigued me? Or was it because she called me "dear" that I came away enchanted?[23]

Several hours after writing my fieldnotes, too elated to sleep, I wrote to David Schneider: "The more I get into the history, the harder hold Cherry Grove has on my imagination . . . I'm embarking, and thrilled about it" (Newton 1986). And then I plunged on, far more confident and confiding than I had been as his closeted graduate student when I was doing fieldwork with female impersonators (Newton 1979) and my "best informant" was a gay man (whom I also adored).[24] "This morning I introduced myself to a woman of eighty plus whom I'd been wanting to meet, as she rolled toward me in her electric cart. Not only was she receptive, she clasped my arm in an intimate embrace and practically pulled me into her lap while we talked . . . and my heart quite turned over. Such are the perils of fieldwork."

After that I went by Kay's cottage every day, and as I talked to other community members, my fascination with her grew. I discovered her powers of seduction were legendary. As one Grove woman told me: "Kay was the first one to walk into the Waldorf and say, 'Send me a bottle and a blonde.' She's a law unto herself; don't think you can compare her to the average lesbian. She could walk into the Taj Mahal and people would think she was the owner." That triggered another reflection, only weeks after our first meeting: "Seeing Kay now, crippled and gasping for breath, I still can imagine it, remembering how her ex-lover Leslie came in and threw her arms around Kay saying, 'Oh Kay, we had some great times on this couch!' and Kay's enormous blue eyes light up to go with the smile—the expensive dentures gleaming—the gesture of a devilish flirt."

The work progressed around and through my crush on Kay. She helped me organize a group of old-timers to reminisce about the Grove, and I followed up in a burst of energy with individual interviews. And despite her often expressed fear that my book would reveal to an unsuspecting world that the Grove was a gay haven, she became ever more helpful. Six weeks later "we had an intense five minutes of smiling at each other. On my way out I gave her my number out here and said 'If there's ever a problem, don't hesitate to call me,' and she seemed very pleased, and asked if she could do anything for me. I said yes, 'Show me your pictures, tell me about the people.' She agreed."

That winter I returned to my teaching job. I spoke to Kay by telephone, and in April I picked her up at her Park Avenue apartment for a lunch date. By then our pattern of flirtation and teasing was established. "Back then Kay, did you get who you wanted?" I asked, as she was insisting on paying for our pricey meal with her American Express gold card. "Yes," she smiled, "and lots of them." She told me that she still got sexual urges but just waited for them to pass. We both flirted with the idea of making love. "Someday I'm going to surprise the hell out of you and really kiss you back," she said once gleefully.

Two summers after I met Kay the fieldwork project was cresting, and although it was tacitly settled that her physical pain and chronic illness precluded sex and we would not actually become lovers our daily visits were affectionate and full of erotic byplay. On July 11, 1988 I wrote, "I don't remember now when I used to sit *facing* Kay across the round coffee table. Probably even that first summer I began to sit next to her on the Naugahyde (so practical for the beach) orange couch, partly because she generally hears me if I speak about six inches from her right ear, and mostly just to get closer. In the last weeks my visits have taken a new pattern. I arrive, I kiss her quickly on the lips and find out what she needs from the store—then I return. Now comes the real visit."

During the "real visit," when she felt up to it, Kay repeated stories about her past life, her many lovers, her marriages, and about the major and minor characters in Cherry Grove's history. I sat enthralled as she recited verses from poems of Edna St. Vincent Millay—she had known the poet—which I guessed had been part of her seduction repertoire. And although I could never persuade her to leave her letters and papers to a university library, she did allow me to copy many valuable photographs and newspaper clippings. She also continued to help me gain access to other old-timers. When I asked Kay to tell one Grover who had resisted an interview that I was a "good guy," she answered, smiling, "Oh, I tell that to everybody." I observed later, "Millions couldn't buy this goodwill. No one's word means more than Kay's to the old-timers here, and she has given me her trust freely. I know Kay's affection has never been compelled or bought. She just likes me, and the beauty of it is I adore her even though I need her and have ulterior professional motives."

Kay never had to say "now let's talk about me" because she rarely asked me about my life. She was used to being the entertaining center of attention, even though she was acutely and painfully aware that her friends—me included—sometimes found her conversation boring because she didn't remember what she had told to whom, couldn't get out, didn't hear gossip, and was preoccupied with her physical problems. But even on days when Kay had no new story, no information or photograph to offer, I enjoyed being with her:

> What's deep about her is almost all non-verbal. It's her bodily presence, bearing—still—and that emotional force, crushing and liquid like an ocean wave . . . Kay once told me that driving out to the Grove with two other lesbians on a cloudy day she had raised her arms to the sky and intoned "Clouds Go Away, Sun Come Out"

several times. Within minutes the clouds split and the sun came out. Kay showed me how the other two women turned around and looked at her incredulously from the front seat. In another culture Kay would have been some kind of priestess.

Her stories and our mutual pleasure in each other constantly led me back to the work:

> The more I think about Kay allowing herself to be seduced in the girls' school the more her life connection to the history I am helping to construct excites me. Kay's beauty and presence would have made me crazy in her younger days, but I wonder if—because she was a party girl rather than an intellectual—I could have loved her deeply. But now, instead of *having* ideas she *embodies* ideas. Kay spans almost the entire period from "smashing" and romantic friendship to the age of AIDS. When I kiss her I am kissing 1903.

My love affair with Kay and with Cherry Grove culminated in 1988 celebrations around her eighty-fifth birthday, which also marked her fiftieth summer as a Grover. At her small birthday party I was proud that her hand on my knee proved she could still attract women. I was her escort at a Cherry Grove theater performance dedicated to "Kay, our national institution." Until the day a year later when Kay had what quickly proved to be a fatal heart attack, our loving relationship continued. To Grovers, Kay's death symbolized the end of an era; for many of us her loss was also a personal one. My fieldwork suddenly felt more finished than it had before, and I decided not to return another summer.

"All Poems Are Love Poems"

This would have been a very different chapter had I set out to "decide" whether ethical and/or strategic considerations should constrain anthropologists from having sexual relationships with informants. If we are to believe that only those who publicly confess to it are tempted, then, Manda Cesara aside, women fieldworkers' vulnerability as women rules out (hetero) sex. In print, and probably much more so in life, the men feel freer. Malinowski struggled to keep *himself* pure, and Rabinow saw no ethical difficulty in his sexual behavior in the field. Yet it is hard to see why, if our power as anthropologists to name the subordinated "other" poses an ethical problem, the power to screw them doesn't. Most of our English sexual vocabulary implies domination to begin with. I doubt that a way out of this problem will be found so long as it is posed in these terms. But if "the burden of authorship cannot be evaded," as Geertz suggests (1988:140), then neither can the burden of being, and being seen as, an erotic creature.

In my case, there was no higher status to take advantage of to buy or attract sexual partners. Almost all my informants were, like me, American, white, and at least middle class. Although some Grovers were apprehensive about what I might write, few were impressed by my being a scholar, and many Grove men considered themselves my superior because of my gender. Far from my being above Kay, in Cherry Grove's lexicon she was a wealthy homeowner and longtime community icon whereas I was a passing blip, a newcomer and lowly renter. Unquestionably, her regard enhanced my status far more than the reverse. Because our loving relationship never became defined as an affair, my strategic anxieties about possible complications from becoming sexually involved with a beloved member of a small face-to-face community were never put to the test. Those fears did advise caution (as did the fact that we both had somewhat absent longtime companions—that is another story) but for Kay, too, the fact of sexual attraction was more compelling than "having sex" and much safer than "having an affair."

As a child who was more comfortable with adults than with other kids, I've often been attracted to older people as friends, advisors, and, in adulthood, as lovers, so it's predictable that the work of writing gay history seduced me and kept me enchanted through Kay, who had lived and created it. If Kay had not existed, I might have had to invent her. For me, intellectual and creative work, including fieldwork and the writing of ethnography, has always been inspired by and addressed to an interior audience of loved ones like informants and mentors. The most intense attractions have generated the most creative energy, as if the work were a form of courting and seduction.

What Kay got was an admirer forty years younger who could run errands, set up appointments, move garden furniture, bring friends by, flirt, and who genuinely wanted to know and hear who her friends had been and what their common experience had meant to her. Kay had other devoted friends who helped with some of the problems old age brings. Perhaps my unique gift was erotic admiration, which must have brought her vital powers back into focus amid the dissolution caused by failing mental and physical strength. Eroticism energized the project—which caught Kay's imagination—of giving her old age shape and meaning by recording the journey of her generation in Cherry Grove and seeing it as connected to my own life.[25]

This manner of working poses the danger of "uncritically adopting Kay's point of view," as one of the *Cultural Anthropology* readers and two colleagues who had read drafts of *Cherry Grove, Fire Island* (1993), my ethnohistory of the Grove, have warned. But until we are more honest about how we feel about informants we can't try to compensate for, incorporate, or acknowledge desire and repulsion into our analysis of subjects or in our discourse about text construction. We are also refusing to reproduce one of the mightiest vocabularies in the human language.

Philosophy, psychology, and literature have reflected on how creativity may be powered and shaped by Eros—I invoke both the glorious and the terrible powers of the winged god, not the debased sweetness of the cuddly Cupid—even if anthropology has not. "The lover is turned to the great sea of beauty," Diotima tells Socrates in that touchstone of Western meditation on Eros, the *Symposium* (Plato 1989:58), "and, gazing upon this, he gives birth to many gloriously beautiful ideas and theories, in unstinting love of wisdom." Freud's theory of sublimation reinterprets Plato's encomium of Eros, albeit darkened by Judeo-Christian pessimism. And in a novel by May Sarton the lesbian protagonist declares, "When I said that all poems are love poems, I meant that the motor power, the electric current is love of one kind or another. The subject may be something quite impersonal—a bird on a window sill, a cloud in the sky, a tree" (1965:125).

The subject might also be a culture, a people, or a symbolic system. Of course, ethnographic texts are not poems, and neither are they diaries. Whatever motivates them, their purpose should be "enabling conversation over societal lines—of ethnicity, religion, class, gender, language, race—that have grown progressively more nuanced" (Geertz 1988:147). The erotic dimension intersects with those lines. To follow Malinowski's lead by including the sexuality of "our" people among the topics worthy of publication, anthropologists will have to surpass him and describe not just in Polish but also in English—in I-Witnessing or any other authorial style of "being there"—where we anthropologists, as encultured individuals like all other humans, are coming from.[26] In the age of Anita Hill and AIDS, can we do less?

Notes

An earlier version of this chapter was read at the "Lesbian/Gay Identity" session at the annual meeting of the American Anthropological Association, Sunday, December 1, 1990, New Orleans. It is reproduced by permission of the American Anthropological Association from *Cultural Anthropology* 8 (February 1993): 3–23. Without the support of my colleagues in SOLGA (Society of Lesbian and Gay Anthropologists) who loved the earlier draft, I wouldn't have had the nerve to try for publication. I also thank Julie Abraham, two anonymous readers for *Cultural Anthropology,* Amber Hollibaugh, Morris Kaplan, Ellen Lewin, Sherry Ortner, Jane Rosett, David M. Schneider, Kath Weston, and Peter Worth, all of whom read drafts of this essay and made helpful suggestions. "Sex sickness" is Marvin Harris's (1967:72) term from his review of Malinowski's *A Diary in the Strict Sense of the Term* (1967).

1   One of my informants, Peter Worth, was shocked by reading here the word *informant* in reference to herself and her friends. I explained that in all my published work on Cherry Grove I intended to use the word *narrator* for those whom I had interviewed, but in this essay, I was addressing an anthropological audience for whom the historical importance of the word *informant* recommended its use.

David Schneider said he had heard the postmodern anthropologist joke from Marshall Sahlins. Later Kath Weston pointed out that Judy Stacey (1990:272) had quoted a slightly different version, attributing it to Sahlins (1991).

2   I think it was only in the later 1960s that I heard rumors that Mead lived with another woman who was thought to be her lover. Partly I doubted it because she had been so publicly and often married, and partly the news had less impact because being more confidently lesbian I needed role models less. Much more important to my survival—I mean that quite literally—from high school on was the forceful advocacy for human variation, gender and otherwise, in both Mead and Benedict's work.

In the acceptance speech upon receiving the Margaret Mead Award at the 1991 annual meetings of the American Anthropological Association, Will Roscoe (1992) expressed the hope that if Benedict and Mead were still living they would not have to hide their sexuality to be credible public advocates for greater tolerance.

3   "Personal interactions and relationships are the stuff of field data collection," asserts sociologist Carol A. B. Warren (1977:105) in an excellent article on fieldwork in the male gay world, but, she ends mysteriously, "They only become a problem when they block access to certain parts of the data." She astutely discusses how the researcher may be stigmatized as gay by "normals" and so lose credibility, how the fieldworker trying to establish trust may be grilled by informants about her own sexual orientation, and even the need for "reflective subjectivity" by the fieldworker (1977:104)—all

without ever tipping her own hand. This is the same illusiveness to which I resorted in my early work on gay men (Newton 1979).

4   Only one of the male anthropologists in *In the Company of Man* chose to write about a female informant—a prepubescent girl (Conklin 1960).

5   Jean Briggs (1970) made her own anger and frustration central to her Eskimo ethnography; Barbara Myerhoff's (1978) elderly Jewish informants got under her skin in a rich variety of ways; Robert Murphy's (1987) account of how becoming paralyzed changed his identity and propelled him toward studying the disabled moved me deeply; Renato Rosaldo (1989) explored how his wife Shelly's death helped him grasp the rage motivating Ilingot head-hunting; and Michael Moffatt (1989) constructs a narrative about college students with himself as a very present participant-observer (whatever one thinks of his initial ethical lapse in fooling the students about his identity). All three of the men's texts do begin to construct the sexuality of the author as a subject, especially Moffatt's, perhaps because he writes extensively about the students' sexuality.

6   Quoted in Geertz (1988:98).

7   Geertz (1988:90) actually observes that in this genre the authorial voice is somehow configured as "an object of desire" but apparently only by readers and from afar. The term *positioned subject* is Rosaldo's (1989:19), and I think he wouldn't mind my adding "sexual" because he alone, of the new ethnographers, includes sexual orientation as a meaningful axis of difference that can help dismantle "objectivism" and add richness to ethnographic accounts (see especially 1989:190–93).

8   See also Geertz (1967), Greenway (1967), Harris (1967), and Hogbin (1968).

9   Recently, I was discussing the *Diary* in a class of undergraduates. One woman student said, indignantly, "Knowing about the *Diary,* why should I read Malinowski's ethnographies?" and another added, after thinking about it, "Maybe if you could put the *Diary* together with *Sex and Repression* you'd have good ethnography."

10   Of those who could be considered in the I-Witnessing school of ethnography, the only woman to rate a mention from Geertz is Barbara Myerhoff in a footnote (1988:101–15). Not comparing Cesara's *Reflections of a Woman Anthropologist* (1982) to Rabinow's *Reflections on Fieldwork in Morocco* (1977) is disappointing to say the least. Note that Rabinow can just be in the field, but Cesara has chosen to accept and acknowledge being in the marked category.

11   For the perspective of an African American man working in the Caribbean see T. Whitehead (1986). For the perspective of a black lesbian anthropologist working in Yemen see the chapter by Delores M. Walters in this volume.

12   Of course, the majority of gay and lesbian anthropologists are in the closet, which by definition precludes them from publicly acknowledging their orientation and generally from even writing about sexuality. And is it necessary to add that in the review of the literature that follows, the work done on gay *culture* is not mentioned unless it deals specifically with erotic issues

and systems? An article about a gay community center, for instance, is not necessarily any more (or less) about sexuality than one on a small-town Elks Club.

13 For an interesting, odd (and perhaps fabricated) account that actually centers on the homoerotic relations between Amazonian Indians and a Western observer-adventurer see Schneebaum (1969).

14 In a conversation at the 1990 AAA convention in New Orleans, Walter Williams confirmed that this was the case and that, although he had written more explicitly about it in his manuscript, friends had advised him to "tone it down" before publication lest too much frankness jeopardize his tenure, which he has since gotten, although only after a struggle.

15 Perhaps emboldened by Read, other anthropologists have followed in his New Guinea trail with important (although less evocative) work on (homo)sexuality (Herdt, ed. 1981, 1984).

16 The authorial presence in Read's ethnography of a gay bar (1980) is far more tortured and dissembling than in the New Guinea work.

17 The diffuse homoeroticism, even in Read's first ethnography on the Gahuku-Gama (1965) *did* disturb at least one "sensitive" anthropologist—Clifford Geertz (1988:86), who in an appreciation of Read's "brilliantly realized," I-Witnessing style can neither give his discomfort plain speech nor restrain a snide remark about Read's description of the farewell hug he shared with Makis.

18 After I began this chapter, Kath Weston sent me her "Requiem for a Street Fighter," which appears in this volume and is about her relationship with a young woman who would have been an informant had she not committed suicide. The fieldwork was conducted in Cherry Grove, Long Island, New York, from the summer of 1985 through the summer of 1989 (Newton 1993).

19 A welcome exception is Serena Nanda's fascinating (1990) work on the gender variant Indian *hijras,* which received SOLGA's Ruth Benedict Prize in 1990.

20 Gay and lesbian anthropologists have discussed these problems in a series of recent panels at the annual meetings of the American Anthropological Association, and many of these ground-breaking and silence-breaking papers are in this volume.

21 I agree with Mascia-Lees, Sharpe, and Cohen (1989:33) that the way anthropologists should work against power imbalance between themselves and their subjects is to make conscious choices to write for them too and to be attentive to research questions they want answered.

22 Kay asked me not to publish her last name. A different version of this narrative is embedded in Newton (1993:3–7).

23 This and all subsequent quotes in this section are from my unpublished fieldnotes, except for the letter to Schneider.

24 The categories "gay" and "straight," no matter how fateful and socially real, cannot be taken literally to mean that people so identified are *never,* as individuals, sexually interested in whichever gender is supposed to be eroti-

cally null. Even at the time of my dissertation fieldwork with female impersonators in the mid-1960s, I recognized that, improbable as it seemed, my
then "best informant's" considerable charms, which included his dresses,
or rather his persona in dresses, had a certain erotic component for me. But
here I allude to a complex subject far beyond the scope of this chapter.

25 Even when we gays are teachers, as many of us are, our identity is the one
thing about which most of us can never teach the young. Many gay people
do not have children who could give them personal and intimate access to
succeeding generations and cannot share their lives even with nieces and
nephews. Kay, for instance, was childless, and in the name of "discretion"
never discussed her homosexuality—all of her living, that is, that formed the
substance and subject matter of our friendship and was the reason why she
had lived in Cherry Grove for fifty summers—with any of her family. Because of the enforced secrecy in which we live, older gays have trouble transmitting our culture to younger ones.

26 Although our cupboard is bare, it isn't empty. In addition to the articles
and books previously referred to, Gregersen (1983) has done a quirky follow-up of Ford and Beach's (1951) early cross-cultural work. For American culture, there is Rubin's (1984) article on the hierarchical stratification
of sexual practices, Vance's (1983) witty essay on the Kinsey Institute, my
effort to develop a more precise sexual vocabulary (Newton and Walton
1984), Thompson on teen girls (1984, 1990), and Davis and Kennedy's
pioneering work on the sexuality of lesbians in Buffalo (1989). For non-
Western cultures, there is the "berdache" controversy (Callender and
Kochems 1983; Roscoe 1991; Whitehead 1981; Williams 1986), the essays
in Blackwood, ed. (1985), and three monographs: Thomas Gregor's account
of the heterosexual Mehanaku (1985), Gilbert Herdt and Robert Stoller's
collaboration on the Sambia (1990), and Richard Parker's (1991) Brazilian work, the winner of SOLGA's 1991 Benedict Prize.

References Cited

Blackwood, Evelyn, ed. 1985. *Anthropology and Homosexual Behavior.* New York:
Hawarth Press.

Bordo, Susan. 1990. "Feminism, Postmodernism, and Gender-Scepticism." In
Feminism and Postmodernism, ed. Linda J. Nicholson, 133–56. New York:
Routledge.

Boswell, John. 1992. "Same Sex Marriages in Medieval Europe." Paper presented
at State University of New York College at Purchase.

Briggs, Jean. 1970. *Never in Anger: Portrait of an Eskimo Family.* Cambridge:
Harvard University Press.

Callendar, Charles, and Lee M. Kochems. 1983. "The North American Berdache." *Current Anthropology* 24(4): 443–70.

Casagrande, Joseph, ed. 1960. *In the Company of Man: Twenty Portraits by
Anthropologists.* New York: Harper and Brothers.

Cesara, Manda [Karla O. Poewe]. 1982. *Reflections of a Woman Anthropologist:
No Hiding Place.* New York: Academic Press.

Clifford, James. 1986. "Introduction." In *Writing Culture: The Poetics and Politics of Ethnography*, ed. James Clifford and George E. Marcus, 1–26. Berkeley: University of California Press.

Clifford, James, and George E. Marcus, eds. 1986. *Writing Culture: The Poetics and Politics of Ethnography*. Berkeley: University of California Press.

Conaway, May Ellen. 1986. "The Pretense of the Neutral Researcher." In *Self, Sex, and Gender in Cross-Cultural Fieldwork*, ed. Tony Larry Whitehead and Mary Ellen Conaway, 52–63. Urbana: University of Illinois Press.

Conklin, Harold C. 1960. "Maling, a Hanunoo Girl from the Philippines." In *In the Company of Man: Twenty Portraits by Anthropologists*, ed. Joseph Casgrande. New York: Harper and Brothers.

Crapanzano, Vincent. 1980. *Tuhami, Portrait of a Moroccan*. Chicago: University of Chicago Press.

Davis, Madeline, and Elizabeth Lapovsky Kennedy. 1989. "Oral History and the Study of Sexuality in the Lesbian Community: Buffalo, New York, 1940–1960." In *Hidden from History: Reclaiming the Gay and Lesbian Past*, ed. Martin Duberman, Martha Vicinus, and George Chauncey, 426–40. New York: New American Library.

Ellen, R. F., ed. 1984. *Ethnographic Research: A Guide to General Conduct*. London: Academic Press.

Ford, Clellan S., and Frank A. Beach. 1951. *Patterns of Sexual Behavior*. New York: Harper and Brothers.

Geertz, Clifford. 1967. "Under the Mosquito Net." *New York Review of Books*, September 14:12–13.

———. 1988. *Works and Lives: The Anthropologist as Author*. Stanford, Calif.: Stanford University Press.

Giovannini, Maureen. 1986. "Female Anthropologist and Male Informant: Gender Conflict in a Sicilian Town." In *Self, Sex, and Gender in Cross Cultural Fieldwork*, ed. Tony Larry Whitehead and Mary Ellen Conaway, 103–16. Urbana: University of Illinois Press.

Golde, Peggy, ed. 1970. *Women in the Field: Anthropological Experiences*. Chicago: Aldine.

Gorer, Geoffrey. 1967. "Island Exorcism." *The Listener*, September 7:311.

Greenway, John. 1967. "Malinowski Unbuttoned." *World Journal Tribune*, March 26.

Gregersen, Edgar. 1983. *Sexual Practices: The Story of Human Sexuality*. New York: Franklin Watts.

Gregor, Thomas. 1985. *Anxious Pleasures: The Sexual Lives of an Amazonian People*. Chicago: University of Chicago Press.

Harris, Marvin. 1967. "Diary of an Anthropologist." *Natural History* 76:72–74.

Herdt, Gilbert H., ed. 1981. *The Sambia: Ritual and Gender in New Guinea*. New York: Holt, Rinehart and Winston.

———. 1984. *Ritualized Homosexuality in Melanesia*. Berkeley: University of California Press.

Hogbin, Ian. 1968. "Review of *A Diary in the Strict Sense of the Term* by Bronislaw Malinowski." *American Anthropologist* 70:575.

Malinowski, Bronislaw. 1955. *Sex and Repression in Savage Society.* Cleveland, Ohio: World Publishing.

———. 1967. *A Diary in the Strict Sense of the Term.* London: Routledge.

Mascia-Lees, Frances E., Patricia Sharpe, and Colleen Ballerino Cohen. 1989. "The Postmodernist Turn in Anthropology: Cautions From a Feminist Perspective." *Signs: Journal of Women in Culture and Society* 15(1): 7–33.

Moffatt, Michael. 1989. *Coming of Age in New Jersey: College and American Culture.* New Brunswick: Rutgers University Press.

Murphy, Robert. 1987. *The Body Silent.* New York: Henry Holt.

Myerhoff, Barbara. 1978. *Number Our Days.* New York: Simon and Schuster.

Nanda, Serena. 1990. *Neither Man nor Woman: The* Hijras *of India.* Belmont, Calif.: Wadsworth Press.

Newton, Esther. 1979 [1972]. *Mother Camp: Female Impersonators in America.* Chicago: University of Chicago Press.

———. 1984. "An Open Letter to 'Manda Cesara.'" *Anthropology Research Group on Homosexuality Newsletter* (Spring).

———. 1993. *Cherry Grove, Fire Island: Sixty Years in America's First Gay and Lesbian Town.* Boston: Beacon Press.

Newton, Esther, and Shirley Walton. 1984. "The Misunderstanding: Toward a More Precise Sexual Vocabulary." In *Pleasure and Danger: Exploring Female Sexuality,* ed. Carole S. Vance, 242–50. Boston: Routledge.

Parker, Richard. 1991. *Bodies, Pleasures and Passions: Sexual Culture in Contemporary Brazil.* Boston: Beacon Press.

Plato. 1989. *Symposium.* Translated by Alexander Nehamas and Paul Woodruff. Indianapolis: Hackett.

Rabinow, Paul. 1977. *Reflections on Fieldwork in Morocco.* Berkeley: University of California Press.

Read, Kenneth. 1965. *The High Valley.* New York: Scribner's.

———. 1980. *Other Voices: The Style of a Male Homosexual Tavern.* Novato, Calif.: Chandler and Sharp.

———. 1986. *Return to the High Valley.* Berkeley: University of California Press.

Rosaldo, Renato. 1989. *Culture and Truth: The Remaking of Social Analysis.* Boston: Beacon Press.

Roscoe, Will. 1991. *The Zuni Man-Woman.* Albuquerque: University of New Mexico Press.

———. 1992. "Comments on Receiving the Margaret Mead Award." *Society of Lesbian and Gay Anthropologists* Newsletter 14(1): 11–12.

Rubin, Gayle. 1984. "Thinking Sex: Notes for a Radical Theory of Politics in Sexualty." In *Pleasure and Danger: Exploring Female Sexuality,* ed. Carole S. Vance, 267–319. Boston: Routledge.

Sahlins, Marshall. 1991. "The Return of the Event, Again." In *Clio in Oceania,* ed. Aletta Biersack. Washington, D.C.: Smithsonian Institution Press.

Sarton, May. 1965. *Mrs. Stevens Hears the Mermaids Singing.* New York: W. W. Norton.

Schneebaum, Tobias. 1969. *Keep the River on Your Right.* New York: Grove Press.

Smith, Carolyn D., and William Kornblum, eds. 1989. *In the Field: Readings on the Field Research Experience*. New York: Praeger.

Smith-Rosenberg, Carroll. 1985. *Disorderly Conduct: Visions of Gender in Victorian America*. New York: Knopf.

Stacey, Judith. 1990. *Brave New Families*. New York: Basic Books.

Thompson, Sharon. 1984. "Search for Tomorrow: On Feminism and the Reconstruction of Teen Romance." In *Pleasure and Danger: Exploring Female Sexuality*, ed. Carole S. Vance, 350–84. Boston: Routledge.

———. 1990. "Putting a Big Thing into a Little Hole: Teenage Girls' Accounts of Sexual Initiation." *Journal of Sex Research* 27(3): 341–61.

Vance, Carole S. 1983. "Gender Systems, Ideology, and Sex Research." In *Powers of Desire: The Politics of Sexuality*, ed. Ann Snitow, Christine Stansell, and Sharon Thompson, 371–84. New York: Monthly Review Press.

Warren, Carol A. B. 1977. "Fieldwork in the Gay World: Issues in Phenomenological Research." *Journal of Social Issues* 33(4): 93–107.

Whitehead, Harriet. 1981. "The Bow and the Burden Strap: A New Look at Institutionalized Homosexuality in Native North America." In *Sexual Meanings: The Cultural Construction of Gender and Sexuality*, ed. Sherry B. Ortner and Harriet Whitehead, 80–115. Cambridge: Cambridge University Press.

Whitehead, Tony Larry. 1986. "Breakdown, Resolution, and Coherence: The Fieldwork Experiences of a Big, Brown, Pretty-Talking Man in a West Indian Community." In *Self, Sex, and Gender in Cross-Cultural Fieldwork*, ed. Tony Larry Whitehead and Mary Ellen Conaway, 213–39. Urbana: University of Illinois Press.

Williams, Walter. 1986. *The Spirit and the Flesh: Sexual Diversity in American Indian Culture*. Boston: Beacon Press.

12. Male Homosexuality in Guatemala: Possible Insights and Certain Confusions from Sleeping with the Natives
Stephen O. Murray

To fully appreciate the activities one is observing, it is necessary to engage in them. . . all the more so when the behaviors being studied are not generally ones about which people will speak openly, which is often the case with respect to sex, or in situations where the opportunities for observing the behaviors are limited, which is usually true in the arena of sexuality.—Bolton (1991:131)

Once upon a time—a time before AIDS, a time before ethnographers were preoccupied with epistemological conundrums or immobilized by self-consciousness about "writing culture," and a time when gay studies were community-based—I was a graduate student interested in ethnosemantics and in varying organizations of homosexuality. Without research funding or any particular research plan, I spent most of the summers of the late 1970s in Mesoamerica. Neither my M.A. nor Ph.D. dissertation research dealt with homosexuality or with Mesoamerica, but the analytical bent and the interest in alternative social, cultural, and sexual organizations that motivated me to undertake graduate work in sociology, anthropology, and linguistics definitely also underlay attempts to understand my own sexuality and various social organizations of male homosexuality, including those in *mestizo/criollo* Mesoamerica.[1] Although I was not in Mesoamerica specifically to "do research," was without funding of any sort, and had no official sanction for research, I think that I am always "on" as an observer, contrasting what I see and feel and hear with the theories and descriptions I know. Research and life are not distinctly compartmentalized for me.[2]

Alas, no one taught me how to go about studying homosexuality. Rather, I was actively discouraged when I tried to focus on the topic in graduate school. Moreover, none of the methodology courses I'd taken taught me about finding—let alone systematically sampling—unenumerated populations. Indeed, the emphasis in my graduate training was on sophisticated reanalysis of data collected by others. We were taught practically nothing about sampling, even from enumerated populations, or about collecting new data, or even about assessing the validity of data.

Not knowing how to locate men interested in sex with men in general (or with me in particular) was an obstacle to any research on homosexuality and (more important to me at the time) to living as a "liberated gay man." This is what I sometimes thought that I was and at other times aspired to be. Although knowing how to cruise is widely supposed to be innate in gay men, what little I knew about it was "book knowledge," mostly from reading John Rechy. I thought it highly unlikely that I could do what his narrators did. Like Edward Delph's description of himself, "The researcher knew very little about the public erotic marketplace. He did not know the extent of public homosexual eroticism or where it was to be found. He was shockingly deficient in the knowledge of what it consisted and how to recognize the subtle, tenuous initial cues that lead to its fruition" (1978:176).

My obliviousness to being cruised during earlier travels in southern Mexico and Guatemala had amused the lover who had "brought me out." Lee claimed that once on the Mexico City subway an attractive young man had done everything short of masturbate in my face yet had failed to get my attention (to convey his intentions). That I didn't notice such blatant nonverbal invitations reassured Lee that I wasn't going to stray from him at the same time that it reinforced his belief that I wasn't "really gay." If I were, I'd know how to cruise, right? So, in Lee's view, the danger was minimal that I'd become involved with another man. Like my mother, Lee thought that I might eventually find the right woman.

They were wrong. After nine years, the first man with whom I'd ever been sexually involved dumped me. I knew that my sexual "orientation" was toward men. Feeling anything but secure in the summer of 1978, however, I was traveling with a *rubia* [blonde woman] friend who attracted plenty of attention. Perhaps it was watching Latino men devour Laurie with their eyes that taught me to recognize the sexual gaze. I was accustomed to knowing from being told more than from seeing that men were interested in my companions of the road—first Lee, now Laurie. I didn't expect anyone to be interested in me. With so little self-confidence I had not tried to learn to distinguish the looks that might be aimed at me from those that were for my companions.

I seemed not to be equipped with the vaunted "radar" by which gay men are supposed to detect interest from other males, or, perhaps, it was impaired by the conviction—carefully nurtured by Lee—that no one but he would have such an interest in me. Thus, I was startled crossing the square across from police headquarters in Guatemala City that a young man sitting alone on a concrete bench locked eyes with me. "So that's it," I thought. *"That's* cruising. He was cruising me! This is a place where cruising occurs. Maybe, if I come back later he'll still be here." (If I'd been more self-confident, the conclusion would have been, "When I come back, someone will be here who will be interested in getting together.")

I dropped Laurie off at the neighborhood cinema later that evening to see *The Exorcist* and walked back through the square. I was disappointed that the man who had locked eyes with me earlier wasn't a permanent fixture. Not knowing what I should do, I decided to sit where he'd been. Probably, I was waiting for him to return.

I wasn't alone long. I wasn't on the bench long—just long enough for my interlocutor to find out that I had a nearby room to which we could go. On the way there, he asked the classic question, "¿Eres pasivo o activo?" [Are you passive or active?] I rejected the question like any liberated *norteamericano:* "Soy gay" [I'm gay], I self-righteously replied. Little did I know that I'd begun a study of the diffusion of "gay" in Latin America (Murray and Arboleda 1987). Miguel did not understand my answer. He did not know the word. (This is not my inference; I asked him.)

In retrospect, the fact that Miguel didn't answer his own question before we started off to my room indicates that he was willing to pitch or to catch. Whatever my expectations were, he was going to be complaisant. Neither choice was the "right answer" in the sense of being a condition of going off together. As it turned out, even though he didn't know the word, his behavior fit my answer. That is, he was *gay* in the sense of "transcending limiting dichotomous roles," as we missionaries of gay liberation in those days thought of it.[3]

After we'd exchanged bodily fluids (which is definitely *not* how we thought then) and I'd fairly casually elicited the small set of terms Miguel knew for the domain of homosexuality, we got dressed. Walking back toward the square, I playfully asked him again, "¿Eres pasivo o activo?"

Probably, I expected that I had converted him to my superior, liberated way of being-in-the-world, or, at least, that his answer would be consistent with his recent sexual behavior. Contrary to such expectations, he answered, "Soy pasivo."

I did not (and do not) know whether he used *pasivo* for his most common desire or as a term for an identity. I could not fail to notice a lack of congruity between such self-designation and my recent observation of his sexual repertoire. Although he labeled himself a *pasivo*, his sexual repertoire included both *pasivo* and *activo* roles. I did not at that point know that there is a term—*internacional*—for someone who is neither *activo* nor *pasivo* or is both. I did know that Spanish has two copulas (*ser* and *estar*) and that Miguel had used a form of *ser*, the one for a permanent characteristic. At the time I didn't think very long about what the disparity between behavior and report meant because I still had another hour before the movie ended. I returned to my "lucky" bench. Again, I did not remain on it long.

Raúl didn't ask the question. He *told* me, "Soy activo." He seemed to me to understand my response of, "Soy gay." At least he didn't ask what I meant, moving on immediately to the more practical aspect of whether I had some space in which to be gay. I did. We were. The second postcoital "interview" elicited more terms than the first had. Raúl mentioned *gay* as a term for a man who prefers men, and as a kind of *pasivo*. With my cum up his ass, he told me that he didn't get fucked and never would. I badly wanted to fuck him again and then ask him again, but I had to get back to the theater and escort Laurie back. I told her something of my own recent exorcism (of the belief that no one but Lee would take any interest in me as a sexual partner).

We walked around instead of through the square. Now I realize that at least some denizens probably noticed all three of the people with whom I'd walked away from there. That my status in this literally shadowy world might be enhanced by the appearance of having a *rubia* with whom to spend the night didn't occur to me at the time.

In contrast, she was consciously using me as a shield from unwanted propositions and harassment. Laurie had instructed me on how a respectable husband was supposed to behave in Latin America before we left the United States. I was supposed to glare at any man who spoke to her and to stare down too-intense gazes I intercepted. I wasn't supposed to keep any for myself. The logic was that if I were interested in men, then Laurie must be available, either because dissatisfied with sexual neglect or because we weren't really a couple. In either case she could legitimately be hit on. We were playing by local rules in which appearances of propriety are everything—feelings, nothing. As long as we were visibly together, our sexual honor was interdependent (see Bowman [1989:88] on another place with similar, Mediterranean meanings read into aliens' sexual availability).

Like most of those who accompanied someone ostentatiously doing "fieldwork," Laurie was invisible in what I wrote (which was not an ethnography, let alone a first-person account of time spent in another culture). Even in the first draft of this chapter, the editors found the motivation for our traveling together mysterious. She was increasingly estranged from her husband, fluent in Spanish, and interested in spending another summer in Latin America so long as she did not have to cope with all the verbal harassment that a lone *gringa* (especially a blonde one) receives. We both wanted company. Neither of us wanted to try to "go native." I wasn't ready for a total immersion in Spanish in 1978. I suspect that I was also applying brakes to all-out cruising. Although these two purposes seem contradictory to me now, I think that I felt them both at the time.

In advance, certainly, I didn't know that I could find company. In my view and previous experience, I could talk some men whom I found desirable into bed. I didn't think my Spanish was adequate to such a task, however, and had no experience with making nonverbal connections. In short, I didn't have the confidence to be on my own. At the same time, I had a fear that I would sink into "depravity" and "indiscriminate promiscuity." Laurie would be there if I struck out. And she would be there to restrain me from tricking my brains out. Of course, these motivations didn't add up, but I don't think that many people have difficulties harboring contradictory notions like these. If what some social psychologists call "cognitive dissonance" exists, it doesn't pain most people. As Paul Veyne put it, "The coexistence of contradictory truths in the same mind is a universal fact" (1988:84).

At the time, I did not rationalize tricking as sampling or as fieldwork. Indeed, "fieldwork" was entirely a post hoc definition of the situation. Eliciting terms was secondary (motivationally as well as temporally) to making sexual contacts. I am confident that I didn't think of sex as a means to elicitation interviews, even though my questions became systematic.[4] I was far more interested in participating than observing; that is, I was more interested in the sex than in what became a recurrent postcoital conversational topic. Homosexuality was a domain I was interested in understanding as the natives did. It seemed a "natural" topic to talk about in the setting. It also quickly became one of the two domains (the other being food) in which my vocabulary matched (or exceeded) that of my native interlocutors. My primary motivation for having sex with Guatemaltecos was *not* to recruit research informants. In only one case did I give even a passing thought to the "representativeness" of my "sample," and even in this instance, it was as much my sample of sexual experience as my sample of informants for a lexicon. I rationalized going off with one man toward whom I felt no sexual attraction partly out of curiosity about how he lived (because he was the one man to approach me who had a place of his own to which to take me) and partly because he spoke English (having attended graduate school in the United States). We ended up talking and not having sex, thus inadvertently preserving the purity (from instrumentality) of my motivations for retrospective scrutiny.

I didn't, and don't, think that I was "prostituting" myself to further social science research.[5] My curiosity about how others live and think was more the motivation to undertake social science study than it was a product of it. To reiterate, I wanted to have sex with those I took to bed more than I wanted to interview them; sex was by no means work I suffered through on the way to interviewing. Insofar as sex was a prelude to conversation, this was a conventional pattern in both Anglo and Latin American homosexual encounters. We got to know one another via sexual rather than verbal exchange.[6] This seems astonishing to later generations of gay men and to women of several generations, but, to us, sex was not just a means to intimacy, it was intimacy.

I did most of the elicitation on which my 1980 paper on Guatemalan gay lexicon was based while Laurie was in Antigua with another friend.[7] Two other times I took men back to the room we shared—well, three. One of them couldn't bring himself to having sex with another person present (or was it with a woman present that mattered?). José decided to fellate me in the hallway instead. I was amused that he found that more private. I was also interested that he initiated fellatio, because Latin American men supposedly don't do that.

That sex is not exclusively anal for Latin American men was evidenced by all three, in fact. One very beautiful man whom I asked to dance at Pandora's Box, a *norteamericano*-style disco, fellated me on one of the couches upstairs from the dance bar.[8] The other, whom I met on the street in front of a popular outdoor restaurant, had just left an introductory-level English class. After we had quietly undressed and climbed into bed, Manuel wordlessly pushed my head down, albeit only as foreplay.

Obviously, all three of these men (and a number of others) knew of oral sex. For Juan and Manuel, and perhaps for José, it was a substitute for anal sex in semipublic—or potentially public—settings. For José, it might have been a preference, as it was for one of my recurrent dates in Mexico City.

Manuel was adamant that he would never put or allow a penis in his mouth.[9] He said that he had fucked men before, but that he had never put his penis in anyone's mouth. Perhaps this was true. The statement is a datum, regardless of its validity. The interpretive problem is whether it is a datum about sexual behavior, sexual norms, fantasy, or identity.

I was sufficiently confused by the disparity between Guatemaltecos' sexual behavior with me and their reports to me of sexual preferences and repertoires not to write about sexual behavior or sexual meaning in Latin America for years. Then a session at the 1986 American Anthropological Association provoked me to challenge what I saw as some Anglo North American anthropologists' romantic fantasies about Latino sexual flexibility by adding a postscript to the book *Male Homosexuality in Central and South America* that was about to be printed (Murray 1987:192–99).[10] Some of the presentations at the 1990 AAA session that seemed to advocate basing comparative sexology on having sex with natives, and Itiel's (1989, 1991) gay guidebooks based on his sex tourism (criticized by Manalansan 1991; Murray 1991), increased this disquiet and led to the present reflection on my experiences of trying to understand sexualities from the puzzling position of a questioning as well as observant participant. It seems to me that in addition to anthropologists' occupational disease of ethnoromanticism (Murray 1981) conclusions based on sexual participation are distorted by confusing the intimacies possible with strangers with natives' everyday intimate lives.[11]

Multiple Motivations for Sex

From experiences with young persons experimenting outside their usual world, foreigners easily overestimate the sexual role flexibility in a culture. Being in a foreign society, and in "intimate contact" with one or more natives, alien observers may not realize that their sexual partners in a significant sense are not playing by the usual rules of their sexual culture. Rather than penetrating the mysteries of another culture's sexual lifeways, both may be outside their own cultures in a (liminal?) interculture.[12] Almost as much as the foreigner, the native who has sex with the foreigner is "away from home" and released to some extent from the cultural constraints that affect intracultural sexual behavior. This is not to say that prior socialization (including culturally shaped fantasies about Latins or Americans) is irrelevant. Foreigners' assumption that they have participated directly in a foreign sexual culture, however, is suspect.

Young (and not-so-young) social scientists may also be finding out what our desires are. I certainly was. But reliance on personal sexual exploration to understand sexuality in other cultures may lead us to generalizing that Guatemaltecos (or whoever) do this or prefer that, with little more sophistication than Latin American sexual partners generalize about *el vicio norteamericano* [the North American vice, i.e., performing fellatio] or "what Europeans like" (receptive anal intercourse). In going to bed with me, Miguel, Manuel, et al. were participant-observers of *norteamericano* homosexuality as much as I was a participant-observer of Guatemalteco homosexuality. At the same time that I was trying to fit my behavior to what I thought were their expectations, they were trying to fit their behavior to what they thought were my expectations. Reciprocity was part of my expectation. My experiences showed that some Latinos enact both *activo* and *pasivo* roles with the same person. With me, that is. But what about with each other?

I am not convinced that "I did x with A, D, J, and K" establishes that x is in the repertoire of A, D, J, and K in any very meaningful sense. Obviously, it is in at least their experimental repertoire of sex with foreigners, whether or not previously tried. And I'll grant that a foreign observer may have intuitions about the previous experiences of A, D, J, and K with x after collaborating in it.[13] But even if D and K seemed to like doing x, I don't think that we can conclude that they are going to do x with their compatriots, let alone that they usually do, or that x is what they prefer to do, and still less that they identify themselves in the category "a person who does x."

D may deny that he does x, even to someone with whom he has done x, as Raúl and Manuel denied ever permitting being penetrated. Such denial indicates that D feels that x is stigmatizing or knows that it is conventionally stigmatized in D's culture. It constitutes some negative evidence about D's sexual identity (if sexual identity is, in fact, a universal domain of categorization). I also take it as calling into question the conditions under which D does x. However, denial of x does not establish that D rarely does it or never had before; it may be another case of a "virgin every morning" pose. Self-reports are not transparent. As much as behavior, they may be manufactured for foreigners' consumption, as some Brazilians have suggested to me is the case for the representations of Brazilian sexuality in Parker (1991).

In a postcoital, soft glow—a state of mind that easily may extend to writing "fieldnotes" or even to writing reports of research and analyses of cultures—it is easy to forget that people engage in sexual acts for reasons other than their desires and preferences (Greenberg 1983; Herdt 1984, 1991; Whitam 1987, 1992). Upward social mobility is an important one. Persons from more affluent countries frequently are conceived to be potential patrons, as many fieldwork memoirs mention, usually in embarrassed passing. "This could be my ticket to America [Holland, Germany, France, etc.], so I'd better do what he wants" is a thought that occurs both to those establishing their first intimacies with a foreigner and to those who have tried before to procure such a ticket. I can't remember anyone saying "take me with you" directly, but the wish was apparent more than once. Estimating the importance of this factor is very difficult for a foreigner. The calculus of patronage in general—and of sponsoring emigration in particular—is not revealed to the potential patron, even (especially?) in answer to a direct query.[14]

I don't think that moving to America was Manuel's primary interest when he made eye contact with me in 1978. If it had been, I think he would have been more sexually complaisant. His younger, bolder brother Jaime, with whom I did not have sex, although from our first meeting I never had any doubts that he was homosexual, plied me with questions about my income and the cost in America of seemingly everything he could think of. WASPs don't talk comfortably about such things.[15] When finally I told Jaime that, he asked, "What do North Americans talk about?" I provided the flip phrase (in English), "Sex, drugs, rock 'n roll." Very seriously, Jaime said that Latinos can't talk about sex and drugs. Did that mean we could only talk about rock and roll? We were curious about each other's cultures, albeit about different domains. I wanted to talk about sex as much as Jaime wanted to talk about microeconomics.

Although some fieldworkers are unwilling to exchange information, curiosity runs both ways in ethnographic encounters, as many narratives about fieldwork report.[16] In an early instance, Mabel Cook Cole wrote, "It must have seemed to them that we asked many questions as, indeed, we did; but they, in turn, asked many of us, and sometimes it would be hard to conjecture which anthropological study would be most complete, theirs or ours. . . . [Our] guests were as interested in us as we were in them" (1929:20, 45).[17] Not having mystified myself as engaged in the priestly vocation of ethnography, I felt that I owed it to the people to whom I asked questions to try to answer theirs as best I could. If their conceptions of America sometimes struck me as irremediably wrong, I was all too aware that they might think the same of some of my conclusions about their culture and society (Hong 1994a, 1994b; Hong and Murray 1995).

Jaime and the whole family wanted to know about life in America at least as much as I wanted to know about life in Guatemala. In that the mother and the youngest son are currently living in Southern California, perhaps they learned something useful from me. On different occasions I have put up the other three siblings while they contemplated staying on as illegal immigrants after their tourist visas to the United States expired. I learned something from being with them, some of which I have been relating here. Nevertheless, I don't think that seeking such knowledge was the primary motivation for our relationships or, specifically, for Manuel in our initial sexual encounter. Rather, various potentials have emerged from our relationship as it has continued.

Although I considered myself economically quite marginal in my society, I could afford more abstract inquiry about a place in which I had no intention of spending my life. Manuel's whole family may have seen me as a potential American patron. Jaime may just have been the most blatant about it. Perhaps what I conceived as hospitality from his family was calculated for some specific future utility. I didn't, and don't, want to think so. My first impression—that hospitality is so deeply ingrained a part of Latino culture as to be "second nature" and unconscious—was probably sound.

My somewhat later interpretation—that they were accepting of Manuel's homosexual relationship—was perhaps true for Jaime. But it became clear to me that sexuality in general and Manuel's sexual involvement with me in particular were not discussed, whether or not they were conceived by family members. Although Manuel and Jaime both slept in the same room, they each told me separately that they never discussed their sexual behavior with each other. I couldn't even elicit an opinion from either about what his brother's sex life was like.[18] If the two young men sexually involved with men didn't discuss sexuality in their tight quarters, certainly the sexual aspect of Manuel's friendship with his *norteamericano* was unlikely to be discussed within the family. That was an important demonstration to me of the possibility of family members' discretion. Not just "don't ask" and "don't tell," but "don't even think about it!"

The unshared homosexuality of Manuel and Jaime demonstrated to me the reality of the impersonality that Sol Tax (1941:33) described as characteristic of highland Guatemala, the force of the formulaic phrase for Mesoamerican families in small spaces, living "juntos pero no revueltos" [together but not scrambled] and of the more general Latino formula "todo hecho, nada dicho" [everything is done, nothing is said].[19] Visiting their apartment showed me how little room there was and how impossible it was for Manuel to take me (or anyone else, male or female) there to have sex. A place to go and have sex is a luxury in Guatemala City and in much of the world. This was an important lesson from having an ongoing gay relationship. More than in observing *fichas'* [tricks'] inability to stay the night and their need to return to their family home, my relationship with Manuel underlies what I have written about familialism precluding the path of development ("evolution") of northern American and European gay homosexuality (Murray 1987:118–28, 1992a, 1995:33–47; cf. Allyn 1991, 1992, and Khan 1990).

In addition to fantasized prospects of mobility (geographical and economic), curiosity can motivate sexual encounters quite apart from deep-seated desires and preferences. In Guatemala (and much of the world) there is no place to explore one's sexuality. Besides providing such a space, a foreigner, social scientist or other, can provide a relatively safe psychological space for experimentation in a culture strongly stigmatizing sexual receptivity, just as the foreign setting may seem a psychologically safer space for the foreigner to explore his or her sexuality.[20]

In Latin America as in other Mediterranean-influenced cultures, one's reputation is important, but it is difficult to be sure how one is regarded: "To be a man in a society where sanctions are discreetly expressed, if at all, and everyone is provided with a 'public' that in a sense 'honours' him, does not make life all that easy. The man must steer a deft and elegant course with very few signals from that public who are his judges. He can never be sure that his value is what he thinks it is, as he observes his bland reflection in his polite spectators" (Wikan 1984:646). Whether machismo is inner-directed or other-directed performance and approval-seeking, there may be elaborate collusions to avoid questioning appearances that could easily be challenged and not to see deviance (gender, sex, or other). Nonetheless, gossip outside the household is pervasive, and therefore a predominant concern in urban Latin America as well as in the countryside, the stereotypical homeland of minding others' business. Moreover, the family's reputation may be compromised by the "dishonor" of any family member, especially by any of those living with their natal family.

Particularly in exploring sexual receptivity, it is safer to experiment with foreigners. In some sense, aliens don't count. Rationalizations of being surprised and pressured into perversions (i.e., "doing what they wanted, not what I wanted to do") are readily available. More important, a foreigner is unlikely to tell the native's family, neighbors, or friends what happened sexually. The few who even visit the neighborhood don't remain around it to gossip about what happened.

In contrast, fellow natives are more likely to hear what happened from the native conquistador, who doesn't move away. His secret knowledge remains a threat to the masculine reputation of the insertee, whose honor may be *quemado* [singed] at any time by reports or rumors of receptivity. Even when obtainable, the luxury of privacy is not as safe with peers as with foreigners. Thus, to say that it doesn't matter what a Latino male does as long as no one finds out (Lacey 1979; Parker 1991) doesn't say much because of the necessary caveat "hardly ever does no one find out." Some things remain hidden [*escondido*], but guarantees of eternal silence are dubious. Anyone especially concerned about his reputation is not all that safe getting fucked under the sheets or between four silent walls [*entre quatro paredes*] when "no one is watching" (Parker 1987:163–66, 1991:100; echoed for Costa Rica by Kutsche and Page 1992). In the words of José, Richard Parker's Brazilian primary informant, "Sometimes one gives [*dá*] first, or sucks or jacks off the other, and then when it is the turn of the one who received pleasure first, he doesn't want to do it for the other. There are some times when this same first person goes about telling others that the second did this or that with him. . . . The active defames the passive, giving rise to fights and shame, if not blows and serious punishments coming from family members" (Parker 1991:128). The walls may not speak, but those cavorting between them tend to do so sooner or later. Such unwelcome leaking of information forms a recurrent theme in Latin American fiction dealing with homosexuality (Foster 1991; Murray 1995:62–19).

Alien visitors are the safest repositories of usually suppressed longings (sexual and other), whether acted on or fantasized (Caplan 1992:71; Gal 1993:349). "It is in the après-sex milieu of casual sexual encounters when people often open up and speak honestly and profoundly about their lives, sharing thoughts with a partner that may never be voiced in any other context," as Bolton (1991:138) noted. This relief is best provided by someone from outside the local pecking order whom one can be certain is going to go away and will not be around to tell family or friends what one did or said in bed.

What occurs or is expressed in this "safe space" cannot be extrapolated to what the person generally does in intracultural encounters, especially not to being a *pasivo* or even an *internacional*. The exploration with the alien of what someone has thought about but never tried may lead to deciding, "So this is it. I don't like this!" and not repeating the experiment, as seems to be the case for Manuel and receptive anal intercourse.[21]

I have suggested some factors other than "sexual nature" and "inherent desire" that may influence people in general and Latin American males in particular to have sex with alien male visitors. Although the question barely occurred to me in Guatemala in the late 1970s, I wish that I knew which of my assets were salient to the Guatemaltecos with whom I was physically intimate. Katherine Ewing noted that "most recent ethnographies that strive to include the ethnographer in the text demonstrate a similar weakness: anthropologists are not trained to be observant of how they actually shape an interaction, and so they substitute 'confessions' about their own background for accurate assessments of specific interactions" (1992:237). I think that this criticism applies to what I'm writing, but I am skeptical that any amount or kind of training would enable human beings to be able to assess accurately how we shape interactions with others, especially sexual ones, even within our native cultures. We have difficulty knowing how we are regarded by "the other" (Crick 1992; Dumont 1978; Gossen 1993; Wade 1993), let alone knowing what the effects of such conceptions are in shaping interaction. Even at home, our surmises about what is going on in the heads of those closest to us frequently are revealed to have been wildly wrong—sometimes years afterward. Questions are replied to with what the other person thinks we want to hear. I find it hard to imagine that, for instance, Manuel or an uninvolved observer could estimate what proportion of his motivation in picking me up was perceiving me as *guapo* [handsome], what part was the novelty of a foreigner, what part the potential advantages of association with a presumably affluent *norteño*, what part was the prospect of some privacy for obtaining sexual relief, what part an opportunity to experiment with stigmatizing behavior, or what other reasons were operative. I would prefer the first of these factors to have been dominant, supplemented by the last. At the time I could barely conceive of the third.[22] The idea that I was accumulating a capital of "exotic" experience that would profit me when I carried it home didn't occur to me, and such an idea is false in regard to intent as well as consequences.

I don't (can't) know what fantasies or what rational calculations I triggered at home in what were once parts of New Spain or in Guatemala. At least I never felt that I was functioning as a Guatemalteco and could generalize about Guatemalteco homosexual behavior from that with which I participated (cf. Bloch 1990; Bolton 1991:133). Raúl shocked me, fomenting a deep, lasting distrust in self-reports that others collect in their own or other societies.[23] Unwilling to trust either what Guatemaltecos did with me or what they said about their sexual repertoires, I have avoided making global statements about what Guatemaltecos do and prefer to do sexually.[24] None of what I have written about homosexual behavior in Mesoamerica has been based on the intercultural sexual conduct in which I engaged. Even the categorizations of roles in published data (e.g., Murray 1980) are based on elicitation rather than on my direct explorations of sexual repertoires. As Bolton wrote, "Averting their gaze from sex itself, with its messiness, complications, and research difficulties, most anthropologists interested in sexuality have opted to concentrate on issues of gender, identity, roles, rituals and symbolism almost to the exclusion of sexual behavior" (1991:132). In my case, identity and collective consciousness have been my focuses although I would not say that I averted my gaze. I certainly looked upon the deeds. I just couldn't figure out the meaning (for the natives) of what they did with me, or of the disparities between what they did with me and what they told me about their sexual conduct.

Conclusion

¿Por qué todos mis pinches actos deben tener un corolario de palabras, tan inútiles como gastadas? Uno devería situarse en lo inmediato, en lo palpable; decir únicamente, cuando mucho: A. estuvo presente en mí hoy; cogimos. O ni siquiera eso: desconfiar de lo que es susceptible de verbalizar. Sólo lo que no puede ser escrito, formulado en palabras, es válido; por lo menos en lo que toca al deseo y a su satisfacción. Lo demás son chaquetas.

[Why must there be a corollary of words for all my useless, tired acts? One should be situated in the immediate and palpable and say, at most, "A. was here in me today. We fucked." Or not even that much. Distrust what can be verbalized! Only that which cannot be written and formulated in words about desire and its satisfaction is valid. The rest doesn't matter.]—Zapata (1985:47)

Seemingly empirical generalization by a traveler (or an ethnographer) that "they're all available" may be mistaken for evidence of undifferentiated desire if no consideration is given to the lack of genuine options for sexual release, or for sexual experimentation, or for upward (and northward) mobility in Latin America and elsewhere. The meaning to them of what others are doing when they are having sex is not transparent to even the best-trained, most sympathetic ethnographer. I greatly doubt that it is clear to the natives, either.

Curiosity, xenophilia, and hopes and expectations of material rewards or some participation in elite culture all may influence sexual behavior more than any particular desire to do what the foreigner wants—or what the native thinks the foreigner wants. Confidence that peers won't find out what happened makes safe behavior that within the culture risks a male reputation. These factors seem to me to make it difficult to extrapolate from the sexual experiences of a stranger to everyday cultural understandings and behaviors. Leaving discussion of ethics to the many others only too eager to serve as judges,[25] I raise this as a point of epistemology for those who suppose they understand homosexuality in alien societies—particularly impoverished ones[26]—from personal sexual experiences in them. The relationship between such data and native intracultural behavior and thought is far from obvious.

Having sex with the natives is not a royal road to insight about alien sexualities. I don't think that there is a royal road. Or even a smooth one. In answering questions or inscribing life histories at a researcher's behest, as in having sex with them, the person whose sexuality is being studied is likely to be guessing what the researcher wants to hear rather than representing his or her most fundamental desires and identities.

I prefer native documents not elicited by foreigners as data,[27] although I am quite aware of the inevitability of genre conventions[28] and of the importance of intracultural variation. Obviously, intracultural representations are still representations influenced by what will appeal to an audience. Although it is useful to know what the imagined audience is, social scientists cannot escape from representations to some firm stratum of directly apprehended nature, even by direct participation in physical intimacies. We need to think about our effect on what we are told and observe at home or abroad, even if we cannot reach definitive conclusions that are not interpretations about such effects or the behavior observed, read about, or heard about.

Notes

This chapter grows out of conversations, some of them verging on arguments, many stretching across more than a decade, with Barry Adam, Eric Allyn, Manuel Arboleda, the late Phil Blumstein, Ralph Bolton, the late Joel Brodsky, Gary Bukovnik, Joe Carrier, Chris Carrington, Norm Dale, Regna Darnell, Wayne Dynes, Kent Gerard, Mike Gorman, Alma Gottlieb, Gil Herdt, Richard Herrell, Keelung Hong, the late Laud Humphreys, Joe Kao, Badruddin Khan, Paul Kutsche, Bill Leap, John Lee, the late Marty Levine, Ellen Lewin, Martin Manalansan, Peter Nardi, Luis Paloma, the late Ken Payne, Ken Plummer, Will Roscoe, Debbie Spehn, Clark Taylor, Pablo Tellez, Dave Thompson, Amparo Tusón, Fred Whitam, Walter Williams, Unni Wikan, Deborah Wolf, and Wayne Wooden. It also grows from reflecting on gay guidebooks by Itiel (1989, 1991) and Allyn (1991). Its readability has been enhanced by editorial suggestions from Ralph Bolton, Paul Kutsche, and Bill Leap. Names have been altered, as is conventional, even when unsought by those "protected" (Crick 1992:186–87).

1   My first gay observant participant research (presented in 1977 and published as Murray 1979a, 1979b) dealt with Anglo Canadians. It was in press before I began what I classified after the fact as "research" and discuss in this chapter. I was not funded or approved by any government; see Hong (1994a), Hong and Murray (1989), and Murray and Hong (1994) on the problems of anticipatory cooperation with oppression that such funding seems to entail.

2   I take comfort in the statement by the pioneer American anthropological observer of *mestizo* Latin America that "in me, man and anthropologist do not separate themselves sharply; I used to think that I could bring about that separation in scientific work about humanity. Now I have come to confess that I have not effected it, and indeed think it is not possible to do so" (Redfield 1953:165). This is all the more comforting since, to me, Robert Redfield is the archetype of looking at idiographic material and seeing the nomothetic—a vision to which fewer and fewer anthropologists even aspire. My title indicates that I do, even though the subtitle signals the epistemological pessimism of my generation. I want to know about male homosexuality in Guatemala, not just to inscribe my homosexual experiences in Guatemala. Although I think that there is too much about the self and not enough about the others in postmodern ethnography, I think that social scientists must risk undercutting confidence that what we generalize from

our experience is true. Also, like Caplan (1992), Dumont (1978), Ewing (1992, 1994), Gossen (1993), and Hendry (1992), I think that trying to figure out who I was (or was fantasized to be) by those with whom I was interacting is necessary to understanding their behavior. See Bolton (1991:136), and Tedlock (1991).

3   I may have been ethnocentric in carrying the opposition between the traditional equation of homosexuality and effeminacy from Anglo North America, as Fred Whitam has charged. I am neither defending nor apologizing for my gay liberationist values, merely stating that my sexual behavior in the 1970s derived at least in part from such values. I considered the Latin American folk model of the *maricón* less valid than the gay organization of homosexuality at the personal and cultural levels. Rather than being a cultural relativist, I was a missionary of sorts for gay liberation, a conscious agent of acculturation to "modern" homosexuality. I was looking *for* as well as *at* change. Writing about obstacles to development of a gay organization of homosexuality (Murray 1987:118–28, 1992a, 1995) followed nearly inevitably. Although, like Bolton (1991), I first tried to ascertain what my sexual partners preferred to do by reacting rather than initiating, I usually tried later in the encounter to see if their sexual repertoire included taking the other role. This, too, was a kind of gay liberation proselytizing.

4   I was asking standardized "Is A a type of B? Is B a type of C?" questions in a white room. Most people, however, do not conceive of asking questions after fucking as "white room ethnography." The locution "white room ethnography" refers to systematic elicitation of cultural data outside the context of a culture in a (bedless) white-walled room near but not in a settlement of indigenous people, prototypically, ethnoscience work with Tenejapaños in San Cristóbal de las Casas, Chiapas, Mexico, during the 1960s (Murray 1982).

5   This work was unlikely to help my career. Studying homosexuality anywhere was more likely to preclude than to advance a career in academic social science in North America during the 1970s and early 1980s, as in the cases of those anthropologists, such as Joseph Carrier, Michael Gorman, David Soneschein, Clark Taylor, and Deborah Wolf, whose dissertations focused on lesbian or gay topics.

6   See Bolton (1991:136–37) and Williams (1993). Especially with regard to research dealing with sex, anthropologists privilege verbal communication, although, as Bolton stresses, nonverbal signals are generally far more important than verbal ones in communicating pleasure, desire, displeasure, repugnance, and so on. Even within a sexual encounter, verbal channels frequently deny what is going on, so reliance on post hoc verbalizations in sex research almost certainly leads to biased estimates of non-normative behavior. For a criticism of wordstruck anthropology together with a plea for experience-near study, see Wikan (1992), although I do not think she had quite this kind of resonating and sharing concerns in mind.

7   In the summer of 1978 I had not read the published articles derived from Carrier's (1972) or Taylor's (1978) unpublished dissertations. I would have

been more confident in the lexical data I was collecting had I seen them.

8   I'm sure that Juan heard plenty about this later. I'm also relatively certain from his later enthusiasm that he preferred receptive anal sex to receptive oral sex.

9   Three years later he was ready to try receptive anal intercourse, but still found the thought of performing fellatio unimaginably repugnant. Thirteen years later he denied ever having been sexual receptive.

10   Some of it has been published in Kutsche and Page (1992), Lancaster (1992), and Parker (1991); on which see Murray (1992b, 1993, 1995:50–56).

11   See Simmel's (1950 [1908]:402–8) classical exploration of the uses of "the stranger." I see considerable dangers of self-delusion that we are "resonating" in intercultural encounters in Wikan's (1990, 1992) "experience-near" ethnography. To expropriate one of her formulas (from 1992:467), the invocation of empathy and resonance can lead to a false sense of security while explaining nothing, especially for those more ethnocentric and less sensitive than she is, particularly young monolinguals out of their own culture for the first time. I think that before getting "beyond words" and feeling the concepts or structures it is necessary to have at least some rudimentary understanding of the words.

12   By no means is sexual conduct the only aspect in which anthropologists are prone to overestimate their participation and ability to represent another culture from inside, ignoring the extent to which those who choose to interact with the alien are innovating or recurrently act as culture brokers (Caplan 1992:71, 80; Crick 1992:180, 188; Hendry 1992). Designation as an "honorary chief" seems especially likely to go to anthropologists' heads and make them believe that they can continue fieldwork intrapsychically. Contrast Dumont's (1978:164) tortured recognition that he "was playing both within and without the system" with Bloch's (1990:194) smug recommendation of introspection following participant observation.

13   For instance, I think it unlikely that someone who pushes a sexual partner's head down to his crotch has had no previous experience of fellatio. Nonetheless, fantasy of what one has only heard about (anticipatory socialization) is a possible alternative explanation. On occasion, two virgins have been known somehow to manage to have sex of various sorts (Daphnis and Chloe are the archetypes).

14   Trying to guess (largely from nonverbal communication) and do what a partner wants is far from being confined to intercultural encounters. In particular, providing sexual access in hopes of improving one's economic or occupational position surely occurs with greater regularity intraculturally than interculturally.

15   However, the very British ethnographer Nigel Barley (1988:61) writes that one of the satisfactions for the fieldworker is "ceas[ing] to belong to the impoverished part of the population and becom[ing], in relative terms, a wo/man of wealth," adding that "left-wing anthropologists are especially prone to the seductions of being able to behave like local gentry and dis-

pense benefaction. It provides an immediate and entirely false feeling that you have got close to the people."

16 See Winkin (1992) on Goffman, and also the overly instrumental view of the obligation of reciprocity in R. Wax (1952). M. Wax (1980) and Thorne (1980) discuss average conclusions that "informed consent" in ethnography is impossible.

17 Also see Barley (1988), Crick (1992:180), Dumont (1978:192), Ewing (1994), Gal (1993:349), Gossen (1993:453), Gottlieb and Graham (1993), Kulick (1992:271–72), Wikan (1990, 1992), and many others. Like it or not, anyone asking about what those socialized in a culture take for granted, or even observing what is unremarkable to "the natives," indicates the possibility of alternative cognitive and social arrangements and raises to consciousness contradictory beliefs and explanations that normally go unquestioned within a society (Goody 1977; Murray 1983). Interrogators and observers are necessarily stimulators of some degree of mental estrangement. The imperviousness of cultural assumptions varies, but the observer is necessarily also observed and the interpreter interpreted. See Hong (1994a, 1994b) for a chilling example.

18 This was still the case on a visit from Manuel in the summer of 1992. Even Jaime's carrying back a copy of my 1987 book on male homosexuality in Latin America for Manuel did not lead to any discussion between them of their involvement in homosexuality or of their place in my text.

19 With regard to another very un-introspective culture, Mulder (1985:64, 71) wrote, "Whatever is to be found deep down in the self is a Thai secret about which one often knows little oneself," but as long as people do not challenge the rules in public, "there is room for some tolerated individual deviation" from the rules. See Murray (1992a) on some parallels between Thailand and Latin America and Allyn (1991) on Thai organization of homosexualities. A will not to know about male-male eroticism and sex seems to be part of the circum-Mediterranean culture area and was carried west by Iberian conquistadors and east by imans (Khan 1990; Murray in press).

20 In addition to the prototypical American in Paris, there has been a long procession of sexual pilgrims from what has been felt to be the stifling repression of England and Germany to what they felt to be the warm and open embraces of Italians, North Africans, and southeastern and southern Asians. I think that there is a certain symbiosis of convenience and space for experimentation in this. I am well aware that other (horrified) views of such exchanges, and of male sexuality in general, exist.

21 When he visited me while I was writing this chapter, I couldn't resist eliciting anew a sexual history. He told me that he had never been penetrated. Although I was barely startled by this denial of behavior in which I had been directly involved more than a decade earlier (in contrast to Raúl's denial within a few minutes of the deed) I still found it impossible to challenge the report with "I know better: *I* fucked you!"

22 Some might think that there was something neocolonial about exploring

my sexuality in Guatemala (see Manalansan 1991). Understanding the role of difference in desire is not the analytic task of the moment. Nonetheless, and at the risk of sounding defensive, I can't avoid noting that I was sexually imprinted on Jesús, the Mexican-American with whom I had my first (extramarital) affair in Tucson before I spent a night south of the U.S. border. He was more affluent than I was, besides being far more attractive, more experienced, and two years older, so I don't think a charge of exploitation could be sustained in the first, shaping instance. And by no means has most of my sexual career been enacted in Latin America or with Latinos. Those eager to judge such matters might also consider the phenomenon of Latinos visiting the United States or Spain to explore *their* desires. Trying out in a foreign country what one does not want discussed by one's family and neighbors is a two-way street (or runway).

23   In particular, my experience of the disparity between participated-in behavior and reported behavior made me dubious about the kind of self-reports about sexual behavior on which AIDS epidemiology relies. Statements of the "I never get fucked" sort may communicate an identity, although I am not convinced that interviewers can distinguish statements about behavior from statements of socially approved identity—what one is supposed to be, do, and not do rather than what one does. Contrary to the initial emphasis on kinds of people rather than kinds of behavior transmitting HIV, identity does not transmit HIV or cause AIDS. Denials of behavior that are statements of identity or are presentations of socially approved behavior not only obscure epidemiology but also impede prevention among those who count themselves out of being at risk (Bolton 1992; Murray 1994; Murray and Payne 1988). Unfortunately, eliciting norms is what anthropologists do best. Elucidating the relationship between ideal norms and actual behavior was not a strong point of Boasian or of functionalist anthropology. The cognitive turn of the 1960s (Lévi-Strauss's proclamations about the savage mind as well as ethnoscience and its successors) rejected behaviorism and ignored behavior. Although occasionally reaching beyond explicating old texts to counterfeiting voices of the other in carefully managed inscriptions of "dialogue," purportedly "postmodern" anthropology has not shown any interest in reclaiming behavior as an object of interest.

24   Although I have generally focused on trying to understand intracultural sexual meaning, I join Manalansan (1991:39) in viewing unequal intercultural sexual encounter as a phenomenon worth trying to understand. We know something of how the alien consumers view their roles and those of their sexual "partners" (Davidson 1988; Itiel 1990, 1991; Kutsche and Page 1992; Kutsche 1995; Lane 1978). We need testimony from the suppliers, not just the consumers' inferences about what their suppliers think. Even if we are to accept that the consumers accurately inscribe what their suppliers tell them, I think that we still should be skeptical about the meaning of what the latter tell those whom they are trying to cast in the patron role.

25   They are particularly so in the case of penetrative sex, although there are a few dissenters against the taboo. Wade (1993:212) argues that "sexual re-

lations between an anthropologist and his or her informants imply the same kinds of ethical or emotional difficulties as any other relationship between these parties. Such problems, while they may be more intense, are not qualitatively different" (also see Cesara 1982 for a woman's rejection of the taboo). Ethnography in general is based on instrumental use of other human beings who rarely (if ever) understand the uses to which the ethnographer is putting friendship, seemingly idle chat, and confidings in order to inscribe culture and advance the ethnographer's career, fame, and occasionally some measure of fortune, especially relative to those inscribed. Thorne (1980:287) rightly noted that fieldworkers often have not tried very hard to explain what observational research means to those they observe, preferring to misrepresent what they are doing. (I actually was learning the language of Mesoamerican homosexuality and didn't at the time define what I was doing as fieldwork.)

26   The lack of private space for sex, the novelty of relationships with North Americans, and the desperate wish to emigrate are less likely to be factors in the sexual relations between citizens of countries of roughly equivalent levels of affluence (Bolton 1991).

27   See Allyn (1992, 1994), Foster (1991), Jackson (1989), and Khan (1990) for examples. Among my elders who have written about male homosexuality in Latin America, Joe Carrier, Paul Kutsche, and Clark Taylor have been exemplary in seeking out and examining what Latin Americans have written about homosexuality. They also supplemented asking questions by observing intracultural relations in semipublic spaces such as bathhouses that either did not exist or that I did not know about in Guatemala in 1978–79.

28   John Boswell (1990:205) suggested the "cum shot" in contemporary erotic films as an example: If these are the only sexual representations that survive, future historians will conclude that coitus interruptus was an invariable part of late-twentieth-century heterosexual and homosexual behavior. This must be the place for the obligatory reference to Bakhtin (1981:425), too, if it isn't too late already. I'm as pro-multivocal and pro-dialogical as the next person, so long as I choose which chunks of the dialogue to reproduce and (like Dosteovsky) what of the polyphony to inscribe.

References Cited

Allyn, Eric. 1991. *Trees in the Same Forest: Thailand's Culture and Gay Subculture*. Bangkok: Bua Luang.

———. 1992. *The Dove Coos: Gay Experiences by the Men of Thailand*. Bangkok: Bua Luang.

———. *The Dove Coos II: Gay Experiences by the Men of Thailand*. Bangkok: Bua Luang.

Bakhtin, Mikhail M. 1981. *The Dialogic Imagination*. Austin: University of Texas Press.

Barley, Nigel. 1988. *Not a Hazardous Sport*. New York: Holt.

Bloch, Maurice. 1990. "Language, Anthropology and Cognitive Science." *Man* (n.s.) 26:183–98.

Bolton, Ralph. 1991. "Mapping Terra Incognita: Sex Research for AIDS Prevention—An Urgent Agenda for the 1990s." In *The Time of AIDS,* ed. Gilbert Herdt and Shirley Lindenbaum, 124–58. Newbury Park, Calif.: Sage.

———. 1992. "AIDS and Promiscuity: Muddles in the Models of HIV Prevention." *Medical Anthropology* 14:145–223.

Boswell, John. 1990. "Sexual Categories, Sexual Universals." In *Homosexuality as Behavior and Identity: Dialogues of the Sexual Revolution,* ed. Lawrence D. Mass, 202–32. New York: Harrington Park Press.

Bowman, Glenn. 1989. "Fucking Tourists: Sexual Relations and Tourism in Jerusalem's Old City." *Critique of Anthropology* 9:77–93.

Caplan, Pat. 1992. "Spirits and Sex: A Swahili Informant and His Diary." In *Anthropology and Autobiography,* ed. Judith Okely and Helen Callaway, 64–81. London: Routledge.

Carrier, Joseph M. 1972. "Urban Mexican Male Homosexual Encounters." Ph.D. dissertation, University of California, Irvine.

Cesara, Manda [Karla O. Poewe]. 1982. *Reflections of a Woman Anthropologist: No Hiding Place.* New York: Academic Press.

Cole, Mabel Cook. 1929. *Savage Gentlemen.* London: Macmillan.

Crick, Malcolm. 1992. "Ali and Me: An Essay in Streetcorner Anthropology." In *Anthropology and Autobiography,* ed. Judith Okely and Helen Callaway, 175–92. London: Routledge.

Davidson, Michael. 1988 [1970]. *Some Boys.* London: Gay Men's Press.

Delph, Edward William. 1978. *The Silent Community: Public Homosexual Encounters.* Beverly Hills: Sage Publications.

Dumont, Jean-Paul. 1978. *The Headman and I: Ambiguity and Ambivalence in the Fieldworking Experience.* Austin: University of Texas Press.

Ewing, Katherine. 1992. "Review of *Notes on Love in a Tamil Family* by Margaret Trawick." *American Anthropologist* 94:237–38.

———. 1994. "Dreams from a Saint." *American Anthropologist* 96:571–83.

Foster, David William. 1991. *Gay and Lesbian Themes in Latin American Literature.* Austin: University of Texas Press.

Gal, Susan. 1993. "Diversity and Contestation in Linguistic Ideologies." *Language in Society* 22:337–59.

Goody, Jack. 1977. *The Domestication of the Savage Mind.* Cambridge: Cambridge University Press.

Gossen, Gary H. 1993. "The Other in Chamula Tzotzil Cosmology and History: Reflections of a Kansan in Chiapas." *Cultural Anthropology* 8:443–75.

Gottlieb, Alma, and Phillip Graham. 1993. *Parallel Worlds: An Anthropologist and a Writer Encounter Africa.* New York: Macmillan.

Greenberg, David F. 1993. "The Pleasures of Homosexuality." Paper presented at the annual meeting of the American Sociological Association, Miami.

Hendry, Joy. 1992. "The Paradox of Friendship in the Field." In *Anthropology and Autobiography,* ed. Judith Okely and Helen Callaway, 163–74. London: Routledge.

Herdt, Gilbert H. 1984. *Ritualized Homosexuality in Melanesia*. Berkeley: University of California Press.

———. 1991. "Representations of Homosexuality." *Journal of the History of Sexuality* 1:603–32.

Hong, Keelung. 1994a. "Experiences as a 'Native' Observing Anthropology." *Anthropology Today* 10(3): 6–9.

———. 1994b. "Anthropology on Taiwan." *Anthropology Today* 10(5): 26–27.

Hong Keelung, and Stephen O. Murray. 1989. "Complicity with Domination." *American Anthropologist* 91:1028–30.

———. 1995. "A Taiwanese Woman Who Became a Spirit Medium: Native and Alien Models of Possession." Manuscript.

Itiel, Joseph. 1989. *Philippine Diary: A Gay Guide to the Philippines*. San Francisco: International Wavelength.

———. 1991. *De Onda: A Gay Guide to Mexico and Its People*. San Francisco: International Wavelength.

Jackson, Peter A. 1989. *Male Homosexuality in Thailand*. Amsterdam: Global Academic Publishers. Revised. 1995. Bankok: Bua Luang.

Khan, Badruddin. 1990. "Not-So-Gay Life in Karachi." *Society of Lesbian and Gay Anthropologists Newsletter* 12(1): 10–19. [Revised version in *Islamic Homosexualities,* ed. Stephen Murray and Will Roscoe. New York: New York University Press, in press.]

Kulick, Don. 1992. *Language Shift and Cultural Reproduction: Socialization, Self, and Syncretism in a New Guinea Village*. New York: Cambridge University Press.

Kutsche, Paul. 1991. "Review of *La formación de una contracultura* by Jacobo Schifter Sikora." *Society of Lesbian and Gay Anthropologists Newsletter* 13(1): 19–20.

———. 1995. "Two Truths about Costa Rica." In *Latin American Male Homosexualities,* ed. Stephen Murray, 111–37. Albuquerque: University of New Mexico Press.

Kutsche, Paul, and J. Bryan Page. 1992. "Male Sexual Identity in Costa Rica." *Latin American Anthropological Review* 3:7–14.

Lacey, E. A. 1979. "Latin America." *Gay Sunshine* 40:22–31.

Lancaster, Roger. 1992. *Life Is Hard*. Berkeley: University of California Press.

Lane, Erskine. 1978. *Game-Texts: A Guatemalan Journal*. San Francisco: Gay Sunshine Press.

Manalansan, Martin F. IV. 1991. "Neo-Colonial Desire" [review of Itiel (1989)]. *Society of Lesbian and Gay Anthropologists Newsletter* 13:37–40.

Mulder, Niels. 1985. *Everyday Life in Thailand*. Bangkok: Duang Kamol.

Murray, Stephen O. 1979a. "Institutional Elaboration of a Quasi-Ethnic Community." *International Review of Modern Sociology* 9:165–77.

———. 1979b. "The Art of Gay Insulting." *Anthropological Linguistics* 21:211–23.

———. 1980. "Lexical and Institutional Elaboration: The 'Species Homosexual' in Guatemala." *Anthropological Linguistics* 22:177–85.

———. 1981. "Die ethnoromantische Versuchung." In *Der Wissenschaftler und das Irrationale,* ed. Hans-Peter Duerr, 377–85. Frankfurt/M: Syndikat.

————. 1982. "The Dissolution of Classical Ethnoscience." *Journal of the History of the Behavioral Sciences* 18:163–75.

————. 1983. "Fuzzy Sets and Abominations." *Man* (n.s.) 19:396–99.

————. 1987. *Male Homosexuality in Central and South America.* New York: Gay Academic Union.

————. 1991. "Sleeping with Natives as a Source of Data" [review of Itiel (1991)]. *Society of Lesbian and Gay Anthropologists Newsletter* 13:49–51.

————. 1992a. "The 'Underdevelopment' of Gay Homosexuality in México, Guatemala, Peru and Thailand." In *Modern Homosexualities,* ed. Ken Plummer, 29–38. London: Routledge.

————. 1992b. Review of Parker (1991). *Journal of the History of Sexuality* 2:679–82.

————. 1993. Review of Lancaster (1992). *Society of Lesbian and Gay Anthropologists Newsletter* 15:32–35.

————. 1994. "The Obdurateness of AIDS 'Risk Groups.'" *Contemporary Sociology* 23:751–53.

————. 1995. *Latin American Homosexualities.* Albuquerque: University of New Mexico Press.

————. In press. "The Will Not to Know: Traditional and Recent Accommodations of Homosexuality in Islamic Societies." In *Islamic Homosexualities,* ed. Stephen Murray and Will Roscoe. New York: New York University Press.

Murray, Stephen O., and Manuel Arboleda G. 1987 [1982]. "Stigma Transformation and Relexification: 'Gay' in Latin America." In *Male Homosexuality in Central and South America,* ed. Stephen Murray, 129–38. New York: Gay Academic Union.

Murray, Stephen O., and Keelung Hong. 1994. *Taiwanese Culture, Taiwanese Society.* Lanham, Md.: University Press of America.

Murray, Stephen O., and Kenneth W. Payne. 1988. "The Promiscuity Paradigm and AIDS." *California Sociologist* 11:13–54. [Revised version in *Homosexuality and Medicine, Health, and Science,* ed. Wayne Dynes and Stephen Donaldson, 119–60. New York: Garland, 1992.]

Parker, Richard G. 1987. "AIDS in Urban Brazil." *Medical Anthropology Quarterly* 1:155–75.

————. 1991. *Bodies, Pleasures, and Passions: Sexual Culture in Contemporary Brazil.* Boston: Beacon.

Redfield, Robert. 1953. *The Primitive World and Its Transformation.* Chicago: University of Chicago Press.

Simmel, Georg. 1950. *The Sociology of Georg Simmel.* Glencoe, Ill.: Free Press.

Tax, Sol. 1941. "World View and Social Relations in Guatemala." *American Anthropologist* 39:423–44.

Taylor, Clark L. 1978. "El Ambiente." Ph.D. dissertation, University of California, Berkeley.

Tedlock, Barbara. 1991. "From Participant Observation to the Observation of Participation." *Journal of Anthropological Research* 47:69–94.

Thorne, Barrie. 1980. "'You Still Takin' Notes?': Fieldwork and Problems of Informed Consent." *Social Problems* 27:284–97.

Veyne, Paul. 1988. *Did the Greeks Believe in Their Myths?* Chicago: University of Chicago Press.

Wade, Peter. 1993. "Sexuality and Masculinity in Fieldwork among Colombian Blacks." In *Gendered Fields,* ed. D. Bell, P. Caplan, and W. Karim. New York: Routledge.

Wax, Murray L. 1980. "Paradoxes of 'Consent' in the Practice of Fieldwork." *Social Problems* 27:272–83.

Wax, Rosalie Hankey. 1952. "Reciprocity as a Field Technique." *Human Organization* 11:34–37.

Whitam, Frederick L. 1987. "Os entendidos: Gay Life in São Paulo." In *Male Homosexuality in Central and South America,* ed. Stephen Murray, 24–39. New York: Gay Academic Union.

———. 1992. "Bayots and Callboys: Homosexual-Heterosexual Relations in the Philippines." In *Oceanic Homosexualities,* ed. Stephen Murray, 231–48. New York: Garland.

Wikan, Unni. 1984. "Shame and Honour: A Contestable Pair." *Man* (n.s.) 19:635–52.

———. 1990. *Managing Turbulent Hearts: A Balinese Formula for Living.* Chicago: University of Chicago Press.

———. 1992. "Beyond the Words: The Power of Resonance." *American Ethnologist* 19:460–82.

Williams, Walter L. 1993. "Being Gay and Doing Research on Homosexuality in Non-Western Cultures." *Journal of Sex Research* 30:115–20.

Winkin, Yves. 1992. "Baltasound as the Symbolic Capital of Social Interaction." Paper presented at the annual meeting of the International Communication Association, Miami.

Zapata, Luis. 1985. *Los jirones.* Mexico, D.F.: Posada.

13. Out of the Closet and into Print: Sexual Identity in the Textual Field
James Wafer

What is "lesbian and gay anthropology"? If one were to define it on the basis of the extant literature, the term would appear to refer to anthropological studies *about* homosexuality. To date, the ethnographies that have dealt with lesbian and gay issues have generally externalized homosexuality as an object of research, which has no necessary or obvious connection with the sexual identity of the ethnographer.

I would suggest that there is a complementary approach to lesbian and gay anthropology, as yet fairly undeveloped but likely to become increasingly important as the field of lesbian and gay studies gains wider acceptance within the academy. This approach takes its inspiration from those theoreticians of gay studies who call for "a gay perspective on society and culture in general" (Aldrich 1992:27). The kind of scholarship being advocated by these writers is not defined in terms of the object of study, which may be homosexuality but also may be anything else. It is characterized rather by the fact that it is based on "the different angle . . . which gay scholars can offer" on any subject of research, an angle that proceeds from a "gay sensibility" (Aldrich 1992:27–28).

What would this mean for anthropology, specifically for researchers engaged in fieldwork and ethnographic writing? Is it possible to imagine a "gay ethnography"?

Anthropologists who have a gay sensibility might think that a gay ethnography is one that sleeps with other ethnographies (the ultimate form of intertextuality). But let me try to characterize it in a more scholarly fashion. A gay ethnography would be one in which the identity of the ethnographer as a lesbian or as a gay man is an explicit and integral part of the text. At the time of writing there have been very few ethnographies that would fit this definition.[1] One of the reasons for this, I suspect, is that the writing of a gay ethnography entails greater risks than the simple matter of coming out of the closet because it threatens cultural norms in a more profound way.

In the Preface to *Mother Camp*, Esther Newton writes that "anthropology (and the other social sciences) are the ideological arms of sociopolitical arrangements. . . . In general, scholarship reflects and molds the sociopolitical system called a university, and universities are not independent from our social order, but are paid and organized to perpetuate and legitimize it. Not all the ways in which we are implicated are obvious, though. Some are so subtly structural that trying to change them is like trying to crawl out of your own bones" (1979:xvi).

One of the ways in which lesbian and gay scholars are implicated in perpetuating and legitimizing the prevailing social order is by acquiescing to the maintenance of a distinction between their professional lives and private lives. This distinction is closely related to the deeply rooted dichotomy between work and home, which, as David Schneider (1980: 45–48) has shrewdly pointed out, is one of the most basic constructs of American culture.

My particular concern is with the way this distinction affects ethnographic practice—that is, fieldwork and the writing that results from it. Any scholar who attempts to write from a "gay perspective" is faced with a difficult problem of identity management. Sexual identity is regarded as part of one's private life, and therefore, according to the prevailing norms of academic culture, not supposed to intrude into one's professional life. For lesbian and gay ethnographers, the problem is compounded by the fact that their writings are based on fieldwork. This means, for a start, that they have to face the question of how to manage their sexual identity in the field as well as in their writing. In addition, they have to find a way of reconciling their field persona with the identity they construct for themselves in their fieldnotes and ethnographies.

The underlying problem is not one that lesbian and gay ethnographers face alone. All ethnographers confront the issue of how to divide their experiences in the field into professional experiences and private experiences and how to translate these experiences into an anthropological text. The ethnographic tradition has bequeathed a fairly standard set of procedures for dealing with this problem, both in the field and in the resulting texts, and these practices merit closer analysis here.

It is common for fieldwork methodology courses to encourage students to believe that they can carry over into a host culture the same compartmentalization of their being into a professional self and a private self that is normative in middle-class Western culture. An important technique for maintaining this compartmentalization is the keeping of two separate sets of notes. Field experiences that belong to one's professional life go into fieldnotes, which are the basis for professional publications. And the experiences that belong to one's private life go into a diary, which, if it ever reaches the eyes of a reading public in an uncensored form, should only do so, as in the celebrated case of Malinowski (1967), after one's death. Alternatively, the diary may provide the material for a work that will be carefully distinguished from "real ethnography" by being called something like an "ethnographic memoir" or "personal narrative" (cf. Gatewood 1984).

The genre conventions of ethnography itself provide another means of maintaining this compartmentalization. In a traditional ethnography the body of the text reflects only one's professional persona—objective, detached, and scientific. But a discreet bow in the direction of one's private life is permitted in the frontmatter and the appendixes.

The most private part of the ethnography is also the briefest—the dedication, if there is one. The dedication may be to an individual or individuals who had no connection at all with the production of the text. In the preface one may acknowledge people who are members of one's private world, such as friends and family, but only on the pretext that one's labors were facilitated by their support. And in the introduction or an appendix one can write briefly and circumspectly about such details of one's private experience in the field as how one got to be there, what it was like, how one managed to establish relationships with people there, and how one comported oneself for the purpose of "gathering data." This is justified on the grounds that it is a discussion of field methodology. But even under such a scientific-sounding rubric, this information is too private to be permitted to leak into the body of the text, which is supposed to be purely professional.

The result of this compartmentalization is, as the literary theorist Mary Louise Pratt points out, that most ethnographic writings "leave out or hopelessly impoverish some of the most important knowledge [ethnographers] have achieved, including the self-knowledge." She continues, "For the lay person, such as myself, the main evidence of a problem is the simple fact that ethnographic writing tends to be surprisingly boring. How, one asks constantly, could such interesting people doing such interesting things produce such dull books? What did they have to do to themselves?" (1986:33).

There are good reasons for this, of course. It is self-evident that in order to make a career in the profession of anthropology one must appear to be a professional. Because one's published accounts are the main evidence of one's professional status, it is important that these accounts do not give away any information about one's private life, in the field or out of it, that could be construed as incompatible with professionalism.

This is a problematic situation for all ethnographers, but particularly so, I think, for those who are lesbian or gay. As I have said, all ethnographers are faced with the difficult question of how to transform their lived experience in the field into a social scientific text. Most opt for the safe course of writing about that experience as though they were not in it, by analyzing the social and cultural environment they lived in as an objective reality separate from themselves.

There has been a fairly recent move toward more experiential ethnographies in which the ethnographer enters the text as just another participant in the social and cultural world being described rather than as an observer with a god's-eye view (Jackson 1989). But the validity of this kind of ethnography is still hotly disputed in some quarters, and the fact that it is routinely referred to as "experimental" indicates that its legitimacy as social science has not been resolved.

Understand that what is at issue here is the simple question of the ethnographer's presence in his or her account of a social and cultural world, not the question of the ethnographer's identity or behavior in that world. In an academic climate where even this is controversial, it is easy to understand why lesbian and gay anthropologists are not rushing to publish ethnographies that give an account of their experience *as* lesbians or gay men in another culture.

The reactions to Tobias Schneebaum's book *Where the Spirits Dwell* (1988) are instructive in this regard. The anthropologists who have read the book (which does not pretend to be an ethnography, even though it provides an account of another culture) generally treat it as a dirty joke. As though it were not sufficient provocation to admit that he is gay, Schneebaum breaks the ultimate taboo by being explicit about the fact that he had sex with the natives. One straight colleague of mine commented that it was obvious Schneebaum's main motivation for going to the field was to get screwed. It is hardly necessary to add that this was seen as sufficient reason for dismissing the writer and his work, whatever the merits or defects of Schneebaum as an ethnographer. But why?

The answer seems to be that the textualized field is one that the ethnographer is supposed to enter as a disembodied and therefore asexual being. Ideally, there would not only be no sex in the text, but also no desire. Yet it is hard to imagine that the actual field experience of ethnographers could be so insipid. Surely eros plays as great a role in structuring their relationships in the field as it does in any other social context.

These difficulties are not insuperable, but there are certainly no ready-made guidelines for dealing with them. For anthropologists who are motivated to explore the possibilities of lesbian and gay ethnography, and thus to challenge the cultural norm that separates professional life from private life, the most difficult task is to mount the challenge in such a way that their writing is still taken seriously as scholarship. There are few precedents from which to learn. I can, however, give some examples from my own experience of the problems to be faced and provide some discussion of my attempts to deal with them.

When I was planning the fieldwork for my doctoral dissertation, I wanted to go to Brazil to study the religions generally known as "Afro-Brazilian" because I knew from the literature that many of the practitioners of these religions are what we would call homosexual. However, when I was applying for research grants, I was advised by the chair of my department that focusing on homosexuality in my research proposal would guarantee that I would not be funded.

I took his advice and transformed my proposal in such a way that my research was to focus on trance and its relationship to conceptions of personhood. This would, I thought, give me a chance to study homosexuality without having to be explicit about it in my proposal. It was a compromise, but one I had to make in order to be able to do fieldwork at all.

I received funding and went to Brazil. Initially, I followed the counsel of my teachers and kept separate sets of notes—one a set of fieldnotes directly related to my research and the other a diary. It was not long before I abandoned this practice because I found it impossible to decide where to draw the line between professional experience and private experience. I could not limit my professional experiences to the business hours of 9 to 5, nor regard the rest of the day as in any way private and certainly not as irrelevant to my professional ethnographic purposes.

I developed a romantic relationship with an anthropology student in the city where I was doing my fieldwork, and he became my "research assistant." This opened many doors. It was not just that he knew and was able to introduce me to members of the religious houses I wanted to study, but also that our relationship seemed to give me quasi-insider status. On the one hand, the simple fact of being known to be gay immediately removed an invisible barrier. On the other hand, there was the additional advantage of being, so to speak, "married into" the culture by virtue of this relationship.

This had other benefits apart from the entrée it gave me. It meant, for example, that I was regarded as "accounted for" within the kinship system. Other ethnographers, particularly women and gay men (e.g., Picchi 1989; Proschan 1990), have written about the problem of being single in the field and therefore being "unaccounted for" in the kinship system. In my case, the fact of being accounted for meant that I was less a threat than I might otherwise have been because I was less likely to be interested in other people's boyfriends, lovers, or husbands. At the same time, it meant that my friendships with other people in the community where I was working were relieved of, if not sexual overtones, at least any serious pressure to become involved in a particular relationship that might have prejudiced my friendships with a wide range of people in the community by upsetting the prevailing arrangement of alliances and balance of power.

Thus, for me, the issues of management of my sexual identity in the field were different from those that face many of my gay and lesbian colleagues who work in cultures where being gay is not so taken for granted. Issues of identity management did, of course, confront me, but they were not related to my sexual orientation so much as to my identity as an anthropologist, a white foreigner, and a person with a source of dollars.

The real question of management of my sexual identity came up in the writing stage. In my fieldnotes I had tried to forget the professional-private distinction. Obviously, I was most interested in particular information that would throw light on my research topic, but this information was woven inextricably into the fabric of daily community life. This made it virtually impossible to keep notes that were immediately related to my research interests in a way that separated them from notes that concerned the rest of my life.

When the time came for writing up these notes in the form of a professional monograph, which was to be my doctoral dissertation and which subsequently appeared as a book (Wafer 1991), I was confronted with issues of identity management that I had never had to face in the field. The division between professional life and private life is a form of implicit knowledge so deeply embedded in American culture that I knew if I ignored the distinction in my ethnography, as I had done in my field-notes, my work would have every chance of being dismissed as unprofessional. I had to find a way of appearing to respect this distinction while at the same time critiquing and subverting it.

My solution was to try to write an experiential ethnography that was not confessional. I wanted to avoid turning the work into an autobiographical episode because that would almost certainly have made it vulnerable to the criticism of being unprofessional or, at least, of falling outside the boundaries of what could legitimately be called ethnography. At the same time, I intended to construct the text in a way that reflected my experience in the field, because I believed it necessary to demonstrate that accounts of other cultures do not have to be "hopelessly impoverished" of self-knowledge (to use Pratt's expression) in order to qualify as ethnographies.

The constraints imposed by the decision not to write confessionally were ones I was not reluctant to accept. I did not want the events in which I had participated during my fieldwork to be seen as mere incidents in the saga of the anthropologist as hero (or, for that matter, anti-hero). The "hero" of an ethnography is, after all, a particular social world, and the anthropologist is only a very minor player in that world. I felt that an excessive preoccupation with my personal concerns would have been out of proportion. It would have limited the attention I could give to the other players and to the collective drama in which we were all involved.

These decisions raised certain difficult questions about how to deal with the matter of homosexuality in the text. My attraction to the Candomblé religion was based on reports that homosexuality was widespread among its practitioners. In the course of my fieldwork, however, I began to doubt that theories of homosexuality provided the most appropriate framework for analyzing what I actually encountered. These theories have been developed in response to a culture-specific taboo that seemed to have little influence in the Brazilian community whose life I shared. I began to believe that to focus on homosexuality in the text would be to allow a personal preoccupation to obscure the subtle ways in which this subculture was different from my own.

It was not just that in this particular community, which I call Jaraci, same-sex relationships were regarded as commonplace and were taken for granted. More important, sexual orientation did not play a part in the formation of significant subdivisions of the social world. It is hard for gays or lesbians in the English-speaking world to appreciate the difference this makes. Their attitudes have been formed through the experience of struggling to have the rights of a minority called "homosexuals" recognized by a majority called "heterosexuals." Classification according to sexual orientation has been essential to this process and has led to the formation of two distinct social categories that are, in principle if not in practice, endogamous. Their separateness has been reinforced through their embodiment in social institutions and practices that profoundly affect interaction across the boundary that separates their members.

In Jaraci it was different. Although some people expressed an exclusive sexual preference for their own sex, they did not belong to a distinct category because there was no single homogeneous opposite category from which to distinguish them. It seemed to be taken for granted that most members of the community were capable of same-sex relationships until proved otherwise. Some people displayed a preference for relationships with the opposite sex, but there was no a priori assumption that such a preference was exclusive. This meant that people's sexual tastes did not lead them to see themselves as fundamentally different kinds of beings.

This had important implications for social relations. It meant, for example, that any interaction between persons of the same sex, as well as between persons of opposite sexes, had a potentially erotic dimension. It would probably not be an exaggeration to say that life in Jaraci was characterized by an atmosphere of imminent sexual adventure.

In my ethnography I wanted to enable the reader to experience something of the flavor of life in Jaraci, and I tried to do this by making local discourse and practice the basis for the text's structure. This meant avoiding the terms *homosexual* and *heterosexual* because the conceptual framework they imply was not part of the local discourse and was not embodied in the local sexual *habitus*.

This is not to argue that the concept of homosexuality is so culture-specific that it has no use in cross-cultural studies (Murray 1984:45), nor that it cannot be fruitfully applied in analyses of the sexuality of adherents of the Afro-Brazilian religions, as it has been, for example, by Fry (1982), Birman (1988), and Teixeira (1986). It is simply to state that my particular aim, which was to write about Candomblé in a way that focused on the operation of native categories in everyday life, precluded the use of the term.

How, then, was I to write about erotic life in Jaraci? It is easy to say that same-sex relationships were taken for granted there, but it is less easy to create a text that induces the reader to take them for granted. My solution to this problem was never to focus on the Jaracians' sexual relationships as a particular issue, but to treat them rather as background information that is distributed throughout the text. For example, the three "fathers-of-saint" (religious leaders of Candomblé) whom I got to know best all engaged in sexual relationships with other men, at least one of them exclusively, but this information is never assembled at a single point in the text. The father-of-saint of the Candomblé house where I was initiated is introduced in chapter 3: "Marinalvo was with his new boyfriend—the fifth, he later told us, he had had in the five nights since *carnaval* had begun" (23). In chapter 6 we learn that his "sexual practices were well known in Jaraci, and no one seemed to pay them much heed, or regard them as in any way unusual, except for his mother, Neuza, who lived a few doors away. She had threatened to kill him if she ever found him in bed with another man. . . . She confided to us that she would not mind so much if Marinalvo settled down with one of his nice middle-class boyfriends. What she objected to was his habit of making out with all the young ruffians of the district" (110).

This provides the background to a subplot that is very minor but that confirms the point that Marinalvo's mother is concerned more with class than with sexual orientation. We soon find out that Marinalvo has a new (middle-class) boyfriend. Delcir is a computer programmer and on friendly terms with Marinalvo's mother (112–13). However by chapter 9 he has become "Marinalvo's ex-boyfriend Delcir" (177).

The sexual tastes of the other two fathers-of-saint are hinted at early in the text but do not become obvious until quite late. In the case of Edivaldo, we learn in chapter 3 that he "receives" (goes into trance with) a female spirit called Maria Eugênia, "an *exua* of exquisite refinement, who dusts off a chair before sitting down, and drinks with her little finger crooked" (43). Whatever suspicions this may arouse are not confirmed until chapter 9, when there is passing mention of Edivaldo's boyfriend (177).

In the case of Biju, we also find out in chapter 3 that he receives a female spirit, called Pomba-Gira (43). The attentive reader will, of course, wonder whether this is the same Pomba-Gira who kisses the narrator in the opening scene of the ethnography (3–4), but this riddle is not solved until the last page of the final chapter (178). In the meantime we learn of Biju that "he had a masculine demeanor; but in the summer he donned the skirts and turban of a Baiana and set up a street-stall in one of the beach-side suburbs, where he sold African food he prepared himself" (164).

These examples could be multiplied because, of course, the fathers-of-saint were not the only people in the community to engage in relationships with the same sex. But the passages I have quoted are probably sufficient to indicate the strategies I used in writing about the erotic life of Jaraci.

There remains the question of how I dealt with the matter of my own sexual identity in the text. I wanted to write an experiential ethnography but not a confessional one. The distinction between the two genres is subtle but important and had significant implications for my approach to textual self-representation.

Fieldwork is recognized in the anthropological community as a kind of rite of passage and thus as a turning point in the life history of the ethnographer. In my own case this was doubly so because it was in the field that I began a relationship with the man who is now my partner. Because he was also my field assistant, and thus intimately involved in most of the events I participated in during my fieldwork, it was not a simple matter for me to write an experiential ethnography without turning it into an ethnographic love story.

My solution to this dilemma was to treat my relationship in the field in the same way as I treated the relationships of the Jaracians—as background information distributed throughout the ethnography. There were also other reasons for this approach. One was that I wanted to write about my sexual orientation in the same way as the Jaracians saw it—that is, as something so commonplace that it did not merit any flourish of trumpets. Another was that by writing this relationship into the text as merely a subplot I hoped to be able to keep the focus of the ethnography on the life of the community as a whole.

I tried to achieve this in the following way: my field assistant, "Archipiado," is introduced in chapter 1 as "an anthropology student . . . [who] had friends who were involved with Candomblé" (10). He appears again briefly in chapter 3 in a discussion of my attempts to find somewhere to live in Jaraci: "I also had to consider Archipiado. . . . From our place in the Pelourinho it had been fairly easy for him to get buses to his classes at the university. If we lived in Jaraci, transport would be a constant problem" (25). This is one of a number of textual subterfuges I used in order not to give my own relationship disproportionate prominence in the ethnography. The subtext of the passage just quoted is, of course, that Archipiado and I lived together.

In chapter 3 there is also a longish account of a "love-magic rite on behalf of a couple who were soon to be separated" (47). The fact that this rite occurs shortly before the narrator's departure from Brazil is intended to be a clue to the identity of the couple involved. Other clues occur later in the ethnography when it becomes clear that the patron deities of the narrator and Archipiado are Oxalá and Oxum, respectively. These are the same two deities who are involved in the rite.

I had a number of reasons for not wanting to be explicit about the identity of the couple so early in the text. One reason was that the description of the rite is intended to reveal a different facet of the character of the *exu* spirits rather than to draw attention to my relationship. Another was that I was attempting to use some rudimentary literary techniques of plot construction, which meant being aware of the importance of allusiveness and timing (or what, in other genres, would be called "suspense") in the creation of a story-line.

There is a series of other clues about the nature of my relationship with my field assistant in the course of the text, but they are not drawn together into a disclosure until chapter 7. I was about to go into ritual seclusion and had already undergone some initial purificatory rites. The priest who was head of the religious center where I carried out my fieldwork said that my field assistant and I could spend the last night before my seclusion alone together, in the center's kitchen, but we could not touch each other and would have to sleep with our bodies in opposite directions, our heads toward each other's feet. The subsequent events I describe thus:

> Archipiado and I rolled out our straw mat on the floor. Archipiado was peeved that I, with my strange notions about what constitutes good faith, insisted on following Marinalvo's instructions concerning our sleeping arrangements. He said that if Marinalvo had really meant us to take them seriously, he would not have left us alone together in the kitchen.
>
> Archipiado was probably right. The next morning Zita roused us early so that the kitchen could be used for making breakfast, and I thought I detected a certain sly tone in her voice when she asked us if we had slept well. In fact, even after Archipiado resigned himself to my intransigence, we had had a very disturbed night. (145)

These various passages make it clear that my identity as a gay man is an integral part of the text. Whether it is also explicit enough for the work to be classified as a gay ethnography depends, I suppose, on the form this embryonic genre takes as it grows to maturity. If gay ethnography turns out to be a genre in which the author is obliged to make a statement to the effect that she or he is lesbian or gay, then clearly my book about Candomblé will fall outside the definition.

Such a narrow definition of the genre would be unnecessarily limiting and also somewhat ethnocentric. Natives of the English-speaking world are not the only ethnographers, and anthropologists from other cultures may wish to write from a perspective that reflects a different construction of sexual orientation. There will probably also be other English-speaking ethnographers who decide that their work will be a more effective demonstration of the relativity of Anglo cultural categories if they try to write about sexual orientation, including their own, from the perspective of another culture.

Notes

This chapter has benefited from my discussion of the issues with Bill Leap and Hédimo Santana, from bibliographic leads provided by Frank Proschan and Dino Hodge, and from editorial comments by Ellen Lewin and Liz Goodman. I would like to thank them for their help.

1   Among those ethnographies that might fit the definition are Goodwin (1989) and Williams (1986).

References Cited

Aldrich, Robert. 1992. "Not Just a Passing Fad: Gay Studies Comes of Age." In *Gay Perspectives: Essays in Australian Gay Culture,* ed. Robert Aldrich and Garry Wotherspoon. Sydney: Department of Economic History, University of Sydney.

Birman, Patrícia. 1988. "Fazer Estilo Criando Gêneros: Estudo sobre a Construção Religiosa da Possessão e da Diferença de Gêneros em Terreiros da Baixada Fluminense." Doctoral thesis, Postgraduate Program in Social Anthropology of the National Museum of the Federal University of Rio de Janeiro.

Fry, Peter. 1982. "Homossexualidade Masculina e Cultos Afro-Brasileiros." In *Para Inglês Ver: Identidade e Política na Cultura Brasileira,* by Peter Fry, 54–86. Rio de Janeiro: Zahar.

Gatewood, John B. 1984. "A Short Typology of Ethnographic Genres: Or Ways to Write about Other Peoples." *Anthropology and Humanism Quarterly* 9(4): 5–10.

Goodwin, Joseph P. 1989. *More Man Than You'll Ever Be: Gay Folklore and Acculturation in Middle America.* Bloomington: Indiana University Press.

Jackson, Michael. 1989. *Paths toward a Clearing: Radical Empiricism and Ethnographic Inquiry.* Bloomington: Indiana University Press.

Malinowski, Bronislaw. 1967. *A Diary in the Strict Sense of the Term.* New York: Harcourt, Brace and World.

Murray, Stephen O. 1984. *Social Theory, Homosexual Realities.* Gai Saber Monograph No. 3. New York: Gay Academic Union.

Newton, Esther. 1979 [1972]. *Mother Camp: Female Impersonators in America.* 2d ed. Chicago: University of Chicago Press.

Picchi, Debra. 1989. "Yare's Anger: Conformity and Rage in the Field." *Anthropology and Humanism Quarterly* 14(2): 65–72.

Pratt, Mary Louise. 1986. "Fieldwork in Common Places." In *Writing Culture: The Poetics and Politics of Ethnography,* ed. James Clifford and George Marcus, 27–50. Berkeley: University of California Press.

Proschan, Frank. 1990. "How Is a Folklorist Like a Riddle?" *Southern Folklore* 47:1 [special issue on "Folklore Fieldwork: Sex, Sexuality, and Gender"], 57–66.

Schneebaum, Tobias. 1988. *Where the Spirits Dwell: An Odyssey in the New Guinea Jungle.* New York: Grove.

Schneider, David. 1980 [1968]. *American Kinship: A Cultural Account.* 2d ed. Chicago: University of Chicago Press.

Teixeira, Maria Lina Leão. 1986. "Transas de um Povo de Santo: Um Estudo sobre Identidades Sexuais." Master's thesis, Department of Social Sciences, Institute of Philosophy and Social Sciences, Federal University of Rio de Janeiro.

Wafer, Jim. 1991. *The Taste of Blood: Spirit Possession in Brazilian Candomblé.* Contemporary Ethnography Series. Philadelphia: University of Pennsylvania Press.

Williams, Walter L. 1986. *The Spirit and the Flesh: Sexual Diversity in American Indian Culture.* Boston: Beacon Press.

14. Requiem for a Street Fighter
Kath Weston

A mon Requiem, peut-être ai-je aussi, d'instinct, cherché à sortier du convenu. Voilà si longtemps que j'accompagne à l'orgue des services d'enterrements! J'en ai par-dessus la tête. J'ai voulu faire autre chose.[1]—Gabriel Fauré

Introït

ho was Julie Cordell?" That's the question I encountered again and again after the publication of my book on lesbians, gay men, and kinship (Weston 1991). I had expected perhaps, "Are mothers really easier to come out to than fathers?" or, "What do you think of gay marriage?" Instead, "Who was Julie . . . Julie . . . Julie . . . ?" echoed off the walls and wound its way through the telephone lines to my home in Arizona. Behind that simple question lay the difficult, unspoken ones: Was she your girlfriend? Your friend? What happened to her? Why did she die so young?

It all started with a dedication. Not the kind required to make it through the seven years it took to research and write the book. No, this dedication was spartan in comparison, a mere three lines sandwiched between the title page and the contents:

> In memory of Julie Cordell
> 1960–1983
> who came looking for community

Like many gay people of my generation, I had attended far too many funerals by the time I reached my late twenties. For San Francisco's "gay community," the 1980s was a decade that witnessed the explosion of the AIDS pandemic, the exacerbation of racial and class tensions, and worsening economic conditions for people caught in the undertow of the wave of financial speculation sweeping the city. As an ethnographer trained to read up on my subject, I knew full well that topics such as class, death, and sexuality would merit attention "in the field." As someone who claimed membership in the community I studied, I knew too well the subtle but no less debilitating effects of living in a society where heterosexuality remains a grounding assumption for social action.

As long as I restricted my voice to that of the researcher, I could not adequately communicate the experience of living under siege in a subaltern population, regardless of how explicitly I brought myself into the text. Claiming "insider" status by coming out in print did not solve my dilemma. A single body cannot bridge that mythical divide between insider and outsider, researcher and researched. I am neither, in any simple way, and yet I am both.

When I write, I can call myself a gay anthropologist or an anthropologist who is gay, a lesbian, a queer, or a human being who has foregrounded homoeroticism in her life for almost two decades now. I can hold class relations constant by introducing myself as a woman from a working-class background, or emphasize the ways that professional employment has repositioned me in the class hierarchy. I can highlight or downplay the contradictions that face an Anglo writer who sets out to research a multiethnic "gay community" that includes people of color who may or may not call themselves gay. Because my subjectivity is neither seamless nor fixed, the queering of my own identity has not always translated into feelings of closeness or identification with the people I study.[2] An ever-shifting self-as-subject has shaped my work in ways that can never be confined to field encounter or text.

In the charged context of analyzing as one lives a stigmatized existence, composing a book has meant writing not only between the lines but also behind the lines. What follows does not fall neatly into any one of the established anthropological genres of ethnography, reflections on fieldwork, or literary critique of a monograph already produced. To address that deceptively straightforward question—"Who was Julie?"—I needed new ways to link observation to participation and context to contemplation. Only then would I begin to convey the effects of a kind of engagement with my research topic that cannot be neatly packaged into a field study of limited duration. Julie Cordell could have been—in some sense was—my "best informant," even though by the time I taped my first interview she was already dead.

Kyrie

As gay writers have experienced increasing success in having their work published, many have paused to take a closer look at the place of writing in queer lives. In recent years anthropologists, too, have scrutinized, in minute detail, what they write, how they write, and the political implications of both. This process of self-examination (some would say obsession) has raised a host of stylistic and ethical issues for the would-be writer of monographs. What should be done about the power inequities set up when a researcher adopts a tone of omniscience or writes in language inaccessible to readers in the places under study?

Many anthropologists have argued for the desirability of letting people encountered in the course of fieldwork "speak for themselves" by giving them voice in the texts that present research results. Others have called for ethnographers, through the narrative *I*, to make an appearance in their own books and articles. No longer is it generally acceptable for anthropologists to conceal or deny the significance of their gender identity, age, class, or ethnicity. (Sexual identity represents a sort of final frontier in this regard.) Instead, contemporary ethnographic writing tends to acknowledge these attributes as factors that shape an anthropologist's interpretations of what she or he observed in the field.[3]

In the midst of all this discussion, few have stopped to wonder how a writer arrives at the dedications that stand like sentinels at the gates to a book or a poem. When it comes to the frontmatter of books, there seem to be two kinds of readers: the ones who skip over the acknowledgments and dedication to "get to the good stuff," and the ones who consider the first few pages of a book part of the good stuff, a place to get the dirt on who's who and who knows who. With the passing years, I must confess that I find myself in the latter group. So I suppose I should not have been surprised when people started asking about Julie.

If a book is dedicated to someone who does not share the author's surname, speculation provides a handy tool for filling in the gaps. Perhaps the person mentioned is a spouse, child, or lover. Perhaps she represents the mythical woman-behind-the-woman, the one who stood by the author through the long hours of writing and revisions. The limited, almost stereotypical character of the images that come to mind suggests just how little an author customarily reveals regarding the events that led to a particular book's dedication.

More than a few writers dedicate their books to relatives. Who can forget *Lesbian Nation* (1973), which Jill Johnston claimed she wrote "for my mother, who should've been a lesbian, and for my daughter, in hopes she will be"? Like many authors, the anthropologist Lila Abu-Lughod (1986) dedicated one volume to her parents; Richard Handler presented *Nationalism and the Politics of Culture in Quebec* (1988) to "my father's sisters Gertrude, Esther, Mary, and Talie." Occasionally a lyric touch breathes life, along with mystery, into these concise formulations, as in the poet Audre Lorde's preface to *The Black Unicorn* (1978), which reads, "For Linda Gertrude Belmar Lorde and Frederick Byron Lorde. The Face Has Many Seasons."

Some dedications embrace (as they construct) entire communities, like the one in Gloria Anzaldúa's *Borderlands/La Frontera* (1987), written *"a todos mexicanos* on both sides of the border," or the one in the Gay American Indians anthology *Living the Spirit* (Roscoe, ed. 1988), which invokes "our ancestors and the memory of our fallen warriors." More obliquely, David Bergman, editor of *Camp Grounds: Style and Homosexuality* (1993), incorporates a quotation from a "gay" poet: "In Memory of Karl Keller: 'Do you think the friendship of me would be unalloy'd satisfaction?'—Walt Whitman."

The most common dedications are brief and cryptic: for "Wendy," "Yangitelig," "The Thirty-Six Sexual Rebels," even "Susan Louise and the Voice Dolls."[4] These allusions may or may not become decipherable once a reader has turned the pages. Sometimes they resonate with the book's topic or hint at some aspect of the fieldwork situation. In a twist on the ubiquitous invocation of kin, Robert Alvarez, Jr., offers *Familia* (1987), in part, "to the memory of my grandparents," who double as subjects of his study. More solemn, but no less restrained, are the inscriptions that open Vincent Crapanzano's *Waiting: The Whites of South Africa* (1985) ("For Tesgemariam Abebe and Rudolph Schmidt, Who Died") and Jonathan Boyarin's *Storm from Paradise: The Politics of Jewish Memory* (1992) ("For Aaron, the brother whom I never knew"). I suspect that behind many dedications are attachments laden with a feeling and a fierceness that seldom come across in the text that follows.

When it comes to my dedication of *Families We Choose* to Julie Cordell, there are many possible stories I could tell by way of explanation.

Julie was not my inspiration for writing the book, although she had labored long hours on her own account of the women's music industry, a project I greatly respected. Julie was not my lover, although she was certainly my friend, and I would be lying to say we never stole a kiss in the back of the clubs where we went to hear jazz and salsa.

Because Julie met her death two years before my formal research project got underway, she technically was not a participant in the field study that provided material for the book. Her name appears at the beginning of *Families We Choose* due to a different sort of connection: an interpretive link between the narratives I constructed of Julie's life and the experiences of an entire generation of lesbians and gay men, a link I made only in retrospect, after the manuscript was drafted and ready to be sent off to the publisher. To understand this connection, you need to know something more about the way Julie Cordell lived and also about the way she died.

Offertoire

I first met Julie at a gathering of women who played conga drums. Although she was younger than I, she had moved to the Bay Area from New Mexico at about the same age I had been when I left the Midwest behind for an unseen city, eager to explore gay San Francisco. Like me, she had grown up white and working-class. At the time of her death, after three years on the West Coast, Julie was twenty-three.

Except for a stint working as a typesetter for local newspapers, Julie found only marginal, dead-end jobs waiting for her in the Bay Area. At times she worked in the underground economy to make ends meet. Julie was one of the few lesbians I've known who, as an adult, lived in a literal closet. The walk-in closet in the Oakland apartment she shared with roommates was just large enough to contain a full-sized mattress; it was all she could afford. I remember that apartment well because it had a staircase leading up to the roof, where we would go with friends to enjoy the spectacular view of the bay and play drums until the sun dipped below the horizon.

In her struggles for survival, Julie was far from alone, although she felt alone with her "money troubles" much of the time. During those years, many young lesbians, gay men, and bisexuals had difficulty getting by on the modest income derived from service-sector jobs in an urban landscape being radically altered by gentrification. Twice roommates kicked Julie out for being late with her share of the rent. After one of these incidents, which left her homeless on the eve of her birthday, Julie camped out in my studio apartment for a month until she was able to locate work and move on. Her parents were Christian fundamentalists who rejected her lesbian identification and called her up on the telephone every so often to urge her to resist the devil's influence by leaving San Francisco, that legendary city of vice and iniquity. In any case, they were not wealthy people and could not have offered much in the way of financial assistance even if Julie had been willing to ask.

"The edge" is not a comfortable place to live. Tired of moving from household to household and job to job, Julie found herself locked into a serious depression. After months of battling the condition on her own, she decided to check herself into a psychiatric hospital. Like many queers, she had first encountered the mental health system when she was coming out, grappling with desires she didn't understand. This time she turned to psychiatry with a sort of desperation, only to find herself further marginalized among her gay friends and in society at large.

Libera Me

The last time I spoke with Julie, she told me she felt the gay community had let her down. In retrospect, her dream of finding a harmonious community that had learned to cope with differences of class, race, gender, age, ability, and sexuality seems naive. At the time, however, many queer migrants to the Bay Area subscribed to similarly utopian visions. As Julie had begun the research for her own book, she had been dismayed to discover in women's music not just a creative endeavor but a business, its stars no more than human. The roommates who had kicked her out were both lesbians. She had expected them to be more understanding, based upon a shared sexual identity.

While Julie was hospitalized, yet another gay roommate attempted to steal all her possessions and refused to return the keys to her car until I leaned on the doorbell for a solid ten minutes. After Julie's release from the psychiatric facility, it took police intervention and an escort from a few concerned friends to get Julie back into her own apartment to gather up her few belongings. As the police officer stood by looking bored and impatient, Julie's former roommate began to taunt her, removing items from boxes as quickly as Julie could pack them, until the two eventually came to blows. Of the friends who offered their assistance on this occasion, I was the only one who identified as gay. This rueful observation was Julie's, not mine. In my preoccupation with keeping the interchange between Julie and her roommate from escalating into a full-scale brawl, I had set aside any inclination to operate as the note-taking anthropologist.

By the fall of 1983 Julie had made a decision to leave San Francisco for the southwestern city in which she had come of age. Her options were limited: she controlled little income, had no savings, and no confidence that she could hold down a job in her depressed and medicated state. Although Julie had turned to friends in the past for help during emergencies, she did not feel she could rely upon them for the basic necessities of life. Instead, she turned to the only people she could name as family: relatives by blood and adoption. Her stepfather agreed to drive to California to pick her up from the hospital where she had undergone a second round of psychiatric treatment. She would be allowed back "home," provided she agreed to leave behind the corrupting influence of "homosexual companions" and return to her parents' version of faith in a Christian god.

The day before her stepfather was scheduled to arrive, Julie and I had planned to meet to say goodbye. When I called that morning to let her know I was running late, the receptionist told me that the hospital had released her to her stepfather's custody the previous afternoon. Disheartened at the lost opportunity to say our farewells, and suspicious of her stepfather's motives, I resolved to call Julie at her parents' house later in the month.

A few weeks later I did call, hoping to reconnect with Julie and to offer her support in what to me looked like extremely adverse circumstances in which to come to terms with her needs, her desires, her depression, and her future. After a long pause, her stepfather informed me, "Julie is no longer with us." I asked for her telephone number, supposing she had found some way to gain a measure of independence with a room or an apartment of her own. "I mean she is no longer *with* us," he repeated. He went on: "After I picked her up from the hospital, she suddenly leaped out of the car as we were driving through the city. We never made it out of San Francisco. The next thing I knew, they told me she had jumped off the Golden Gate Bridge."

What happened in the car that late autumn day only Julie's stepfather knows. The report filed by the Coast Guard crew that picked her up off Baker's Beach said she was still alive when they hauled her aboard the boat. Even as she hit the water, her body fought to live, to draw in one more breath. It was to be her last battle.

In Paradisum

Why did I dedicate *Families We Choose* to Julie Cordell? One reason is thoroughly embedded in desires that spring from my own cultural context: a wish to restore to Julie her chosen name, coupled with a determination that her memory endure at least a few years beyond a life that was much too short. When all is said and done, I miss her deeply, and I still rage at the way she died. Read another way, the story behind my dedication bears a message and a moral. In what has often been characterized as a "post-AIDS" and "new gay" era, queers are still dying of some very old-fashioned causes. We still grapple with pervasive heterosexism in our encounters with employers, religious institutions, medical providers, and members of our straight families. Despite the visibility of gay organizations in urban areas, many of us still struggle to come out and to gain a modicum of self-acceptance. Suicide rates remain disproportionately high among gay and lesbian youth (Miller 1992; Remafedi, ed. 1994; Rofes 1983). Class conflict and racism cut a wide swath through "our" communities.

As the writing and rewriting of the manuscript for *Families We Choose* progressed, the prospect of opening the book with a reference to Julie acquired new significance for me. I began to rework my interpretations of what had happened to Julie in light of what I had learned while I was officially studying the gay community in the Bay Area. It was this back-and-forth movement between the stories of Julie I had told since her death and the stories of lesbians and gay men who had never met my friend that finally convinced me to dedicate the work to her.

Families We Choose chronicles the historical emergence of the concept of gay families, a category that scarcely existed when Julie jumped from that bridge in 1983. Before the 1980s, "gay people" and "family" tended to appear as mutually exclusive categories in the United States. Lesbians and gay men were supposed to represent either an ominous threat to "the family" (in New Right rhetoric), or a group capable of creating exciting new alternatives to "the family" (in the rhetoric of many gay liberationists). Both formulations located queers somewhere outside kinship. To speak of gay families, lesbian families, chosen families, and families of friends was not the commonplace then that it has since become.

In the book I trace the appearance of gay families to two related developments of the 1970s and 1980s. The first was the unprecedented impact of the gay movement's call for all gay people to come out to heterosexuals, including relatives by blood and adoption. Within a matter of a decade it became customary for self-identified gay men and lesbians at least to consider disclosing their sexual identities to parents and other close kin. But did coming out necessarily imply membership in something called a gay community? Disillusionment set in as queers began to recognize what later seemed obvious: their different positioning within a population defined in terms of sexuality but crosscut by lines of race, ethnicity, gender, age, ability, and class. More and more people dissociated themselves from the sanitized and masculinized gayness represented by the image of the "Castro clone." Some even questioned whether the concept of coming out applied in the same way to people of color and working-class whites.

Julie was not the only one in the early 1980s who had sought acceptance from parents only to be told to fend for herself unless she was prepared to "go straight." And Julie was far from the only one who had failed to find, in the gay mecca that was supposed to be San Francisco, the vision of community that had originally brought her to the Bay Area. For Julie, as for many others, "community" turned out to be an entity too abstract, too encompassing, and too homogenizing to provide the face-to-face relationships, the tolerance for conflict, and the emotional sustenance that could have seen her through a difficult life transition. In Julie's eyes, neither the gay community nor the women's community had ever come to terms with the class differences that had contributed to her precarious financial condition, or with the stigmatizing label of mental illness.

What would have happened if Julie had been born a few years later, or held on until there was a cultural construct—a "family of friends"—that might have allowed her to turn to her peers for the validation and material support that her parents were never able to provide? Sometimes I tell myself it's wishful thinking to believe that a simple category like "family" could have carried the weight of the problems and oppression that Julie faced at that point in her life. Other times I tell myself to have more faith in the power of human creativity. I remember all the days when Julie discovered whatever intangible resources she needed to bounce back from seemingly overwhelming chaos and despair.

Julie Cordell was not a working-class hero; neither was she a passive victim of circumstances. She could be demanding. From time to time, as she put it, she "got on people's nerves." Then again, in a culture that values the trappings of self-sufficiency, it's not easy to have to ask for the things you need to live. Sometimes Julie tripped over her own stubbornness and insecurities only to pick herself back up and try again. Sometimes she stayed down for the ten-count. More than once, friends stepped in to help. After a while, some of them grew tired of helping and left her lying there in the mess that she and society had made. No, Julie was nothing like a working-class hero. There was a time when she fought, she danced, she ate, she kissed, she breathed. She doesn't do those things any more.

Would a chosen family have given Julie the support she needed to bounce back one more time? Would "once more" have been enough in the absence of a meaningful job and adequate mental health care services? I've often wondered, though I'll never know. What I do know is that Julie's parents took her ravaged body back to New Mexico without consulting her friends about the disposition of her remains or even informing us of her death. Under prevailing statutes, which grant great powers to relatives narrowly defined through marriage or blood, they had every legal right to do so.

Today Julie's ashes lie in a vault under a surname that she rejected as a young adult. Julie chose for herself the name "Cordell," and this was the name under which her friends marked her passing when we gathered to beat drums and read poetry at the ocean's edge. It took me a long time after the ritual to feel anything but anger and pain and loss whenever I looked at the Golden Gate Bridge. It has taken even longer to remember the unparalleled beauty of that bridge against the setting sun the evening Julie and I played congas on a rooftop in Oakland.

Notes

Many thanks to Esther Newton and Geeta Patel for their insightful comments on an earlier draft of this chapter. Versions of the essay were presented at the 1992 annual meetings of the American Anthropological Association in San Francisco and the 1991 OutWrite: National Gay and Lesbian Writers Conference.

1   "As to my *Requiem,* perhaps I have also instinctively sought to escape from what is thought right and proper, after all the years of accompanying burial services on the organ! I know it all by heart. I wanted to write something different" (translated in Orledge [1979]:113). On Fauré's attempt to de-

velop a composition that could meld classical structure with artistic inno-
vations, see Nectoux (1991). Subheadings in this chapter derive from the
expanded orchestral version of Fauré's *Requiem*, Opus 48.

2   On the lack of any necessary correspondence between "insider" status and
nearness to the people who end up at the focus of a research study, see
Limón (1991) and Sarris (1991). Kondo (1990) discusses her experience
of a "collapse of identity" as a Japanese-American woman conducting research in Japan. For Behar, fieldwork precipitated a "personal crisis of representation" that entailed situating herself as (among other things) "another
new mestiza who has infiltrated the academy" (1993:339). On the ever-
shifting category "self," see also Butler (1991).

3   The annual OutWrite conference for lesbian, gay, bisexual, and transgender writers is a case in point. For a range of contributions to this discussion
within anthropology, see Clifford and Marcus, eds. (1986), Geertz (1988),
Mascia-Lees, Sharpe, and Cohen (1989), Rosaldo (1989), Sangren (1988),
and Thomas (1991).

4   Taken from Butler (1990), Lutz (1988), Sears (1991), and Povinelli (1993),
respectively.

References Cited

Abu-Lughod, Lila. 1986. *Veiled Sentiments: Honor and Poetry in a Bedouin Society*. Berkeley: University of California Press.

Alvarez, Robert R., Jr. 1987. *Familia: Migration and Adaptation in Baja and
Alta California, 1800–1975*. Berkeley: University of California Press.

Anzaldúa, Gloria. 1987. *Borderlands/La Frontera*. San Francisco: Spinsters/Aunt
Lute.

Behar, Ruth. 1993. *Translated Woman: Crossing the Border with Esperanza's Story*.
Boston: Beacon Press.

Bergman, David, ed. 1993. *Camp Grounds: Style and Homosexuality*. Amherst:
University of Massachusetts Press.

Boyarin, Jonathan. 1992. *Storm from Paradise: The Politics of Jewish Memory*.
Minneapolis: University of Minnesota Press.

Butler, Judith. 1990. *Gender Trouble: Feminism and the Subversion of Identity*.
New York: Routledge.

———. 1991. "Imitation and Gender Insubordination." In *Inside/Out: Lesbian Theories, Gay Theories,* ed. Diana Fuss, 13–31. New York: Routledge.

Clifford, James, and George E. Marcus, eds. 1986. *Writing Culture: The Poetics
and Politics of Ethnography*. Berkeley: University of California Press.

Crapanzano, Vincent. 1985. *Waiting: The Whites of South Africa*. New York:
Random House.

Geertz, Clifford. 1988. *Works and Lives: The Anthropologist as Author*. Stanford:
Stanford University Press.

Handler, Richard. 1988. *Nationalism and the Politics of Culture in Quebec*.
Madison: University of Wisconsin Press.

Johnston, Jill. 1973. *Lesbian Nation*. New York: Simon and Schuster.

Kondo, Dorinne. 1990. *Crafting Selves: Power, Gender, and Discourses of Identity in a Japanese Workplace*. Chicago: University of Chicago Press.

Limón, José. 1991. "Representation, Ethnicity, and the Precursory Ethnography: Notes of a Native Anthropologist." In *Recapturing Anthropology: Working in the Present*, ed. Richard G. Fox, 115–35. Santa Fe: School of American Research Press.

Lorde, Audre. 1978. *The Black Unicorn*. New York: Norton.

Lutz, Catherine. 1988. *Unnatural Emotions: Everyday Sentiments on a Micronesian Atoll and Their Challenge to Western Theory*. Chicago: University of Chicago Press.

Mascia-Lees, Frances E., Patricia Sharpe, and Colleen Ballerino Cohen. 1989. "The Postmodernist Turn in Anthropology: Cautions from a Feminist Perspective." *Signs* 15(1): 7–33.

Miller, B. Jaye. 1992. "From Silence to Suicide: Measuring a Mother's Loss." In *Homophobia: How We All Pay the Price*, ed. Warren J. Blumenfeld, 79–94. Boston: Beacon Press.

Nectoux, Jean Michel. 1991. *Gabriel Fauré: A Musical Life*, trans. Roger Nichols. New York: Cambridge University Press.

Orledge, Robert. 1979. *Gabriel Fauré*. London: Eulenburg Books.

Povinelli, Elizabeth A. 1993. *Labor's Lot: The Power, History, and Culture of Aboriginal Action*. Chicago: University of Chicago Press.

Remafedi, Gary, ed. 1994. *Death By Denial: Studies of Suicide in Gay and Lesbian Teenagers*. Boston: Alyson Publications.

Rofes, Eric E. 1983. *"I Thought People Like That Killed Themselves": Lesbians, Gay Men, and Suicide*. San Francisco: Grey Fox Press.

Rosaldo, Renato. 1989. *Culture and Truth: The Remaking of Social Analysis*. Boston: Beacon Press.

Roscoe, Will, ed 1988 *Living the Spirit: A Gay American Indian Anthology*. New York: St. Martin's Press.

Sangren, P. Steven. 1988. "Rhetoric and the Authority of Ethnography: 'Postmodernism' and the Social Reproduction of Texts." *Current Anthropology* 29(3): 405–35.

Sarris, Greg. 1991. "'What I'm Talking about When I'm Talking about My Baskets': Conversations with Mabel McKay." In *De/Colonizing the Subject: The Politics of Gender in Women's Autobiography*, ed. Sidonie Smith and Julia Watson, 20–33. Minneapolis: University of Minnesota Press.

Sears, James T. 1991. *Growing Up Gay in the South: Race, Gender, and Journeys of the Spirit*. New York: Haworth Press.

Thomas, Nicholas. 1991. "Against Ethnography." *Cultural Anthropology* 6(3): 306–22.

Weston, Kath. 1991. *Families We Choose: Lesbians, Gays, Kinship*. New York: Columbia University Press.

Afterword
Sue-Ellen Jacobs

We're all made up of little secrets,
No one knows who we really are.
—Lilly Harper, in *I'll Fly Away* (1994)

T he autobiographies, "ethnographic memoirs and narrative ethnographies" (Tedlock 1991:81), presented in this book are part of a tradition relatively new to American social and behavioral sciences. They assign authoritative voice to individuals about whom a text is constructed, let the informants speak for themselves, and construct their own professional and personal life histories. By doing so they seek recognition on their own terms as daring anthropological innovators in a field of inquiry that has eluded anthropology since its beginning and to claim the space and recognition to which they are entitled—in spite of the fact that the academic and nonacademic worlds in which they operate still have at their core dangerous homophobia. What they do is a good thing for the discipline of anthropology, for science, and for the larger cultural worlds in which these important personal stories have been constructed.

In all of the chapters, positionality or the standpoint (Hartsock 1989, esp. 240–47) of the ethnographer is elucidated in a way resembling "feminist critical theory, which, when it denies the split between epistemology and politics, is simultaneously reflexive and political" (Tedlock 1991:82). All authors treat themselves as objects of study (cf. Strathern 1993:153), not unlike the process involved in life history collection where the informant or subject controls those portions of the life story that will be revealed in the interview and presented to the public (cf. Kuper 1979 in Langness and Frank 1981:143–154; McBeth 1993:145; Personal

Narratives Group, ed. 1989) or in other collections of ethnographic autobiographies. The difference, as noted by Lewin and Leap in the Introduction is, of course, that all but one of the contributors positions herself or himself as a lesbian or gay ethnographer.[1] In addition, most of the contributors pay more attention to sex and sexuality than contributors to other collections have in spite of urgings by editors of those collections.[2] Some contributors (e.g., Williams and Bolton) take the brave stance of revealing their memories of sex in the field, examining the notion that the gay male world is defined by sex and can only be understood through *participant* observation. Other contributors (e.g., Newton) describe their attraction to informants, their ambivalence about their feelings and issues concerning the implicit fieldwork rule of "no-sex-with-the-natives" or issues of personal identity management in the field. Unlike the contributors to Bell, Caplan, and Karim (1993), most of the contributors to this volume make "mention of homosexual attraction or relations in the field [breaking] the silence in the literature with respect to this topic [which has been] even more deafening than that concerning heterosexual relationships" (Caplan 1993:23). In addition to these silences, there are others that lead to invisibility of sexuality and gender variance within the anthropological community. It has been very rare to find published declarations of sexual identity, and until recently most of those which have appeared have done so in postmortem biographies (Bateson 1984; Caffrey 1989).

There are certainly important sociocultural reasons why this silence has prevailed. Homophobia, along with sexism, racism, and ageism within departments of anthropology and the American Anthropological Association (both of which, for the most part, constitute microcosms of conservatism in the society at large), has required people to appear as mainstream and undifferentiated as possible. For gays and lesbians this meant striving to pass as straight or heterosexual with interest in traditional topics. But, as several contributors have noted (see especially Bolton), although the 1969 Stonewall Rebellion in New York City paved the way for the international gay pride movement, it was the AIDS pandemic that became the catalyst for opening the field of anthropology to "urgent" research into homosexuality in the United States in particular.[3] Colleagues whom I had known for fifteen to twenty years as mainstream or passing-straight males began to raise their voices as gay liberation activists within anthropology, mainly in response to AIDS, although the first effort to get attention within the AAA came in 1970 when Clark Taylor addressed the business meeting at the annual meeting in San Diego, calling for an end to discrimination against homosexuals in anthropology.

The response of the AAA membership at that meeting was not welcoming. In the years following, stories of harassment, denial of tenure, discrimination against gay topics by professional journals, and lack of funding for research at the graduate and postdoctoral levels circulated widely among members of the Society for Lesbian and Gay Anthropologists (SOLGA; formerly ARGOH, the Anthropology Research Group on Homosexuality) as well as among other lesbian and gay members of the association. Only in 1993 did the American Anthropological Association form a Commission on Lesbian and Gay Issues in Anthropology, nearly twenty years after the Commission on the Status of Women in Anthropology (COSWA) was formed in response to issues of discrimination against women throughout the domains of the discipline.[4]

In spite of the lack of support from funding agencies, departments, and mainstream publishers of journals and texts, studies of homosexuality, lesbian and gay cultures were conducted and published (see Weston [1993] for the first critical review of the history and contemporary status of lesbian and gay studies in anthropology to be published in a mainstream anthropological source). Feminist anthropology grew out of the feminist movement, contributed to the development of feminist theory, and continues to benefit from the interdisciplinary theories of feminist studies; lesbian and gay anthropology grows out of the gay pride movement and contributes to and grows in complexity through its relationship to "queer theory" and "queer studies" (Weston 1993:360). The remaking of anthropology, especially ethnographic fieldwork, is likewise enhanced by lesbian and gay anthropologists' work. The autobiographies in this volume reveal how gay and lesbian anthropologists contribute to the general debates and discourses within the discipline. The contributions are shaped by the politics of the discipline and the location of these "subaltern" members within the discipline (Spivak 1988). As with other marginalized anthropologists, there are lesbian and gay anthropologists who appear to have the dual consciousness or double-sightedness gained through the process of adjusting to stigma and to having been marginalized in society at large as well as within the discipline.

> Anthropologists with dual or multiple vision may be uniquely able to convert their "extra eyes" into useful research tools and effective political weapons. . . . ethnographic research, upon which an-

thropological discourse is based, is intrinsically political, regardless of immediate or intended research focus. The ethnographer studying an apparently politically innocuous and neutral phenomenon, nonetheless, carries the dirty laundry-filled baggage of a research tradition which usurps the authority to construct the Other as object of national- , class- , and gender-biased inquiry. When the ethnographer chooses to investigate more overtly political phenomena in an intensely political climate, ethnography as praxis and as political agency is forced into bold relief. (Harrison 1991:90–91)

Dual vision may lead to sensitive and insightful accounts of culture regardless of where the fieldwork is conducted; it may also produce a radical approach to fieldwork that insists on the right to conduct it in one's own culture (Lewin and Leap in this volume).

This book is valuable to a number of people, be they undergraduate students seeking information about identity management as they mature in their educational and professional fields or practicing professionals who have also struggled with issues of sexuality and gender identity in fieldwork and current occupations.

Becoming an Anthropologist: A Personal Narrative

My adventures into studying sexualities and gender variance began when I was a graduate student and conducted research on the "North American berdache." My "serious scholarship" was to take place in Suriname, where I had expected to spend no less than eighteen months living with and trying to understand Saramaccaner culture in a time of dislocation and rapid change. After two years of language preparation, large amounts of correspondence with Dutch anthropologists and Surinamese governmental officials, and training in fieldwork by my faculty at the University of Colorado, I wrote to the official who had been encouraging my preparations to explain that I would be ready for fieldwork in several months and ask for the forms necessary for a work permit. He replied in formal Dutch that because I was a single woman who would be entering an area of "unrest" his government could not let me enter the country for fieldwork. Unlike Delores Walters (in this volume), who used a brilliant strategy for entering a field that might otherwise have been off-limits to a "single woman researcher," it never occurred to me to mention that I would be accompanied by my longtime partner.[5]

I was angered and sorely disappointed by this denial of entry to Suriname.[6] I thought that my years of study and preparation for that fieldsite were now simply a waste, and that, with no other prospects in mind, I might as well drop out of anthropology and go back to nursing. But the chair of my committee, Dorothea V. Kaschube, suggested an alternative project, and I wound up writing a dissertation based on a comparative study of communication styles and strategies in a small urban hospital (a "bounded community") and an "unbounded" ethnic community that defined itself as a "poverty" community, then gave several papers about the work over the years (Jacobs 1970a, 1970b, 1970c, and 1971). Subsequently, I had the opportunity to work as an applied anthropologist in a midwestern African American community, trying out some of the things I had learned in my dissertation research (Jacobs 1974a, 1974b, 1975, 1979).

But something was missing. The romance of anthropology eluded me, and I wanted at least a chance to try fieldwork in a difficult space. I had only to wait a couple of years before the serendipitous events that led to twenty-three years of relationship with a New Mexico pueblo, thanks entirely to the goading and challenge Harry Hay posed in the summer of 1970 (see Timmons [1990:236–7] for Hay's view of how he made and I responded to this challenge; see Jacobs [1993] for my view). However, even after I began my work in New Mexico, I could not present myself as a lesbian to anyone outside my small circle of gay and lesbian friends, and I rarely see the need to do so today.

"Discovering" the "North American Berdache" and Facing Homophobia

The course of discovering the literature on North American "berdache" (as an intellectual construct, not as an empirical reality) began for me in 1965 when I was a first-year graduate student at the University of Colorado and enrolled in Omer C. Stewart's course "Acculturation of American Indians." As part of the requirements for the course, Stewart assigned students topics about which he needed or wanted to have current information. I was told to investigate "berdache." Because I had never read or heard of the term before, I felt a bit intimidated by the assignment, but being a dutiful graduate student I went to the library to begin my work. Searching through the guides to periodicals, literary indexes, anthropological field guides, and other reference materials the librarians recommended, I continued to find no sources. I had to wonder after several weeks of (now) frantic searching whether I had fallen into the proverbial traps of new graduate student enthusiasm and innocence.

Gathering my courage, I went to Stewart and told him that I was not having any success in locating sources on "berdache." He asked me where I had looked. After I told him, he then said (something like), "Hmm, I suspected as much. Well, you'll just have to start with my collection in the files in the other room." He had sent me out to see if maybe some mainstream sources had dealt with the topic since his 1960 articles published in the *Mattachine Review.*[7] They had not. He knew three traditional "berdaches" still living in 1965: a *winkte* (Lakota), a *nadle* (as the term has been spelled in most literature on Navajo third gender [e.g., Martin and Voorhies 1975:89–93]), and a person at Taos (*lhunide* according to Roscoe 1987:144). He knew of other people who were males living and working as women, males who were ceremonial transvestites and homosexuals, and others who were "mixed" or androgynous in appearance, behavior, and cultural classification.

I was given a key to his office and invited to work with his "berdache" files. Until I opened the file that afternoon, I did not know that I was being asked to deal with homosexuality. Had Stewart said to me in class in 1965, "and Miss Jacobs, I want you to investigate homosexuality and American Indian acculturation" instead of, "I want you to investigate berdache and American Indian acculturation," I probably would have fainted. As it was, I had some serious moments of fear as I began to read through the files: Could it be that Professor Stewart knew that I was a lesbian? If so, what would that mean for my future in anthropology? Why had he assigned this topic to *me* if he didn't know? How could he know? My "roommate" and I were very careful about our private life. We knew no other "couples" at the university and maintained our lesbian connections in Denver. What would be the outcome of this research in terms of my future prospects for a career in anthropology? My concerns remained with me as I worked, but soon the files laid open for me a wondrous world of information I could not have imagined nor seen elsewhere. Stewart's files contained the articles he had published in the *Mattachine Review,* along with related articles from the *Review* written by nonanthropologists, including Harry Hay. There were copies of fieldnotes from Alfred Kroeber, references to obscure items to be found in the anthropology library at Berkeley (Stewart had earned his Ph.D. at

UC-Berkeley under Kroeber), and odds and ends of other references that were good leads to other sources.

Once I began to feel confident that I might get a twenty-page paper out of the assignment after all, under Professor Stewart's challenge to do "something new" I became obsessed with finding materials as close to the original sources as possible. Because I had a reading knowledge of French, Stewart sent me to the basement of Norlin Library, where the university's copy of the Jesuit Relations was kept. Had I not been obsessed, I would have stopped there because the full collection was on hand and I did not have a clue about which volume would contain the first reference to "berdache." But with assistance from a very knowledgeable librarian, I found it and painstakingly copied that and other references by hand to put in Stewart's file (where it remains today, I assume).[8]

My paper came together in 1965 at the end of my first year as a graduate student in anthropology. In 1968 the inaugural issue of the *Colorado Anthropologist* was put together by faculty and students, and Stewart kindly suggested that my paper be included. I was pleased. It was my first publication in anthropology. Unbeknown to me, the paper was copied and circulated in the "gay underground" for the next twenty-something years. It became a beacon for people who were looking for self-affirming studies of homosexuality. But when my initial homophobia subsided, or maybe as a survival measure to get me through it, I took a "distant position" to the material I read about Native Americans. I am not a Native American, had not lived in any Native American community, and had no empirical reference point from which to consider the possible universality of what was described by missionaries, trappers, government officials, and only a few anthropologists among others over the course of several hundred years of colonial intrusions into and writings about Native American communities. Consequently, I did not consider "berdache" a form of homosexuality when I wrote that first paper. My sources sometimes referred to "sodomy" and "sodomites," but more often the materials I read placed emphasis on Native American cross-gender and transgender behavior rather than sexuality. This is close to the same conclusion Sabine Lang reached in 1991, when she conducted far more extensive research than I had done for her dissertation; thus her title *Men as Women and Women as Men*.

At the end of my graduate school residency in 1968, as I began my first teaching job at Sacramento State University (now California State University at Sacramento), I focused my "real work" on issues of culture and poverty. In ignorance and innocence, I did not see a need to follow-up on my original research, but others did: Paula Gunn Allen (1981, 1986), Evelyn Blackwood (1984), members of Gay American Indians of San Francisco (Roscoe, ed. 1988), Judy Grahn (1984), Sabine Lang (1991a, 1991b, 1992, 1993), Terry Tafoya (1992), Will Roscoe (1987, 1991), Walter Williams (1986), and others. Nor did I understand that my own sexuality and gender identity would frame and inform my research no matter where or what I undertook to study.

During this time, I practiced the same "unconscious arrogance" mentioned by Geoffrey Burkhart (in this volume), which allows anthropologists to think that we can separate who we are personally from how we will be perceived in the communities where we conduct fieldwork and, finally, who we are and become professionally. In the late 1960s my colleague Clark Taylor tried to help me understand more about these matters, but I glossed them as too personal, convinced that I should keep separate my "real anthropology persona" and my personal life. But many "emerging from the chrysalis" during the late 1960s and early 1970s also understood that something was not right about what came to be known as "colonial anthropology."

Feminism, Applied Anthropology, and a Return to Studies of Gender Variance

In spite of knowing that something was not right about the ethnographic record and theories in anthropology, I was not prepared for being swept up into feminist anthropology. I viewed my civil rights activism of the 1950s and 1960s as part of my duty as a citizen-of-conscience that should be kept separate from my emerging professional status as anthropologist. My latent anger about Suriname, the preferential treatment of male graduate students in my graduate school cohort, the discrimination by male colleagues, and more came spilling out in a way that drove me to search for theories about women's statuses and roles cross-culturally.[9] I became active in the Women's Liberation Front in Sacramento and was soon taking what I learned there into the classroom, where, in 1970, I taught the first course on "Women Cross-Culturally" to be offered at CSUS. In the research for this course I gained a great curiosity about the way gender is constructed in various cultures. This would lead to the core theoretical issues I continue to work with under the label "gender variance."

My use of the term *gender variance* is not intended as a gloss for study-ing women. I use the term precisely to mean the study of the diversity and range of gender categories found cross-culturally. I am interested in emically or endogenously (literally, internally) defined gender categories; that is, since my earliest immersion into feminism I have focused on the ways cultures organize, label, and define gender (Jacobs and Cromwell 1992; Lang in this volume provides an excellent but brief description of my meaning). The fact that homosexuality may accompany one or more emically defined categories of gender has been of secondary interest to me, and with one brief exception I have not studied homosexuality.[10] My fascination continues to be with the ways cultures construct gender types and the way individuals express gender identities within those construc-tions. Sex and sexuality issues may enter the discussion as part of cultur-al definitions of gender types, or these terms (and emic equivalents) may be used outside of definitions of gender.

I carried my interest in gender variance into my work as an applied anthropologist when working with health problems in the black com-munity in the midwestern United States. In my ethnohistorical research and ethnographic fieldwork in the Southwest it was the focus of my re-search. Thus it was probably inevitable that I would find myself once again confronting issues of gender variance in cross-cultural perspective as related specifically to Native Americans. But before returning to this work, I had learned through feminist studies and the community engage-ments that were part of my applied projects that *gender* behavior could be more dangerous to men (if they were "feminine" in work, walk, and talk) than sexual behavior (unless performed in "dangerous" environ-ments) (cf. William Leap, Ralph Bolton, Walter Williams, and Stephen Murray in this volume and elsewhere). The same is true regarding women who "act like men" in unguarded places (cf. Kennedy with Davis in this volume and 1993; Newton in this volume and 1993). In other words, it is dangerous to behave in "alternatively gendered" ways in Anglo-American society.

Early feminism taught us that we who believed in and worked for freedom and equal rights for women and racial minorities must be pre-pared to pay a price for acting in ways inappropriate to the contempo-rary, regional constructions of appropriate gendered behavior. Although I knew about the dangers for lesbians because of my experiences in a range of cities, after my 1968 article I clung to a romantic notion that in Native communities it would be different. My naiveté, romantic notions, and just plain ignorance about the safe cultural location of "alternatively gendered" people called "berdache" was shattered when I finally learned, after years of fieldwork in a Tewa community, about the dangers of being considered *kwidó* (literally, "woman-man," colloquially, "womanly-man"). It was not until I did fieldwork designed specifically to study women's changing roles and statuses that I began to appreciate how carefully, yet serendipitously, gender is constructed.

How Long-term Fieldwork Changed My Life and Theory

In 1972 I fell in love with a culture, a people, and lots of women (Underhill 1979, esp. x, 91–94). Answering Harry Hay's call in 1970 (Jacobs 1991; Timmons 1990) to conduct ethnohistorical and ethnographic research on women's changing statuses and roles in the Tewa community in New Mexico changed my life forever, more than I have been able to acknowledge. The lines quickly blurred between researcher, friend, and family member. Geoffrey Burkhart (in this volume) notes how the interpersonal intimacy of friendship in the field introduces problems for carrying ethnographic fieldwork to an ethnographic text: "It has raised for me acute questions about privileged grounds of ethnographic knowledge and about appropriate ways to write about information gained through friendship." This dilemma continues to perplex me in my writing about the Tewa. William Leap (in this volume) comments about elements of secrecy that enter fieldwork relationships. How well I know this. I have been trusted with many secrets, most of which I will not reveal in any format. It would be absolute betrayal of trust to do so, even though some whose secrets were shared are now deceased.

At the outset of my relationship with the Pueblo, I was asked to help answer an endogenously constructed question: "When did we women lose our rights in this pueblo?" To facilitate my research, I was taken in as a guest-member by elders of a large extended family. I was not expected to become, nor did I expect to become, a fully enculturated member of the tribe; I was expected to behave like an adult member of the community. From the beginning, gender issues were at the core of my fieldwork. Starting with questions about "what women and men do" on the reservation to those concerned with child-rearing and socialization gender roles, I continually avoided asking deliberate questions about gender variance. Harry Hay often told me stories about the "traditional *kwidó*" and the non-Indian gay men who came to visit on weekends and special occasions. But I kept this information separate from my "real purpose" of studying women's changing statuses and roles.

After seventeen years of relationship with the community, I met a woman my age who had retired from the service to one of the urban centers of the state with her woman "friend." Young women and men who had grown up without establishing heterosexual relationships were following paths that were different from age-mates. One woman, A, was living with a "friend" in an adjacent community; one young man, M, had survived brutal beatings first by his father (who caught him "playing sex with another boy"), then by other men in the community. The last time I talked with M was in 1993, the day before a man at a party cut open his abdomen with a knife in a violent attack, driven at least in part by the frenzy of drugs and alcohol. When his father nearly killed him in 1978, his aunts asked if I would take M to Seattle because the world was too dangerous for him on the reservation. I agreed to do so but wondered how I was going to be able to keep him safe there. I never got to find out, however, because over the course of the next few days the tribal elders settled the matter by telling the father that he must never again treat his son with disrespect, that he must never again harm him, that to do so could mean the father would be asked to leave the reservation.[11] The aunts told me that the elders also told the father that his son was special and would have to be protected within the reservation for the sake of the Pueblo.

It was during this time that I learned about an oral tradition that accounted for people like M and J (the male elder *kwidó*). It was said that the child's genitalia were accidently exposed to the full moon, and this made them "like that"—*kwidó*, women-men. When I asked if they knew of any women who were like that I was told no. Until 1993 (that is, after twenty-two years of close and sometimes intimate relationship with friends and family on the reservation), I used the word *lesbian* only during the time I was pursuing the issues surrounding M's and J's origins, never in self-disclosure. The last time I tried to talk about *kwidó* the topic had to be put aside because of the potential problems I felt it would raise for my relationship with primary friends and consultants. Over the course of the years, the stories have changed. In the first instance I had been told how J came to be as he was; in the second, I was told that M and the young women I mentioned were "special"; in the third instance, after J had died from "pneumonia," I was told that I had "not got that right. We don't have people like that here" and more. The hard work on these issues continues, but it might not have had I not had the good fortune to meet three people who helped refocus my work on issues of Native American sexuality and gender variance.

From 1990 to 1992, first Jason Cromwell, then Sabine Lang, then Wesley Thomas drew me back to my original and subsequent (published and unpublished) work on gender variance, glossed originally as "ber-dache" but now referred to as "two-spirit people," a term preferred by Native Americans. Our collaborations have resulted in two Wenner-Gren Foundation conferences and one AAA symposium that have brought together Native American writers, scholars, and activists of the two-spirit tradition and anthropologists who have written about Native American sexuality and gender variance largely under the rubric "berdache" (Jacobs, Lang, and Thomas 1993, 1994).

In the Introduction to this volume, Lewin and Leap note that Myer-hoff's observation that she would never become a Huichol woman but she would become a "little old Jewish lady" led her to study women and men in an older Jewish community. This is an interesting approach to fieldwork in that it situates fieldwork as a way to learn to become a new self, even treating the future self as other. In my experience of working with Native Americans, African Americans, and Chicanos, I have never thought about *becoming* a member of the defined ethnic group; however, in each instance, I was taught how to become a member of the *communi-ty,* to do my share of the daily work, carry out my social responsibilities, and use my talents or expertise as other educated people from the community were expected to on behalf of the community, at least while I lived there. As I became integrated into daily life, I forgot more and more of the details of how I lived my life elsewhere. In my fieldnotes from this time I wrote about being puzzled by my inability to answer women's questions about my everyday life in Illinois and in Washington.

Becoming part of the social matrix of more than 150 people was exciting, chaotic at times, but hardly what I expected for doing "science." As the years passed, the research required to answer various tribally defined problems was carried out in ways necessary to file reports or monitor sociocultural change. But at the same time, I became more and more aware that I had become a stranger in too many places. Sometimes there is a wash of confusion, similar to that several authors in this volume describe, about separating myself from my field persona.

By listening carefully within the Tewa world and to the Native American and other colleagues working in the area of two-spirits/berdache research I am learning new ways of situating myself in relation to my identity and interests in gender studies. Reading the chapters in this book also has had a powerful, sometimes disturbing, effect on my attempts at personal and professional realignments. They reaffirm my belief in collaborative ethnographic research by diverse anthropological fieldworkers in cross-cultural studies of gender, sex, and sexuality and also strengthen my commitment to continuing to converse about human sexuality and gender variance cross-culturally, my approach to research, and my position within anthropology.

The chapters in this collection have provided me with a multileveled appreciation of the work being done by lesbian and gay anthropologists who are out. First, they remind me of difficulties I have faced confronting and dealing with my private and public sexual and gender identities over the years. Second, as hard as this retrospective has been for me, each author's work serves to affirm my right and obligation to be a fully functioning individual, to work conscientiously and diligently to overcome my own internalized homophobia, and to work harder to facilitate the acceptance of research interests of students and junior colleagues who are lesbian or gay. Third, each chapter informs my continued efforts to understand how ideas and realities are constructed and how people negotiate the presentation of themselves at various times. This is part of what I call "autoethnography"—looking at oneself looking at others, looking at oneself working with others, looking at oneself as other, and reflecting on the process of gaining self-understanding. This is more complicated than reflexive ethnographic writing or writing a personal or professional autobiographical narrative. It means turning the tools of the discipline on oneself and asking, "How do I construct my self in diverse situations? What is the difference (if any) between what I do as a lesbian or gay person and what colleagues who are not lesbian and not gay do in fieldwork and ethnographic writing?" Because all of these have to do with identity management, the next interesting question for me is whether there are differences in approach to research if one is already "other" (Harrison 1991) as one goes to the field, writes the ethnographies and theoretical articles, and works within an academic or other environment.

These chapters reveal great diversity in their authors' reflections and assessments of how their sexuality and gender identity affected their fieldwork, as well as a variety of strategies used for identity management. There are interesting thematic sets that coalesce along sex lines: the gay male anthropologists here describe sexual arousals, encounters, and relationships in more graphic terms than do the lesbian anthropologists, who tend not to describe sexual aspects of fieldwork at all (this is also true among the contributors to Bell, Caplan, and Karim, eds. [1993]). Development of personal relationships and maintenance of distance and closeness are more often described by both lesbian and nonhomosexual females in all forms of writing, from literary works to ethnographic monographs and other social science works. An essentialist's observation of this tendency or generalization could lead to the conclusion that females who work in Western writing traditions are socialized to focus on relationships, socialization that is brought to the field of scholarship. Whether in the sciences or the arts, most females will try to develop a "feeling for the organism" (Barbara McClintock as reported by Keller [1983]) and then explain the organism from this empathetic stance. But as one becomes more like the studied subject, the subjectivation of self becomes clouded, even murky.

Each of the contributors to this book differs in terms of scholarly approach, personal and political motivations, and standing in the discipline. Yet we may all be seen as "them" because we have chosen to gather together as lesbian or gay anthropologists. Our work is important to the future of anthropology because we dare to take on topics that are under assault in the general public as well as within many institutions of higher learning in the United States, Canada, and Europe. The study of the rise of anti-gay rights activism in these locales will require the same courageous approaches that Ginsburg undertook in her fieldwork among the religious right and right-to-life/pro-life communities (see Ginsburg [1993] for a discussion of how she worked within the "enemies' camp").

Most lesbian and gay anthropologists I know do not study gender variance, sex, or sexuality. Most gay and lesbian anthropologists I know are still closeted, even though a number of them are senior scholars at their respective universities. Most will give cautious encouragement to undergraduate and graduate students who want to express their sexuality openly but dissuade "serious scholars" from studying their own "subculture" for practical reasons: They may never get a teaching job in anthropology if they focus on their own community or if they study lesbian and gay topics. Junior faculty are expected to "stay away from controversial issues" until after they have tenure. "Lesbian/gay/queer studies" is still controversial. Yet how can anthropologists ever understand homosexuality, gender diversity, homophobia, heterosexism, and even heterosexuality if they leave this work to psychologists, sociologists, historians, and those who work in literary criticism? We have much to learn if we are going truly to understand human diversity. Many anthropologists have worked diligently to recruit students who will conduct fieldwork in gender studies. I have been fortunate in having students and junior colleagues seek me out to ask for help in doing this kind of anthropology, but on my campus there have been searches conducted in other departments specifically for colleagues who specialize in queer theory, gay studies, and lesbian studies. Where are the job notices for anthropologists who want to or have conducted such studies? What must be done to open the doors to gain the recognition that this research and these researchers are serious contenders in restructuring anthropology?

The retrospectives on fieldwork in this book are based on careful reconsideration of life in the field informed by current debates within anthropology, gay and lesbian studies, gender studies, ethnic studies, and women's studies about positionality, the self, and others. The contribution that this volume makes is its insertion into ongoing conversations that suggest that because of fieldwork anthropology may be a special type of humanistic social science.

Anthropology may have a colonial heritage, and there are certainly still remnants of a colonial style (Harrison 1991) within these chapters as well as others, but anthropologists are trying to get over that fact, as they have been doing for several decades (Jacobs 1982). Not only that, but we who are lesbian and gay ethnographers have had to position ourselves in our fieldwork as well as our daily lives in relation to the level of stigma associated with our ilk, our kinds in the cultures where we conduct ethnographic fieldwork, where we wish to report that fieldwork, where we hope to have jobs, and where we position ourselves concerning our identity. Lewin and Leap use a brilliant analytical strategy when they remind us of the important work of Goffman (1963) and resurrect his extremely valuable notions of stigma and marginality to help us define positionality, our respective standpoints. When we use "stigmatized" and "marginalized" to describe ourselves, we are acknowledging a central aspect of our self-definition, the internalized homophobia resulting from experiences in personal and professional communities. It is not appropriate for others to use these terms when talking about gay and lesbian ethnographers, according to current professional etiquette (see Williams [1991] for an interesting discussion of the legal implications of social naming by self and others).

The reality is that lesbian or gay members of society face stigmatization, marginalization, and overt and covert discrimination, the effects of which correspond to those of ordinary racism—"everyday occurrences, casual, unintended, banal perhaps, but mortifying" (Williams 1991: dust jacket)—experienced by people marked as members of minority racial and ethnic categories in the United States. The difference is that sexual and gender minorities (irrespective of race and ethnicity) may blend into the sexual and gender dominant group by simply denying sexual or gender identities that diverge from the dominant. These are universal phenomena, not confined to the West nor to the North. Discovery of the pervasiveness of such cultural manipulations (or adaptive strategies), has been ongoing in several fields, although anthropology, with a few notable exceptions, has not done well in working with the concepts inherent in the cross-cultural puzzles embraced by the terms *sexuality, sex,* and *gender* (Blackwood 1984; Caplan, ed. 1987; Lancaster 1992; Nanda 1990; Williams 1986).[12]

The contributors to this volume remind us that the work of ethnographic fieldwork into gay and lesbian topics must be done, and lesbian and gay anthropologists should do it. They should be supported in their efforts and rewarded for studying gay and lesbian topics. On the other hand, gays or lesbians should not *have* to study their own cultures or communities. As is evidenced by the publications of contributors to this book, they have the credentials to be, but only some are privileged to be, part of the mainstream of anthropology, irrespective of where they work.

Notes

Portions of this chapter are also included in "Introduction: Is the 'North American Berdache' Merely a Phantom in the Imagination of Western Anthropologists?" in "Revisiting the 'North American Berdache' Empirically and Theoretically," a Wenner-Gren Foundation Conference and American Anthropological Association session, both held in November 1993.

Special thanks to Ellen Lewin for so patiently guiding me through the development of this chapter and for her skillful editing of its previous versions.

1 Will Roscoe is the exception; he deliberately chose to identify himself as an ethnohistorian rather than an anthropologist in his dealing with the Zunis.

2 The most interesting collection that tried to achieve this goal is Bell, Caplan, and Karim, eds. (1993). In her "Introduction 2: The Volume" Caplan observes, "Not all authors tackle sexuality directly, although there are sometimes hints that preoccupation with clothes, hair and jewelry is part of a concern for an appropriate projection, or even a disguising of sexuali-

ty. . . . Several authors discuss the question of sexuality in the field more openly, although it is striking that, while all three men consider this topic (and for two—Abramson and Wade—it is a major focus), only one of the women (Karim) is courageous enough to discuss it at any length and no woman acknowledges a sexual experience in the field. This perhaps indicates that for women sexual activity or, even more so, 'confessing' it, still has very different consequences than for men. Furthermore, none of the ethnographers in this collection makes any mention of homosexual attraction or relations in the field, and indeed, the silence in the literature with respect to this topic is even more deafening than that concerning heterosexual relationships" (1993:23).

3   Because of the incidence of AIDS in the U.S. gay population, federal funds became available for research to track, not treat or cure or prevent, HIV transmission. This emphasis on epidemiology rather than prevention and cure has led to numerous publications reporting demographic studies but very few on ethnographic research in communities with high HIV incidence. Bolton (1991, 1993) and others have been urging that funding be made available for ethnographic fieldwork, including participant observation.

4   The Commission on Lesbian and Gay Issues in Anthropology expects to be able to accomplish, at minimum, the following goals: (1) formal documentation of discrimination against lesbian and gay anthropologists in hiring and promotion, publication, research funding, and other environments; and (2) presentation of scholarship through a series of readings or modules that can be incorporated into teaching about human diversity, whether in introductory or upper-division courses.

5   This was the case, despite my having read Alice Marriott's *Greener Fields* (1952) and *The Valley Below* (1949) and knowing that Marriott traveled with her "longtime companion," as was often recounted by "paired women" of her generation and many in mine. I thought someday I would be like her. My companion and I would travel the world together doing exotic fieldwork, she an artist, me the ethnographer. This was before Stonewall, before the Vietnam War, before the feminist movement, and well before the move to reinvent anthropology would lead to my politicization and determination to do relevant anthropology in the United States.

6   Terry Tafoya has told me about an article written by an African American lesbian feminist anthropologist (Wekker 1993), who had done her dissertation research in Suriname. Reading the article brought tears to my eyes, as I recalled once again the deep anguish over being denied access to a field site because I was a "single" (i.e., not escorted by a male) woman.

7   The *Mattachine Review* was the official magazine of the Mattachine Society, an American homophile organization with chapters in many states.

8   Carl Stewart, Omer's son, has been cataloguing his father's files for placement in Norlin Library at the University of Colorado, Boulder. These files are rich sources of information on Ute, Paiute, Shoshone, and other tribes with whom Stewart worked, as well as the vast record he kept on his research with members of the Native American Church.

9   One day in 1969 I arrived at my office to find that a poster had been placed
    on the *inside* of my office door. It read, "The Army Needs Nurses! See your
    local recruiter." It was not meant to be a joke. I had been an antiwar activ-
    ist in graduate school and still was in my private life; before I became an
    anthropologist, I was a practicing registered nurse. I did not disguise these
    facts when I was hired at Sac State. After some snooping, I found "who-
    dunit" and confronted this senior white male. He tried to pass it off and
    said I was "too sensitive" and "couldn't take a joke," and to this day he has
    not apologized. I was angry, but more, I was terrified that the incident sig-
    naled the end of my chance to get tenure at Sac State.

10 I worked as a consultant to an AIDS Research Project located in the Alcohol
    and Drug Abuse Institute at the University of Washington. As part of my work
    I was to provide a mentoring relationship to a gay graduate student who was
    hired to conduct ethnographic interviews in the gay community. Because he
    was not from Seattle, I made appointments for him to meet friends and ac-
    quaintances in Seattle's gay community so he could get to know the bars and
    other locales where he could make contacts for his research. We coauthored
    one paper (Jacobs et al. 1988), and I gave another (Jacobs 1988) based on
    early findings of the research team. I withdrew from this very important yet
    personally disturbing project at the end of the first year.

11 Corporal punishment is strongly sanctioned in the Tewa world, and until
    recently parents who spanked, slapped, or beat their children could expect
    public criticism during ceremonial occasions.

12 Some people even still write as though "gender" means "women" rather
    than women and men, at minimum. In India it means, women, men, *hijras*,
    and *sadhin*, at minimum. In some Tewa communities it means women, men,
    and *kwidó* at minimum. In Navajo it means women, men, and *nadleeh*, at
    minimum, ad infinitum.

References Cited

Allen, Paula Gunn. 1981. "Lesbians in American Indian Cultures." *Conditions*
    7:67–87.
———. 1986. *The Sacred Hoop: Recovering the Feminine in American Indian
    Traditions.* Boston: Beacon.
Bateson, Mary Catherine. 1984. *With a Daughter's Eye: A Memoir of Margaret
    Mead and Gregory Bateson.* New York: William Morrow.
Bell, Diane, Pat Caplan, and Wazir Jahan Karim, eds. 1993. *Gendered Fields:
    Women, Men and Ethnography.* New York: Routledge.
Blackwood, Evelyn. 1984. "Sexuality and Gender in Certain Native American
    Tribes: The Case of the Cross-Gender Females." *Signs: Journal of Women
    in Culture and Society* 10:27–42.
Bolton, Ralph. 1991. "Mapping Terra Incognita: Sex Research for AIDS Pre-
    vention: An Urgent Agenda for the 1990s." In *The Time of AIDS: Social
    Analysis, Theory and Method,* ed. Gilbert Herdt and Shirley Lindenbaum.
    Newbury Park: Sage.

———. 1993. "Sex, Science and Social Responsibility: Cross-Cultural Research on Same-Sex Eroticism and Sexual Intolerance." Presidential address, Society for Cross-Cultural Research, February. Revised version in *When They Read What We Write: The Politics of Ethnography*, ed. Caroline E. Brettell. Westport: Bergen and Garvey.

Caffrey, Margaret M. 1989. *Ruth Benedict: Stranger in this Land*. Austin: University of Texas Press.

Caplan, Pat, ed. 1987. *The Cultural Construction of Sexuality*. New York: Tavistock.

———. 1993. "Introduction 2: The Volume." In *Gendered Fields: Women, Men and Ethnography*, ed. Diane Bell, Pat Caplan, and Wazir Jahan Karim, 19–27. New York: Routledge.

Ginsburg, Faye. 1993. In *When They Read What We Write: The Politics of Ethnography*, ed. Caroline E. Brettell, 163–76. Westport: Bergen and Garvey.

Goffman, Erving. 1963. *Stigma: Notes on the Management of Spoiled Identity*. New York: Simon and Schuster.

Grahn, Judy. 1984. *Another Mother Tongue: Gay Words, Gay Worlds*. Boston: Beacon.

Harrison, Faye V. 1991. "Ethnography as Politics." In *Decolonizing Anthropology: Moving Further toward an Anthropology for Liberation*, ed. Faye V. Harrison. Washington: Association of Black Anthropologists/American Anthropological Association.

Hartsock, Nancy. 1989. "Standpoint: Toward a Specifically Feminist Historical Feminism." In *Money, Sex and Power*, ed. Nancy Hartsock, 235–50. New York: Longman.

Jacobs, Sue-Ellen. 1968. "Berdache: A Brief Review of the Literature." *Colorado Anthropologist* 1:25–40

———. 1970a. "Clinical Anthropology: Some Techniques for Problem Analysis in Urban Systems." Paper presented at the annual meeting of the Southwestern Anthropological Association, Asilomar.

———. 1970b. "Analysis of Social Systems in Terms of Communication Processes." Paper presented at the annual meeting of the Society for Applied Anthropology, Boulder.

———. 1970c. "Anthropology and Nursing: Small Community Hospital Research." Paper presented at the annual meeting of the American Anthropological Association, San Diego.

———. 1971. "Communication Networks among Hospital Staff Personnel." Paper presented at the annual meeting of the American Anthropological Association, New York.

———. 1974a. "Action and Advocacy Anthropology." *Human Organization* 33:209–15.

———. 1974b. "Doing It Our Way and Mostly for Our Own." *Human Organization* 33:380–82.

———. 1975. "Our Babies Shall Not Die." Paper presented at the Symposium on Black Adaptive Strategies at the annual meeting of the American Anthropological Association, San Francisco.

———. 1979. "'Our Babies Shall Not Die': A Community's Response to Medical Neglect." *Human Organization* 38:120–33.

————. 1982. "Unraveling the Threads of Oppression: Notes on the Development of Ethical and Humanistic Anthropology." In *American Social and Cultural Anthropology 1980: A View from Spring Hill*, ed. E. Adamson Hoebel, Richard L. Currier, and Susan Kaiser, 379–404. New York: Garland Publishing.

————. 1988. "The Results of Ethnographic Research on AIDS and IV Drug Users in Seattle and Implications of Our Research." Presented at the Northwest Area Indian Health Conference, Seattle.

————. 1991. "The Predicament of Sincerity: From Distance to Connection in Long-Term Research." *International Journal of Moral and Social Studies* 6:237–245

————. 1993. "Introduction: Is the 'North American Berdache' Merely a Phantom in the Imagination of Western Anthropologists?" Paper prepared for the first Wenner-Gren Foundation Conference on Revisiting the North American Berdache Empirically and Theoretically, presented at the 92d annual meeting of the American Anthropological Association, Washington, D.C.

Jacobs, Sue-Ellen et al. 1988. "Intervention Ethnography in Two Communities at High Risk for AIDS." Paper given at the annual meeting of the Society for Applied Anthropology, Tampa.

Jacobs, Sue-Ellen, and Jason Cromwell. 1992. "Visions and Revisions of Reality: Reflections on Sex, Sexuality, Gender and Gender Variance." *Journal of Homosexuality* 23(4):43–69.

Jacobs, Sue-Ellen, Sabine Lang, and Wesley Thomas. 1993. Wenner-Gren Foundation Conference on "Revisiting the 'North American Berdache' Empirically and Theoretically." 92d annual meeting of the American Anthropological Association, Washington, D.C.

Jacobs, Sue-Ellen, Sabine Lang, and Wesley Thomas. 1994. Second Wenner-Gren Foundation Conference on "Revisiting the 'North American Berdache' Empirically and Theoretically," Chicago.

Keller, Evelyn Fox. 1983. *A Feeling for the Organism: The Life and Work of Barbara McClintock*. San Francisco: W. H. Freeman.

Kennedy, Elizabeth Lapovsky, and Madeline D. Davis. 1993. *Boots of Leather, Slippers of Gold: The History of a Lesbian Community*. New York: Routledge.

Kuper, Hilda. 1979. "An Interview with Hilda Kuper, 1979." In *Lives: An Anthropological Approach to Biography*, ed. L. L. Langness and Gelya Frank. Novato, Calif.: Chandler and Sharp.

Lancaster, Roger N. 1992. *Life Is Hard: Machismo, Danger, and the Intimacy of Power in Nicaragua*. Berkeley: University of California Press.

Lang, Sabine. 1991a. *Männer als Frauen—Frauen als Männer: Geschlechtsrollenwechsel bei den Indianern Nordamerikas*. Hamburg: Wayasbah.

————. 1991b. "Women and Not-Women: Female Gender Variance Among North American Indians." Paper given at the 90th annual meeting of the American Anthropological Association, Chicago.

————. 1992. "Two-Spirited People: Gender Variance and Homosexuality among North American Indians Today." Paper given at the 91st annual meeting of the American Anthropological Association, San Francisco.

————. 1993. "Masculine Women, Feminine Men: Gender Variance and the Creation of Gay Identities among Contemporary North American Indians." Paper prepared for the first Wenner-Gren Foundation Conference on "Revisiting the 'North American Berdache' Empirically and Theoretically" and presented at the 92d annual meeting of the American Anthropological Association, Washington, D.C.

Langness, L. L., and Gelya Frank. 1981. *Lives: An Anthropological Approach to Biography.* Novato, Calif.: Chandler and Sharp.

Marriott, Alice. 1949. *The Valley Below.* Norman: University of Oklahoma Press.

————. 1952. *Greener Fields: Experiences among the American Indians.* Garden City: Doubleday.

Martin, Kay, and Barbara Voorhies. 1975. *Female of the Species.* New York: Columbia University Press.

McBeth, Sally. 1993. "Myths of Objectivity and the Collaborative Process in Life History Research." In *When They Read What We Write: The Politics of Ethnography,* ed. Caroline B. Brettel, 144–62. Westport: Bergen and Garvey.

Nanda, Serena. 1990. *Neither Man nor Woman: The Hijras of India.* Belmont: Wadsworth.

Newton, Esther. 1993. *Cherry Grove, Fire Island: Sixty Years in America's First Gay and Lesbian Town.* Boston: Beacon.

Personal Narratives Group, ed. 1989. *Interpreting Women's Lives: Feminist Theory and Personal Narratives.* Bloomington: Indiana University Press.

Roscoe, Will. 1987. "Bibliography of Berdache and Alternative Gender Roles among North American Indians." *Journal of Homosexuality* 14 (3–4):81–171.

————, ed. 1988. *Living the Spirit: A Gay American Indian Anthology.* New York: St. Martin's Press.

————. 1991. *The Zuni Man-Woman.* Albuquerque: University of New Mexico Press.

Spivak, Gayatri. 1988. "Can the Subaltern Speak?" In *Marxism and the Interpretation of Culture,* ed. Cary Nelson and Lawrence Grossberg, 271–313. Urbana: University of Illinois Press.

Starn, Orin. 1994. "Rethinking the Politics of Anthropology." *Current Anthropology* 35(1):13–38.

Strathern, Andrew. 1993. *Landmarks: Reflections on Anthropology.* Kent: Kent State University Press.

Tafoya, Terry. 1992. "Native Gay and Lesbian Issues: The Two-Spirited." In *Posively Gay: New Approaches to Gay and Lesbian Life,* ed. Betty Berzon, 135–41. Berkeley: Celestial Arts Publishing.

Tedlock, Barbara. 1991. "From Participant Observation to the Observation of Participation: The Emergence of Narrative Ethnography." *Journal of Anthropological Research* 47(1):69–94.

Timmons, Stuart. 1990. *The Trouble with Harry Hay: Founder of the Modern Gay Movement.* Boston: Alyson Publications.

Trinh T. Minh-ha. 1989. *Woman, Native, Other: Writing Postcoloniality and Feminism.* Bloomington: Indiana University Press.

Underhill, Ruth M. 1979. *Papago Woman*. New York: Holt, Rinehart and Winston.

Wekker, Gloria. 1993. "Mati-ism and Black Lesbianism: Two Idealtypical Expressions of Female Homosexuality in Black Communities of the Diaspora." In *If You Seduce a Straight Person, Can You Make Them Gay? Issues in Biological Essentialism versus Social Constructionism in Gay and Lesbian Identities,* ed. John P. DeCecco and John P. Elia, 145–58. New York: Harrington Press.

Weston, Kath. 1993. "Lesbian/Gay Studies in the House of Anthropology." *Annual Reviews of Anthropology* 22:339–67.

Williams, Patricia J. 1991. *The Alchemy of Race and Rights: Diary of a Law Professor.* Cambridge: Harvard University Press.

Williams, Walter. 1986. *The Spirit and the Flesh: Sexual Diversity in American Indian Culture.* Boston: Beacon.

Contributors

RALPH BOLTON is a professor of anthropology at Pomona College, Claremont California, where he teaches courses on human sexuality and medical anthropology. His research interests include societal responses to AIDS and the sexual behavior and sexual cognition of gay men. He is the editor of *The AIDS Pandemic: A Global Emergency, Rethinking AIDS Prevention: Cultural Approaches* and numerous publications on gay men, sex, and AIDS.

GEOFFREY BURKHART is the chair of the Department of Anthropology at the American University, Washington, D.C. His research in southern India has focused on social relations and identity issues in rural and urban settings. His interests are in gender-related issues in the South Asian diaspora.

MADELINE DAVIS is the chief conservator of the Buffalo and Erie County Public Library System, Buffalo, New York. She is a singer, songwriter, and actress and is the coauthor, with Elizabeth Kennedy, of *Boots of Leather, Slippers of Gold: The History of a Lesbian Community*.

LIZ GOODMAN received her Ph.D. in anthropology from the University of California, Riverside, after doing field research in North Yorkshire, England. Trained in economic anthropology and agricultural economics, she eventually discovered that she liked economics better than anthropology and now works in investment management. She lives in San Francisco.

SUE-ELLEN JACOBS is an associate professor of women's studies at the University of Washington. She is a prominent figure in feminist anthropology and was president of the Society for Applied Anthropology in 1984. She is a coeditor of the forthcoming collection *Two-Spirit People: Perspectives on Native American Gender and Sexuality*.

ELIZABETH LAPOVSKY KENNEDY is a founding member of women's studies at the State University of New York, Buffalo, and a professor in the Department of American Studies. She was trained as a social anthropologist at the University of Cambridge and did two years of fieldwork with the Waunan in Colombia, South America. Since the early seventies she has worked to build the field of women's studies and has coauthored *Feminist Scholarship: Kindling in the Groves of Academe*. She is the coauthor (with Madeline Davis) of *Boots of Leather, Slippers of Gold: The History of a Lesbian Community*, which won the Jessie Bernard Award of the American Sociological Association in 1994, the Lambda Award for Lesbian Studies in 1994, and the Ruth Benedict Prize from the Society of Lesbian and Gay Anthropologists in 1993.

SABINE LANG received her Ph.D. in anthropology from the University of Hamburg. She is the author of *Männer als Frauen—Frauen als Männer: Geschlechtsrollenwechsel bei den Indianern Nordamerikas.*

WILLIAM L. LEAP is a professor in the Department of Anthropology and a member of the core faculty in women's and gender studies at the American University, Washington, D.C. He is cochair of the American Anthropological Association's Commission on Lesbian and Gay Issues in Anthropology. Recent publications include papers on gay discourse strategies, gay language socialization, and the language of AIDS; a monograph on gay men's English; and an edited collection of papers on lavender linguistics. He is studying the language of the gay city.

ELLEN LEWIN, an independent scholar working in San Francisco, is affiliated with the Stanford University Institute for Research on Women and Gender. Her book *Lesbian Mothers: Accounts of Gender in American Culture* (1993) won the Ruth Benedict Prize from the Society of Lesbian and Gay Anthropologists. She is the editor of a forthcoming collection, *Inventing Lesbian Cultures in America,* and is working on an ethnographic study of lesbian and gay commitment ceremonies and weddings, tentatively titled *Recognizing Ourselves.*

STEPHEN O. MURRAY's dissertation research (republished as *Theory Groups and the Study of Language in America*) was based on participant observation of linguistic anthropologists. Following postdoctoral training in linguistic anthropology at Berkeley, he has worked as a consultant to California county public health departments. His books include *Male Homosexuality in Central and South America, Oceanic Homosexualities, Latin American Male Homosexualities,* and *Standing Out: American Gay De-Assimilation and Diversity.*

ESTHER NEWTON is a professor of anthropology at the State University of New York College at Purchase. Her major interest is in American culture, especially in lesbian and gay ethnohistory and representational practices, and she is a founder of the lesbian and gay studies program at the college. She is the author of *Mother Camp: Female Impersonators in America* and *Cherry Grove, Fire Island: Sixty Years in America's First Gay and Lesbian Town,* winner of the 1994 Ruth Benedict Prize from the Society of Lesbian and Gay Anthropologists.

WILL ROSCOE is an affiliated scholar at the Institute for Research on Women and Gender at Stanford University and a research associate at the Center for Education and Research on Sexuality at San Francisco State University. He is author of *The Zuni Man-Woman* and the coordinating editor of *Living the Spirit: A Gay American Indian Anthology.*

JAMES WAFER is a lecturer in the Department of Sociology and Anthropology at the University of Newcastle, Australia. An Australian anthropologist, he completed his graduate studies in the United States and carried out fieldwork in Brazil. He has written *The Taste of Blood: Spirit Possession in Brazilian Candomblé,* as well as articles on homosexuality in Australian Aboriginal cultures and Islamic cultures. His research interest is in gay and lesbian alternative religious movements.

DELORES M. WALTERS has taught anthropology courses on the East and West Coasts and in the Midwest. Her students worked in grass-roots organizations in various multicultural communities. She is an administrator in a diverse low- and middle-income neighborhood housing cooperative in Syracuse, New York. She continues to pursue research in Yemen on diverse women's roles and identities, on which the analysis in this volume is based.

KATH WESTON is an associate professor of anthropology at Arizona State University, West, in Phoenix. She is the author of *Families We Choose: Lesbians, Gays, Kinship* and a coeditor of *The Lesbian Issue: Essays from SIGNS*. Her next book is titled *Render Me, Gender Me: Lesbians Talk Sex, Class, Color, Nation, Stud-muffins and Such*.

WALTER L. WILLIAMS is a professor of anthropology in the Program for the Study of Women and Men in Society at the University of Southern California. He is also the director of the ONE Institute Center for Advanced Studies. He was a cofounder of the Committee on Lesbian and Gay History for the American Historical Association, president of the International Gay and Lesbian Archives, and a Fulbright Scholar in Indonesia. His most recent book (with W. Dorr Legg) is *Homophile Studies in Theory and Practice* (1994).

Index